Comparative Literature and Literary Theory:
Survey and Introduction

Comparative Literature and Literary Theory ✍ ✍ ✍

Survey and Introduction

by ULRICH WEISSTEIN
*Translated by William Riggan
in collaboration with the author*

INDIANA UNIVERSITY PRESS
Bloomington • London

This is an authorized Taiwan edition
published under special agreement with
the proprietor for sale in Taiwan only.

Published by Bookman Books, Ltd.
5, LANE 62, ROOSEVELT RD. SEC. 4, TAIPEI,
TAIWAN 10764

有著作權　◇　不准翻印
臺內著字第　　　　號

定價： 150 元

出版者／書　林　出　版　有　限　公　司
發行人／蘇　　　　　正　　　　　隆
門市部／臺北市羅斯福路四段62巷5號
電　話／３９２‐４７１５・３９２‐８６１７
郵　撥／０１１４５７０‐４・書林書店
新聞局登記局版臺業字第一八三一號
中　華　民　國　七　十　七　年　九　月　出　版

German edition, *Einführung in die Vergleichende Literaturwissen-
schaft,* copyright © 1968 by W. Kohlhammer, Stuttgart
English edition copyright © 1973 by Indiana University Press
All rights reserved

Published in Canada by Fitzhenry & Whiteside Limited, Don Mills,
Ontario
Library of Congress catalog card number: 73–81716
ISBN: 0–253–31388–0 cl.　0–253–20171–3 pa.

Manufactured in the United States of America

With even more justification than for the original German text, this English version of my book is dedicated to the Comparative Literature majors at Indiana University who have been enrolled in the courses C-501 (Introduction to Graduate Studies in Comparative Literature) and C-545 (Problems in Comparative Literature), and, especially, to my wife, Judy.

comparaciones . . . odiose reputantur

—JOHN FORTESCUE
(1471)

NOT SO ODIOUS

—Title of editorial on
Comparative
Literature in *TLS*

Contents

 Preface

Although there are quite a number of books which carry the term "Comparative Literature" in their titles (see the entries for Aldridge, Brandt Corstius, Gifford, Posnett, Stallknecht/Frenz and Wrenn in the appended bibliography), this is the first systematically conceived and historically as well as theoretically oriented survey of our field in English. It thus takes its place beside the existing manuals in Dutch, French, Japanese, Romanian, Serbo-Croatian, Slovak, Slovenian and Spanish. As *Comparative Literature and Literary Theory: Survey and Introduction* is here presented, it is, in fact, a work not originally written in English, but a translation of my *Einführung in die Vergleichende Literaturwissenschaft* (which was commissioned by a German publisher, W. Kohlhammer in Stuttgart, and first published in 1968). A literal translation of that book was made by William Riggan, to whom I am extremely grateful for this labor, which I personally might never have undertaken. Using his faithful rendition as a basis, I have refined and, on occasion, slightly modified the text, to the point that I myself must take full responsibility for the present version.

Following the lead of Benedetto Croce and René Wellek, among others, the preface to the original German version states that Comparative Literature does not have a methodology of its own but must be regarded as a specialized branch of literary history and theory. Hence the deliberate change of title and the concomitant rearrangement of chapters in this version, where Chapter One and the two appendices will appeal primarily to the student of Comparative Literature, while Chapters Two to Seven, which form the core, should appeal to all students of literature interested in theoretical and historical questions. Throughout I have taken pains to account for the special application of a given view or concept to Comparative Literature as a discipline.

Regarding the text, then, herewith submitted to the reader, while basically it conforms to its German model, certain deviations and discrepancies were unavoidable and, at times even desirable. Thus the bibliography has been brought up to date (as of June, 1973), and pertinent information has been added to various sections of Appendix One and certain footnotes. Throughout, I have dropped sentences or phrases which struck me as being inappropriate or overly assertive. In general, taking my cue from the English language, I have adopted a slightly more cautious attitude, gauged to precision. Since I have also corrected some of the minor errors of the German text, I am hopeful of having produced a better book.

Perhaps the most vexing problem encountered by Mr. Riggan and myself was the terminological confusion prevalent in the parlance of literary theory, history and criticism seen from an international vantage point. Often there simply is no exact foreign equivalent for a term firmly entrenched in the technical jargon of a given language; and real synonyms are as rare as butterflies in the winter. Therefore, although one has to make certain concessions to current (or past) usage, an arbitrary but uniform application is, occasionally, preferable to the existing chaos. For example: I use Comparative Literature, throughout, as a term equivalent to *Vergleichende Literaturgeschichte* on the one hand, and *Vergleichende Literaturwissenschaft* on the other; at the same time—especially in Appendix One—pointing up the semantic and historical difference.

Similarly, and more importantly as far as the methodology of our discipline is concerned, my use of the plural "themes" for *Stoff* is somewhat idiosyncratic. But "subjects" would seem to be too general, and "subject matter" is an inveterate singular. The madness implicit in this method could have been circumvented if there existed a standard reference work to be consulted in cases of uncertainty or doubt. Unfortunately, the *International Dictionary of Literary Terms*, edited by Robert Escarpit under the auspices of the AILC/ILCA, has not substantially progressed beyond the rudimentary stage reached three or four years ago. And the *Literaturwörterbuch in Deutsch, Englisch und Französisch mit griechischen und lateinischen Ableitungen für Studenten der allgemeinen und vergleichenden Literaturwissenschaft* by W. V. Wittkowski and R. E. Blake (Berne/Munich: Francke, 1969) is almost useless for my purpose because it offers no historical, semantic or etymological explanations. For instance, the thematological matrix encompassed in its Chapter Seven is presented in the following manner: "342 Stoff; Thema; Inhalt; Fabel// Subject; Theme; Topic; Fable// sujet, thème."

While in the German version all quotations from French, English and German were given in the original (in the case of Italian, they were immediately followed by their German equivalents), translations have been used in the present text. They are our own unless other translators are specifically identified. The titles of literary and scholarly works are usually cited in the original, except when couched in ancient, Slavic or non-Western languages. In cases where quotations are not fully footnoted but are identified only by their authors and the appropriate page number, the reader is asked to consult the bibliography for the title of the work from which the passage has been drawn.

At various stages in the preparation of the manuscript, I have enjoyed the benefit of professional and professorial counsel from my colleagues at Indiana University, notably from Giancarlo Maiorino and Heitor Martíns. Special thanks are due to Mrs. Anna Strikis, who is not only an expert typist and proofreader but could easily double as an editor. Chapter Five has previously appeared in the second edition of *Comparative Literature: Method and Perspective*, eds. N. P. Stallknecht and H. Frenz (Carbondale, Illinois, 1971). It is here reprinted with the permission of the editors.

Bloomington, Indiana   ULRICH WEISSTEIN
June, 1973

Postscript: As the book goes to press, Mouton in The Hague announces the publication of the first fascicle (L) of the *Dictionnaire international des termes littéraires* (eighty-five pages comprising twenty entries, including those on *littérature, littérature comparée, littérature générale* and *littérature modiale*).

Comparative Literature and Literary Theory:
Survey and Introduction

ABBREVIATED REFERENCES

ACLA	American Comparative Literature Association
AILC/ICLA	Association Internationale de Littérature Comparée/International Comparative Literature Association
B/F	Baldensperger/Friederich, *Bibliography of Comparative Literature*
Escarpit	Robert Escarpit, *Sociologie de la littérature*
Etiemble	René Etiemble, *Comparaison n'est pas raison: La Crise de la littérature comparée*
Forschungsprobleme I, II	Fritz Ernst & Kurt Wais, editors, *Forschungsprobleme der vergleichenden Literaturgeschichte*, vols. 1 and 2
Frenzel	Elisabeth Frenzel, *Stoff-, Motiv- und Symbolforschung*
Guyard	Marius-François Guyard, *La Littérature comparée*
P/R	Claude Pichois and André M. Rousseau, *La Littérature comparée*
Proceedings, II, III, IV	Proceedings of the Second, Third and Fourth Congress of the AILC/ICLA
RLC	*Revue de littérature comparée*
S/F	Newton P. Stallknecht and Horst Frenz, editors, *Comparative Literature: Method and Perspective*, second ed., 1971
Trousson	Raymond Trousson, *Un Problème de littérature comparée: Les études de thèmes*
Van Tieghem	Paul Van Tieghem, *La Littérature comparée*
W/W	René Wellek and Austin Warren, *Theory of Literature*
YCGL	*Yearbook of Comparative and General Literature*

All other abbreviations follow the usage established by the annual *MLA* bibliography.

One ⟋ Definition

$\mathcal{A}$ N essential task of a work of introduction to Comparative Literature such as this one must be to define the term which denotes this specific branch of literary scholarship. In moving toward a definition, we would do well, within the self-imposed limits of our study, to take a middle road between the rather narrow conception held by the orthodox representatives of the Paris school (especially Paul Van Tieghem, Jean-Marie Carré, and Marius-François Guyard) and the more liberal views embraced by the exponents of the so-called American school. I make this choice not because I wish to put shackles on our discipline—which is as yet far from having reached a state of maturity—but rather because, in the systematic study of a rich body of material, too little is always better than too much.

At one extreme we have the definition that emerges in the brief foreword which Carré has placed at the beginning of Guyard's *La Littérature comparée*, where we read:

Comparative Literature is a branch of literary history: it is the study of international spiritual relations, of *rapports de fait* between Byron and Pushkin, Goethe and Carlyle, Walter Scott and Alfred de Vigny, and between the works, the inspirations and even the lives of writers belonging to different literatures. (p. 5)

We shall discuss subsequently the notion of Comparative Literature as a branch of literary history, a classification which Carré seems to take for granted. For the mo-

3

ment, however, let us consider his emphasis on *rapports de fait*.

Carré's emphatic stress on factual, that is, clearly distinguishable and measurable connections and influences makes sense if one recalls the situation of comparative studies in particular, and literary historiography in general, which prevailed at the end of the positivistic nineteenth century, especially the overriding interest in folklore and thematology, which today is regarded as either obsolete or as needing complementation. If the study of literature is degraded to a mere amassing of material, it loses its dignity, since the aesthetic aspects of the literary work of art are no longer valued.

For a number of reasons (the most important being the inevitable lack of perfect continuity), the patriarch of French comparatism in our century, Fernand Baldensperger, took strong exception to the folkloristic gathering of material. He felt that such a procedure altogether ignored the individual, creative element, the personality, initiative, and originality of the writer. As he put it, "this *folklore* or *Stoffgeschichte*, toward which a whole branch of Comparative Literature tends to gravitate, represents a mode of investigation which is more interested in subject matter than in art, and for which the hidden survivals are of greater concern than the craftsman's initiative."[1] Embracing a similar view and excluding folklore altogether from Comparative Literature—because of the anonymity of its products, even where these are literary, as in the case of the fairy-tale, the myth, the legend, and hagiography—Van Tieghem, following this precedent, asserted:

This is folklore, and not literary history; for the latter is the history of the human mind viewed through the art of writing. In this subdivision of thematology, however, one considers only the subject matter, its passage from one country to another, and its modifications. Art plays no part in these anonymous traditions whose nature it is to remain impersonal, while Comparative Literature studies the actions and influences exerted by individuals. (p. 89)

This attitude explains, at least in part, the ostracism of ancient and medieval literature which, though never theoretically grounded, has long been practiced at the Sorbonne. For in the writings of those eras the author (of, for instance, the Homeric epics or the *Nibelungenlied*) cannot always be properly identified:

Comparative Literature aims primarily . . . at studying the works of various literatures in their interrelationship. Conceived in such general terms, it comprises—to speak only of the Western world —the mutual relations between Greek and Latin literature, the debt of modern literature (since the Middle Ages) to ancient literature, and, finally, the links connecting the various modern literatures. The latter field of investigation, which is the most extensive and complex of the three, is the one which Comparative Literature, in the sense in which it is generally understood, takes for its province. (Van Tieghem, p. 57f.)

That this position is no longer tenable and that ancient and medieval literatures reside squarely in the realm of Comparative Literature need hardly be stressed in an age which has learned to concentrate on belles-lettres proper and to consider the study of the raw materials of literature and the psychology of creative genius as auxiliary rather than major disciplines.[2]

In contrast to many of his predecessors and contemporaries, Carré considered the study of literary influences to be dangerous because here one is frequently forced to deal with intangibles. He therefore warned his students and colleagues: "Perhaps there has been too great a proclivity toward influence studies. These are difficult to manage and often deceptive, since one sometimes deals with imponderables" (Guyard, p. 6). Safer and more gratifying, he continues, would be the study of "the history of the success of works, of the fortunes of a writer, of the afterlife of a great figure, of the mutual interpretations of various peoples, of travels and of *mirages*: how we see each other, Englishmen and Frenchmen, Frenchmen and Germans. . . ." Here we find ourselves, from a literary point of view, on a highway leading in the direction of sociology, along a route where travelers attain their goal only by studying the survival of works, the fame (René Etiemble would say the "myth") of the writer, and the images peoples fashion of each other by the means and on the basis of literary documents.[3]

This pseudo-literary conception of Comparative Literature is rejected by René Wellek, who, in his sharp rejoinder to Carré, points out that such a substitution is methodologically questionable since "the comparative psychoanalysis of national myths demanded by MM. Carré and Guyard" is "not a part of literary scholarship" but "a subject belonging to sociology or general history."[4] I share this view, especially since Guyard himself provides the key to this approach in what are essentially extra-literary terms by stating, with reference to genology (the theoretical and historical study of literary genres):

> To study the fortune of a genre demands rigorous analysis, a very strict historical method, and genuine psychological insight. Far from being arid, such studies ultimately can and should be the work of a moralist. Comparative Literature here expands, as so often, into comparative psychology. (p. 20f.)

"L'Etranger tel qu'on le voit" is the title of the eighth and last chapter of Guyard's survey, where the future of Comparative Literature is depicted in broad colors. To be sure, in view of the development which had taken place in the meantime, the French scholar felt urged, in the postscript to the second, revised edition of his book (1961), to modify his position in such a way as to account for the stance taken by the "rebels" Etiemble and Escarpit.[5] Still, the damage had been done and was, in some respects, irreparable. Thus, studies like Simon Jeune's overview of American types as personified in modern French literature seem anachronistic at a time when their methodological bases are no longer valid.[6]

If a definition of Comparative Literature based exclusively on the study of *rapports de fait* does too little, its polar opposite—the deprecation of factual links and the elevation of mere analogies—overshoots, in my opinion, the scientifically justifiable goal. I share in principle the generosity of Henry H. H. Remak, according to whom "the French desire for literary *sécurité* is unfortunate at a time which cries . . . for more (not less) imagination."[7] But I should also like to stress the disadvantages of such generosity, even at the risk of being called a reactionary. Viewing the potential and actual excesses of mere parallel hunting, one should not let Baldensperger's warning go unheeded. Nearly fifty years ago, he, the founder of the *Revue de Littérature comparée*, offered the following comments:

No explicatory clarity results from comparisons restricting themselves to a glance cast simultaneously at two different objects, to that recollection, conditioned by the play of memories and impressions, of similarities which may well be *erratic* points furtively linked by the mind's caprice.[8]

Like so many of his colleagues, Carré would like to banish such analogy studies from Comparative Literature, while Van Tieghem admits them at least insofar as they point to a common trend (*courant commun*).[9] But even thus, in his view, they pertain more properly to General Literature (*littérature générale*) than to Comparative Literature conceived in the narrower sense of the term.

Once again: I admire Remak's enthusiasm but do not wish to desert the *terra firma* of scholarly security without taking steps to prevent the sliding off into the bottomless pit of mere speculation. I do not deny, for example, the relevance of Etiemble's call for a comparative study of such aspects as metrics, iconology, iconography, stylistics, but hesitate nevertheless to extend the study of parallels to phenomena pertaining to two different civilizations. For it seems to me that only within a single civilization can one find those common elements of a consciously or unconsciously upheld tradition in thought, feeling and imagination which may, in cases of a fairly simultaneous emergence, be regarded as signifying common trends, and which, even beyond the confines of time and space, often constitute an astounding bond of unity, as illustrated by the emotional value of color epithets, the conception of landscape, or with regard to individual or mass psychology, even where there can be no question of a common *Zeitgeist*. Thus, studies of the kind represented by comparisons between Rainer Maria Rilke and Antonio Machado or Rilke and Wallace Stevens (which are so popular in our universities) are more easily defensible from the point of view of Comparative Literature than is the attempt to discover a likeness of pattern in Western and Mid- or Far-Eastern poetry.[10]

To what extremes a comparison of East Asian and European poetry may lead is shown, with marked naiveté, by a senior scholar well acquainted with both traditions, Etiemble, who makes the point that "the comparative study of the structure of poems (whether or not the civilizations in question are linked by historical relations) might enable us to ascertain the conditions *sine qua non* of the poem" (Etiemble, p. 102). These conditions, however, can at best pertain to such basic features as can be reduced to commonplaces, such as the answer to the question "When and under what circumstances does a novel cease to be a novel?" With slight reservations I, therefore, underwrite the programmatic view held by the editor of *Arcadia*, Horst Rüdiger, who affirms that his periodical will "avoid the discussion of all ahistorical parallels based solely on speculation and likely to damage the reputation of Comparative Literature at the time of its consolidation."[11]

To return, once more, briefly to the problem of *rapports de fait*: it would seem to be obvious that such factual links primarily concern the *historian* of literature. Thus, our discipline, in voluntarily restricting itself to the study of such connections, would limit itself to the realm of Comparative Literary History. That this no longer corresponds to the "progressive" view conforming to the present state of scholarship is demonstrated by the change in German usage. As is evident from the descriptive subtitle of *Arcadia*, the tendency for some time has been to give preference to the term *Vergleichende Literaturwissenschaft* over the more narrowly conceived *Vergleichende Literaturgeschichte*. Only the representatives of the older, philologically-minded school—such as the Romanist Werner Krauss in the title of his address to the East Berlin Academy[12]— still insist on the old usage. Political factors may also play a part, as can be gauged from Evamaria Nahke's report on the fourth ICLA congress in the journal *Weimarer Beiträge*.[13]

In the more familiar tongues, the name of our discipline does not always match the subject matter dealt with and the method used in studying it. In an essay published as early as 1901, the English scholar H. M. Posnett was complaining that the term "Comparative Literature" (derived from the French) designates the object of study rather than the method employed. Thus he himself was compelled, as he put it, "to make the name of the subject-matter do service for the uncoined name of the study of the subject-matter."[14] The French term *littérature comparée* and its Italian, Spanish and Portuguese equivalents (*letteratura comparata, literatura comparada, litteratura comparada*) are similarly unsatisfactory from a semantic point of view, even if one takes into account the fact that they were derived, by analogy, from the natural sciences (*anatomie comparée*, etc.).[15] "Comparable literature" (= Comparative Literature) and "literature compared" (*littérature comparée*) are only shorthand for designations like "the products of one national literature compared with those of one or several others." Like the Dutch term (*vergelijkend literatuuronderzoek*), the German label is much more descriptive.

Literaturwissenschaft, it should be emphasized, is more inclusive than *Literaturgeschichte*; for it involves, in addition to the study of literary history, that of literary criticism and theory as well as poetics, while excluding aesthetics as a branch of philosophy using literature to illustrate *a priori* theorems.[16] In the fourth chapter of their *Theory of Literature*, René Wellek and Austin Warren deal at some length with the division and limitation of these branches and offer the following conspectus:

Within our "proper study," the distinctions between literary theory, criticism, and history are clearly the most important. There is, first, the distinction between a view of literature which sees it primarily as a series of works arranged in a chronological order and as integral parts of the historical process. There is, then, the further distinction between the study of the principles and criteria of literature and the study of the concrete literary works of art, whether we study them in isolation or in a chronological series. It seems best to draw attention to these distinctions by describing as "literary theory" the study of the principles of literature, its categories, criteria, and the like, and differentiating studies of concrete works of art as either "literary criticism" (primarily static in approach) or "literary history." (p. 30)

Accordingly, the sector "Comparative Literature" would have to be divided into the segments "Comparative Literary History," "Comparative Literary Criticism," and "Comparative Literary Theory." If our subject is defined in this manner, the relevance of comparing, for instance, A. W. Schlegel and Coleridge, or Aristotle and Corneille (as the author of the *Discours sur les trois unités*), is as obvious as that of scrutinizing the relationship between, say, Gerhart Hauptmann and Tolstoi. In 1973, only a pedant can believe that one must—as the orthodox theoreticians of Comparative Literature demanded two or three decades ago—avoid all "criticism," since it forces one to make value judgments.[17]

In postulating that Comparative Literature is concerned with confronting the products of different national literatures, we did not specifically state what circumstances must be attendant upon this activity. It is now time to make up for this omission, first of all by defining the links in the chain of the phenomena known as national literature, Comparative Literature, and World Literature respec-

tively. To these may be added, for the sake of completeness, the term General Literature which, as we have seen,
Van Tieghem put into circulation and endowed with a
specifically comparatist meaning.

To begin with, the term "national literature" needs to
be defined in a way that is binding for Comparative Literature since, by its very nature, it refers to the units which
form the basis of our discipline. Thus the question arises
as to precisely what constitutes the literature of a country
and what specific limits are imposed upon such an entity.
We must also decide whether the definition should be
made according to politico-historical or linguistic criteria.
After thorough reflection, one is likely to conclude that
the latter must be given precedence, since in the course of
time and under the pressure of historical circumstances
political boundaries have a way of changing more often
and more quickly than linguistic ones. Take just one example from recent history: the partition of Germany in
1945 violently split a linguistically unified nation into two
states with a common cultural and literary heritage. But
even today, some twenty-odd years after the division, one
hesitates to call a study of writings produced, respectively,
in the German Federal Republic and the German Democratic Republic unqualifiedly comparative.

Just how irrelevant political aspects may be within the
domain of Comparative Literature is shown by the relative
indifference with which questions of citizenship or resi-
dence would have to be treated in most cases. One need
only think of the fate suffered by the German emigré writers in the 1930s and 1940s. Heinrich Mann, for instance,
fled to France, became a Czech citizen and spent the final
decade of his life in the United States. Should he then, because of historico-geographic circumstances, be regarded
as a German/French/Czech/American author? Obviously
not. However, on the basis of his affinity with France, his
intimate knowledge of French, and his choice of a French
subject for his novelistic masterpiece, *Henri Quatre*, an
elective *esprit gaulois* can be discerned in his oeuvre, the

latter portions of which are shot through with French phrases, expressions, passages or even chapters. In other writers bilingualism is even more strongly evident, and men who, like Rilke and the Portuguese poet Fernando Pessoa, are equally conversant with two different languages and literary traditions, are in fact suitable objects for comparative study.

If, in following the majority of theoreticians, we prefer linguistic to political and geographic criteria, we are sure to run into other difficulties. For instance, the question whether French literature also encompasses works produced by Belgian, Swiss, Canadian and African authors writing in French gives one pause. The same applies to German literature, which extends to Austrian letters as well as to the works of German-speaking Swiss authors like Max Frisch and Friedrich Dürrenmatt and the members of the Prague circle around Max Brod and Franz Kafka. And what are we to do about continental Spanish literature in its relation to Central and South American (excluding Brazilian) letters, or about Arabic literature as the repository of a cultural heritage to which Egypt, Iraq, Syria, Lebanon, and Saudi Arabia are equally indebted?

In this connection, the arguments offered by Wolfgang von Einsiedel in the foreword to the one-volume survey of one hundred and thirty literatures which he edited are worth pondering. Einsiedel reports that the literatures covered in the book are named "primarily according to linguistic families (*Sprachgemeinschaften*), which do not coincide with nations, and only in exceptional cases according to religious or ethnic families (*Glaubensgemeinschaften* and *Bevölkerungsgruppen*)."[18] In his view, one of the basic features of each entity treated in the volume is that it possesses "a more or less distinct physiognomy, which becomes clearly recognizable only when, taken as a whole, it is compared with other literatures."[19]

Each of the above-mentioned problems constitutes a special case and calls for a solution carefully gauged to the historical circumstances and the current usage of literary historians. For the prospective comparatist, the study of several histories of the same national literature is, therefore, especially instructive, since he will find the comparison to be a practical tool for fixing boundaries. By way of illustration, we refer to a practice common among French literary historians and commented upon by Van Tieghem:

> In France, where the national unity is so old and the sense of this unity so profound and vivid, the question is resolved with an often fumbling and sometimes absurd timidity. For obvious reasons, we regard the Genevan Rousseau and the Savoyard [Xavier] de Maistre as French authors. We generally admit the Swiss writers [A.] Vinet, [Edmond] Schérer, [Edouard] Rod, and [Victor] Cherbuliez, and the Belgians [Georges] Rodenbach and [Emile] Verhaeren, since they more or less gravitated toward Paris as the center of their literary activities. But we leave [Rodolphe] Toepffer to Switzerland and Camille Lemonnier to Belgium because they voluntarily remained in their respective homelands. In order to be logical, it is, therefore, necessary to consider the influence of Emile Zola on Lemonnier as a subject for Comparative Literature. The same applies to Romanticism in Geneva and in the Vaud, and to the French influence on the French-language literatures of Canada, Haiti, etc. (p. 58f.)

The literature of the developing African countries, often framed in Western languages, must also be duly taken into account by the comparatist. Here, once again, the question arises whether a particular world view or a specific local color may be regarded as producing national literary traits.

That the question raised here is not purely academic but has immediate practical applications will be apparent to readers of Baldensperger/Friederich's *Bibliography of Comparative Literature*, where Friederich's native Switzerland and Baldensperger's native Alsace occupy special niches, whereas Austria and Canada are "annexed" to German, French, and English literature respectively.

It would be equally questionable to separate, for the sake of a misguided methodological purism, Irish from English literature; for by such a sleight-of-hand writers like Swift, Yeats, and Shaw would be artistically uprooted for the sake of a nonliterary principle. A problem of especially great concern arises from the close kinship between English and American letters; for here is a case of two countries or nations which, culturally (and, therefore, literarily), have gone their own ways, at least since the early nineteenth century. Thus, although they continue to use a common language (minor linguistic variations excepted), the products of their respective literatures considered, by general consent, as "national," could be the legitimate object of comparative studies.

Our choice of linguistic difference as decisive in solving the question of whether a case is to be treated by the specialized philologies or within the confines of Comparative Literature is bolstered by a glance at the situation prevailing in those countries which are politically unified but linguistically divided, and which as a result possess no one exclusive national language. This group includes Switzerland (in regard to whose total literary output François Jost prefers to speak of Swiss letters rather than Swiss literature in the ordinary sense),[20] India, and the Soviet Union, where linguistic minorities abound. That a comparison between the novels of Gottfried Keller and Charles Ferdinand Ramuz, for example, belongs, fairly and squarely, to the realm of Comparative Literature would seem to strike most Western readers as self-evident. And the same viewpoint must be taken with regard to studies involving works written in the various Indian tongues (Hindi, Bengali, Urdu, Tamil, for instance), as well as the bodies of literature couched in Russian, Ukrainian, Estonian, Latvian, Georgian, Buryat, and Kirghiz—to name only a few of the numerous languages spoken in the USSR which can boast of their own literary traditions.[21]

Even within an essentially monolingual nation such as France or England, however, there exist "foreign" admixtures and pockets whose relation to the koiné of the country-at-large may necessitate a truly comparative analysis. We think of the nineteenth-century Provençal poet Frédéric Mistral, of whom Van Tieghem says that "our literary histories grant him no place whatsoever, and in order to consider his link with French writers one must, therefore, turn to Comparative Literature" (p. 170), and of the Scottish poet Robert Burns, whose literary citizenship Louis Cazamian defined as *semi-étrangère*.

The latter case demonstrates that even literature written in what we ordinarily call dialect (that is, a tongue which is not, or not readily, understood by compatriots speaking and writing the standard vernacular) may well be considered as offering a welcome opportunity for the comparatist. It must be kept in mind, however, that the boundaries between "dialect" and "language" are relatively fluid, and that, in the absence of strictly scientific means of differentiation, the pragmatic test of intelligibility must determine to which category a given piece belongs. Methodologically, it is worth noting that the Low German novels of Fritz Reuter and the Sicilian comedies of Eduardo de Filippo must be regarded as foreign works since they require translation into High German and "High" Italian respectively in order to attract a truly national audience.[22] Here we seem to have reached a dead end, however, for nobody will seriously maintain that, for instance, Reuter's *Ut de Stromtid*, the original version of Hauptmann's drama *Die Weber*, and Ludwig Thoma's uproariously funny Bavarian *Filserbriefe* are not part and parcel of German *Nationalliteratur*.

In stressing linguistic criteria and their importance for Comparative Literature, we must take note that they should be used with extreme caution whenever distinct phases in the "organic" development of a given language are concerned, as in the case of Anglo-Saxon or Old High German, which the Englishman or German of today has to learn like a foreign language. A comparison between works originally written in Old English, Middle English and modern English (say between *Beowulf*, Chaucer's *Canterbury Tales* and a novel by Dickens) cannot be regarded as falling within the province of our discipline.

Having explained, at some length, what problems arise

when one seeks to define the essence of a national literature, delimit the various literatures, and mutually relate them to one another, we must now look at the terminological and conceptual links between Comparative Literature on one hand, and General Literature on the other. As it turns out, this division is an artificial one, to which no methodological significance should be attached. Van Tieghem defines *littérature générale* (signifying general history of literature) in the third and final part of his book. In his opinion, Comparative Literature confines itself to the study of "binary links between two elements, whether these elements be individual works and writers, or groups of works and men, or entire literatures" (p. 170). Literary phenomena encompassing three or more elements, on the other hand, are assigned to the province of General Literature, "a discipline which bears on facts common to several literatures, considered as such, be it in their mutual interdependence or by analogy (*dans leur coincidence*)" (p. 174).[23] Claude Pichois and André Rousseau, in their recent handbook, do not totally reject this distinction, but wisely limit the realm of General Literature to studies involving no *rapports de fait* (P/R, p. 95).

As Wellek has pointed out, Van Tieghem himself actually fails to draw a clear line between the meanings of these terms. In his essay "The Concept of Comparative Literature," the former observes:

[Comparative Literature] is now an established and comprehensible term, while "general literature" is not. "General literature" used to mean poetics, theory of literature, and M. Van Tieghem has tried to give it a new and special sense. Neither meaning is well established today. M. Van Tieghem drew a distinction between "Comparative Literature" which studies the interrelationship between two or more [sic!] literatures and "general literature" which is concerned with international movements. But how can one determine whether e.g. Ossianism is a topic of "general" or "comparative" literature? One cannot make a valid distinction between the influence of Walter Scott abroad and the vogue of the historical novel. "Comparative" and "general" literature merge inevitably. (*YCGL*, 2 [1953], p. 5)

Among the topics to be dealt with under the heading of *littérature générale*, Van Tieghem (p. 176) lists the study of international currents, like Petrarchism and Rousseau- ism; the preoccupation with problems of *Geistesgeschichte* and the history of ideas, as exemplified by Humanism, the Enlightenment, and the Age of Sensibility; the analysis of far-flung literary movements, like Naturalism and Sym- bolism; and the so-called *formes communes d'art ou de style* (genres), like the sonnet, classical tragedy, and the rustic novel. But in Part Two, Chapter Two, of his survey, he treats the question of style and genre as a province of Comparative Literature, thereby implicitly canceling the artificial division into two separate disciplines. It should also be borne in mind that several of the topics which Van Tieghem assigns to General Literature belong more prop- erly to intellectual history (*Problemgeschichte*). The divi- sion, however, would be tenable only if truly literary phe- nomena were clearly separated from things philosophical, religious and scientific, and if the History of Ideas were classed as an auxiliary but independent discipline.[24]

The inadequacy of Van Tieghem's definition is under- scored by the fact that Guyard blatantly contradicts his master when, in Chapter Seven of his survey, entitled "Grands courants européens: idées, doctrines, sentiments," he laments this contamination and, while accepting it as a necessary evil, pillories the methodological error com- mitted by his predecessor:

Paul Van Tieghem proposed to call *littérature générale* that superior form of comparatism which goes beyond the level of binary relations by taking a truly international (or, at least, European) point of view regarding the history of ideas or the currents of sensibility. [But] in his view *littérature générale* also embraces properly literary facts: the history of genres, forms, and themes. This book carefully avoids theoretical discussions, which are often useless, in this area. . . . To the ignorant, or simply indifferent, witness of these verbal battles it must be pointed out, however, . . . that if the term *littérature générale* is to have any meaning at all, that meaning applies precisely to the comparative approaches discussed in the present chapter. (p. 96f.)

Having ascended from national literature to Comparative Literature and, from there, to Van Tieghem's *littérature générale*, we now arrive at world literature. This term, like its foreign equivalents (such as *littérature universelle, Weltliteratur*), is less controversial than General Literature, but still offers a number of interpretive cruxes. In the present context, it is impossible to account for the full range of its possible meanings and nuances. (For such a survey, the interested reader is directed to the rich body of secondary literature on this subject listed in the bibliographical appendix.)[25] Here we are solely concerned with covering those shades of meaning which touch upon, or overlap with, Comparative Literature.

As can be seen from his remarks on the subject—compiled by Fritz Strich—Goethe considered *Weltliteratur* to be a historical phenomenon linked to the social, political and technological developments of the immediate past and conditioned by the "present and extremely turbulent period" as well as "greatly improved communications."[26] This "extremely turbulent period," however, was the legacy of Napoleon, "for all nations, jumbled together in the most terrible wars and then restored to themselves, realized that they had observed and absorbed many unfamiliar things" and had begun to feel "certain previously unknown spiritual needs."

Thus, for all practical purposes, *Weltliteratur* to Goethe meant only that the various nations (or, more precisely, the contemporary writers residing in different European countries) should "notice and understand each other, and, if they do not wish to love each other, at least learn how to tolerate one another." Goethe sincerely hoped that the uniqueness of national literatures would be preserved in this process of mutual exchange and recognition. He expressly stated "that there can be no question of the various nations thinking alike." Rather, by means of these worldwide contacts, a harmonization was to ensue within the individual literatures—but not in the form of a general leveling. On October 12, 1827, Goethe wrote to his friend Sulpiz Boisserée: "I should also like to observe that what I call *Weltliteratur* is most likely to come about when the differences prevailing within one nation are reconciled through the views and judgments of the other nations."

Goethe wisely refrained from advocating universal conformity. On the contrary: he thoroughly hated this kind of cultural *sansculottisme*, the inevitable consequences of which—thanks to the frightening efficiency of the mass media—we are facing today. To be sure, in ages of narrow-minded nationalism literary world citizenship (cosmopolitanism) is to be welcomed, but its extremes must be avoided at all costs. As an object of study in the context of Comparative Literature, *cosmopolitisme* has always held —at least with the French—a special position because, naturally, it is a soil in which our discipline flourishes.[27] Thus Van Tieghem stresses the importance of the four cosmopolitan ages in European letters:

In the Middle Ages, the identity of the religious faith and the Latin culture—an immense reservoir of pious, chivalric and popular legends—created between all the clerics and scribes of the West innumerable points of contact and caused them to regard themselves as citizens of the same divine and human city. In the sixteenth century, the Renaissance, in offering as common sources of thought the great Greek and Latin thinkers, closely linked all the humanists of the countries subscribing to the same ideals and nourished by the same food, as well as all the writers who were trying to rival the ancients by imitating them. In the eighteenth century, the wide dissemination of French caused admiration for the French writers to spread through the upper classes all over Europe . . . and the similarity of literary tastes and philosophical trends united the men of letters and the enlightened public of all nations in a rationalist cosmopolitanism. In the nineteenth century, finally, under the influence of revolutions, wars, and emigrations, . . . under the influence of historical and philological studies . . . and, above all, through the impact of Romanticism, many critics considered the modern European literatures as a whole whose various parts offer contrasts or similarities. (p. 26f.)

Inspired by Rousseau, Sebastien Mercier applied the concept of cosmopolitanism to literature, and Joseph Texte subsequently accorded it full status in literary historiography.[28] As a branch of Comparative Literature, however, this phenomenon (to which the participants in the Fribourg congress of the ICLA [1964] paid special heed)[29] must be viewed with caution, for it carries a distinctly political flavor. In literary sociology, on the other hand, cosmopolitanism operates under the mask of erudition (*Belesenheit*), as will be apparent to the reader of the Fribourg Proceedings.

Because of its stress on international contacts and fruitful literary interrelationships, barring the eradication of distinctive national traits, Goethe's concept of *Weltliteratur* is extremely useful for our discipline. This is true also because the notion entails a focus on the role of the intermediary which, according to the "classical" theory of Comparative Literature, is appropriate. In this sense, both French and non-French comparatists have long interested themselves in the activities of translators, travelers, emigrants, political refugees, salons, and journals contributing to the international exchange of literary products.

The richly varied and somewhat ambiguous concept of world literature has by no means been exhausted by our reflections up to this point. By way of precaution, I take note of still another shade of meaning which is rather common in the United States and popular in our academic circles. This application extends the term to cover the literary masterpieces of all ages and places as presented and analyzed, more or less professionally, in courses in world literature, freshman literature, great books, or humanities.[30] In order to stave off any confusion between this usage and the Goethean sense of *Weltliteratur*, it might be well to substitute the term "classics" in this case, without restricting, with T. S. Eliot, the application of this label to a handful of uniquely seminal works, such as the *Aeneid* or the *Divine Comedy*. Instead, with Matthew Arnold, we should include in this category "the best that is known and thought in the world." It is methodologically significant that, in the pedagogical context, these masterpieces are rarely presented in a truly comparative manner, and that comparative methods are usually applied only where generic or thematic links are present (as in courses on the modern novel or the anti-hero in modern fiction). Moreover, the presentation of the Great Books often forms part of a collaborative effort in the guise of a general introduction to cultural history—a practice which precludes a truly comparative analysis.

In concluding, I must not forget to mention the use of the term "World Literature" as an abbreviation for "history of world literature," which presupposes an analogy with Comparative Literature (= comparative *history* of literature) and General Literature (= general *history* of literature). The history of world literature must be understood as a history of all literatures of the world, regardless of their scope and aesthetic or historical significance. However, since on a universal scale the major literatures are more popular and more familiar than the minor ones, the ICLA has made it its special duty to stress the—often intermediary—role of the younger or less fortunate siblings in its official transactions. Thus a sizable portion of the papers read at the Utrecht congress of 1961 was devoted to this particular topic.

Despite the vast body of knowledge and the vast range of information they presuppose, there is no lack of overall surveys of world literature (*vide* the large number of items listed in the *Bibliography of Comparative Literature* and the informative survey of the most recent efforts presented by Jan Brandt Corstius in an essay entitled "Writing Histories of World Literature").[31] Within the framework of his exposition, the Dutch scholar calls attention to the fact that the vast majority of the overviews he has scrutinized are of the analytical kind and that, in most of them, the literatures are treated sequentially according to geographic, linguistic or chronological criteria. The Kindler volume *Die Literaturen der Welt* offers a cogent example of this practice, although the many literatures of India, for example, are dealt with in a single chapter—a procedure which tends to confuse the reader and prevents a proper assessment of proportionate values.

Attempts to write the history of world literature in such a way that the interrelationships of the various literatures participating in the making of the tradition are synthetically dealt with are as yet few and far between. The last major undertaking of this kind was the *Outline of Comparative Literature from Dante to O'Neill* by Werner P. Friederich and David H. Malone, which is by no means wholly successful.[32] Thus, until fairly recently, Brandt Corstius' stricture applied:

> After what has been said it seems obvious that the time for writing a history of world literature in the synthetic manner has not yet arrived. There is some difficulty in using the term "world literature" in connection with literary historiography. The term surely cannot be understood in the Goethean sense of the conditions favorable to cosmopolitanism in literature. For the history of world literature is neither a history of the preliminaries of a cosmopolitan literature nor the history of that literature itself. It cannot be taken in the canonic sense of the Great Books; the history of world literature cannot use this concept as an organic principle because we do not possess the knowledge demanded by such a task. It would perhaps be better simply to speak of the history of literature.[33]

In the last five years, however, there has been a new departure. Whether or not the plan of a jointly written Comparative History of Literatures in European Languages, outlined by the ICLA and now on the point of showing the first tangible results, can ever be realized *in toto* remains to be seen. But it can be assumed that at least the preliminary phase of this comprehensive survey—the projected series of analytical studies of different periods, currents, and international movements—will be completed in the foreseeable future.[34]

In discussing General Literature in the sense ascribed to that term by Van Tieghem, we moved into a fringe zone, a kind of scholarly no man's land that stretches between the domain of literature proper and other branches of learning which either tend in the direction of literature or are reflected by it in one way or another. One important border area of considerable interest for the comparatist is known as the history of ideas, and links belles-lettres with philosophy, theology and other systematic patterns of abstract thought. Since literature is a reservoir for the preservation, and a vehicle for the transmission of intellectual values, and thus occupies a central place in every culture, there is an abundance of such tangents. Therefore, whether or not he is a comparatist, the student of literature must determine their exact position. For eminently practical reasons, the comparatist must, moreover, decide whether to subscribe to the rigorous French conception of our discipline or to the more generous views expounded by Remak, in whose eyes

Comparative Literature is the study of literature beyond the confines of one particular country, and the study of the relationships between literature on the one hand and other areas of knowledge and belief, such as the arts, . . . philosophy, history, and the social sciences, the sciences, religion, etc., on the other. In brief, it is the comparison of one literature with another or others, and the comparison of literature with other spheres of human expression. (S/F, p. 3)

For brevity's sake, I shall temporarily skip the problems relating to the interaction between, and mutual illumination of, literature and the other arts (music, painting, sculpture, architecture, the dance, the film, for example), because I am going to raise this issue in the concluding chapter, where I shall also be concerned with the so-called semi-literary genres, such as the libretto, the emblem, and the screenplay. Let it be said here by way of anticipation, however, that insofar as literature is an art, that is, the product of a nonutilitarian, creative activity, it has certain natural affinities with the realms presided over by the other Muses, which makes it plausible, and even probable, that common denominators (which, in turn, may serve as a solid basis for comparison) exist in spite of the different media involved. If only for this reason, I am inclined to qualify as "comparative" the study of belles lettres in their cross-relation with the other arts, especially when an actual linking-up or fusion has occurred, as in the Wagnerian *Gesamtkunstwerk* or in the case of *Doppelbegabungen* (multiple talents) of individual artists working in two or more different media. To the purists among my colleagues, who wish to see Comparative Literature contained within strictly literary confines, it may be reassuring if I promise always to use literature as the starting point and goal. Even in this particular instance, however, I tend to doubt the wisdom of separating scholarship from pedagogy, as Friederich has proposed we do in order to salve our philological conscience.[35]

To my mind the answer is not nearly as simple in the case of studies involving the connections between literature and nonaesthetic or primarily nonaesthetic "spheres of human expression" such as philosophy, sociology, theology, historiography, and the pure or applied sciences. Before reaching any conclusions in this regard, one might pose the seemingly naive question as to what actually constitutes literature. This very problem, which von Einsiedel briefly touches upon in his introduction to *Die Literaturen der Welt* (pointing out that, in medieval Latin, at least beginning with St. Jerome, *litteratura* designated chiefly secular works, whereas the sacred writings were called *scriptura*),[36] was significantly raised by Escarpit in his contribution to the still unpublished International Dictionary of Literary Terms.[37]

In this context, we can trace the etymology of the term and the historical evolution of its meaning only in broad outline. This much is certain, however: in English as well as in French, the word "literature" was originally used in the sense of learning (*Bildung*) or erudition. Voltaire, for instance, speaks of Chapelain as having had "une littérature immense," and it was not until the eighteenth century that the focus was finally shifted from the subject to the object of study. But even at this relatively late stage of the development, "literature" included practically all published writings, regardless of their nature (as in English, French and German, the noun is still frequently used in the sense of "secondary literature"). Especially in the eighteenth century, nonutilitarian writing was often qualified as "poesy" or its cognates. Not until the nineteenth century were pragmatic writings systematically syphoned off from nonpragmatic ones. Only when this distinction becomes universal do we arrive at the definition of literature furnished by Raymond Queneau in his foreword to the *Encyclopédie de la Pleïade*, where we are told that it is a "manner of writing opposed to the functional use of the written word" in an age in which the "technicians have gradually raised their specialties to the dignity of sciences." Let us not forget, however, that even as late as the turn of the century, the Nobel Prize for literature was repeatedly conferred upon prominent natural scientists and philosophers.

Since the split between scientific and "aesthetic" literature is now a *fait accompli* (borderline cases like science fiction notwithstanding) the interrelationship of the two spheres is definitely a methodological crux. Let it be said at the outset that here, as so often in the intellectual realm, a perfect line of demarcation cannot always be drawn, since we are inevitably faced with hybrid forms—for instance the historical novel, the essay, the diary, the autobiography and other literary or semi-literary genres, to which renewed attention has recently been drawn. To be more specific: how, for example, should we classify Søren Kierkegaard's *Either/Or*, which at least one contemporary critic regards as a psychological-erotic novel? And what about Rousseau's *Confessions*, Goethe's *Dichtung und Wahrheit*, André Gide's diaries, La Bruyère's *Caractères*, and Montaigne's *Essais*? And can one regard the study of Sigmund Freud's impact on the French Surrealists as a literary and/or "comparative" topic?[38] In the context of German cultural history, for instance, it is generally taken for granted that Nietzsche should also be treated as a *Dichter*

—not only because of the poems he wrote or the literary nature of his prose style, but also on account of his influence on many German and non-German writers—the young Gide, Gabriele d'Annunzio and the brothers Heinrich and Thomas Mann among them. However, in the case of mystics like Meister Eckhart and Jakob Boehme, as in that of philosophers like Arthur Schopenhauer and Henri Bergson, such a label would be somewhat more questionable. Kant's, Hume's and Aristotle's writings, finally, would seem to be too technical in most instances to deserve a prominent place in literary history.

The French, whose intellectual life is more unified and better integrated than that of Germany (for in France almost all written utterances are judged according to style), view Descartes, along with Montaigne, Pascal and Bergson, as literary authors in good standing; whereas the names of John Locke or John Stuart Mill are conspicuously absent from most histories of English literature. Theoretically, literary scholarship, if it wishes to be reckoned with, should probably refrain from studying other than literary phenomena. But in actual practice an extension of the area of presumed competence is unavoidable, as in the case of the Brechtian *Lehrstück* and Lucretius' didactic poem *De rerum natura.*

Clearly, in comparing literary works with nonliterary ones, the floodgates to dilettantism are thrown open as often as the literary historian or critic demonstrates a lack of incisive first-hand knowledge of the scientific disciplines he seeks to study in their literary applications. Remak's proposal to annex this no man's land to Comparative Literature rests on the benevolent assumption that in every case one can, and must, distinguish between pragmatic and systematic criteria. In other words, "We must make sure that comparisons between literature and a field other than literature are accepted as 'comparative literature' only if they are *systematic* and if a definitely *separable, coherent discipline* outside of literature is studied as such." As the few examples which Remak adduces demonstrate, however, such a view is methodologically untenable. Moreover, it is unique in the history of our discipline, since neither the French nor the American school of Comparative Literature, in its chief representatives, has endorsed it.

Few comparatists, for example, would assent to the notion that the study of the historical sources of a Shakespeare drama waxes comparative the moment "historiography and literature are the main poles of the investigation," or that the study of the function of money in Honoré de Balzac's novel *Père Goriot* would be comparative "if it were principally . . . concerned with the literary osmosis of a coherent financial system or set of ideas." Clearly, the former topic is the sole concern of the critic or historian of English literature, and the latter issue is of interest only to the Romance scholar on the one hand and the economic historian on the other. To use a Faustian metaphor, carrying colonization that far means, in my opinion, dissipating the very forces that require consolidation; for as comparatists we are not a people lacking space but rather one having too much of it, and suffering from a kind of intellectual agoraphobia.

Convinced that, in the long run, the call for historical/ philological *sécurité* is compatible with Remak's call for "more imagination," I shall deal, first of all, with the methodologically "safe" topics of influence (Chapter Two) and literary fortune (Chapter Three). The important question of translation and translators (which extends to all other types of intermediaries as well) can be touched upon only in this connection, although it evidently belongs in a survey of this kind. For information regarding this important field of investigation the reader is referred to the vast body of secondary literature produced primarily in the last two decades. These "orthodox" chapters will be followed by those devoted to periodization (Chapter Four), to the history and theory of genres (Chapter Five), and to the freshly rehabilitated subject of thematology (Chapter Six). This solid chunk of literary theory relevant to Comparative Literature studies will be followed by a chapter focusing on the interrelationship of the arts (Chapter Seven), by a lengthy appendix detailing the history of our discipline (Appendix I), and a brief survey of the bibliographical situation (Appendix II). No separate chapters have been assigned to the comparative study of oral (folk) literature,[39] to the question of parallelism (to which a recently completed dissertation addresses itself),[40] and to comparative metrics and stylistics.[41] All these matters, and others as well, will be discussed, passim and in passing, whenever the need or the occasion arises.

Two 𝒮 Influence and
Imitation

THE notion of influence must be regarded
as virtually the key concept in Comparative Literature
studies, since it posits the presence of two distinct and
therefore comparable entities: the work from which the
influence proceeds and that at which it is directed. At this
point, I hardly need to stress that, as Wellek notes, the difference between the study of influences occurring within
a national literature, and that of influences which transcend linguistic boundaries is not a qualitative and hence
methodological one. The two approaches are merely distinguished by the fact that, in the latter case, works written in two different languages are scrutinized, which generates an urge to account for the language barrier.

In Ihab H. Hassan's opinion, it is unfortunate that often,
in literary studies, "the concept [of influence] is called
upon to account for any relationship, running the gamut
of incidence to causality, with a somewhat expansive
range of intermediate correlations."[1] In recent years, this
question—which is vital for the comparatist—has repeatedly been the focus of scholarly attention, especially in the
United States. Besides Hassan, scholars like Anna Balakian, Haskell Block, Claudio Guillén, and Joseph T. Shaw
have participated in the lengthy and animated discussion.[2]
The controversy reached its temporary climax at a symposium held during the First Congress of the ACLA.[3] In
the following pages, the views of the scholars referred to

will be discussed with a view toward clarifying the concept of influence.

To prevent undue methodological complications I shall at the outset disregard the fact that often the "emitter" and the "receiver" of a literary influence are not in direct touch with each other but are linked by "intermediaries" or "transmitters," such as translators, reviewers, critics, scholars, travellers, or vehicles like books and journals. The function of the intermediary is ignored here, as a matter of principle, but will be briefly dealt with in the following chapter. Two examples will serve to draw the reader's attention to the fact that, in the case of influences, the question is not invariably one of simple cause/effect relationships.

To begin with, Mikhail Lermontov was a Russian poet who borrowed from Pushkin the model of the Byronic verse tale, but at the same time went back to Byron's own works in order to utilize certain characteristics of the English poet which had been overlooked or rejected by the author of *Eugene Onegin*. Byron's influence on Lermontov was thus twofold. This situation elicited the following comment from J. T. Shaw:

One of the most complex problems in the study of literary influence is that of direct and indirect influence. An author may introduce the influence of a foreign author into a literary tradition, and then, as in the case of the Byronic tradition in Russia, it may proceed largely from the influence of the native author. But as the tradition continues, it may be enriched by another native author going back to the foreign author for materials or tonalities or images or effects which were not adopted by the first author. (S/F, p. 94)

A.O. Aldridge, on the other hand, uses the example of Benjamin Franklin and his collection of moralizing commonplaces, *Poor Richard's Almanac*, to show that "one author may be influenced by parts of another's work without being aware of his predecessor as an artist or of the totality of his work" (CLS, Adv. Issue, p. 146). Some of the

maxims included in the almanac originated with La
Rochefoucauld; but it would be hard to prove in each case
whether Franklin borrowed them directly from the Frenchman or whether he derived his knowledge of them from
an English-language compilation.

I turn to the systematic study of the problem with the
proviso, in the form of a warning, that in principle the
comparatist should make no qualitative distinction between the active (giving) and passive (receiving) factors of
an influence, for there is, or should be, as little disgrace in
receiving as there is honor in giving. In most cases, at any
rate, there is no direct lending or borrowing, and instances
of literal imitation are probably rarer than more or less
creative transmutations.

Schools and movements would seem to constitute an
important exception to this rule of thumb; for, in such
configurations, emission and reception, characterizing the
relations between a master and his pupils, or a leader and
his followers, are often closely attuned to each other. This
relationship, however, constitutes not influence but imitation. It should also be noted that, in this present theoretical discussion of the problem, less attention needs to be
paid to the emitter, since his contribution is to be weighed
in the chapter on reception. In reception studies, however,
purely aesthetic criteria play a relatively minor role since,
chronologically, reception can best be characterized as a
preliminary step to the kind of assimilation known as
influence.

For the moment, I bypass the question whether, and to
what extent, literary influence is a conscious or unconscious form of appropriation. In terms of their mutual interdependence, we might tentatively and dialectically define influence as unconscious imitation, and imitation as
directed influence. As Shaw aptly remarks: "In contrast to
imitation, influence shows the influenced author producing work which is essentially his own. Influence is not
confined to individual details or images or borrowings or
even sources—though it may include them—but is some-

thing pervasive, something organically involved in and presented through artistic works" (S/F, p. 91). Aldridge, who defines influence as "something which exists in the work of one author which could not have existed had he not read the work of a previous author," corroborates Shaw when stating: "Influence is not something which reveals itself in a single, concrete manner, but it must be sought in many different manifestations" (CLS, Adv. Issue, p. 144). In other words: Influence cannot be quantitatively measured.

If one wishes to exhaust the range of possibilities opening up to the student of influences, one may conceive of a series of steps which, beginning with literal translation, proceeds in an ascending order through *adaptation, imitation,* and *influence* to the original work of art. "Originality" applies to creative innovations in form or content as well as reinterpretations and combinations of ingredients borrowed from diverse models. In this regard, I am in agreement with Wellek and Warren, who note that

Originality is usually misconceived in our time as meaning a
mere violation of tradition, or it is sought for at the wrong place,
in the mere material of the work of art, or in its mere scaffolding
—the traditional plot, the conventional framework.... To work
within a given tradition and adopt its devices is perfectly
compatible with emotional power and artistic value.[4]

The dialectic of originality and imitation has long pervaded cultural history. Thus imitation (whose sibling is eclecticism) is generally praised in classicist periods and invariably damned by such anticlassical "movements" as Storm and Stress, Romanticism, and Surrealism. As plagiarism, that is, as imitation on the sly or quotation without reference to the source, it is generally unacceptable; yet exactly where plagiarism ends and creative imitation begins is often doubtful, as in the case of Brecht's "impudent" use of K. L. Ammer's Villon translations in his *Dreigroschenoper.*[5]

"In the case of imitations," says Shaw, "the author gives

up, to the degree he can, his creative personality to that of another author, and usually of a particular work, while at the same time being freed from the detailed fidelity expected in translation" (S/F, p. 88). *Adaptations*—which, when they involve works written in a foreign tongue, are often based on literal translations—range all the way from congenial reworkings of a model to more or less commercial attempts at making a work palatable to foreign audiences, as in the case of Maurice Valency's English version [*The Visit*] of Friedrich Dürrenmatt's play, *Der Besuch der alten Dame*. The resulting product often amounts to "creative treason" (*trahison créatrice*). In recent years, some leading American poets—Robert Lowell, for example—have employed an unusual form of poetic recreation which they themselves tout as imitation. Like Goethe in his *West-Östlicher Divan*, or Pound and Brecht in their reworkings of Chinese poetry, they have, using available translations, produced lyrical paraphrases that are "original."

Another kind of imitation is not based on a particular model but aims at the style of a single poet, a whole movement, or even an entire period. In scholarly parlance, this technique is known as "stylization" (the German *Pastiche* and French *pastiche*): "Related to an imitation but perhaps best considered separately is a *stylization*, in which an author suggests for an artistic purpose another author or literary work, or even the style of an entire period, by a combination of style and materials" (Shaw, in S/F, p. 89). Shaw cites the example of Pushkin's epitaph for Byron and his use of the old Russian style in certain portions of *Eugene Onegin*. In this context, one might refer to the familiar practice, common in turn-of-the-century secondary schools, of requiring students to write poems in the style of certain classics or contemporary works (see T. S. Eliot's youthful exercises as described by Rudolf Germer).[6]

As a comic variant of stylization, we should mention the *burlesque* which (say in the operettas of Gilbert and Sullivan) ridicules a style by means of a comically distorted imitation. In the *pastiche* (which is not humorous), on the other hand, formal traits and, more rarely, traits related to subject matter and extracted from different works, are loosely but not ludicrously mixed. If an imitation pokes fun at specific literary models, one speaks of *parody* in the strict sense. Whereas in literary *satire* and pictorial *caricature* life itself furnishes the model, art serves the same function in the case of parody.[7] In this connection, it should be emphasized that parody and satire are frequently found side by side, and often complement and enhance each other. Moreover, it sometimes happens that in parody the consciously distorting imitation of a model results in an original product. Unconscious parody, on the other hand, is a contradiction in itself, although it is tempting to think of *Stilblüten*, *Kitsch*, and literary clichés in precisely these terms.

As creative genres, parody and travesty form a bridge to the so-called negative influences, by which latter term scholars like Anna Balakian signify the emergence of new trends and beliefs within a national literature, often inspired by foreign models in protest against prevailing artistic theories and practices. Literary history offers a wealth of relevant examples, such as Victor Hugo's repudiation of the Neoclassicism of Corneille and Racine in the foreword to his drama *Cromwell*, and Filippo Marinetti's unmitigated Futurist rejection of the art "of the museums."

As Professor Balakian points out, such "negative" influences are felt mostly within a national literature, as when rebellious sons rise in protest against their literary fathers:

It is interesting to note that very often the influences of authors of the same nationality and language upon each other are negative influences, the result of reactions, for generations often tend to be rivals of each other and in the name of individualism reject in the work of their elders what they consider to be the conventions of the past. (*YCGL*, 11 [1962], p. 29)

Thus, she continues, Comparative Literature will be rather indifferent to this remarkable and characteristic phenomenon of literary history, all the more so since, in the case of importation, "there is no longer a question of rivalry, and particularly as the reading of foreign literature is done generally at a more mature age when one may be more aware of the need for models and direction."[8] An interesting variant of negative influence, the phenomenon known as "counter-design" (Gegenentwurf), a term coined or at least popularized by Brecht, should perhaps also be mentioned. Here, a literary model is changed into its opposite, as it were, through a reversal of the polemic thrust, much as Brecht at one point intended to do with Beckett's drama Waiting for Godot.

It is necessary to draw still further lines of demarcation, in order to avoid pitfalls in terminology and semantic overlaps. The urgency of such regulation is underlined by the fact that the French theoreticians of Comparative Literature were singularly reluctant to distinguish between "influence" and "effect" (impact). Thus, Van Tieghem writes: "Moreover, in practice, the study of a writer's influence on a foreign writer or country is so closely linked to the study of his appreciation or his fortune . . . that it is often impossible to separate them from each other" (p. 117).

In his rather eclectic survey, Guyard even goes so far as to regard "influence" as one of several phenomena to be treated under the heading "The Fortunes of Authors." Although he expressly states that one must differentiate between diffusion, imitation, fortune, and influence, he indiscriminately lists the cult of Rousseau, the effect of Shakespearean drama on the French Romantics, and the European dissemination of Voltaire's ideas among the "several kinds of influence." Guyard opens Chapter Five ("Influence and Success") of his compendium with the equally ambiguous sentence: "The fortunes of authors outside the countries of their origin have certainly kindled, in France and among foreign adherents of the French comparative school, more studies than any other branch of Comparative Literature" (p. 58).

By comparison, Carré shows better sense, for in his foreword to Guyard's book, he speaks of influence studies as
being "difficult to manage" and "often deceptive" and has
a marked preference for straightforward reception studies.
In the article Anna Balakian wrote for *Yearbook of Comparative and General Literature*, as well as in the above-
mentioned symposium, she bemoans the contamination
of influence and reception studies and demonstrates how
very different are the data to be accounted for in each case.
Reception studies, that is to say, may well succeed in shedding new light on the artistry of the emitter, but in most
cases they operate on sociological, psychological, ethnic or
even statistical levels. Generally, their unity depends on
the unity of the emitter whose fame and reputation are to
be accounted for. With influence studies, on the other
hand, the primary interest is in tracking the sources of
creativity, a task in which quantitative criteria are replaced
by qualitative ones. Here, too, the dialectic of originality
and imitation is at work:

One is sometimes led to wonder whether any study of influence
is truly justified unless it succeeds in elucidating the particular
qualities of the borrower, in revealing along with the influence,
and almost in spite of it, what is infinitely more important: the
turning point at which the writer frees himself of the influence
and finds his originality. (*YCGL*, 11 [1962], p. 29)

In an aperçu of Gustave Lanson's, quoted by Guyard, the
line separating quantity from quality is even more clearly
drawn, with reference to the determinism of the Natural-
ists: "The great works are those which Taine's doctrine
does not entirely dissolve."
The use of quotes or allusions offers a special case of
influence. Literal correspondences (unless they are coinci-
dental) constitute an extremely superficial form of influence; indeed, they still belong within the realm of reception studies. The qualitative leap occurs in situations of
the kind which Hermann Meyer studies in *Das Zitat in
der Erzählkunst*, i.e., in extended prose works where quo-

tations are used in the manner of *leitmotifs* and thus assume the function of structural props.[9] Very informative, in this respect, is the Naturalistic sketch "Papa Hamlet," published by Arno Holz and Johannes Schlaf under the pseudonym Bjarne P. Holmsen. For, in pursuing their parodistic and satiric intents, these authors place literal or not-so-literal quotes from Shakespeare's drama in the mouth of their rather seedy protagonist. Unintentional or half-intentional quotes, such as the numerous *Faust* echoes in modern German literature, can hardly be counted as genuine influences, simply because they occur randomly and are merely proof of the speaker's formal education.

At this point, reference should perhaps be made to that type of negative influence which Escarpit has named creative treason.[10] The French champion of literary sociology alludes thus to the well-known fact that literary works are often misunderstood by a subsequent, or even their contemporary, public. Escarpit speaks of "recoveries" or "resurrections" which enable a work "to surmount social, spatial, or temporal barriers and achieve surrogate successes with audiences other than those originally contemplated." He continues,

We have seen that the foreign audiences do not have direct access to the work. What they see in it is not what the author wanted to express. There is no coincidence or convergence between their intentions and those of the author, but there may be compatibility. That is to say, the author did not expressly wish to put something in or did not even dream of its being there. (p. 111)

As typical examples of such shifts in emphasis due to social, historical, or cultural differences, Escarpit cites the fate of Swift's *Gulliver's Travels* and Defoe's *Robinson Crusoe*, books which are now popular among children, whereas Lewis Carroll's classic *Alice in Wonderland* attracts many adult readers and critics. This whole trend is effectively parodied in F. C. Crews's book *The Pooh Perplex* (New York: Dutton, 1965).

In the case of translation, creative treason is almost unavoidable, and there is a popular Italian saying which
speaks, not incorrectly, of the *traduttore* as a *traditore*.
Seen from the standpoint of the receptive and receiving
literature, a literal translation (especially of lyric poetry)
is, in any case, indefensible. The transfer of a poem from
one idiom to another is justifiable only when it is congenial to the new audience so that "it gives the work a new
reality by furnishing it with the possibility of a new literary exchange with a larger audience, because it enriches
the work not simply with survival, but with a second existence" (Escarpit, p. 112).

The treason is clearly most creative when the recasting
of the model is not limited to mere translation, although,
even on this level, translation often plays a major role
(witness Baudelaire's versions of Poe). Anna Balakian
draws our attention to a chain of *trahisons créatrices* that
is firmly anchored in the nineteenth-century tradition, but
which can be seen as pointing in either direction: namely,
that of French Symbolism, which extends from the German Romantics (mainly Novalis) through A. W. Schlegel,
Coleridge, and Poe to Baudelaire and Mallarmé, and continues past Symbolism to Surrealism.

Twice more we must briefly pause on our way to the
core of the present chapter. First of all, it should be stressed
that in the case of the so-called analogy or parallel studies
there can be no question of influence in the proper sense,
but only of "affinities" or "false" influences. Witness the
following example, given by Van Tieghem:

There are very marked affinities which at first it seems plausible
to attribute to an influence; thorough investigation shows that
there is none. There are two classic examples of this kind. "That
fellow Ibsen, who is so much talked about, is not original," said
Jules Lemaître in 1895. "All of his social and moral ideas are
found in George Sand." Georg Brandes . . . replied that Ibsen had
never read Sand. "That makes no difference," said Faguet to
M. Huszar. It makes a lot of difference: they moved in the same
current but are not indebted to each other: hence there was no

influence. The other example is that of Alphonse Daudet, considered, on the basis of *La Petite Chose*, to be an imitator of Dickens. But he firmly denied having read Dickens. However strange it may seem, there was, then, no influence but only a common trend. (p. 136f.)

From such evidence Van Tieghem would infer that one must treat the relationship of Ibsen to George Sand, and of Daudet to Dickens, under the heading of General rather than Comparative Literature. I, for one, eschew a pat solution while sharing, in principle, Ihab Hassan's view that one must clearly differentiate between affinity and influence:

When we say that A has influenced B, we mean that after literary or aesthetic analysis we can discern a number of significant similarities between the works of A and B. . . . So far we have established no influence; we have only documented what I call affinity. For influence presupposes some manner of causality. (*JAAC*, 14 [1955], p. 68)

For all the plausibility of this statement, it must be observed that the two phenomena are not always distinct, since affinities and influences are often intertwined. For instance, Claudio Guillén, in a footnote to his article "Literatura como sistema," points out that there are, in the *Celestina*, attributed to Fernando de Rojas, textual echoes of other Spanish works; on the whole, however, these "influences" are less significant than the impact of the Stoic tradition evidenced in Petrarch's *De remediis*—even though there are no verbal parallels to Petrarch.[11]

The scholar dealing with the problem of influence will be forced to draw, on many occasions, upon the concept of *source* (*Quelle*), which looms especially large in nineteenth-century literary historiography. A connection between influence and source exists, semantically, by virtue of the fact that both terms relate to the flow of liquid, the source being the origin of that flow, and the influence or influx (the German noun *Einfluss* covers both) its goal, that is, the point at which the movement ceases. In literary scholarship, one would do well to distinguish between these concepts and to use "source" only with regard to thematic models, subjects which furnish material but are, themselves, nonliterary. Shaw justly speaks of "source" as the matter "providing the materials or the basic part of the materials—especially the plot—for a particular work" (S/F, p. 90). Thus Holinshed's *Chronicles* and Plutarch's biographies of the great Greeks and Romans, as well as news reports which serve as stimuli for literary works, would constitute bona fide sources.

In insisting on this distinction, one staves off any conflict with the usage designating the word "source" as a preformed literary model. But here, too, there are instances where confusion is unavoidable because the source itself is literary, as in the case of many mythological or legendary subjects which, even at their most elemental stage, are known only in their poetic guises. (Here the concept of Simple Forms, to be discussed in Chapter Five, comes in handy.) To put it even more bluntly: Aeschylus and Sophocles serve both as models and as principal sources for all Prometheus dramas and Oedipus or Antigone plays, respectively.

After this extended introduction, I now give the floor to a comparatist who refuses to accept the traditional concept of literary influence and who flatly asserts that the term is insofar inappropriate as it presupposes a dearth of creativity and poetic imagination. Since influence implies a passive role, Guillén—the scholar referred to—banishes this term and what it implies from the realm of aesthetics and wishes to retain it only *in psychologicis*, as a fragile link between a source and an original work of art. Seen in this way, source—newly merged with influence—is reduced to the role of a mere substratum, demonstrating that a true *creatio ex nihilo* is impossible.[12]

Using this thesis as my point of departure, I proceed following Guillén's argument with the hackneyed observation that in a study of literary influence the works as well as their authors must be accounted for, although generally greater emphasis will be placed on the works themselves. With his customary acumen, Ihab Hassan reminds us, however, that "no literary work can be said to influence another without the intermediacy of a human agent" (Hassan, p. 69). Thus, in determining influences, we are, in fact, compelled to proceed psychologically, even if we would prefer to steer clear of psychology. For it is clearly as dangerous to maintain that influences occur only between works (Zhirmunsky) as it is to state axiomatically that they involve only their authors (Guillén).

At the beginning of his article "The Aesthetics of Influence Studies in Comparative Literature," Guillén poses the question: "When speaking of influences on a writer, are we making a psychological statement or a literary one?" (*Proceedings* II, Vol. I, p. 175). In his contribution to the ACLA symposium, he subsequently called upon ordinary usage to support this view. After all, we like to say that author B was influenced by author A, whereas we should in all honesty assert that work B^1 shows traces of work A^1. "Thus," Guillén comments, "we prefer to retain the equivocal 'X was influenced by Y,' where we blend the psychological with the literary" (*CLS*, Special Advance Issue, p. 150).

In the course of his systematic presentation, Guillén seeks to resolve this apparent paradox, which has long been a topos in literary historiography. He objects, firstly, to the underlying assumption that a solid chain of causes and effects lies at the root of all influence, and maintains that actually we deal with two entirely different series pertaining to two different kinds of affinity. Thus the psychology of the creative process operates in the space intervening between an author A and his work A^1, the psychology of the receptive process in that separating work A^1 from author B, and the psychology of the creative process—this time enriched by the reception—once more between an author, B, and his work, B^1. At the same time, however, A^1 and B^1 should, ideally, transcend psychological subjectivism and interact in a strictly aesthetic manner. This, at least, is alleged by those scholars who castigate the "intentional fallacy" (Hassan calls it the "expressionist fallacy"), and will not be persuaded that a work of art is the conscious or unconscious expression of an individual and, therefore, bound to him with iron bands.

Two solutions to the problem at hand have, so far, been suggested and discussed in literary criticism. A simplistic one, cherished especially in the nineteenth century, sought to raise the barrier between art and psychology by a series of causes and effects subordinated to the ironclad law of causality—as if the step from A to A^1 were, in every way, equivalent to the steps leading from A^1 to B, and from B to B^1. This quantified, mechanistic conception of the creative process rests on the assumption that, basically, there is nothing new under the sun and that the imagination, too, is only a synthesizer. As might be expected, Taine is the chief defendant in the case which Guillén brings against this critical *modus operandi*:

Taine's interpretation of the creative act is not as explicit as his view of the nature of art or of the relationship between an artistic work and the people or the environment which produce it; to indicate a starting-point and an end-result, a cause and a product, is not the same as to show how the distance between the two is eliminated, that is to say, as to question the process of creation itself. We know that in Taine's system every work of art is determined by a cause and should be explained by it; but to indicate, again, that A controls B is not to show how the artist went from A to B. (*Proceedings* II, vol. I, p. 176)

Like most of his contemporaries, Guillén rejects this positivist solution. He is far more sympathetic to Croce's theory, which is based on the belief that a work of art is always *sui generis* and that it is, by its very nature, monadic:

At the moment in which a new work of art is born those of its predecessors which were present in the poet's mind, whether perfect or imperfect, great, mediocre or poor, turn inevitably into matter [i.e., raw material].[13]

In Croce's wake, similar views emerged in the late thirties and early forties among the New Critics and, in the German-speaking world, in the writings of Emil Staiger, whose book *Die Kunst der Interpretation* conveys the notion that the positivist who wants to know what is inherited and/or acquired abuses the law of causality by forgetting that the creative act—because it is creative—is nonderivative.[14]

Guillén shares this view in principle, but qua comparatist he does not like to scotch the concept of influence. (By the way, the practice of T. S. Eliot and Ezra Pound, the very poets acclaimed by the New Critics, contradicts Croce's puristic theory, as in the montage of the "Waste Land" and the "Cantos," as well as the various techniques described by Joseph Frank under the general heading of "reflexive reference.")[15] In his divided loyalty, Guillén eases his conscience by trying to strike a compromise between the two extremes, that is, he condones the use of psychological categories without abandoning his firm belief in the qualitative leap. For, in the execution of his program, influence is simply shunted onto the psychological track and appears as a moment or phase of the creative process:

Our idea of influence . . . would define [it] as a recognizable and significant part of the genesis of a literary work of art. . . . The writer's life and his *creative* work exist . . . on two different levels of reality. Influences, since they develop strictly on the former level, are individual experiences of a particular nature: because they represent a kind of intrusion into the writer's being or a modification of it or the occasion for such a change; because their starting-point is previously existing poetry; and because the alteration they bring about, no matter how slight, has an indispensable effect on the subsequent stages of the *genesis* of the poem. (*Proceedings II*, Vol. I, p. 181)

Guillén thus recognizes influence in the *process* or influx, but not in its *product*. Under these circumstances, however, he is wrong in regarding influence as a recognizable component of the genetic process. The example he uses clearly demonstrates how rarely a literary critic succeeds in penetrating to the inner sanctum of genius. It is, in fact, pure chance when the biography of a poet offers us clues to this type of influence.

The fact that the problem raised by Guillén is a logical rather than a poetological one is affirmed by his own admission, in a footnote pertaining to Block's objection, that it is difficult to determine "the exact moment in which a work of art becomes independent of its creator and assumes an aesthetic vitality of its own" (Ibid., p. 182, note 14).

Guillén in his attempt to create a new foundation for the study of literary influence has committed a sin of omission, or *petitio principii*, which rocks the scaffold he has erected. For he conceals or overlooks that what he calls influence and wishes to see upheld against all objections as the object of serious scientific study goes, more properly, by another name—that of *inspiration*. He actually speaks of "genetic incitation," and, in so doing, echoes Amado Alonso, who maintains that "literary sources must be related to the act of creation as incitations and forces of reaction."[16]

Inspiration, however, is in fact a psychological category; it presupposes, as an effect upon the poet, a personal experience which leaves visible traces in exceptional cases only. Even there where one honors it as a gift from Heaven it is always that ingredient of art which, by definition, is neither transferable nor communicable. It designates rather the point at which, out of the mass of available themes and techniques, the essence of the work-to-be-conceived suddenly flashes like lightning in the poet's mind. Moreover, inspiration is often extra-literary, drawing its nourishment from painting, music, history, or life itself.

Guillén himself refers to a poem written by his father ("Cara a cara") which received its basic impulse from the rhythmic *Gestalt* of Ravel's *Bolero*: "The stubborn, unrelenting, obsessive quality of this piece's rhythm—but only its rhythm—fired the poet's initial desire to write his tenacious response to the more chaotic aspects of life" (*Pro-

ceedings II, vol. I, p. 185). In the case of Valéry's "Cimetière Marin," it was, by the poet's own admission, a rhythmic figure totally devoid of specific musical models which obsessed him and led him, step by step, to the discovery of a metrical and strophic form and, finally, of a subject suited to that form.

In the case of "inspiration," then, we are dealing with a mood about which we know nothing unless the poet himself furtively permits us to peer into his soul. By definition, such a mood is not subject to scientific proof. Under these circumstances, the approach suggested by Guillén is truly impracticable.

Whether in determining literary influences we may overstep the bounds of literature proper is a question which, as far as the other arts are concerned, will be clarified in Chapter Seven. What stance we should take concerning the status of nonartistic influences, however, is difficult to say. Without probing into the matter deeply, I would point out that, although the scientific discoveries and theories of a Darwin, Marx, or Freud have had a powerful impact on literature (in such aesthetic doctrines as Naturalism, Surrealism, and Socialist Realism), this force should not be overrated, for, in these cases, an influence "will usually be upon content, rather than directly upon genre and style, upon *Weltanschauung* rather than upon artistic form" (Shaw in S/F, p. 93). Methodologically it seems therefore appropriate to separate this kind of effect from the purely aesthetic one and to distinguish, accordingly, in the study of Surrealism between the role of Freud and Charcot, on one hand, and that of Arnim and Lautréamont,[17] on the other.

I shall conclude the present chapter by analyzing Guillén's views regarding influences that are recognizable in the art work. Not unpredictably, Guillén assigns all factually ascertainable influences to the realm of literary *tradition* and *convention*, by which terms he means shared forms, types, subjects, or techniques (*topoi*, form and content of the elegy, the external structure of the five-act

drama, mythical and legendary figures, etc.) which cannot
—or at least can no longer—be credited to a specific writer
but have, in a manner of speaking, become public property
and now serve as useful vehicles within a given civilization.

Aldridge regards tradition and convention as "resem-
blances between works which form part of a large group
of similar works held together by a common historical,
chronological or formal bond" (*CLS*, Special Advance Issue, p. 143), while Guillén notes that traditions are dia-
chronic and conventions synchronic:

One tends to think of conventions synchronically, and of
traditions diachronically. A cluster of conventions forms the
literary vocabulary of a generation, the repertory of possibilities
that a writer has in common with his living rivals. Traditions
involve the persistence of certain conventions for a number of
generations, and the competition of writers with their ancestors.
(*CLS*, Special Advance Issue, p. 150)

To be distinguished from "tradition" and "convention"
are concepts like "program" or "manifesto," which presuppose an individual's, or group's, deliberate focus on a
clearly delineated goal, whereas tradition and convention
are characterized precisely by the fact that where they operate specific intentions can no longer be assigned.

Guillén poses what is certainly not intended, or not
solely intended, as a rhetorical question, namely: "Did a
Renaissance poet have to have read Petrarch in order to
write a Petrarchan sonnet?" And since the answer is clearly
in the negative, he surmises that "literary conventions are
not only technical prerequisites but also basic, collective
shared influences." Little fault can be found with this con-
jecture, which does not free us, however, from the obliga-
tion of scrupulously investigating, in every instance,
whether collective influences suffice to explain correspondences in form or subject matter.

My critique of Guillén's views has shown that the attempt to solve the problem of literary influence in this

manner, with the help of the dialectic of inspiration and tradition-convention, must ultimately fail on terminological and semantic grounds. Simultaneously with Guillén, but without dabbling in psychological categories, Hassan has attempted to take the bull by the horns. In his essay "The Problem of Influences in Literary History. Notes Toward a Definition," he tries to prove "that the ideas of Tradition and of Development provide, in most cases, a sounder alternative to the concept of Influence in any comprehensive scheme of literature" (*JAAC*, 14 [1955], p. 66). It will be noted that Hassan replaces "convention" with "development," and thereby dissolves spatial coexistence into temporal succession.

Hassan succeeds in unraveling the Gordian knot formed by the numerous intertwined strands of the complex subsumed under the concept of influence, which Guillén tries in vain to cut. To be sure, this solution, too, was not arrived at without the use of generalizations; for Hassan seeks to come to terms, at whatever price, with the plethora of historical, biographical, sociological, and even philosophical findings. His reflections culminate in the assertion that, in its full ambience, influence should no longer be understood as "causality and similarity operating in time," that is, as *rapports de fait* and parallels, but as a network of "multiple correlations and multiple similarities functioning in a historical sequence, functioning . . . within that framework of assumptions which each individual case will dictate" (p. 73). This definition furnishes, concurrently, an answer to Guillén's futile attempt at using Beelzebub to drive out the Devil. For only when the interpenetration of *rapports extérieurs* and *rapports intérieurs*, and the interrelation between specific influences and general conventions or traditions is fully considered, is it possible to reconstruct the chain A—A^1—B—B^1 satisfactorily.

Three ✍ Reception
and Survival

IN the preceding chapter, I have dealt at
some length with the view, embraced by Claudio Guillén,
that *influence* is a psychological phenomenon which
leaves no visible traces in the influenced work. I considered this theory to be both logically and methodologically
suspect because its originator introduced the concepts of
inspiration on the one hand and tradition and convention
on the other. A satisfactory solution of the problem would
seem to be possible, however, only after the borders separating "influence" from "reception"—a term for which
Horst Rüdiger, raising the matter to a more strictly aesthetic plane, would like to substitute survival (*Wirkung*)
or "appropriation" (*Aneignung*)[1]—have been clearly de-
marcated. "Influence" should preferably be used to denote
the relations existing between finished literary products,
while "reception" might serve to designate a wider range
of subjects, namely, the relations between these works and
their ambience, including authors, readers, reviewers, publishers and the surrounding milieu. The study of literary
reception, accordingly, points in the direction of literary
sociology or psychology.

A special kind of reception is the fortune (*succès*) of a
work, which may serve as a gauge of its popularity and can
be measured with the help of bestseller lists or performance statistics. Literary success, like any other, is often
superficial and short-lived. It may depend on a momen-
tary fashion or on external events, such as the awarding of

an honor like the Nobel Prize, the premature death of a writer, resulting in the formation of a legend, or, as in the case of Andrej Sinyavsky (Abram Tertz), the punishment meted out to an individual who has dared to censure a totalitarian regime. The fact that a work which wins public acclaim tends to attract imitators and emulators for commercial reasons goes without saying. In this way, success sometimes turns into quick but fleeting influence: the *Werther* fever led to *Werther* sequels in which the sensational and sentimental aspects of Goethe's novel were exploited. Regarding the literary consequences of this phenomenon, which is akin to plagiarism in the thematological realm, Elisabeth Frenzel notes:

It is characteristic that many works of the highest artistic merit use an established theme, and that relatively few have an original plot. These few are mostly works that capture the spirit of their time and in which the typical features of an age are most cogently presented. *Don Quixote, Simplicissimus, Robinson Crusoe, Werther*—such works, because they are truly topical, have initiated no true *Stoffgeschichte* but have merely found their emulators, who copied many specific traits of the model, such as the characters and their relations, the situations, and the plot.[2]

It need hardly be emphasized that popularity is not necessarily a prerequisite for literary influence. As a particularly flagrant case of an influence lacking popular support, we might mention the *Divine Comedy*, which has failed to make a lasting impression either with the general public outside Italy or with the bulk of foreign writers, but which, through the mediation of the few poets who were profoundly affected by it (as, later, a Baudelaire and an Eliot), became assured of its firm place within the literary tradition. Actually, conclusions of considerable sociological and—indirectly—literary merit can often be drawn from the lack of receptivity on the part of a given reading public, and the notion of *infortune* (P/R, p. 26) parallels the concept of *noninfluence*, introduced by Anna Balakian (*YCGL*, 11 [1963], p. 26).

If one attempts, as I shall do in the following pages, to distinguish *reception* from *influence,* one does so in full awareness of the obstacles which stand in the way of such a task. The fact that we will come across many marginal cases of partial or total overlap must not scare us off, however. Let us, rather, plunge *in medias res* by turning our attention to the phenomenon of "erudition" (*Belesenheit*), an important factor in the hierarchy of literary values. In the theatrical world, its equivalent would be the familiarity with the repertory, as exemplified, for instance, in the case of the Swiss playwright Max Frisch, who, a regular patron of the Zurich *Schauspielhaus* in his youth and early manhood, saw many productions of plays by Brecht, Claudel, Thornton Wilder, and Tennessee Williams, among others, which obviously affected him as a writer and were later to exert one or another kind of—sometimes latent—influence on his own dramas.

As an illustration of the literary outgrowth of erudition, I shall use Heinrich Mann's historical novel, *Henri Quatre,* in which the figure of Michel de Montaigne plays such a prominent role.[3] As the inventory of Mann's library reveals, he owned a copy of the *Essais,* some of which he graced with marginal notes. Several quotes from these pieces return like leitmotifs intermittently throughout the extended narrative, which, taken as a whole, breathes the spirit of Montaigne—i.e., enlightened skepticism. In addition to channeling Montaigne's writings into his own novel, however, Heinrich Mann also digested the historical facts, with which he familiarized himself by studying documents and other contemporary sources. Yet, for all the historical authenticity of the work, the fictional Montaigne—who liberally quotes from his own essays—is clearly a product of Mann's imagination. In this historical novel, then, the fusion of reception (here, erudition), influence, and originality would seem to be almost perfect.

The difference between influence and *Wirkung,* as far as literature is concerned, can be illuminated with the help of Franz Kafka's letters and diaries, which were not intended for publication and can therefore be regarded as genuinely autobiographical documents. The question concerning the influence of foreign authors upon Kafka (which interests the comparatist) has been more or less intelligently treated by scholars on both sides of the Atlantic. Thus, in a most instructive essay, Mark Spilka has demonstrated that the beginning of the novella "Metamorphosis" is directly related to Gogol's story "The Nose" and Dostoevsky's novel *The Double*, and that certain elements of its plot were apparently borrowed from *David Copperfield*.[4] But, if one turns to Kafka's letters and notebooks and examines which foreign authors are most frequently mentioned there, one discovers that the place of honor is not accorded to Gogol, to Dostoevsky or to Dickens, but to Gustave Flaubert, whose life and work fascinated Kafka to the point of obsession.

To date, no one, as far as I know, has attempted to prove a literary (stylistic or thematic) influence of Flaubert on Kafka. Such an attempt would probably fail, at any rate; for, as various entries in Kafka's diary show, the kinship of the two writers was primarily psychological and emotional. Thus, while working on his novel *Amerika*, Kafka wrote on June 6, 1912: "I am now reading in Flaubert's letters: 'My novel [he meant *L'Education sentimentale*] is the rock to which I cling, and I know nothing of what happens in the world.' Similar to what I said about myself in my diary on May 9th." The affinity alluded to by Kafka lies in the relation of the two authors to their works *in statu nascendi*, and in their compulsion to write at the expense of living. Flaubert literally withdrew from the world into physical isolation in order to continue the laborious work on *Madame Bovary* to the bitter end; but Kafka was saddled with a profession which was a torment to him, because it left him only weekends and nights for writing. Thus, in spite of its grim medical implications, the tuberculosis, diagnosed in 1917, was a virtual godsend.

The biographical significance of this spiritual affinity between Kafka and Flaubert is underscored by a second parallel within the psychological realm. At the end of July, 1913, Kafka wrote to his friend, Max Brod, regarding his planned marriage to Felice Bauer: "Everything gives me cause for reflection. Every joke in the humor magazines, the thought of Flaubert and Grillparzer, the sight of night-shirts on my parents' bed prepared for the night, Max's marriage."[5] The poet rightly considered the psycho-physio-logical inhibitions which surface in this passage as insur-mountable. He shared them, moreover, with Flaubert, who, on October 28, 1872, had written to George Sand: "Women have never fitted into my life; moreover, I am not rich enough, moreover . . . moreover . . . I am too old . . . and also too neat to inflict myself forever upon some-body else."

Our example proves that Flaubert's direct influence on Kafka was not—at least not exclusively or primarily—lit-erary; and it is perhaps only because both men are major authors of truly universal stature that this psychological "reception" is important for literary history and fruitful for Comparative Literature as well. In the ties linking Kafka to non-German authors, influence and reception combine more happily in the case of Strindberg—partly because the Swedish author, too, embedded his personal Inferno in his novels and plays, albeit much more directly so than the author of *The Trial*.

If one projects the psychological aura surrounding a writer into the sociological realm, one approaches per-sonal myths or legends of the kind which begin to form when biographical facts are twisted or simplified to the point of distortion. Quite often, new, fictitious traits are added in such cases. Thus it was that, in the Middle Ages, Dante came to be regarded as a sorcerer, largely on ac-count of a passage in the twentieth Canto of the *Inferno* concerning the origin of the name of his native city, Man-tua.[6] Similarly, Byron and Rimbaud may suffer as poets because posterity has crowned them with a martyr's wreath.[7] From the literary point of view, the accretions of personal myth sometimes operate in such a way that a poet is read or esteemed for a single work, and that his fame rests, accordingly, on too narrow a basis. Outside Germany, for instance, Goethe is, or was for a long time, most widely known as the author of *Werther*, whereas in the case of Christian Morgenstern, even within his native country, he became the "victim" of his *Galgenlieder*.

In contrast to the kind of psychologically "tainted" appropriation, the reception of a foreign work on the part of an author writing in a different tongue is a methodologically safe object of study for Comparative Literature, and that regardless of whether such reception has direct, indirect, or questionable literary results. Thus Klaus Schröter does not make a convincing case for his contention that Balzac greatly influenced the novels and novellas of young Heinrich Mann; but by adducing biographical evidence he shows why, despite Mann's intimate knowledge of Balzac's works, the latter wrote no major essays about the author of the *Human Comedy*:

The reasons for his failure to do a study on Balzac are external ones. They can be deduced from excerpts of Heinrich Mann's letters reproduced in an auction catalogue. In 1908, when Mann corresponded with the Insel-Verlag concerning the publication of his collected works, he offered to write an introduction to an edition of *La Comédie humaine* which was being published that same year. He submitted his proposal through the lawyer Maximilian Brantl to Anton Kippenberg, who replied on August 10, 1908: "We do not concur with your opinion as regards the introduction. To be sure, we believe, like you, that Heinrich Mann would have acquitted himself most honorably of the task, but, unlike yourself, we find that the introduction by Hugo von Hofmannsthal is also extremely subtle and accomplished."[8]

The simplest mode of the kind of appropriation referred to above is that where, thanks to his linguistic skill, the writer who does the receiving has direct access to the works of a foreign literature. To be sure, here too we must count on qualitative differences, according to the expertise of the recipient. If the latter's knowledge of the foreign tongue is scant or imperfect, misunderstandings are likely to occur and may result in involuntary creative treason. In such cases, it is not always easy to make out where, in a given instance, the creative transformation ends and the conscious manipulation begins. Brecht's relation to English and French literature, for example, must be viewed from this double perspective. Questions such as "Did he have access to the original texts?", "Did he avail himself of this opportunity?", "Was he, in recasting a model, concerned with being faithful to it?" force themselves on the investigator and enable him to establish the proper balance between the various shades of influence and reception.

Reception studies are especially attractive when the recipient also acts as an intermediary. In her article "Influence and Literary Fortune," Anna Balakian, using Baudelaire's translations of Poe and Gide's recasting of Blake's poems as examples, demonstrates what creative possibilities are inherent in the distortion of a model undertaken by the poet-translator. Two passages from Hölderlin's version of *Antigone* and its Brechtian *Gegenentwurf* bring this aspect of reception studies into focus.

Hölderlin's German translation of the Greek tragedy is faithful to the original insofar as—apart from a few "objectionable" passages[9]—it reproduces the text literally verse by verse. Nonetheless, his contemporaries noted the obscurity of certain phrases and constructions. The contorted quality of Hölderlin's diction can be explained in two ways: on the one hand, by the poet's well-meaning intention to furnish a literal version instead of reproducing the sense in accordance with the state of the German language in his own time, that is, by modernizing and thus inevitably "adapting" it. This might well account for Ismene's archaic-sounding remark: "You color for me, it seems, a red word." ["Du färbst mir, scheint's, ein rotes Wort." (verse 20)], which, through the Sophoclean use of the verb *kalkhaínein*, is etymologically linked to the hunt for the purple fish (sepia).

On the other hand, Hölderlin's knowledge of Greek was probably inadequate for an understanding of certain passages, such as the portion of a choral ode which he renders (line 599f.) as "Denn jetzt ist über die letzte Wurzel gerichtet das Licht in Oedipus Häusern" ("For now the light in Oedipus' houses is cast over the last root"); the same line is translated by Dudley Fitts and Robert Fitzgerald as "So lately this last flower of Oedipus' line drank the sunlight." Brecht, who did not know Greek (as he did Latin), transposed approximately one third of Hölderlin's text, including the above-mentioned, recrudescent lines, into his 1947 version of the drama. The effect he achieved in this particular instance was not the intellectual detachment usually resulting from alienation (his favorite technique), but, rather, contrived unintelligibility. Brecht's "alienation through classicality" is revealed here as a two-edged sword.

The image of foreign authors and their works projected by the writer-as-critic adds another dimension to the kind of "reception" we are presently concerned with. Quite illuminating, in this respect, are the successive levels of appropriation in the case of Flaubert, who, in German literary criticism of the late nineteenth and early twentieth century, was praised or blamed first as a Realist or Naturalist (mostly, one suspects, on account of the scandal resulting from the publication of *Madame Bovary*), and then as a Romantic and Parnassian.[10] Only gradually did it dawn on his German admirers or detractors that these divergent aspects of his *oeuvre* were not mutually exclusive, but that the Romanticist and the Realist (*Madame Bovary*) or the Decadent and the Parnassian (*La Tentation de Saint Antoine*) were coexistent and often dialectically present within one single work.

In his essay "Aufgaben und Möglichkeiten der Rezeptionsforschung" the German comparatist Klaus Lubbers addresses himself to what are, methodologically, the most pressing questions pertinent to that topic.[11] *Rezeptionsforschung* is a branch of historical scholarship, especially dear to the Germans, which is primarily concerned with the problem of literary survival and with showing how a literary canon is formed and how it changes. Such a demonstration necessitates a close scrutiny of the role which political and social factors play in the process of crystallization. That it is not always the "fittest" works which survive is shown by the fact that the preservation of ancient works (like most of the extant Euripidean dramas) is sometimes due to the chance discoveries of papyruses. On the other hand, only the "canonic" seven tragedies of Aeschylus and Sophocles have been passed on to posterity.

Rezeptionsforschung thus understood and practiced will, for instance, seek to explain the constituency of the circle of poets assembled in the Limbo of Dante's *Inferno* by raising the question as to why Lucian, Ovid, and Horace outscored the three Greek master tragedians, why the now almost forgotten Statius is Dante's leader in the *Purgatorio*, and how it happened that only beginning with the seventeenth century has Homer been accorded a European fame equaling that of his "imitator" Virgil.

Need it be emphasized that scholarly reception studies must be historical rather than critical if they aim at recording, *sine ira et studio*, the variations wrought upon the image of a poet's art? "The dialectically trained historian of literature, who specializes in reception studies," says Klaus Lubbers, "does not proceed judgmentally but descriptively. He yields his right to judgment to a representative sampling of critics from the various epochs" (p. 301f.).

Criteria of the kind which T. S. Eliot uses in his essay "What is a Classic?"—the linguistic and moral maturity of the nation which produces a classic author, and the existence of earlier stages in the history of the national literature which are the platform on which he erects his work —are of interest to the comparatist only insofar as they say something about the capacity and willingness to receive on the part of this English poet, who finds Homer, Dante, and Shakespeare to be less exemplary than Virgil, and who shocks German readers by his indifference toward, and proudly vaunted ignorance concerning, Goethe. Even in his Hamburg lecture, delivered after the presentation of the Goethe Prize, Eliot did not altogether dispel this impression.

As the *Rezeptionsforscher* knows only too well, the classic writer is, essentially, the one who resurfaces from the limbo to which he finds himself banished immediately after his death, and who is extolled by subsequent generations. As Escarpit puts it,

> Quantitatively, the decisive and most severe selection occurs in the first generation beyond the biographical zone. Every writer has a rendezvous with oblivion either ten, twenty, or thirty years after his death. If he crosses that formidable threshold, he joins the literary population and is assured a virtually permanent survival—at least as long as the collective memory of the civilization which witnessed his birth endures. (p. 31)

The oversimplifying tendency of this dogmatic statement will be apparent to those who know their world literature. For this rule suffers significant exceptions, as in the case of Brecht, who did not have to wait for ten, twenty, or thirty posthumous years before crossing the threshold to immortality, since the universal acclaim he had won in his lifetime continued unabated beyond his death, although more recently a reassessment of his contribution to literature in the twenties and a general realignment of values has begun. The matter is different with Kafka, the great unknown of the twenties and thirties, whose work is now practically buried under the weight of his commentators and imitators, and whose very fame threatens to choke its source.

There is no end to variations on this theme. Escarpit, for instance, notes the "resurrections" and rediscoveries of neglected artists staged by writers or critics who find a forgotten masterpiece congenial or topical and restore it to prominence. Thus T. S. Eliot helped to give the metaphysical poets, Donne, Marvell, Herbert, and Crashaw, a new lease on life; and the New Critics, who were profoundly indebted to Eliot, used the works of those very poets as touchstones for their own poetics. The Existentialists, in turn, brought new esteem not only to Dostoevsky, but to certain lesser works by Ibsen (*Brand*) and Tolstoy (*The Death of Ivan Ilych*) as well. For the comparatist tilling this soil, the discovery of writers hitherto unknown in foreign countries is equally tantalizing. It is his special duty, for instance, to show why in France Kafka was enthroned by the Surrealists and why Brecht's international fame arose partly in the wake of Beckett, Ionesco, and the Theater of the Absurd.

Seen from the vantage point of world literature, to be read by many generations means to be read anew in every age. This historically conditioned perpetuation of creative treason seems to subvert the scholarly cry for the kind of philological accuracy (historicism) which seeks to place the work of art in its natural context before explaining it. If one holds the entirely justifiable view that each age needs its own Goethe, Schiller, or Kleist, one must pity the fatherland of great poets, for the simple reason that this avenue is closed to the native audience, even though new interpretations may well fill the gap created by the absence of new translations. Only in the event of a radical change in a still evolving language does the need for a subsequent translation arise, as with *Beowulf* and (perhaps) with Chaucer in English literature (whereas Shakespeare's plays are still accessible to the cultured Britisher, who would, nevertheless, ask for explanatory footnotes).

In present-day Germany, for example, publishers offer "bilingual editions" of the *Nibelungenlied* and the poems of Walther von der Vogelweide; and even the original text of Grimmelshausen's *Simplicius Simplicissimus*—like that of Rabelais' *Gargantua* and *Pantagruel*—must be adjusted for the contemporary reader. Similar circumstances obtain with regard to Ernst Elias Niebergall's Hessian dialect comedy *Der Datterich* and Carl Zuckmayer's Rhenish "Volksstück" *Der fröhliche Weinberg*.

These dialect pieces can, naturally, be transposed into High German; but in the process of translation an important (one might even say: the decisive) element—what we might call their authenticity, atmosphere, or tone—is almost invariably lost. In addition, there are works which are, literally, untranslatable because linguistically they are so idiosyncratic that any transplantation would be fatal. Such is the case with James Joyce, whose *Ulysses* may still be on the borderline, but whose *Finnegans Wake* is "foreign" even in the original.[12] Much the same could be said of German Expressionist writing in its most radical manifestations—August Stramm's terse *Wortkunst*, Johannes R. Becher's futuristic word cascades, and Gottfried Benn's syntactical acrobatics in poems like "Karyatide." Even the syntactically orthodox Georg Trakl often overtaxes the translator's patience and ingenuity. Witness the English version of "Trompeten" ("Trumpets") by Robert Bly and Jerome Wright, where the latent sense of the verse "Fahnen von Scharlach stürzen durch des Ahorns Trauer" turns into the virtual nonsense of the corresponding line "Banners of scarlet rattle through a sadness of maple trees."[13]

If, on one hand, the periodic need for a retranslation of foreign classics serves as a measure of their vitality—especially since, in every round of the "competition," the weaker contestants are eliminated—we have, on the other, translations which have, themselves, emerged as classics. To name but a few, there are the perennial and perennially challenged Shakespeare of Schlegel and Tieck, C. K. Scott-Moncrieff's tenacious version of Proust, and the French *Faust* by Gérard de Nerval. And the more extensive the foreign work to be translated, the more difficult it is to supplant an established rendition. Such is the case with the German and English versions of Homer by Voss and Dryden, respectively, which only lately were seriously challenged by Rudolf Alexander Schröder, Robert Fitzgerald (*Odyssey*) and Richard Lattimore (*Iliad* and *Odyssey*). Finally, the lack of authoritative translations may, in some cases, account for the fact that a classic author of one national literature has been unduly slighted in another. (Especially the products of the "minor" literatures are prone

to suffer this fate.) This may help to explain such anoma-
lies as Eliot's curious lack of appreciation for Goethe, and
the German indifference toward Chaucer.

Translations sometimes succumb to the kind of triviali-
zation previously referred to with regard to *Gulliver's
Travels* and *Robinson Crusoe*. This is often the case when
the translator lives by the motto "Omnia recipiuntur
secundum recipientem."[14] Falsifiers by choice, such adapt-
ors have the knack of appealing to current fashion or presumed ethnic peculiarities. Fortunately, commercial products like Maurice Valency's version of Dürrenmatt's *The
Visit*, previously referred to, are rarer than condensations
or garblings, such as the omission of the "technical" chapters in the German version of *Moby Dick* or the elimina-
tion of entire sections in the authorized translation by
Michael Bullock of Max Frisch's novel *Stiller*. In the latter
instance, the onus is all the greater, since the excisions
largely involve symbolic or allegorizing passages, whose
absence is a slap in the face of the intelligent reader. To
summarize our reflections on this topic, it might be said
that a book remains alive only so long as it can still be
misunderstood. And Lubbers agrees with Escarpit in concluding that the hallmark of great literature is its capacity
for being "betrayed."

The limited scope of our book does not permit an exhaustive treatment of either *doxologie* (as Frank Baur calls
the scholarly study of the fate of books and their authors),
or *mésologie*. The task of the latter branch of Comparative
Literature is defined by Van Tieghem as follows:

Among the modes of the literary exchange between two nations,
a place, and an important one at that, must be granted to the
intermediaries who have facilitated the diffusion in a given
country, and the adoption, on the part of a literature, of works,
ideas and forms pertaining to a foreign literature. (p. 152)

In the present, limited context, I must resist the urge to
examine the literary or sociological role of intermediaries,
such as professional translators. It should be remembered,

however, that a public's knowledge of a particular foreign literature depends, in large measure, on nonliterary factors: the publishers' economically weighted criteria of selection, the changing political scene (as exemplified by the history of literary relations between Germany and France after the wars of 1870–71, 1914–18, and 1939–45), and the role of the mass media (radio, television, film, etc.). In addition, the economic status of the translator should not be overlooked in an evaluation of international literary exchange; for, while in Germany, for instance, these professionals are widely recognized and earn a relatively decent living—although they, too, frequently work under the pressure of rigid deadlines—in the United States they are often poorly rewarded and forced to reel off their work at a dizzy pace. This, among other things, accounts for the poor quality of the authorized English versions of important novels by Gide, Hesse, and Robbe-Grillet, whereas the unevenness of Edwin and Willa Muir's translation of Kafka's *Der Prozess* would seem to be due more to the pair's insufficient knowledge of German. A rare combination of linguistic naiveté and blatant commercialism is apparent in Wirt Williams' "new" English version of Heinrich Mann's novel *Professor Unrat* which shamelessly plagiarizes an earlier and more faithful rendition.[15]

Unfortunately, the selection of translators for a given project is sometimes governed by the provisions of the international copyright. For in many instances this legal privilege is monopolistically exploited by its owners, so that some translators enjoy, until the copyright expires, a status which, on the grounds of their qualifications and accomplishments, they may not deserve. In such cases, the public may well be at the mercy of individuals whose qualifications are dubious, and the products of whose pens may give an entirely false impression of the original. Until very recently this was the lamentable fate of, for example, several plays by Brecht and Pirandello.

Returning to the study of reception in the narrow sense, I should like to review a number of cases in which the "received" writer affected the receiving author indirectly by means of a translation. Thus in his book *Thomas Mann und die Welt der russischen Literatur*, Alois Hofman comes to the conclusion:

Thomas Mann lacked the advantage of knowing Russia by personal experience. Unfavorable circumstances thwarted his plans for a lecture tour through Russian cities and prevented an encounter with Tolstoy. The sensuous world of the Russians was closed to him, and even their language remained alien. He therefore had to rely on secondhand information and insights furnished by intermediaries and critics. These, as well as the translations, are often unreliable tools, especially if we consider that in the process of transmission the national peculiarities, colors, and nuances are often obscured. (p. 75)

Hofman goes on to say that Thomas Mann's image of Russia and his conception of Russian literature (especially Dostoevsky) relied rather heavily on the views of Dmitrii Merezhkovsky. Since these views were subjectively colored, however, the alleged influence of Dostoevsky on Mann is largely based on misconceptions. While scoring a point in this particular instance, the Czech scholar contradicts himself when, elsewhere in his book, he states that Thomas Mann might well illustrate the fact that geographic "distance and linguistic barriers are no major obstacles in the process of literary reception" (p. 334, note 1). This paradox brightly illumines the flaws of the historical-critical method used by Hofman. In her book *Literary Origins of Surrealism*, Anna Balakian introduces another example of creative treason, which involves a passage from Achim von Arnim's novella "Die Majoratsherren" that was misunderstood by the French translator, Théophile Gautier, Jr., who changed the intended meaning into its opposite.[16] Precisely this subverted passage, however, so strongly appealed to André Breton and his Surrealist clique that they elevated Arnim to the position of a forerunner.

The fact that even professioanl reviewers and critics are not always blameless in this respect is underscored by the history of the reception of Brecht's plays in the United

States.[17] Even such sensitive and cultured critics as John Gassner and Stark Young, for instance, were at a loss when confronted with the adaptation of Gorky's *The Mother* at its New York premiere in 1935, because Brecht's theory was then, to them, a book with seven seals. And when the notes to *Aufstieg und Fall der Stadt Mahagonny* were finally published in a fragmented English version, they were received with great misgivings.

As the historian of literature may often observe, many successful and accomplished reception studies rely exclusively on the echo sounded by professional critics or scholars and, in doing so, ignore the sociological dimension of this phenomenon. Pertinent examples are offered by Bernard Weinberg's study of the reception of French Realism and by Winthrop H. Root's book on German criticism of Zola in the last quarter of the nineteenth century.[18] Root frankly admits that his

investigation has limited itself further to a study of the criticism which we may call the public criticism of Zola. It has attempted to find the majority opinion at any given time as it was expressed in the leading journals, the popular literary histories and essays, and in the monographs which, as manifestos of the opposing schools of criticism, had a wide hearing. (p. xii)

Especially in the United States, literary criticism (including its academic wing), to this day, often commits the mortal sin of linguistic ignorance. The grave consequences of this can be illustrated by means of an example drawn from the secondary literature on Kafka. In the chapter "The Road to Ramses" of the novel *Amerika*, for instance, we read the sentence: "Dann nahm (Rossmann) die Photographie der Eltern zur Hand, auf welcher der kleine Vater hochaufgerichtet stand, während die Mutter in dem Fauteuil vor ihm, ein wenig eingesunken, dasass."[19] In this way, the author informs his readers of the dominating role of Karl's father and the submissive attitude of the mother, who is willing to forgive and forget her offspring's alleged moral transgression. In Mark Spilka's essay "*America*: Its

Genesis," the following interpretation is placed upon the passage: "The photograph shows [Karl's] father standing 'very erect' behind his mother. . . . What these images suggest is borne out in the novel: his repulsion for sex is rooted in his love for his mother; his insecurity in his father's sharp disapproval and his phallic power."[20] The nature of this "creative" treason, obviously committed in good faith, lies in the fact that a psychoanalytically oriented critic, who seeks to unearth subconscious complexes and repressions, employs the literal translation of a word (*aufrecht* = *hochaufgerichtet* = erect) but overlooks that the English connotation is absent in its German equivalent. Without in the least intending to do so, the translator has thus sprung a trap for the unsuspecting critic.

In concluding the present chapter, which (to state it once again) is not intended as an introduction to literary sociology, I call attention to a branch of Comparative Literature à la Carré and Guyard which is now often termed outmoded or methodologically suspect: the study of the so-called *images* or *mirages* (meaning distorted images), which may be taken as the national phenomena corresponding to the myths and legends springing like halos around individual writers. This subdiscipline was still unknown to Van Tieghem, whereas Guyard devotes an entire chapter to it, although he admits, in the latest edition of his book, that the most recent developments have pushed this kind of investigation into the background. Nonetheless, Pichois/Rousseau still offer a section entitled "Images and National Psychology" (pp. 88–92), even while candidly admitting: "Here, we are at the crossroads of literature, sociology, political history, and ethnic anthropology" (p. 90). In a review of a book by Simon Jeune, I have tried to show how easily *image/mirage* studies slip into extra-literary territory,[21] and I quote the author as saying: "The literary type has favored the evolution of the human type. Art has rejoined life."[22]

With some success, Hugo Dyserinck recently sought to rehabilitate this fringe zone of Comparative Literature. He proceeded from the assumption that, even from a literary standpoint, the true or distorted image of a foreign people often plays such an important role within a given work, that one is forced to study this phenomenon.[23]

In the second part of his essay, Dyserinck adduces the example of Georges Bernanos' novel *Journal d'un curé de campagne*, where a totally one-sided, cliché-like image of the Flemish national character is presented. Similarly, topics such as "Brecht's Image of America and Its Literary Upshot" can be meaningful within the context of a discussion of plays like *Im Dickicht der Städte, Mahagonny, Die heilige Johanna der Schlachthöfe,* and *Der aufhaltsame Aufstieg des Arturo Ui.* Here, the task would be to investigate to what extent the poet's portrayal of Chicago, for instance, owes a debt to certain literary models (Upton Sinclair's *The Jungle* and Johannes V. Jensen's *The Wheel*), and in what sense it results from nonliterary prejudices.

Four ☞ Epoch, Period, Generation, and Movement

$\mathcal{S}$ LIGHTED for decades in deference to the rising fortunes of criticism, literary history has only recently come to the fore in American scholarship. And those scholars who have concerned themselves at all with the historiography of literature have paid little or no heed to its theoretical framework. Thus, writing in 1940, Wellek could still state with impunity: "Only a very few writers of literary history indicate the principles which underlie the formation of periods in literary history. I cannot find an express discussion of our problem in English, though many historians make, of course, incidental remarks and reflect on the nature of specific periods such as 'Romanticism.' "[1] The slim change for the better in recent years is exemplified by a periodical called *New Literary History*, founded at the University of Virginia (its second issue, published in the winter of 1970, actually contains a "Symposium on Periods"). Claudio Guillén has also published a collection of his essays under the auspicious title *Literature as System: Essays Toward the Theory of Literary History* (Princeton, 1971). Overseas, a series of relevant papers, originally presented at a conference in Bordeaux, has just appeared. The book, *Analyse de la périodisation littéraire* (Paris: Editions universitaires, 1972), is rather disappointing, however, insofar as its contributors restrict themselves to a more or less dogmatic sociological point of view or, where they come to grips with the problem as an aesthetico-literary one, simply ignore the existing secondary literature in English and German, a circumstance which greatly diminishes the value of their contributions.

Since, among other things, Comparative Literature is a branch of literary history, it is, like all historical disciplines, faced with the thankless task of bringing order into the seeming chaos of ceaselessly unfolding and constantly flowing events, "the directionless flux," as Wellek calls it. Those who, like Croce and his ilk, take works of art to be ahistorical, to lack any sort of meaningful precedent or frame, are wont to sever them bluntly from their natural context, and tend to be blind to the ineluctable fact that the movement is continuous and complex, and that if we wish to define the major phases of the progression we must find an ordering system which permits them to be extracted for the purpose of inspection and analysis.[2] Taking my cue from R. M. Meyer, I would like to present the criteria subsumed under the label "period" as the ones most congenial for this purpose, at least in the initial stages of the investigation. As Meyer points out in his still eminently readable essay, the *period*, as a mode of classification, corresponds, in the historical disciplines, to the *concept* in philosophy and to the *class* in natural science.[3]

To the extent to which we ascribe any significance at all to it, history is by no means merely the sum total of more or less random data. Historiographically it is, rather, constituted by our knowledge of such events as phenomena that have occurred at a specific time, at a particular place, and in a certain unique manner. A true apprehension of history results from the attempt to explain, after reconstructing the scene, what *happened* in the context of what *might* have happened. Originally, it was the Occidental awareness of history as a remembrance of things past which, dawning in the Hellenistic age, necessitated some sort of division—at first often with distinctly religious overtones in a nostalgic or teleologically apocalyptic manner.[4] This stratification was, at first, effected by a rough separation into epochs, and it was not until the nineteenth century that a more subtle and systematic (though flexible) arrangement according to periods was undertaken, as in Wölfflin's distinction between Renaissance and Baroque styles, culled with the help of categories from the history of art.

From the prophetic books of the Old Testament, a direct line of descent leads to the Revelation of St. John, and from there to the writings of the Church Fathers. "The division according to periods," says Meyer, "generally applies only since the time when, with St. Augustine, universal historiography made the empires of the prophet Daniel the guide to the history of mankind." The reference is to Nebuchadnezzar's dream, which the Biblical prophet interprets in the second chapter of the book bearing his name. The head of the statue which appeared to the king of Babylon, we are told, "was of fine gold, his breast and his arms of silver, his belly and his thighs of brass, his legs of iron, his feet part iron and part clay." Daniel reads the vision thus: "Thou art this head of gold. And after thee shall arise another kingdom inferior to thee, and another third kingdom of brass." As suggested by the feet of the monument, the last-named kingdom is no longer powerful and united.[5] In a secularized vein, a similar division and sequence is presupposed by the topos of the Golden Age —of which Goethe's Tasso says he knows not where it fled —and, by a reversal of perspective, in the notion of Utopia, the happy No-Place of an indeterminate, longed-for future.

What Meyer calls a *period* should perhaps be more aptly termed an *epoch*, however, for the latter term customarily encompasses the larger, and the former the smaller segment.[6] While making this distinction, we should also take note of the fact that *period* may, at times, overlap with *age*—the difference being that an age is frequently determined by a great individual—for instance, a Shakespeare, Goethe, or Napoleon—dominating a timespan of some length. It is unfortunate that scholars generally—and German scholars in particular—tend to use the above terms indiscriminately. The clearest articulation of the problem comes from H.P.H. Teesing's book *Das Problem der Peri-*

oden in der Literaturgeschichte: "The term *epoch* would
be preferable if it did not have a somewhat weightier
meaning, and should, therefore, be applied only to larger
units of time" (p. 9). What constitutes the "weightier
meaning" is the circumstance that, etymologically, epochs
are primarily determined by an "event or time of an event
marking the beginning of a relatively new development"
(to quote from Webster), which implies, historically, a certain indifference with regard to their length and their conclusion. We sometimes speak of an epoch-making event,
and Goethe, quibbling on the term, once scathingly referred to his own time as an "epoch without an epoch"
(*Epoche ohne Epoche*). *Era*, like *epoch*, stresses the beginning, rather than the duration, of a time span of considerable length, for, as defined by Webster, the term signifies
"a chronological order or system computed from a given
date as a basis, as, the Christian era." Semantically, it is
thus not entirely suitable as a periodizing concept.

Equally regrettable is the circumstance that, semantically, *period* may suggest periodicity, that which returns
at certain specified intervals. This is a slant which the true
historiographer—who views history as a series of irrevers-
ible and inimitable events and is, as a matter of principle,
opposed to all cyclical or even rhythmic thinking in such
matters—would like to avoid. The periodic period, as
Meyer calls it, is indeed an intellectual construct which
sadly presses the facts into a Procrustean mold.

Although the term *epoch* is probably less significant for
Comparative Literature studies than are either *period* or
movement—largely because direct, measurable influences
play a minor role when we think of literary phenomena in
relation to so vast a backdrop—I should, nonetheless, like
briefly to dwell on it. Wellek defines *period* as "a time section dominated by a system of norms, whose introduction,
spread and diversification, integration and disappearance
can be traced."[7] To be sure, it is theoretically possible to
apply the same criteria to *epoch* as well. In doing so, however, we must consider the likelihood that a pattern of in-

dividual traits reducible to a system of norms, such as Wellek has in mind, will scarcely remain constant for so long a stretch of time.

If we consider our Western culture, for example, the triad Antiquity-Middle Ages-Modern Age (*Neuzeit*) immediately springs to mind. This threefold division, however, is a product of the Renaissance, in whose eyes the Middle Ages were truly dark ages, across and through which a return to the ancients, and a renewal of their art, was to be effected. This pattern, by the way, may well exist, analogously, in certain non-Western cultures, as has recently been suggested by Earl Miner and Etiemble, at least with a view toward the Far Eastern *medium aevum*.[8]

The tripartite division just referred to is still in force, at least by implication, although the *Neuzeit* has to be redefined and remeasured as time passes. In German we already distinguish between *Neuzeit* (the era beginning with the Renaissance) on one hand, and *neuere Zeit* and *neueste Zeit*, on the other. The *neuere Zeit* might be said to have begun with the French Revolution, whereas the *neueste Zeit* (roughly corresponding to "present age") would seem to have been ushered in around the turn of the century. What follows is the immediate present or *Gegenwart*, the contemporary age, or that which happens in our lifetime. Life ends with death, however; and with our passing away the present turns into the past.

However great the temptation, I gladly refrain from elaborating on the concept of modernity, but would like to point out in passing that what is called modern is always seen in contrast to the ancient, the familiar or the classical. Ernst Robert Curtius has sketched the prehistory of this term, from its inception with the Alexandrine *neóteroi*, through the *poetae novi* mentioned by Cicero, to the *moderni* of Cassiodorus and the *seculum modernum* of Charlemagne, up until the twelfth century,[9] and subsequently, by way of the "Battle between the Ancients and Moderns" (late seventeenth and early eighteenth centuries) to the quarrel between Classicism and Romanticism

in Germany and to the real *Moderne* of the 1880's and
1890's.[10]

It should further be noted that even though epochs are
theoretically qualified by their capacity for being period-
ized, as regards ancient and medieval literature, this is
possible only to a very limited extent. With the beginning
of the *Neuzeit*, on the other hand, we run (at least in the
retrospective view embraced by recent scholarship) into
increasingly smaller zones of demarcation with constantly
shifting and highly flexible limits. The closer we come to
our own time, that is to say, the shorter are the time-spans
we have to cover—or, at least, that is how Teesing argues.[11]
After 1870, the periods are altogether replaced by movements and avant-garde splinter groups; and immediately
before World War I the waves follow each other in such
rapid succession that we are faced with programs and manifestos in a jungle which is nearly impenetrable for the
purpose of scholarly periodization.[12] Could this impression
be the result of an error in perspective caused by our manifest lack of detachment? I personally would not regard the
progressive decrease in the length of measurable units as a
mere optical illusion but am inclined to think that the reduction in size, and the frequency of change, is partly due
to the fact that, beginning with Romanticism, at the latest,
art has become increasingly self-conscious and programmatic, and that, consequently, the modern artist is virtually forced to seek out new, unprecedented solutions that
will call attention to himself and his products. Eduard
Wechssler, incidentally, supports Teesing's—and my own
—view when he points out that in cultural history the gap
between generations is constantly narrowing as well.[13]

When studying epochs—like all entities abstracted from
the historical flux—the scholar is faced with the need of
setting them off from one another and marking the tran-
sitions as neatly as possible. As students of literature,
though not as art historians, we can forgo the consideration of prehistory and primitive history—the stage of
"oral" literature—which have only recently entered our

field of vision. However, even the archeologist and the anthropologist have little choice but to periodize these early stages. On the whole, art history has always had an easier time than literary historiography, as for example in the treatment of Greek antiquity, whose course can be charted with the aid of period styles broadly defined as geometric, archaic, classical and Hellenistic. The series epic poetry/ lyric poetry/drama, frequently postulated in the nineteenth century, on the other hand, is little more than a skeleton; and within the individual genres we have, at best, the development from Old to New Comedy.

In the Renaissance, the question regarding the beginning of Antiquity was relatively easy to answer, since, with the possible exception of Egyptian hieroglyphics, only the Greco-Roman culture was then familiar. The Near East was, therefore, never considered as an important source of rejuvenation. For us moderns as well, literary history actually begins, not with the Egyptian Book of the Dead or the Gilgamesh epic, but with the *Iliad* and the *Odyssey*.

Nor does the question as to the end of Antiquity appear to create much of a problem. This should not, however, be construed to mean that the onset of the Middle Ages is easy to determine, for every attempt at periodization is rendered more difficult by the fact that the periods, as categories, must not leave any remnants behind, and that, ideally, their sum, as Meyer puts it, "must coincide with the content of their entire course, for otherwise, the whole purpose of the division fails" (p. 19).

Antiquity ended—one would like to imagine—not with the emergence of Christianity, but with the fall of Rome or the founding of Constantinople, but certainly no later than with Boethius and St. Augustine. Yet it survived in the static-hieratic culture of Byzantium, that Yeatsian "artifice of eternity," in which, in the course of a whole millenium, no radical changes from one epoch style to another occurred either in literature or the other arts. In one part of Europe, then, Antiquity was still kicking, while elsewhere the Middle Ages had already been "born."

Next, the fundamental question arises as to whether the Middle Ages, seen from the perspective of cultural history, partake at all of the nature of an epoch, whether they are divisible into clearly marked periods. In considering this matter, we must keep in mind that, as a matter of principle, we cannot assume a temporal concurrence of the arts and that at times a division into periods is, therefore, easier in one artistic realm than in another. (The possible preeminence of certain arts over certain other arts, as postulated by some scholars, is a matter of no concern to us in the present context.) It should nonetheless be noted that, in the history of medieval German art, for instance, the succession of styles has been precisely fixed by means of the series *Frankish, Carolingian, Ottonian, Romanesque,* and *Gothic*. In literature no similar stylistic-historical articulation of this epoch has, unfortunately, emerged, although Guillén (*Literature as System*, p. 448) refers to a recent attempt on the part of the historian M. Seidlmayer. The linguistic tension running throughout the Middle Ages between the vernaculars and the Latin *koiné* may be partly responsible for this condition.

In his lucid book, Professor Teesing bemoans the fact that in most literary histories medieval literature is staggered primarily according to sociological or philological viewpoints, and that criteria derived from *Geistesgeschichte* or stylistics are only hesitantly used:

But now a question we expressly wish to pose as such arises: is it perhaps not so much the material as the treatment of the material in our discipline which prevents such a periodization of medieval literature? It is a well-known fact that the literatures of the Middle Ages and the *Neuzeit* are handled differently: in the treatment of medieval poetry, the emphasis lies on the philological method, whereas with modern literature it lies on stylistics and *Geistesgeschichte*. (Teesing, p. 120)

The *Deutsche Vierteljahrsschrift für Literaturgeschichte und Geisteswissenschaft,* founded in 1928, among other tasks, set itself the specific goal of remedying this situation.

If, according to Meyer's theoretical construct, the end of

the Middle Ages must coincide with the beginning of the Modern Age, the question concerning the precise moment of transition could be solved by fixing the birthdate of the Renaissance. But was there, actually, such a point? Seen from a pan-European, i.e., comparative, viewpoint, a single date means nothing under the circumstances, as is proven by the discrepancies between various histories of national and world literature in the fixation of this vital moment.

Let us adduce a few examples. In doing so, we will, for methodological reasons, refrain from examining Erwin Panofsky's persuasively argued thesis that numerous renascences but no genuine Renaissance had already occurred during the Middle Ages.[14] Following the example set by a famous essay of A. O. Lovejoy, "On the Discrimination of Romanticisms," Panofsky's essay could have been entitled "On the Discrimination of Renascences," although the phenomena it describes were successive rather than simultaneous. Panofsky is at pains to show that many of these medieval reform efforts were half-hearted and largely inconsequential attempts to bring the surviving heritage of the ancients (as surveyed by Jean Seznec in his book *The Survival of the Pagan Gods*)[15] back into focus. As a true Renaissance, meaning a systematic revival of the spirit of Antiquity in all spheres of cultural activity, he recognizes only the Carolingian Renaissance of the ninth century.

If we compare the principles of periodization used in three different literary histories chosen at random—Buckner B. Trawick's *World Literature*, Philippe Van Tieghem's *Histoire de la littérature française*, and Fritz Martini's *Geschichte der deutschen Literatur*[16]—the following picture emerges: Trawick marks the beginning of the Italian Renaissance as 1321, the year of Dante's death. Thus Dante is treated as a poet of the Middle Ages, whereas Boccaccio and Petrarch are no longer "in the dark." Actually, the author of the *Divine Comedy* does not fit too well into the Renaissance mold when one considers that, although he turned to Antiquity for his model, he wished to have his poem understood as a vast allegory illustrating the Christian doctrine of salvation.

As we examine Dante's style, we discover that his full-fledged realism—as Erich Auerbach has so convincingly demonstrated—must be seen as part of a figurative style, and that the faithful rendering of surface reality is the top layer of a stratified depth which must be plumbed for its symbology. The unsuspecting reader of the *Divine Comedy* all too easily forgets that it is the embodied souls and not the real bodies of the sinners which roast in Hell. The realism of Boccaccio's *Decameron* and even of Chaucer's *Canterbury Tales* is equally deceptive, and a thorough reading of both works leads to the conviction that here, too, reality is heavily stylized or symbolically enriched. In this context, the *topos* quality of the depiction (for example, of the gardens and parks in the *Decameron*) plays a role the significance of which should not be underrated.

Nor must we forget that both Dante (in his famous letter to Can Grande della Scala of Verona) and Boccaccio (in the introduction to the fourth Decade of the novellas) found it necessary to apologize for their use of the vernacular. Even Chaucer in the Prologue to his *Canterbury Tales*, where he appeared in the guise of a pilgrim, ironically defended the "realism" in the structure and the language of his poem by pointing out that, being uneducated, he was unable to meet the standards of high literature. It would be equally justifiable, then, to assign Boccaccio, like Chaucer, to the Middle Ages, and to have the actual Renaissance start with Petrarch, who learned Greek expressly in order to read the Classical writers in the original.

Even in France, chronologically the third country—after Italy and Spain—where the Renaissance took hold, the situation is by no means as clear-cut as the literary historian would like. Trawick, for instance, who has the Spanish Renaissance begin with the marriage of Ferdinand of Aragon to Isabella of Castille in 1469 (its first significant literary achievement was the *Celestina* of Fernando de Rojas), regards 1494—the year of François Rabelais' birth and of the invasion of Italy by Charles VIII—as the *terminus post quem*. Van Tieghem, on the other hand, relegates Villon and Rabelais to the Middle Ages (1050–1550!) and treats Montaigne and the poets of the Pléiade as the first writers of the Renaissance, for which he reserves a time-span of no more than forty (!!) years, 1550–1590.

Martini altogether eschews the use of the label "Renaissance," which, in Germany, is not easily applicable to belles-lettres, and is content with using the para-literary terms *Humanism* and *Reformation* to characterize the period in question. Like Trawick, he limits both to the sixteenth century. In England, lastly, the transition from the Middle Ages to the Renaissance was not completed until well after 1500, with poets such as Spenser, Wyatt, and Sir Philip Sidney; while Shakespeare—like Cervantes in Spain —already seems to reach beyond (meaning into the Baroque).

Certain difficulties in coordinating the epochs and in attempting to set up guiding principles for the purpose of a universal assignment of periods arise when one examines literature internationally. The system of norms which would seem to characterize the Renaissance emerges at different times and often after such long delays that, viewed comparatively, one must constantly take "unusual developments and temporal displacements" into account. Viewed *in toto*, the Renaissance, as a European phenomenon, virtually extends from the fourteenth century well into the sixteenth, without ever being in full swing in all countries simultaneously. Indeed, as the Dutch historian Jan Huizinga sought to show in his book *The Waning of the Middle Ages*, the *medium aevum* lingered on. In a comprehensive presentation of the Renaissance, then, Comparative Literature, notwithstanding its usual preference for the synchronic approach, will have to proceed diachronically as well.

I now turn to the examination of periods in the proper sense, that is, of more strictly limited and more tightly structured divisions in the history of Western culture since the Renaissance. Periods, according to Teesing, are time spans of varying length, "which are, in themselves, relatively unified and which distinguish themselves markedly from others" (p. 8). The question arises, therefore, of what forces are involved in shaping the profile of a period.

At the outset, all organizing principles based on the conviction that an inexorable law governs the course of history must be repudiated. For good reasons both von Wiese and Teesing are wary of the polar, phasic, or cyclical ("periodic") constructs of a Vico, Spengler, and Cazamian, whose theories make either openly or tacitly deterministic pretensions. In his cogent essay, von Wiese deals with two other unreasonable approaches to the problem of periodization. Firstly, he repudiates any attempt at transforming it into a metaphysical category. Such attempts, in his view, arise from the erroneous belief, shared by Herbert Cysarz among others, that the period is a true essence (*Wesensform*) instead of being merely an ordering principle (*Ordnungsform*). This ahistorical dogmatism causes Cysarz and his sympathizers to posit the existence of a Gothic or Renaissance Man combining all the typical features of a period style. Like Werner Milch, I, too, deplore this cancerous outgrowth of German *Geistesgeschichte*.

Through manipulations of the sort which Cysarz undertakes, the period concept becomes abstracted and the resulting patterns are rigid and inflexible. Actually, the periods of cultural and intellectual history do not follow each other "in a calculable single file, but rather in a constantly changing permeation, in such a way that each normative unit contains within itself a profusion of other units" (von Wiese, p. 144). Cogent proof for this contention is furnished by the works of what one might loosely call the Romantic Realists—not only in Germany (Gottfried Keller, Theodor Storm, among others), but also in France (Victor Hugo's foreword to *Cromwell*, Flaubert's *Madame*

Bovary) and England (Wordsworth's foreword to the second edition of the *Lyrical Ballads*). And what applies to periods goes for epochs as well. Thus, E. M. W. Tillyard, in his book *The Elizabethan World Picture*, shows how medieval thought lurks hidden in the works of Shakespeare and his contemporaries.

If undue abstraction in the formulation of concepts is the Scylla of literary historiography, the setting up of ideal types (*Idealtypen*) is its Charybdis. Viewed closely, a classification based on ideal types is only a variant of the cyclical or phasic scheme, although this kinship is not always evident. This scheme is based on the assumption that certain normative systems are typical, not only for single, nonrecurrent units of time, but also for historically unconnected periods separated by other units (and perhaps even in other civilizations). According to this view they can therefore be not only abstracted but also extracted and transplanted. We thus arrive at a Greek Rococo (the Hellenistic Tanagra style) and a medieval Baroque. This metaphorical usage is a sure sign that the norms selected by historians were not sufficiently distinct to serve their purpose. The fact that there are entities such as Neoclassicism and Neo-Romanticism (*Neuromantik*) does not invalidate this claim, since such movements imply the imitation or revival of past tendencies, so that, chronologically, the cart is not hitched before the horse.

Any purely nominalistic definition of "period" should also be avoided in our attempt to make the term palatable to students of Comparative Literature. This conception corresponds to the pragmatic view, embraced by Huizinga, that periods are artificial constructs of extremely limited value. Since periodization is necessary but bound to be arbitrary, "colorless designations of epochs, with random caesuras, are preferable," according to the Dutch historian.

In the definition of individual periods, one should not be dismayed by the need for resorting, at times, to circular logic, a mode of reasoning to which the humanities are necessarily subject. "There is," says Wellek, "a logical circle in the fact that the historical process has to be judged by values, while the scale of values is itself derived from history" (*English Institute Annual for 1940*, p. 89). In our case, this means that the norms which serve as guidelines in the identification of periods have actually been abstracted from the historical process, usually by the investigator himself. As von Wiese knows,

> as a matter of principle, one must adhere to the epistemological insight that such epoch concepts are historical categories rather than historical substances; they are conceptual schemes, designed to aid us in comprehending and ordering the historical flow, but not real entities, which the scholar's genius, in a particularly original "vision," has at last discovered and defined. (*DVLG*, 11 [1933], p. 137)

In the present context, I do not wish to play logical games, but am content with stating that period concepts are, in Teesing's words, "conceptūs cum fundamento in re"[17] (*Reallexikon*, p. 77), manifestations of the historical object as perceived by a given subject. This explains why no conclusive, binding definitions can ever be obtained. New facts are constantly being unearthed, and unknown aspects of the past discovered (the *fundamentum in re*); and, beginning with the self-interpretation of periods like the Renaissance or Romanticism, the standpoint of the observer (the *conceptūs*) markedly changes from generation to generation. Thus, every period—like every work of art—will be seen with fresh eyes and in a new manner, since each generation calls for its own Goethe and its own Baroque. Even with the accumulation of specialized studies and monographs, we will, therefore, never completely *exhaust* Neo-Classicism or Mannerism.

It is only one step—though, at times, a bold one—from the theory to the actual practice of periodizing. At the outset of my investigation, I referred to the traditional tripartite division of the history of Western culture. Following in this vein, I would now like to consider quite simply, into how many periods the *Neuzeit* can be broken down.

Naturally, a few of the most familiar labels (Baroque, Rococo, Neoclassicism, Romanticism, and Realism) immediately come to mind; but when, as comparatists, we seek to do justice to all of European literature and culture, we soon run into unexpected difficulties.

If we look backward from Romanticism or forward from the Renaissance, for instance, we notice that a considerable number of period terms are indeed available, but that few of these are readily applicable to simultaneous developments in different national literatures. The term Baroque, for instance, which was first applied to literature thanks to the efforts of the literary historians among Wölfflin's disciples, and which, at times, has served to designate the entire literary production of the seventeenth century, has since met competition from "Mannerism," a term just as intrinsic in art history. The newer coinage has not yet ousted the older, however, although Curtius took this substitution to be *de rigueur* and his disciple, Gustav René Hocke, tested it in two monographs.[18]

Especially in France literary historians continue to dispute whether Baroque and Mannerism are proper designations for literary period styles. Both, however, are now on the point of being firmly entrenched. Philippe Van Tieghem still gave the chapter of his book which is devoted to the time span 1590–1656 the title "From Malherbe to the *Provinciales*" but added the cautionary subtitle "Style Précieux (Baroque)." The following section of his survey treats the age of the Sun King and of the *Grands Classiques*, Pascal, Molière, Racine, and Boileau, among whom, even in France, Racine, at least, is now frequently assigned to the Baroque.

Classicism (Neoclassicism, *Klassik*, *Klassizismus*), too, has its drawbacks as a period term, since the age of the French *Grands Classiques* is not at all synchronic with English Neoclassicism (from Dryden to Pope) and German Classicism in the last third of the eighteenth century (ca. 1775–1795). Similarly, in the case of the Enlightenment, there are temporal overlaps with Rococo and Pre-Romanticism. If one wishes to carry finesse to the extreme, one

could even argue that there is no literature of the Enlightenment, properly speaking, since whatever was "enlightened" in the belles-lettres of the first half of the eighteenth
century belongs more properly to "the history of ideas."
Just how difficult it is to reconcile the often contradictory
and intersecting tendencies of the eighteenth century is
shown by the Protean figure of Denis Diderot, who was at
once enlightened, "sentimental" and irrationalist, as well
as by G. E. Lessing, whose *Hamburgische Dramaturgie*
seeks to vindicate Shakespeare by an appeal to Aristotle.

Even for the well-informed student of European culture,
it is thus almost impossible not to get lost in the tangle of
period terms. Additional confusion results from the fact
that their number is not fixed but is constantly raised by
attempts to let smaller segments ascend to the order of
greater magnitude or to regroup the available periods.
Many of these newly propagated terms are, again, derived
from art history. With the "Baroque," the maneuver succeeded, as we have seen, whereas "Mannerism" and "Rococo" have not been fully acclimatized in literature. With
"Biedermeier" (Early Victorian), over which a lively battle
was fought in the thirties, the attempt has failed for all
practical purposes, despite Jost Hermand's concerted efforts.[19] More recently, Norbert Fuerst has made a stab at
applying the term Victorianism—which Wellek, speaking
of English literature, says has acquired its own flavor and
is no longer restricted to those works which were created
during the lifetime of the Queen—to German literary history as well:

The term "Victorianism" needs all the indulgence of the reader.
It is not much more than a chronological and ideological
approximation. What little more it contains is a reminder that in
the main the waves of nineteenth-century German literature did
not flow with the revolutionary current of French (and in part
even Russian) literature; that its artistic tides and its moral
groundswell were more with English and American literature.[20]

In periodizing one should, at all costs, avoid such com-
promises as are struck in the case of *pré-romantisme* and

Post-Impressionism. The label "Pre-Romanticism" represents a grand-scale attempt, undertaken largely by Van Tieghem, to summarize the irrationalist undercurrents in the Age of Enlightenment, and to view Rousseau, Diderot, Richardson, Sterne, Goldsmith, and the German *Stürmer und Dränger* as the vanguard of Romanticism, that is, as writers whose works approximate the system of norms of which the sum total is Romanticism. What we have here, however, is not a genuine period style, but merely an anticipatory current or trend. Following this precedent, Panofsky could have subsumed the medieval renascences under the term "pre-Renaissance," and Auerbach could have epitomized certain stylistic traits of ancient and medieval literature under the corresponding term "proto-Realism."

The term "Post-Impressionism" offers a singularly unattractive example, which fortunately is limited to painting, since Impressionism remains an ambiguous term in literary history, insofar as its lines of demarcation with Symbolism have not yet been satisfactorily drawn.[21] The prefix "post" is, in this case, doubly misleading, because it does not mean that, after the death of the movement called Impressionism, the latter's stylistic peculiarities were retained by a cohesive group of painters. It means, rather, the exact opposite, namely that the "big four" (Seurat, Cézanne, van Gogh, and Gauguin), having been influenced by the Impressionists, developed counter styles prefiguring the art of the twentieth century: Cézanne that of Cubism, van Gogh that of Expressionism, and Gauguin that of *art nouveau* and Symbolism, whereas the pointillism of Seurat, who died in his early manhood and whose experiments remained inconclusive, may best be regarded as a transitional style. Post-Impressionism is, in fact, neither a sequel to (*Noch-Impressionismus*) nor a recurrence of Impressionism (*Wieder-Impressionismus*) but in many ways already a Counter-Impressionism (*Gegen-Impressionismus*). These few examples could be multiplied at will with others drawn from the history of music, literature, and the visual arts. One need only recall the alleged Proto-Expressionism

of Ernst Stadler, Georg Heym, and Georg Trakl, which
haunts so many recent German literary histories.

Before I turn to the question concerning the genesis of
literary periods and the fixing of their duration, I would
like, following René Wellek, to comment briefly on the
labeling of these units. In his essay "Periods and Movements in Literary History," Wellek rightly decries the fact
that, in national as well as international periodization, extra-literary viewpoints are often used. Realizing that it is
no longer possible to eradicate these *faits accomplis*, he
still expresses the hope that, sometime in the distant future, the norms might be derived from literature itself:

We must try to derive our system of norms, our "regulative
ideas," from the art of literature, not merely from the norms of
some related activity. Only then can we have a series of periods
which would divide the stream of literary development by literary
categories. Thus a series of literary periods can alone make up, as
parts of a whole, the continuous process of literature, which is,
after all, the central topic in the study of literary history. (*English
Institute Annual for 1940*, p. 93)

It is doubtful, however, whether purely literary norms
can be found in every instance. If, for example, in a fit of
puristic fervor, the comparatist were to toss out designations like Baroque or Mannerism, he would be forced to
find substitute terms placing such diverse national phenomena as Gongorism, Euphuism, Marinism, Concep-
tismo, Metaphysical Poetry, bombastic literature
(*Schwulstdichtung*), among others, under one terminological umbrella, a task that might well prove impossible.

If, then—especially in Comparative Literature—one
cannot adjust the period term to the class of objects it represents, one should at least attempt to strike a workable
compromise by insisting that the appellation of a period
in literary history support the claims of a cultural activity
then prevalent. Thus, the labels *Reformation, Humanism,*
and *Enlightenment* justly indicate that the literature so
designated is not aesthetically weighted.

In cases where the period term or the name of a literary movement has been borrowed from another art, one should be tolerant if that art was actually in the ascendant. With the Baroque, for instance, one must consider that, within the span so designated, architecture and painting were either more prolific than literature or at least more representative. The pre-eminence of terms from art history in the naming of literary periods may also be justified by the fact (not nearly as obvious as might appear) that the language of visual art—like that of music, which only subsequently voiced its claim of leadership—is more universal and requires little or no translation.

Of the most important literary movements of the last one hundred years or so, relatively few derive their names from literature: as, for instance, Naturalism (which was practically stillborn in music and painting), Symbolism, and Surrealism. In the case of Realism, an approximate concurrence of origin can be assumed, even though it was clearly Gustave Courbet's exhibition *Le Réalisme* which started the ball rolling. With Expressionism and Impressionism, on the other hand, the priority of the plastic arts is undisputed. It would thus be wrong if in analyzing the literary offshoots of these styles we used literature as our point of departure, or totally ignored the other arts.

Of the many kinds of periodization, the one which is to be most emphatically rejected, in addition to the purely philological classification (which has its place in the individual national literatures and will, therefore, be suspect to the comparatist) is the annalistic approach. Unfortunately, it cannot be altogether ignored, because its use has become second nature to philologists. Only in its excrescences— instances where the dates are lined up mechanically—it should be resolutely attacked. Fortunately, in the synoptic tables prepared by Paul Van Tieghem and Adolf Spemann in their repertories, as well as in the ninth volume of Bompiani's *Dizionario letterario*, the aim is to *identify* simultaneous events rather than to *order* or *periodize* them.[22]

Arithmetically computed time spans can also serve as a

basis for the organization of historical data, as was demonstrated by R. M. Meyer, who admits that he was prompted
to reflect on techniques of periodization by critiques of his
presentation of nineteenth-century German literature according to decades. In a book about the reception of American literature in Germany between 1861 and 1872, for
instance, Eugene F. Timpe rises only slightly above the
level of the annalistic approach.[23] Although he claims that
"the dates designating this period are of some significance
because they encompass the most important years of an
interval of American poetry sandwiched between two eras
of prose [sic] (p. 2)," the true reason underlying the choice
of this particular time span may well have been the existence of a chronological gap between the segments already
covered by his predecessors.[24] With greater historical sensi-
tivity, Simon Jeune, in his book on American characters in
French fiction and drama, chose a time span (1861–1917)
which may be regarded as a relatively coherent phase in
the history of the political ties between France and
America, for it stretches from the outbreak of the Civil
War to America's entry into World War I.

Even today, the favorite kind of annalistic periodization
is the display of literary wares according to centuries. The
catalogues of our colleges and universities literally bulge
with titles like "English Seventeenth-Century Literature"
or "Deutsche Literatur des 19. Jahrhunderts." It is seldom
realized that such labels and the content of the academic
package do not necessarily coincide. And yet, when as
comparatists we speak of the nineteenth century, we
scarcely think of the calendar years 1801–1899, but rather
of the Victorian Age or of the realistic-naturalistic period
beginning, roughly, with Goethe's death and the revolution of 1830, and ending with the public protest by five
"disciples" of Zola against the publication of La Terre, and
with the proclamation of literary Symbolism.

A partial abstraction from chronology without repudiation of the chronological framework is found not only in
the periodization according to centuries but also in more

differentiated alignments according to strictly historical viewpoints, such as the reign of a monarch and the duration of a war or a political alliance. In pragmatic England, this seems to be the preferred method, although it is by no means consistently applied; for example, there is no literary period named after Henry VIII or George V, corresponding to those named after Elizabeth or Victoria. This can probably be explained by the fact that the two latter monarchs had a stronger impact on, or were more representative of the culture and literature of their age, or that important changes in the social and intellectual life of their country occurred during their reigns.

Here, also, the distinction between national and international viewpoints must be made, however, since English literary history favors the term "Jacobean Drama," while, in a pan-European view, the dramatic production of that time segment would still seem to belong to the Elizabethan Age. After all, Shakespeare continued to write plays even after the death of Queen Elizabeth (for example, *The Tempest*). And the entire reign of a monarch need not be designated by a period term: this is shown by Jost Hermand's recent attempt to introduce the stylistic label *Gründerzeit*, to cover the years 1870–1890 in German cultural history.[25]

In determining the length of periods in literary history, it might be wise to use the dialectics of "generation" and "period" as a starting point. If, for simplicity's sake, one assumes that these terms pertain to different orders of magnitude, one can proceed on the basis that one generation represents either thirty years or one-third of a century, and in this manner set what might be termed the lowest temporal limit of a period. Helmut Kreuzer's recent attempt at periodizing German post-World-War-II literature borders, admittedly, on the absurd. Most periods in literary history—with the exception of the more extended Renaissance, which almost rises to the level of an epoch—last probably between two (Romanticism, Realism) and three (Baroque) generations. The term "period" should not be used in connection with German Classicism, for example, because the quantitative minimum is not reached in this particular instance.

The equation "period equals generation" must be rejected in principle because it mixes biological criteria with historical and stylistic ones. According to Wilhelm Pinder, physiognomies of style are, however, "basic formal units spanning several lifetimes and not bound by the limits of individual existence."[26] Periodization on the basis of generations is also undesirable because a man's life normally covers sixty to eighty years; therefore, if one discounts his childhood and early youth, the individual writer is creative on the average for two generations. In fact, it is unwise to periodize by generation precisely "because its representatives undergo further development, which separates them from their origins."[27]

Goethe's literary career offers ample proof of the fact that the generation is "no regular yardstick furnished by the average length of the individual's creative career."[28] The author of *Faust*, for instance, belonged to the generation of the Storm and Stress; stood, initially, under the stylistic influence of the Rococo; turned into a Classicist in his fourth decade; came to grips with Romanticism in the second part of his *Faust*; and, at the end of his career, had a brush—however fleeting—with Realism. A single poet can, therefore, belong to several literary generations and his writings can exemplify various period styles, which need not, however, follow each other in strict chronological order. Rather, overlaps or rhythmic alternations may occur, as was the case with Gerhart Hauptmann, whose sudden "conversion" from Naturalism (*Die Weber*) to Neo-Romanticism (*Hanneles Himmelfahrt*) can scarcely be explained as an organic development, since subsequently Hauptmann more than once returned to Naturalism. This particular phenomenon, by the way, can perhaps also be accounted for by the fact that the German writer—in whose breast there "dwelled two souls"—grew up at a time of stylistic transition; for when he wrote *Vor Sonnenaufgang*, the most Naturalistic German drama from the European viewpoint,

Naturalism in France and Scandinavia was already on the decline, and barely two years elapsed before Hermann Bahr, the living barometer of his age, announced *Das Ende des Naturalismus* to the Germans.

According to Wylie Sypher, similar occurrences abound in English literature. In *Four Stages of Renaissance Style*, Sypher even sought to prove that the four styles touched upon in his book (Renaissance, Mannerist, Baroque, and High Baroque) overlap, in the work of a single writer like Shakespeare:

> Especially in any period as fertile as the Renaissance two or more different styles can be current at not only the same moment in different artists but even in the same artist; for in certain phases Caravaggio utilizes simultaneously mannerist and baroque techniques, and Shakespeare within the same year (c. 1604–05) wrote both *Measure for Measure* and *Othello*, the first Mannerist, the second Baroque, in style. Shakespeare's course is so alternating, various and questing that any effort to contain his art within the category of a single style is self-defeating; like Milton, he demonstrates the coexistence of unlike styles and the intricacy of their relations.[29]

Even a single work may, through the length of its gestation, or changes wrought in the creative process, combine several period styles within its frame, as is demonstrated by the evolution of *Faust* from its original Storm and Stress *Gestalt*, through the Classicist Helena act and the subsequent fusion of Classicism and Romanticism to its mystic-baroque apotheosis. Especially revealing in this respect is the fate of the Expressionist writers, most of whom were born in the 1880's and who, after 1920, either fell altogether silent or began to write bourgeois comedies. The art of the twenties (especially the *Neue Sachlichkeit* [New Objectivity]), is, accordingly, no longer an art to be credited to the Expressionist generation, that is, to a group of contemporaries (*Altersgemeinschaft*) whose *élan vital* had petered out, with their movement, by the time they had reached the age of thirty.

More appropriate than a chronological periodization according to generations, in Teesing's opinion, is the view of a generation as the "spearhead of a period" (Teesing, p. 73), a band of likeminded innovators who succeed in displacing the art of their predecessors.[30] If such experimenters are humanly and artistically united and have developed a specific program, they constitute a literary *movement*, a body which normally consists of a nucleus of writers enjoying roughly equal status, and sometimes strengthened by representatives of the older generation.

If—as often happens fairly quickly—a movement loses its momentum, it may be replaced by a new wave or may receive, like Surrealism, a second impetus through the introduction of new techniques or arts. Since a movement represents a "fresh group of youths" (Petersen), it seldom lasts for an entire generation. However, if it is spared a struggle with a counter-movement or triumphs over new opponents, the dominant system of norms it has established may, under certain conditions, carry over into the following generation and even to the one after that; actually it may expand into a period.

When speaking of representatives of a generation, one usually thinks of individuals who were born within five or, at the most, ten years of each other, thus involving a group of contemporaries linked by age (*Altersgemeinschaft*), not by experience (*Erlebnisgemeinschaft*). This view was upheld by Wilhelm Pinder who stubbornly believed in the "priority of growth over experience" and broached the hypothesis "that the movement of art history results from the combination of dominant entelechies born in a mysterious natural process" (Pinder, p. 145).

For the student of Comparative Literature, Pinder's notion is, negatively, relevant because it seeks to level all racial, political, religious, and social differences, and makes all contemporaries, regardless of their origin and talent, operate under a single star. The attempt to write a history of world literature, according to contemporaries rather than nations, periods, or movements, however, would run into opposition from conservative as well as progressive practitioners of our discipline. For, apart from the fact that *rapports de fait* are meaningless in such a context, the uneven (early, normal, or late) development of the individual artists whose works we study—precisely the "non-contemporaneity of contemporaries" with which Teesing counters Pinder's "contemporaneity of non-contemporaries"—is obviously disregarded.

The nature of the relationship between coevals (biological age-groups) and contemporaries (sociological age-groups) was studied by Eduard Wechssler, who attached greater significance to the latter than to the former. By *Altersgenossenschaft* Wechssler meant

a group of contemporaries in a nation, who, as a consequence of their near-simultaneous birth and the similar experiences of their childhood and youth under the impact of a certain spiritual-moral situation and certain socio-political conditions, have fairly identical desires and aspirations. (*Die Generation . . .*, p. 6)

Wechssler justified his preference for contemporaneity with the argument:

The fate of a person is decided by the years of his youth rather than by the date of his birth. By youth is meant that point of experience around which a new generation crystallizes in the life of its people, announces its presence and makes itself felt. (Ibid., p. 25).

At first glance, it would appear that such common points of experience exist only within a nation. Here, too, the paths of Pinder and Wechssler part, particularly since Pinder, with his ill-concealed belief in spontaneous generation (*Würfe*), succumbs to an irrationalism which ill befits the serious scholar. Books such as Henri Peyre's *Les Générations littéraires* prove that Wechssler's view, on the other hand, is shared by many literary historians.[31] I do not altogether deny that the concept of *Erlebnisgemeinschaft*, as well, can be rendered fruitful for Comparative Literature. This is especially true when experiences are shared by several nations or continents, like the global military conflicts from the Thirty Years War onward to World War II, and the universal threat posed by atom, hydrogen, and cobalt bombs. As the pertinent example of an international movement in which a generation emerges as an *Erlebnisgemeinschaft* we might mention Dadaism, a movement which should be seen as a reaction against the misguided nationalism and chauvinism of the early war years, and also as an anarchist protest against a decadent civilization digging its own grave. In stressing *Erlebnisgemeinschaft* as a factor shaping the profile of a generation, however, we begin to skirt the realm of thematology, which will be treated in Chapter Six.

In closing, I should like to cast a glance at Brunetière's conception of the nature and division of literary periods, namely his opinion that, in periodizing, one should use the date of publication of important works, in other words, their initial shock or impact, as a point of departure. In this way, the center of gravity would be shifted from individuals to the *effect* engendered by their works:

Actually, literary epochs should only be dated according to what are called literary events—the appearance of the *Lettres provinciales* or the publication of the *Génie du Christianisme.* . . . This not only conforms with reality, but it is still the only means of imparting to the history of a literature that continuity of movement and life without which, in my opinion, there is no history.[32]

A periodization in the sense of a nationally or internationally valid system of norms could scarcely be achieved, however, in the sociological manner suggested by Brunetière, since, at different times, different works obviously produce different effects. Moreover, the quality of artistic constructs cannot be measured by the effects which they produce, as Brunetière seems to assume, since the *Wirkung* differs from case to case and is often dependent on mere chance. What period, as a system of norms, could have begun in the year 1857, for instance, which saw the publication of Baudelaire's *Fleurs du Mal,* as well as Flaubert's *Madame Bovary* and Champfleury's collection of essays,

Le Réalisme? (In Germany, as was pointed out in Chapter Three, Flaubert was alternately characterized as a Romantic, Symbolist, and Realist.)

I have treated the problem of periodization so thoroughly from a comparative viewpoint because I wished to show how much work remains to be done in this domain. My survey is also intended as a counterweight to the prevailing French opinion—still shared by Pichois/Rousseau—that it is more profitable to study currents than periods or movements:

Is it, therefore, necessary to renounce all periodization by epochs? Yes, if one wishes to cut up the development into fine pieces and to place walls between them. Yes, if, in availing oneself of this static aspect, one neglects the dynamic element, those currents which do not stop at any barrier. (P/R, p. 111)

Guillén would agree wholeheartedly. In fact, at the conclusion of his essay "Second Thoughts on Literary Periods" he opts for an "alternative" which relies on the use of a "noninterpretative" chronology and "stresses essentially the confrontations, within such chronological units, of a plurality of durations, movements, systems, schools, institutions, and other temporal processes" (*Literature as System*, p. 469). I, too, believe that one should not dismiss this warning out of hand. At the same time, however, I am convinced that studies like those offered by René Wellek in his volume *Concepts of Criticism*[33] are, from a comparative point of view, at least as rich and as suggestive as the large syntheses of Paul Hazard (*La Crise de la conscience européenne, La Pensée européenne de Montesquieu à Lessing*) and of Paul Van Tieghem (*Le Préromantisme*). Unfortunately, unlike the periods, the international literary movements have, so far, been rarely surveyed in their full scope. Thus, the study of Symbolism by Anna Balakian does not treat the dispersion of the movement throughout Europe with the same authority with which it discusses the French antecedent; the monograph on Dada by Manuel Grossman is largely restricted to France and Germany; and Lillian

Furst's recent survey of Romanticism fails to account for the Slavic literatures. As for universal portrayals of Naturalism and Surrealism, little more than bibliographical beginnings and fragmentary investigations have been made.[34]

The theoretical basis for the comparative study of literary movements lies, as I have already indicated, in the dialectic of *movement* and *period*. By a "movement" one understands—to repeat it once again—the conscious and, in most cases, theoretically founded attempt, on the part of like-minded persons, to illustrate and propagate a new conception of art. A *movement* differs from a *school* particularly in the sense that it is usually constituted by coevals, so that no teacher-pupil relationship exists. A movement has a distinct personality as its leader, but not necessarily as its master. Customarily, that is to say, the leaders are just as firmly bound to the projected program as are their fellow members, whereas the voice of the master speaks almost with the authority of law. The term *school* also (and particularly) implies a longer duration, since the disciples usually represent the younger generation and regard it as their mission to preach the gospel of their master.

The *movement* differs from the *cénacle* in that it is no mere literary club or coterie which meets regularly in a café or some other public place but does not require the close-knit unity possessed by the artistic community (*Künstlergemeinschaft*), which evidences genuine collaboration, the effect of which may be enhanced by communal living (*die Brücke* in Dresden and, as a composite of academy and *Künstlergemeinschaft*, the Weimar *Bauhaus*). The *salon*, which outwardly differs from the *cénacle* by virtue of the fact that an intellectually keen lady of high social rank presides over it, pursues artistic ends only by the way and often achieves unity of purpose only within the politico-ideological sphere.

The differentiation of historical concepts such as the above proves especially useful in the exploration of such hybrid phenomena as Romanticism and Expressionism. In German letters, for instance, Romanticism should be regarded as a movement only to the extent that like-minded writers participated, at given times and in specific places (such as Jena, Heidelberg, and Berlin), in common enterprises, as did the brothers Schlegel and Novalis in the case of the periodical *Athenäum*, or Achim von Arnim and Clemens Brentano in the lyrical anthology known as *Des Knaben Wunderhorn*. But there were also individualists like E. T. A. Hoffmann, who presided, at most, over a *Stammtisch* at Lutter and Wegner's, or Heinrich von Kleist, who moved briefly in the Dresden circle.

If one speaks of a Romantic School—as Heine and, later, Rudolf Haym have done—one should be prepared to name its master. But given all the divergent trends of Romanticism from Ludwig Tieck to Ludwig Uhland and from Zacharias Werner to Joseph von Eichendorff, who among them should be accorded that particular honor? When speaking of a Romantic period in German literature, one means the time span between 1795 (Schiller's essay "On Naive and Sentimental Poesy") and, roughly, Goethe's death; but one has to exempt immediately such prominent writers as Goethe and Schiller, who had little or no liking for the Romantics, taken individually or as a group. The disadvantage of this particular concept becomes apparent, comparatively speaking, in light of the French and Anglo-Saxon preference for treating Goethe and Schiller as Romantics or pre-Romantics.

If one examines Romanticism in the other European countries, the difficulties in coordinating the known facts increase immeasurably. In France, for instance, after a modest prelude with Chateaubriand and Bernardin de Saint Pierre, a full confrontation with German Romanticism resulted only from Madame de Staël's travels in Germany and the literary distillate of her trip, *De l'Allemagne*. The word *romantique*, however, did not come into use until the end of the second and the beginning of the third decade of the nineteenth century, and Stendhal was the first major writer who styled himself a Romantic, though chiefly for political reasons. French Romanticism only

jelled into a movement around 1830, mainly in the wake
of Victor Hugo's plays and the scandals caused by their
production. But the movement did not flourish for long.
Strong countercurrents soon asserted themselves, and Realism, in many ways already presaged by Balzac, had its way
at the latest with the Revolution of 1848.

In England (to bring a third national literature into play)
the situation was still different, for there simply was no
English Romantic movement, since even the so-called
Lake School (which was no school in the sense referred to
above) was so incohesive as hardly to deserve that name.
Yet Wordsworth's foreword to the second edition (1800) of
the *Lyrical Ballads*, co-authored with Coleridge, is a program of Poetic (Romantic) Realism in its British strain.
That there was a phenomenon called the Lake School was
known to Byron, who, in the introduction to his satirical
verse epic *Don Juan*, harps on one of its members, Robert
Southey, in particular:

> Bob Southey, you're a poet—poet laureate
> And representative of all the race;
> Although it's true that you turn'd out a Tory at
> Last—yours has lately been a common case;
> And now, my Epic renegade, what are ye at?
> With all the Lakers in and out of place?
> A nest of tuneful persons to my eye
> Like "four and twenty blackbirds in a pye."

Byron never dreamed that, like Southey, he himself
might be a Romantic and was quite surprised, in fact,
when he learned that he was considered as such in Germany. In the following passage, Wellek underscores this
anomaly:

We all know that Romanticists did not call themselves
Romanticists, at least in England. So far as I know, the German
scholar Alois Brandl, in his book on Coleridge (1887) first
connected Coleridge and Wordsworth definitely with the
Romantic movement and grouped them with Shelley, Keats, and
Byron. In her *Literary History of England Between the End of the*

Eighteenth and the Beginning of the Nineteenth Century (1882),
Mrs. Oliphant never uses the term, nor does she conceive of
the "Lake" poets, the "Cockney" school and the "Satanic" Byron
as one movement. (*Concepts of Criticism*, p. 79)

Even if we disregard Italian Romanticism with Manzoni
and the collaborators of the *Conciliatore*, as well as its
Spanish, Scandinavian, and Russian counterparts, we
would still have to admit that European Romanticism possesses little enough unity when viewed from an international perspective. This lack of coherence distinguishes it
from the more clearly profiled Naturalistic movement,
which constitutes an ideal test case for the periodizing
comparatist.

In view of the fact that almost everywhere in Europe Romanticism finds itself "in a consistently changing process
of permeation" in which (as von Wiese puts it) "every normative unit contains within itself a plethora of other
units," it cannot be reduced to a system of norms that is
simultaneously, or even consecutively, valid for all of Europe. One could also say that there are too many norms
here to form a system.[35]

In the case of Expressionism, which I should like to use
as a second illustration of the dialectic of movement and
period, the circumstances are somewhat different. From
the outset, the brief time-span usually assigned to that
phenomenon—within the literary realm, the years 1910–
1920 (according to Gottfried Benn) or 1925—would seem
to preclude its usage as a period term.

In the plastic arts, German Expressionism, which had its
forerunners in foreign painters like van Gogh and Munch,
was concentrated in two essentially different groups, the
Brücke and the *Blaue Reiter*, which were active in Dresden
and Munich, respectively. As an artistic commune, the
Brücke for several years had the character of a movement,
so that it was able to regroup even after resettling in Berlin.
Unfortunately, the chronicle in which its members intended to outline their program remained incomplete for

personal reasons. Like the *Fauves* in France, the members of this *Gemeinschaft* developed and cultivated a common, clearly recognizable style.

The *Blaue Reiter*—descended from the *Neue Münchner Künstlergemeinschaft*—on the other hand, was no true artistic commune. In matters of art, its chief exponents, Franz Marc and Wassili Kandinsky, were individualists and initially joined forces only for the organization of an exhibition and the publication of the almanac which bears the group's name. This almanac was no manifesto, however, and the various contributions contained in it are only expressions of a common desire to foist primitive, popular, and exotic art onto the tradition of Western painting. The *Blaue Reiter* adherents were fairly unanimous also in their craving for pictorial abstraction, which in Kandinsky is lyrically spiritualized; while Marc took the more concrete Cubism as his point of departure. However, idiosyncratic painters like Paul Klee and Alfred Kubin also belonged temporarily to this group.

In literature, Expressionism was even more disparate than in the plastic arts. Admittedly, a hard core of word- and sound-poets, who—from a purely linguistic point of view—represented the radical wing of so-called ·Expressionist literature, gathered around Herwarth Walden. Through the founding of the *Sturm* school and the *Sturm* theater, Walden solidified his position as arbiter and spiritual head of a movement which he himself had launched and for which he recruited such "forced" talents as August Stramm. The fact that, in his critical efforts at clarifying the issue, he did not clearly differentiate between Expressionism, Futurism, and Cubism should not be held against him, since elsewhere too (with Theodor Däubler and later with Benn, who looked at everything with a view towards the destruction of reality) Expressionism served as a catch-all term.

Naturally, there were further groupings in the Expressionist and Activist camps. *Die Aktion*, *Das Ziel*, and *Die weissen Blätter* were, essentially, organs of the political

Left, whereas the book series *Der jüngste Tag* and *Tribüne der Kunst und Zeit* were more pronouncedly literary. However, the publisher Kurt Wolff later vigorously denied that he had either triggered or propagated the movement through the publications of his firm. The hectic activity and constant reshuffling of alliances renders it even now impossible to bring order into the chaos of Expressionistic voices.

Moreover, until a few years ago, Expressionism was rarely, if ever, treated as an international phenomenon but was generally regarded as a uniquely and characteristically German product. With the publication of the first volume in the ICLA-sponsored History of Literatures in European Languages, this gap has been filled, in part, by a sequence of essays devoted to the impact of literary Expressionism on, and its transformation in, countries like England (Vorticism), the United States, Russia, Yugoslavia (Zenitism), Rumania, Poland, Belgium and Holland.[36]

Methodologically, the historical concepts treated in the present chapter are essential tools in the hands of those wishing to strengthen Comparative Literature as a scholarly discipline. In closing, I would like to reiterate, however, that it would be foolish to employ terms like era, age, movement or period statically and mechanically instead of dynamically and flexibly, since, by their nature, historical phenomena remain fluid even in retrospect; hence, the vital interpenetration of literary theory and history.

Five  Genre

*T*HE student who considers literature from a comparative point of view will find that, like the notions of period, current, and movement, the concept of genre offers an extremely fruitful field of investigation.[1] In cultivating this branch of literary theory, the scholar must proceed historically as well as critically if he is to discover principles that make possible a systematic arrangement of his material. At the same time, he must endeavor to operate descriptively rather than prescriptively; for due to the relativity of all things historical a clearcut and unambiguous delimitation of genres is practically unattainable, so that no true atomic model of genology is likely ever to emerge. Yet such a model has been envisaged down the literate centuries.

In classical antiquity, Cicero was one of the first writers to stress the segregation of literary genres in his essay *De optimo genere oratorum* (52 B.C.), and Quintilian followed suit in the *Institutio Oratoria*, his famous handbook of rhetoric.[2] Horace's letter to the brothers Piso (*Ad Pisones*, commonly known as *De arte poetica*) contains what may be regarded as the classic formulation of this view in the admonitions "denique sit quodvis, simplex dumtaxat et unum" (no matter what the subject, let it be simple and uniform) and "singula quaeque locum teneant sortita decentem" (each particular genre should keep the place allotted to it).[3] Such demands for generic purity, are, as a rule, characteristic of the classical or neoclassical frame of mind, which is inured to tradition and wishes to preserve the established order. Thus Schiller writes to Goethe, alluding to their joint attempt to ascertain the true nature of the drama and the epic:

Your present business of separating and purifying the two kinds is surely of the greatest significance. But, like myself, you will be convinced that, in order to exclude from a work of art everything that is foreign to its kind (*Gattung*), one would have to include everything that is germane to it. Precisely that we cannot do, however, at present. And since we are unable to convoke all the conditions proper to each of the two kinds, we are forced to mix them.[4]

This fusion (or confusion), which Schiller regarded as a necessary evil, is often exalted in periods inimical to tradition (as in the case of synesthesia and the Romantic *Gesamtkunstwerk*).

So far in the course of the history of our discipline, comparatists have, unfortunately, been remiss in their duty toward the history and theory of genres. Especially since the failure of Brunetière's attempt to establish a fixed pattern for the evolution of certain literary forms (almost in the terms of biology), hardly anyone dared for a generation or two to till this furrow.[5] Even the third International Congress of Literary History, held in Lyons in late spring 1939, did little to improve the picture, although the problem of literary types was its principal topic of discussion.[6] There was simply too much diversity in the views presented to allow for the necessary synthesis on a universal scale.

Until recently, *Comparative Literature* was the only specialized journal in the West to show an interest in genology, although (in all fairness) it must be added that relatively few relevant contributions have appeared in the first twenty years of its existence. Neither *Comparative Literature Studies*, the *Revue de littérature comparée* or *Arcadia*, emphasize the subject, and the *Proceedings* of the triennial meetings of the ICLA make no amends in this respect. In

Eastern Europe, on the other hand, the Polish periodical
Zagadnienia Rodzajów Literackich—published since 1958
at the University of Lodz—constitutes an important outlet. All the more welcome was the founding of *Genre*, a
quarterly edited by members of the English Department
faculty at the University of Illinois in Chicago. The second
issue of this journal contains the text of three papers read
at a forum held during the 1967 meeting of the Modern
Language Association in Chicago, together with brief eval-
uative comments by three discussants.[7] Of the three speak-
ers, Eliseo Vivas displayed by far the soundest understanding of the logical and historical problems involved, whereas
Sheldon Sacks' paper was more psychologically oriented,
and Germaine Brée's suffered from a certain lack of consistency in the use of such key terms as *theme, motif,
mode,* and *genre.*[8]

In most of the available handbooks and surveys the theory of genres is either totally ignored or treated with more
or less disdain. Wellek and Warren's *Theory of Literature*
(Chapter 17) is a notable exception. Especially, German
scholarship often fails to do justice to the topic, as will become evident in the course of my argument. The most
radical position regarding this matter was, not unexpect-
edly, taken by Benedetto Croce, who considered generic
classification a waste of time.[9] As for the French comparatists of the old school, they could never properly focus on
the issue, largely because they treated genology from the
double perspective of *littérature comparée* and *littérature
générale.* To the latter sphere Van Tieghem assigned the
study of classical tragedy, romantic drama, the sonnet, and
the rustic novel (Van Tieghem, p. 176) and, elsewhere, that
of pastoral poetry and the sentimental novel.[10] Yet *genres
et styles* are also treated at length in Chapter Two of the
main part of his survey (pp. 70–86), where the major kinds
are listed and discussed in the mechanical sequence *genres
en prose, genres poétiques,* and *le théâtre.* The superficial-
ity of this treatment can be explained—though hardly excused—by the fact that, following the practice of Com-

parative Literature then current at the Sorbonne, Van Tieghem restricted his survey to modern literature, thereby avoiding the tricky question regarding the survival of ancient genres.

In his brief eclectic guide, Guyard devotes a scant five pages (pp. 44–48) to our subject. Like his master (though in different order), he deals with drama, poetry, and fiction. Pichois and Rousseau further reduce the scope, and half of the limited space they grant to genology (pp. 96–99) is taken up by their explanation of the difference between monogenesis (*vide* Walter Scott and the historical novel) and polygenesis (*vide* the rustic novels of George Sand, George Eliot, and Jeremias Gotthelf). Three additional pages are devoted to genre under the subheading "Formes de composition" of the section "Morphologie littéraire" in Chapter Five. A cautious reversal of this trend is noticeable in the latest French manual, Jeune's *Littérature générale et Littérature comparée*, where an entire chapter (pp. 72–82) revolves around the study of literary genres, albeit under the heading of General Literature.[11]

Given this state of affairs, one can hardly exaggerate the importance attaching to the place of genre studies within the general framework of Comparative Literature. For in this branch of our discipline—perhaps even more so than in the case of thematology and periodization—a confrontation of literary history and theory occurs on a broad, international basis. In the present context we may, naturally, ignore such forms as have developed exclusively within a national or regional literature, without significantly reaching beyond its confines: such as the many complex metrical and strophic patterns of Provencal poetry, the Alpine *Schnadahüpfl*, and—in spite of some brave efforts at imitation in the German tongue—the English limerick. Hundreds of such "provincial" genres from the literatures of all five continents are catalogued and described in dictionaries like the Princeton *Encyclopedia of Poetry and Poetics*.[12] Equally beside the point are the historical surveys of specific universal genres evidenced solely within a national literature, since, by their very nature, they are bound to remain fragmentary and disjointed. It is sad that few truly international studies of such universal forms have, so far, been undertaken. They are, accordingly, an urgent desideratum of comparative scholarship. Of the major kinds it is undoubtedly the drama which has been most adequately treated in this respect, whereas neither the novel (or fiction as a whole) nor lyric poetry have as yet been surveyed *in toto*. One of the finest recent exceptions, in spite of its specialized approach, is Peter Dronke's book *Medieval Latin and the Rise of the European Love-Lyric* (Oxford, 1968).

As Johannes Hösle notes in his preface to the *Festschrift* for Kurt Wais (Tübingen, 1972), Wais is close to completing a comprehensive survey of European epic poetry from the Middle Ages to the Renaissance, the first volume of which, *Frühe Epik Westeuropas und die Vorgeschichte des "Nibelungenliedes"* appeared as early as 1953.

I have mentioned the problems facing the scholar who is interested in studying the survival of ancient Greek or Roman genres or their revival in the modern age. Difficulties often arise from the lack of direct evidence; for while it is sometimes erroneous to assume that genres flourishing since the Renaissance have no antecedents in antiquity, the existence of such models is, at times, purely hypothetical, the only proof being that furnished by references or quotations in ancient literary criticism. A good case in point would be the dithyramb, especially since, even in antiquity, it underwent repeated changes.

One must also consider the possibility that a genre known and cultivated in antiquity has actually vanished, but that its name persists and serves as the label for a modern genre that may, or may not, be its correlate. In such a case, the comparatist among literary historians is charged with the responsibility of investigating and analyzing the changing conditions responsible for this survival, and the process by means of which the label was severed from the original content. The reverse is true in cases where a genre passes from one national literature to another without retaining its original name. A special study could, and should, be made of what happens when such changes occur, and of how adequately the generic terms have been translated from one language into another; for, etymologically, a change of name usually implies a change of meaning, often imperceptible. One need think only of the somewhat fluid relationship between *cento* and *pastiche* or of the English version of Boileau's *Art Poétique* by Sir William Soame and John Dryden, where *rondeau* appears as *round*, *ballade* as *ballad*, and *vaudeville* as *lampoon*.

Equally significant for the student of comparative genology is the phenomenon known as contamination—a historical situation in which the essential difference between two genres, or even kinds, of literature is obscured by the presence of terms that are similarly spelled or pronounced. A truly classic example is that of satire; for although Quintilian (*Institutio Oratoria*, bk. 10, chap. 1, sec. 93) proudly asserts "satira quidem tota nostra est" (satire is altogether our own), Horace wavers between *satira* and *satura* and points to the Old Comedy as a model of the genre.[13] With a little ingenuity, then, the roots of Roman verse satire could be assumed to lie in the Greek satyr play, which, for all we know, the Greeks themselves did not regard as a separate genre. As in so many other instances, it was Isidore of Seville, the Webster of the early Middle Ages, who incurs much of the blame for this confusion, which it took many centuries to dispel. For he and his avid emulators enshrined the error by calling the masters of Roman satire (Horace, Persius, Juvenal, among others) comic playwrights.

While this contamination, fraught with serious consequences for the medieval theory of literature (whatever its worth), was primarily the result of a linguistic parallelism, the confusion surrounding the major "kinds" has other and, generally, more complex causes. We need only call to mind Dante's discussion of tragedy and comedy in his letter to Can Grande della Scala of Verona. In order to see the validity of this argument, one must realize that in the Middle Ages drama was not necessarily intended for stage performance. On the contrary, it was often designed for recitation, a *genus narrationum*—probably in emulation of Seneca's attitude toward his own closet dramas. In his epistle, Dante states the following reasons for calling his work a comedy:

For if we consider the subject-matter, at the beginning it is horrible and foul, as being Hell; but at the close it is happy, desirable, and pleasing, as being Paradise. As regards the style of language, it is unstudied and lowly, being in the vulgar tongue, in which even women hold their talk. And hence it is evident why the work is called a comedy.[14]

Continuing my survey, I should like to call attention to still another quirk in the history of literary genres. In the Wellek/Warren *Theory of Literature* we are told that " 'genre' in the nineteenth century and in our own time suffers from the same difficulty as 'period': we are conscious of the quick changes in literary fashion—a new literary generation every ten years, rather than every fifty: in American poetry, the age of *vers libre*, the age of Eliot, the age of Auden."[15] Pondering the significance and relevance of this assertion, I conclude, with Guyard, that this state of affairs is attributable not so much to a constantly accelerated generic turnover as to the rapid perfection of new literary techniques and modes of presentation:

The notion of genre, formerly so important, fades in light of the notion of technique. Whether he is a novelist, poet or playwright, the [modern] writer is no longer as much concerned with adhering to the conventions of a well-defined genre as he is with establishing a certain perspective from which to view the events. Whether this perspective be that of duration [Bergson's *durée*] or psychoanalysis, one must, if one wishes to embrace it, adhere to certain rules. Thus one discovers that the generic problem has been shifted rather than abolished.[16]

That such collisions between genre and technique are fairly common is, once again, shown by the changing views on satire. For in spite of several recent attempts (such as Alvin Kernan's book) to salvage satire as a genre, the label is now ordinarily understood to refer to a technique pressed into the service of didacticism and applicable to various literary genres.[17] *Mutatis mutandis*, the same is true of parody, travesty, the burlesque and the grotesque. Especially the last two phenomena deserve close scrutiny on the part of those scholars who wish to retain the crucial distinction between genre and technique or mode (*die Groteske* and *die Burleske* as opposed to *das Groteske* and *das Burleske*).[18]

Much work in this area of specialization remains to be done by the comparatist; and it is hoped that the International Dictionary of Literary Terms, now slowly in the making under the auspices of the ICLA, will furnish the clarifications needed in so many cases. Such elucidations, however, should not be restricted to Western culture but ought to include comparisons involving different civilizations.

As for actual genological *rapports de fait* between East and West, for instance, it cannot be denied that, notably since the middle of the nineteenth century, European and American writers (as well as painters and composers) have been impressed and influenced by Oriental models. Thus the prototype of the Japanese *haiku* has inspired the Imagists, as well as Paul Claudel and many avant-garde poets of today. And the formal properties of the Noh play (much less frequently their content) have found admirers in playwrights like Yeats, Claudel, and Brecht. Their imitations prod the question as to what extent such re-creations are compatible with their models and whether the pressure exerted by the Western tradition has caused a distortion of the originals. In search of an answer, Etiemble notes:

Claudel published some would-be *dodoitsu*, and *haiku* flourished in Europe. It remains to be seen whether poems published under that name still deserve an "appellation" which the cheese and wine merchant would call "contrôlée" (trade mark) and the manufacturer of socks and brassieres "registered." When they read those of our would-be *haiku* which strive for the conciseness of the original, the Japanese I know find in them nothing like theirs. Does this deception depend on economic or political conditions? On philosophical or religious superstructures? On traditional imagery? On phonetics or syntax?[19]

Etiemble has no ready answer but suggests that it is impossible to transplant a genre which is so firmly anchored in a specific historico-geographical context. On the other hand, the study of such unsuccessful experiments may demonstrate the gap which separates East and West, and suggest some of the underlying causes. Pure analogy studies in comparative genology may fulfill a similar function and are likely to benefit Oriental scholars even more than their Occidental colleagues. For, until very recently, no systematic effort to classify literary phenomena according to their generic qualities was made in most Far Eastern countries, while the theory of genres has long been a basic concern in Indian esthetics.

In his inaugural lecture at St. Petersburg, Alexander Veselovsky, harking back to A. W. Schlegel, championed the theory of an inevitable step-by-step progression of the three major literary "kinds." In his opinion, the successive flowering of epic poetry (Homer), lyric poetry (Pindar), and drama (Aeschylus), in the early stages of Greek literary history was the necessary correlate of a historical movement leading from the objective to the subjective, and from there to a fusion of the two modes in a state perhaps most aptly described as that of reflection. Thus, in the Russian scholar's view, "what we might call the epic, lyric and dramatic world view actually had to occur in the particular succession indicated, determined by the ever greater development of individualism."[20] This is a theory not unparalleled in the age of positivism; for it finds its more strictly sociological analogue in Posnett's book *Comparative Literature* (1886) and—with greater literary sophistication—in the writings of Brunetière. However, contemporary scholarship justly rejects such simplistic—evolutionary or teleological—schemes of historical progression.

If, continuing to treat our problem historically, we consult the Greeks themselves, we find that, for them, a tripartite division of the major kinds was theoretically possible but practically unfeasible. Thus, for Aristotle, the epic and the drama were the only two "kinds" identifiable as such, while—for reasons still to be accounted for—lyric poetry remained amorphous and therefore hard to classify. When the Stagirite posed the question as to the superiority of one kind over the other, the choice was only between tragedy and the epic. Aristotle opted for the former by arguing:

And superior it is because it has all the epic elements . . . with the music and scenic effects as important accessories; and these afford the most vivid combination of pleasures. Further, it has vividness of impression in reading as well as in representation. Moreover, the art attains its end within narrower limits; for the concentrated effect is more pleasurable than one which is spread over a long time and so diluted.[21]

In modern times, the epic has lost most of its glamor (just as lyric poetry has won esteem), and the *poème héroique* is as extinct as is the Romance, its subspecies, which although conceptually differentiated and ultimately transformed into a prose genre is historically tied to it. It is all the more regrettable that today there does not seem to exist a universally valid name for the literary kind which embraces all narrative genres, whether couched in poetry or prose; for even the English term *fiction* applies only to such prose forms as the novel, the novella, the short story. On the other hand, a division of imaginative literature into prose and poetry is no longer feasible, since, in the meantime, numerous intermediate genres—such as the verse novel, the Lyrical Novel,[22] the *poème en prose*—as well as mixed forms such as Dante's *Vita nuova*, Boccaccio's *Decameron*, Goethe's *Faust*, and Strindberg's *Dream Play*—have been constituted.

A quadripartite division of literature into epic poetry, lyric poetry, drama, and didactic writings has also been suggested from time to time, without ever catching on. This failure most likely results from the fact that the didactic is a *mode* rather than a *kind* or *genre* and, as such, relates primarily to an author's intentions and the effect which his work seeks to achieve. As a mode, however, it has its place in many genres, although some of these—the verse satire, the fable, the parable, the Morality, and perhaps even the legend and the fairy tale—show a marked predilection for pedagogy. On the other hand, such patently didactic works as the lost poems of Empedocles, Lucretius' *De rerum natura*, and Brecht's unfinished versification of the Communist Manifesto belong to literature partly for formal (metrical) reasons and partly—as in the case of Brecht's experiment—because they were authored by a poet. Aristotle stated, vehemently objecting to the *ars metrica* cultivated in his time:

Even if a treatise on medicine or natural philosophy be brought out in verse, the name of poet is by custom given to the author; and yet Homer and Empedocles have nothing in common except the meter: the former, therefore, is properly styled poet, the latter physicist rather than poet.[23]

In addition to defining the often tenuous relation between didactic and nondidactic elements in a given class or species, the theory of literary genres is also charged with circumscribing and defining such marginal forms as are often excluded from the realm of belles lettres. We think, for example, of the essay, the biography, and the autobiography and, among the miniature forms, the maxim, the aperçu, the aphorism, the Character (*caractère*), and perhaps even the Romantic fragment—many of which forms are just beginning to gain a measure of scholarly recognition.[24] To these hybrids we must add those phenomena which Baldensperger and Friederich somewhat loosely group under the heading of semiliterary genres and which are keys to our understanding of the mutual illumination of the arts: the libretto, the screenplay, the radio play and the emblem.[25]

A manner of classification particularly congenial to the student of the arts and their interrelationship is the division according to what Aristotle calls the *means* of imitation. This criterion is used in the opening passage of the *Poetics*, where literature is confronted with those other arts with which it shares one or several of these means. Indeed, no genological study would be complete without a reference to music—not because language, too, makes use of sounds, but primarily because music (literally, the art inspired by the Muses) was originally wedded to the verbal arts. I specifically exclude epic poetry, although the bards or minstrels recited the verses to [their own?] musical accompaniment; for even in Antiquity this practice has a bearing only on the actual presentation, since no music was specifically composed to go with the poetry. For this reason Aristotle justly includes the epic among the strictly literary "kinds," since it is one of the arts which "imitate by means of language alone, and that either in prose or verse—which verse, again, may either combine different meters or consist of but one kind."[26]

Oddly enough, Aristotle concludes by stating that this art "has hitherto been without a name." This statement is essential for the understanding of his (and the Greek) approach to the theory of genres; for it shows, as O. B. Hardison, Jr., has recently demonstrated,[27] that the ancients did not have a collective term for the kind of nondramatic literature that was not symbiotically fused with music. Among the genres which use several means of expression (meaning, in our context, words as well as sounds), Aristotle differentiates between those in which these are employed simultaneously (the dithyramb and the nome) and those in which they figure alternately (tragedy and comedy). Unfortunately, it is no longer common knowledge that Greek tragedy was, in every way, a *Gesamtkunstwerk* (total work of art), so that actually the standard texts handed down to us are merely the librettos of multidimensional plays akin to operas. This fact is corroborated by the survival of two lines from Euripides' *Orestes*, together with their musical notation.[28]

The problems of generic classification looming for the student of lyric poetry—now generally regarded as the third major kind of literature—are particularly excruciating. Its ties with music are etymologically fixed; for lyric means "accompanied by the lyre." Similarly, several ancient and modern poetic genres, such as the ode (*ode* = song), the song (*Lied, chanson*), and the sonnet presuppose an intimate relationship in degrees varying from age to age and from literature to literature. Greek literary criticism—at least in the classical and postclassical ages—was not yet prepared to assign a collective name to the lyric "kind." The reasons are succinctly stated in the following entry, signed G. L., from the *Lexikon der alten Welt*:

> What today, in contradistinction to the epic and the drama, we call lyric poetry was not uniformly conceived in antiquity. For one thing, the ancient drama contained lyrical passages as well, and ancient literary theory distinguished between lyrical and elegiac poetry. This is due partly to the closer ties which existed between languages, music and the dance in ancient times.[29]

The Greeks themselves, using the manner of performance as a yardstick, separated choric from monodic poetry, which latter carried the label "melic." It was only in Hellenistic times that a clearcut, though rather pedantic division was created, which persisted well into the Middle Ages. This feat was accomplished with the help of a canon of nine classic poets (Alcaeus, Alcman, Anacreon, Bacchylides, Ibycus, Pindar, Sappho, Simonides, and Stesichorus) upon whom the honorific title "lyricists" was bestowed. From that point on, the term *melic* was primarily used to designate noncanonic poetry. Attempts to enlarge the canon of classic poets were, on the whole, unsuccessful, except in some cases where major poets of subsequent ages continued to use the traditional forms. The term "lyrical poetry" (*lyrike*) first appears in the *techne grammatike* of Dionysius Thrax (ca. 170–90 B.C.) as a label for the major "kind."

Horace, too, was unable to cope with these terminological difficulties; for in the *Ars Poetica* he alternately calls

himself *lyricus* and *fidicen* (from *fides* = lyre); and well
into the eighteenth (Germany) and nineteenth (France)
centuries the term *ode* was widely used as a synonym for
"lyrical poem." However, it always applied to consciously
and individually created art (*Kunstdichtung*) and excluded
the popular (folksong) elements. Even so perceptive a critic
as Herder still wavered in his usage and called the ode the
"vein of the drama and the epic, the only three kinds
(*Arten*) of true poetry."[30] It was only with the writings of
the German Romantic poets and critics (Novalis, the
brothers Schlegel, and Schelling) that the tripartite scheme
became universally accepted.

Not to be forgotten in our survey of the various approaches to the theory of genres is the precarious use of
"lyrical," "dramatic," and "epic" in their adjectival rather
than nominal guise—a practice which still enjoys considerable favor, especially in the German-speaking countries.
The purpose underlying this usage is to show that literary
genres are improper groupings and that the best one can
do in the way of drawing generic distinctions is to extract
certain basic qualities, moods or states of mind—which
brings the theorizing about genres dangerously close to being a psychological puzzle game, quite apart from the fact
that the practitioners of this method sin, like Croce, by
deliberately cutting themselves off from the historical
stream in which genres, after all, develop.

In his "Noten und Abhandlungen zum *West-Östlichen
Divan*," Goethe observes that there are too many different
points of view from which to consider the various kinds of
literature. The solution he offers is based on the assumption that there are three *Naturformen*, namely the lucidly
narrative, the enthusiastically excited, and the personally
active (*die klar erzählende, die enthusiastisch aufgeregte*
and *die persönlich handelnde*), in other words, attitudes
relevant to the epic, to lyric poetry, and to the drama. Goethe goes on to say that these *Naturformen* may exist by
themselves or in conjunction with each other, and that
they are often joined even in the shortest poem. In partic-

ular, he seemed to regard the ballad as a kind of literary protozoan where the three natural forms exist *in nuce* and from which they can split off.

In order to relate the individual genres to each other and to the natural forms (*Urformen*), Goethe proposed to arrange them schematically in such a way as to produce a circular pattern in which their proximity to one, two, or all of the *Urformen* is graphically demonstrated. Models for each species were to be found until the circle containing all the possible genres was completed. Goethe himself never played this tedious game; but Petersen subsequently executed the maneuver in his book *Die Wissenschaft von der Dichtung*.[31]

The notion that this approach is more fruitful for literary criticism than the historical study of the genres has been most doggedly advanced by the Swiss Germanist Emil Staiger. Like Goethe, Staiger believes "that every genuine literary work partakes of all genres, though in different degrees and manners, and that it is this proportionate difference which accounts for the abundance of the historically evolved genres."[32] He justifies his rejection of the usual poetics of genre by protesting that in modern times the number of form-content configurations has so rapidly increased that it has gotten out of hand. According to Staiger, however, a theory of genres is meaningful only if each species can look up to an acknowledged model:

Since Antiquity, however, the models have increased a thousandfold . . . (and) if the theory of genres is to remain fair to all individual examples, it must—to speak only of poetry— compare ballads, songs, hymns, odes, sonnets and epigrams with each other, trace the history of each of these genres through one or two thousand years and find a common denominator qualifying them as lyrical poetry. But what is common to all such poems can only be something indifferent. Moreover, it ceases to be valid as soon as a new poet appears and presents an as yet unfamiliar model.[33]

We have already indicated that Staiger's view is shared by several of his German colleagues, notably by the late

Wolfgang Kayser, whose influential and widely used book *Das sprachliche Kunstwerk* also concerns itself with the structure (*Gefüge*) of genres. In the chapter on genres (Chapter Ten), one notes with dismay that the individual genres are hardly touched upon since "what they add to our understanding of a work has been discussed in earlier chapters, especially the ones concerned with techniques (*Darstellungsweisen*)."[34] Consulting these earlier chapters, however, one discovers that in them the major kinds of poetry are summarily, and rather unsystematically, dealt with in a total of twenty-five pages (of which only four concern themselves with lyrical poetry and five with the drama), whereas Chapter Ten extends to nearly sixty pages.

Let me now call attention to a book written by the Dutch scholar André Jolles and published in German (1930) under the title *Einfache Formen* (Simple Forms).[35] The forms in question are what we might call preliterary genres best considered as "specific kinds of mental activity constituted by the changing attitudes which man, creating form by means of language, adopts towards the objects he encounters."[36] Jolles lists nine such basic types, which he takes to be building blocks for the more intricate and demanding genres: *Legende* (legend in the sense of a saint's biography), *Sage* ("a story popularly taken as historical but not verifiable"), *Mythe, Rätsel* (riddle), *Spruch* (proverb), *Kasus* (case, as in "court case"), *Memorabile* (a personal record of noteworthy events and experiences, news account), *Märchen* (fairy tale), and *Witz* (joke). He did not regard the series as complete, but thought, for example, of including the fable.

I have stated that the common feature of Jolles' simple forms is their preliterary or extraliterary character; for a *Kasus* becomes literary only as a salient anecdote (Goethe's "unerhörte Begebenheit") or by expansion into the theme of a longer narrative or dramatic work, the *Memorabile* by its insertion into a diary or autobiography, the *Mythe* by its transformation into a plot (= *mythos*). As far as their subject matter is concerned, these simple forms have relatively little in common with each other, whereas structurally they tend to be rather less complex than most of the established literary genres. However, even among themselves, they vary considerably in scope, extending as they do from the microcosm of the joke or riddle to the rich structural articulation of some fairy tales and legends.

Having so far primarily concerned myself with the literary "kinds," I now turn to the actual genres and the various ways of fixing them in an aesthetic cosmos. For it is understood that some such systematic arrangement must be attempted, since a mere cataloguing of the diverse phenomena, whose number is legion, would yield no genological insight but would amount to acquiescence in chaos. The need for clarification is underscored by the lists furnished by Goethe and Kayser. In his Notes to *Der West-Östliche Divan*, Goethe alphabetically (in the German order) enumerates "allegory, ballad, cantata, drama, elegy, epigram, epistle, epic, novella (*Erzählung*), fable, heroid, idyl, didactic poem (*Lehrgedicht*), ode, parody, novel (*Roman*), romance, satire,"[37] whereas Kayser places his entries in the more hierarchic order "novel, epistolary novel, *Dialogroman*, picaresque novel, historical novel; ode, elegy, sonnet, *alba* (dawn song); auto, vaudeville, tragedy, comedy, Greek tragedy, melodrama."[38]

While Goethe indiscriminately catalogues literary genres belonging to different classes and representing different orders of magnitude, Kayser clearly orients himself toward the major kinds. However, instead of listing the novel, the novella, the short story, the epic, the romance, he singles out the novel together with certain of its subspecies, thereby moving from a higher to a lower level of genological discourse. Goethe attaches the following comments to his random catalogue:

If we scan the above list carefully, we notice that the types are sometimes named after their formal appearance and sometimes after their subject matter, but rarely according to their essential

form. Moreover, one quickly realizes that some of them can
be grouped together while others may be subordinated to
each other.[39]

Goethe attempted a more expedient grouping—with
questionable results—in the section "Naturformen der
Poesie." From E.-M. Voigt's discussion of Greek lyrical
poetry in one of his contributions to the *Lexikon der alten
Welt* we learn that, in effect, Goethe's problem was not, as
Staiger maintains, a specifically modern one; for in Hel-
lenic practice

the terms themselves denote the poems according to different
criteria: according to the refrain (paean, hymeneus), the action
they accompany (hyporcheme, prosodion), the content or the
occasion (encomium, epinicion), the chorus (partheneion), the
meter (iambus) or simply as song (hymnus, melos).[40]

In discussing the various principles of classification, I
shall seek to establish their value for the historical-critical
study of genres from a comparative point of view. From
the very beginning, it should be clear, however, that it is
virtually impossible to arrange all regional, national, and
supranational forms in an encompassing scheme. Since
every survey of this field is bound to be more or less strin-
gently selective, the quest for completeness is futile and
must be abandoned in favor of an attempt to clarify the
reasons that in their poetics Aristotle, Horace, and Boileau
refer to certain genres but leave others untouched. Such
an inquiry should throw new light on the historical circumstances surrounding their survival or their disappearance.

It seems fair to assume that generic classifications based
on psychological criteria are ordinarily to be taken with a
grain of salt, no matter whether it is a question of testing
the psychology of the author or that of his public (reader,
spectator, or listener); for here, in spite of the reference to
archetypal patterns, the subjective element is bound to
prevail. A good case in point is Schiller's distinction between the naive and the sentimental (better, the reflexive),

and his citation of the various genres illustrating these polar attitudes, in his famous essay "Über naive und sentimentalische Dichtung" (1795). The naive, according to Schiller, is "nothing but the voluntary being, the existence of things by themselves and in accordance with innate and immutable laws," whereas the sentimental results from the fact that "in modern times man has lost touch with nature, and nature, in its full truth, is to be found only outside of society in the inanimate world."[41] The further mankind departs from the naive condition (and we know that it does so with ever-increasing speed), the greater will be the preponderance of "sentimental" over "naive" genres. If only for this pragmatic reason, a modern poetics of genres based on Schiller's dichotomy would be decidedly lopsided and fall far short of its goal.

Far more familiar, and far more serious in its consequences is the division of literary genres by their intended effect. Adopting this perspective, Aristotle defines tragedy as the imitation of a serious action "through pity and fear effecting the proper purgation of these emotions." Two things should be noted in this connection. First of all, the author of the *Poetics* apparently does not assign the same aesthetic value to the effects produced by the work of art as he does to the means, the subject matter, and the mode of expression; for fear and pity enter our field of vision only in Chapter Six of his treatise, whereas the other elements are scrutinized in Chapters One to Three.

Secondly, we should remember that pity and fear are *feelings* most strongly evoked in public performance and, hence, of less immediate significance in the composition and consumption—to use a sociological term—of fiction or poetry which, at least in modern times, impinge upon us in the privacy of the study.[42] Indeed, it can be argued that, traditionally, generic designations derived from the intended effect of the literary product are more frequently encountered in drama (*Lustspiel, Trauerspiel, Rührstück*) than in fiction (sentimental novel, *Schauerroman*) or poetry.

For the student of Comparative Literature this approach is especially unproductive, since twentieth-century man is fully aware of the fact that the same event or object is judged variously, and produces diverse effects, not only in different cultures but also at different times—and in different places—even within the same culture. What the Australian bushman calls beautiful or touching may seem ugly and repulsive to the Watussi, and the Aztec's heroic deed appear contemptible to the Dutchman. In a passage of his *Stephen Hero*, Joyce articulates this view by stating

No esthetic theory . . . is of any value which investigates with the aid of the lantern of tradition. What we symbolise in black the Chinaman may symbolise in yellow; each has his own tradition. Greek beauty laughs at Coptic beauty and the American Indian derides them both. It is almost impossible to reconcile all tradition.[43]

It is ironic that, this anthropological insight notwithstanding, young Dedalus continues to build his theory of art around the Aquinatic dictum *pulcra sunt quae visa placent*, which he interprets to mean that "though the same object may not seem beautiful to all people, all people who admire a beautiful object find in it certain relations which satisfy and coincide with the stages themselves of all esthetic apprehension."[44] In other words: Joyce seeks to operate with psychological constants.

The oldest and most venerable way of classifying genres is to be found in Plato's *Republic* (392^b–394^d), where particular emphasis is placed on what we now tend to call "point of view." Thus Socrates, speaking to Adeimantus, observes:

I suppose that all mythology and poetry is a narration of events, either past, present or to come. . . . And narration may be either simple narration or imitation, or a union of the two. . . . [Thus] poetry and mythology are, in some cases, wholly imitative, instances of this being supplied by tragedy and comedy. There is also the opposite style, in which the poet is the only speaker— of this the dithyramb affords the best example. And the combination of both is found in the epic and in several other types of literature.[45]

The value of this definitional method is appreciably reduced by the underlying pedagogical intention; for Plato regards imitation as potentially dangerous for the state, since in the mimetic genres the poet voices his own ideas through the mouths of his characters, thereby presenting as objective fact what is actually his own opinion. If one disregards the didactic aspect of Plato's theory, on the other hand, the distinctions made by Socrates clearly relate to technical or stylistic devices which are also mentioned in the *Poetics* (1448[a]), where, however, no major genological significance is attached to them. Their full meaning emerged only in the second half of the nineteenth century, first with Flaubert and then with Henry James. Following Guyard's suggestions, a latter-day Plato would have to record all the refinements of fictional perspective which have been wrought in the last half-century, adding information about such phenomena as the stream of consciousness and the *style indirect libre* (*erlebte Rede*, narrated monologue).[46]

Perhaps the most frequently used methods of classification are those oriented toward form or content. The more's the pity that these two elements cannot always be cleanly separated. Hence the following recipe offered in the *Theory of Literature*:

Genre should be conceived . . . as a grouping of literary works based, theoretically, upon both outer form (specific meter or structure) and also upon inner form (attitude, tone, purpose—more crudely, subject and audience). The ostensible basis may be one or the other (e.g., the "pastoral" or "satire" for the inner form; dipodic verse and Pindaric ode for the outer); but the critical problem will then be to find the other dimension to complete the diagram.[47]

In light of the dialectic embraced by Wellek and Warren, it is instructive to look, once more, at Horace's epistolary treatise where, in the case of both lyric poetry and the epic,

the genre is identified by its preferred subject matter rather
than by its formal trappings; for the bard is said to have
described *res gestae regumque ducumque et tristia bella*
(the actions of kings and rulers and sad wars), and the poet
is charged with celebrating *divos puerosque deorum/et
pugilem victorem et equum certamine primum/et
iuvenum curas et libera vina* (gods and the sons of gods and
boxing champions and Derby winners, the desires of
young people and the liberating wine).[48]

Particularly instructive for the comparatist is the gradual fusion of formal and conceptual qualities offered by the
elegy and the iamb, both of which genres, in the peripatetic
aesthetic subscribed to by Horace, were distinguished from
lyric poetry because they lacked the musical element. In
the fourth chapter of the *Poetics*, we are told that the iamb
was originally regarded as the meter most suitable for satiric poetry but that, since it imitates the rhythm of col-
loquial speech, it was later used in the dialogue passages of
the drama, thereby becoming neutralized and abdicating
its role as a generic label. Today, the genological attrition
is complete, and the iamb leads a prosodic shadow existence as the most ubiquitous meter.

Polemicizing against the abuses of the *ars metrica*, Aristotle states, in the first chapter of the *Poetics* (1447[b]), that
"people do indeed commonly connect the idea of poetry
or 'making' with that of verse and speak of elegiac poets or
of epic (that is, hexameter) poets; implying that it is not
imitation that makes them poets but the meter that en-
titles them to the common name." Formally, the elegy is a
poem couched in elegiac distichs—one dactylic hexameter
followed by one dactylic pentameter. As for its content, it
was originally used as a vehicle expressing sorrow over the
loss of a beloved person, although subsequently the elegiac
poets were increasingly preoccupied with amatory matters
as Ovid had treated them in his *Amores*. The combination
of love and death seems later to have become a hallmark
of this tradition, as witnessed by Rilke's *Duino Elegies*. In
the course of this development, however, the genre lost

its formal properties and was no longer couched in distichs. Wellek and Warren note that in England "Gray's
'Elegy'," written in the heroic quatrain, not in couplets,
effectually destroys any continuation in English of elegy
as any tender personal poem written in end-stopped
couplets."[49]

As for the classification of genres according to their subject matter, the strict application of this criterion is likely
to produce a proliferation of subspecies without distinct
physiognomies. Kayser's list of types, quoted earlier, could
easily be enlarged to include such forms of the novel as the
Bildungsroman, the pastoral, the political,[50] the courtly
(of the German Baroque), the utopian. It is obvious that,
given such a large body of works constituting a major literary kind, some sort of breakdown is necessary. But how
is one to square this circle?

Actually, Kayser's list is by no means entirely gauged to
content; in the case of the epistolary novel, for example,
the manner of presentation is already more or less clearly
implied. Even the *Bildungsroman*—with its patently didactic overtones, which become more pronounced as we
proceed, for instance, from Goethe's *Lehrjahre* to his
Wanderjahre—presupposes a basic pattern insofar as the
growth and education of the hero unfold in a definite, ir-
reversible biological and pedagogical order. Conversely,
the picaresque novel requires a relatively loose structure
and a frequent change of scene.[51] In the case of the murder
mystery and the detective thriller, the structure is less rigidly predetermined, except that, suspense being used as a
chief device, the identity of the criminal must not be revealed until just before the end. The Gothic novel, finally,
comes much closer to constituting a *bona fide* literary
genre; for here the setting and many of the props are pre-
scribed by a closely knit convention established by a generally acknowledged model, Horace Walpole's *The Castle
of Otranto*.

The *Bildungsroman*, the picaresque novel, the Gothic
novel, the epistolary novel and their ilk may perhaps qual-

ify as genres for still another reason: they have no direct counterparts in the other major *kinds* of literature, whereas the whodunit and the historical novel do have their exact dramatic equivalents. With the Utopian and the rustic types we approach the realm of sociological classification, which would also have to include the (often satirically barbed) novel of school life, and the proletarian novel. In this kind of narrative, the setting is usually the determining factor, and a rather superficial one at that. Of the historical novel—to which Georg Lukács and Lion Feuchtwanger have devoted critical-historical treatises[52]— Wellek and Warren would like to make an exception, "not merely because its subject is less restricted . . . but primarily because of the ties of the historical novel to the Romantic movement and to nationalism—because of the new feeling about, attitude towards, that past which it implies."[53] Pichois/Rousseau would probably agree, since the historical novel, in their opinion, is essentially monogenetic, that is, derived from a single prototype or author.

One would think that purely statistical criteria of genre classification require no comment, insofar as they are quantitative. Thus there is no problem in grouping plays according to the number of acts into which they are divided (but where would we place Greek tragedy?) and in arranging various kinds of narrative according to their length (such as 50,000 words constitute a minimum for the novel, 10,000 words a maximum for the novella, with the short novel, the novelette, and the long novella falling in between, and the anecdote and short story occupying the lowest rungs of the arithmetical ladder). Although such divisions would seem to be altogether mechanical, quantitative criteria—like the annalistic labels attached to period styles—may sometimes acquire a qualitative flavor. This is certainly true of such lyric genres as the sonnet in general and the Petrarchan sonnet in particular, and although like Aristotle I would reject the *ars metrica* in principle, I grant that on occasion the specialist may well associate distinct generic properties with specific metrical patterns, as in the case of the *endecasillabo*, the *terza rima*, the *Alexandrine*, and the *Schüttelreim* (poetic spoonerism). The same applies, with even greater force, to lyrical poetry, as Paul Valéry demonstrates in his persuasive essay on *"Le Cimetière Marin."*[54]

I started out by saying that, given the enormous range and complexity of the literary phenomena known variously as kinds, types, genres, and classes, the historiographer among the students of genology as a branch of Comparative Literature will find it next to impossible to fashion a frame of reference in which a distinct place is assigned to each of these. The best he can hope for is to disentangle some of the knottiest problems, reveal anachronisms and shed light on a few of the many errors perpetrated in the course of literary history. In addition to handling the various approaches to genre definition in as deft and flexible a manner as the circumstances may require, he must also see to it that generic qualities are separated from those relating primarily to technique (as in satire) and from those infringing on thematic categories (as in Northrop Frye's *modes*). Thus, while in our post-Romantic age it would be vain to insist, with Horace, that "each particular genre should keep the place allotted to it," we should nevertheless endeavor to draw lines of demarcation where conditions are suitable and make sure that our terminology is as consistent as is humanly possible, and as is compatible with the historical context.

Six ✑ Thematology
(Stoffgeschichte)

F R O M Benedetto Croce to German *Geistes-geschichte* and the Anglo-American New Criticism, it was widely believed that subject matter (*Stoff*) was merely the raw material of literature, which acquires aesthetic valence only after it has been shaped or fashioned in a given drama, epic, poem, or novel. Thus, when viewed historically, the branch of literary scholarship known as thematology or *Stoffgeschichte* is so strongly discredited from the outset that it would seem to be difficult to overcome the deeply-rooted prejudices. Under the influence of folklore studies, our nascent discipline, at the end of the nineteenth century, was being pushed so much in a positivistic direction that, following the abrupt change in the intellectual climate around the turn of the century, it found itself suddenly under heavy fire, which has abated only in the last decade or so.

In laying the theoretical basis for *littérature comparée*, Van Tieghem and the other representatives of the Paris School found themselves moving in a kind of ideological backwater, whereas their predecessors—Max Koch and the Turin School, for instance—had swum with the stream while holding the same views. Only recently, new life has been breathed into this seemingly dead body by way of *topos* studies and a re-emerging interest in questions of tradition, convention, and *Wirkung*. Raymond Trousson in Belgium, Elisabeth Frenzel in Germany, and Harry Levin in the United States, each in his or her own fashion, has resurrected thematology by seeking to adduce scientifically sound arguments for the cultivation of this branch of learning. Their first and foremost task was to overcome the terminological uncertainty which arose from the fact that the technical terms used in the context of different national literatures did not always coincide semantically. What German scholars refer to as *Stoff- und Motivgeschichte*, for instance, is called *thématologie* in France, while in the English-speaking countries the term *Stoffgeschichte* is often used by way of compromise,[1] at least as long as Harry Levin's coinage "thematology" remains an obvious neologism.[2] In view of this Babylonian confusion, the first step in the critical analysis of thematological methods involves a careful distinction between subject matter (*Stoff*) and theme (*Thema*).

What is usually meant by *Stoff* is revealed in one of Goethe's maxims:

The poet's conscious activity focuses primarily on the form. The world liberally supplies the subject matter (*Stoff*), while the meaning (*Gehalt*) arises spontaneously out of the fullness of his soul. The two meet unconsciously, and ultimately it is impossible to tell which is responsible for the result. But the form, even though it is innate in the mind of genius, must be realized and pondered. Great circumspection is required in blending and integrating form, content and meaning with each other.[3]

Goethe, then, distinguished between subject matter (= content), meaning, and form, and maintained that only the shaping of form is a truly aesthetic act. The fact that he attributes relatively little significance to the choice of subject matter may surprise us, for it appears that Germany's prince of poets was unaware of how much the greatness and unity of a literary work depend on the affinity between subject matter on the one hand, and form and meaning on the other. It is equally striking that Goethe views "meaning" as a psychological (rather than morphological) category. In this he was emulated by Curtius, who further muddled the issue by calling this psychological component *Thema*:

The theme is everything which concerns the individual's unique
attitude toward the world. A poet's thematic range is the
catalogue of his typical reactions to specific situations into which
life casts him. The theme is in the subjective realm. It is a
psychological constant. It is innate to the poet.[4]

For Curtius, as for Goethe, then, the meaning of a literary work results from the poet's personal experience,
which forms a kind of basic pattern for which he seeks a
corresponding subject during the creative process.[5] (In
psychoanalytically oriented studies, these basic strains are
known as motives, which gives rise to further terminological confusion. I will shortly return to this knotty problem.) The idea that this catalysis occurs "spontaneously"
and "unconsciously" is extremely modern; for to contemporary critics of thematology art lies neither in the *Stoff*
nor in the experience, but solely in the writer's esemplastic
imagination, as Coleridge would have called it.

The threefold division of the literary cosmos suggested
by Goethe is still valid, although "content" (*Inhalt*) is now
often substituted for "subject matter" (*Stoff*), and, especially in German scholarship, *Gestalt* (= shape) for
form. My most urgent and immediate task will be that of
demarcating the three spheres. To begin with, the heading
of *form* clearly implies the subheadings of *style* and *structure*. In the current chapter, however, I am not at all concerned with style—a term difficult to define but distinctly
gauged to the personal manner of expression[6]—but only
with what we would like to call the internal correlate to
external structure. By "external structure" I mean, in this
particular context, the interdependence and integration of
the parts of an epic, dramatic, or even (as in the case of the
ballad) lyric piece: the sequence and concatenation of
scenes, the sequel and arrangement of chapters or stanzas,
and the various strands of action—in short: what, in regard
to the drama, is commonly known as fable or plot. Plot is
that part of an action which can be summarized or, as
Petersen puts it, "a reduction of the content of an epic or
drama to the combination of motifs which forms the hub

of its action."[7] Thus, while plot refers to a specific content, it always does so in the manner of a simplified, foreshortened account of a sequence of events. One begins to approach subject matter (*Stoff*) proper only when one ceases to look at an action in terms of a more or less regularly flowing movement and—once more abstracting—observes it from a bird's-eye-view. Now the plot is reduced to a *synopsis*, digest, or epitome (the Shakespearean plat), and its latent dynamism has come to rest. Such a summary of the most important components of an action helps to uncover the themes and motifs which lie at the root of the action and are illuminated by it. Motifs and themes, however, are thematological categories rather than units of meaning.

According to ordinary usage, "meaning" (*Gehalt*) refers to those aspects of a literary work which relate to problems or ideas—in short, the "philosophic-ideational tenor, the ethical bases" of a work.[8] The "idea" may appear in the abbreviated form of the so-called *moral*, an aphoristic phrase offering a solution to the problems at hand. The concluding lines of Schiller's *Braut von Messina*, for example, read "Der Leben ist der Güter höchstes nicht,/ Der Übel grösstes aber ist die Schuld" ("Life is not the greatest good,/ But guilt is the greatest evil"). Taking his cue from Karl Jaspers, Petersen in his methodological survey characterizes this highest level of poetic intent as follows:

With the plot, as well as with the characters and their psychology, it is the posing of problems that proves itself to be the connecting link in the chain in which these elements are linked with the principal idea. Every problem signals the posing of a question, which must find an answer in the idea; and an idea can find poetic formulation only in the solution of problems. As regards the problems, what Jaspers exemplified as the "antinomic structure of existence" in the so-called *Grenzsituationen*, applies to literature as well: "Each of these cases—conflict, death, chance, guilt—implies an antinomy. Strife and mutual help, life and death, chance and design, guilt and the sense of redemption are tied together, as the one does not exist without the other."

The problem always implies an either-or, no matter whether it is a question of practical life or theoretical insight, of ethical principles, human psychology, basic ideological decisions, or metaphysical truths. (*Die Wissenschaft von der Dichtung*, p. 239)

In the elevation of *problem* and *idea* to the level of *meaning*, the subject matter and, in fact, any direct relation to the individual work of art is gradually lost sight of. This was one of Croce's points of departure for his critique of thematology in particular and comparative influence studies in general. For the Italian scholar was convinced that "poetry is essentially form, and form alone cannot influence culture. But the material of poetry, detached from its form, may operate as an influence; it is, then, no longer art, but emotion or ideas." Harry Levin also seems to take it for granted that thematology serves (inevitably?) as a vehicle of *Problemgeschichte*, for he calls the theme an "avenue for a progression of ideas, whose entrance into literature it invites and facilitates." In other words: "Themes, like symbols . . . are polysemous: that is, they can be endowed with different meanings in the face of differing situations. This is what makes an inquiry into their permutations an adventure into the history of ideas."[9]

In the realm of *Gehalt*, the literal meaning—still a content category—tends to give way to deeper significance. In literature, for example, the relation between content and meaning is mirrored in the dichotomies of image and symbol, motif and problem, theme and idea. Thus, for both logical and methodological reasons, I most emphatically disagree with Elisabeth Frenzel, according to whom—

Stoff, motif and symbol are regarded as components of that structural element of literature which pertains to subject matter and content. They represent three levels in the spiritualization of the material encountered by the poet or placed at his disposal. The *Stoff* can be condensed into the motif, and the motif can be raised to the symbolic level.[10]

Harry Levin also "take[s] the symbology for granted in this connection, since it involves interpretations of *Stoff* and *Motiv*." In contrast, I shall exclude symbology from this survey, since it more properly fits into the realm of meaning, and focus instead on the genuine content categories present in, or suggested by, the literary work. To the best of my knowledge, these include, besides subject matter (*Stoff*) itself, theme, motif, situation, image (*Bild*), trait (*Zug*), and *topos*.

In this connection, it should be pointed out that, for Comparative Literature, *Stoff*, theme and *topos* are of considerably greater interest than, for example, motif and situation, although—or because—these latter features are more universal and archetypal than the former. The image and the trait, on the other hand, are too limited in size to lend themselves easily to monographic inquiry. Finally, the leitmotif, a structural device, differs from the motif, which is content-oriented. Being an internal feature, it is of little interest to the comparatist *sensu strictu*.

Fortunately, I can be brief in sketching the historical outline of the joy and sorrows of thematology which must precede the theoretical discussion, since pertinent remarks on this subject have been, and will be, offered in Chapters One and Appendix One respectively. I would like to reiterate, however, that thematology has, traditionally, been considered a German preserve—primarily because in the nineteenth century it was nourished and sustained as a consequence of the German folklore mania. For the study of folk literature, "which, especially in its beginnings, focused mainly on the genesis and evolution of an often fragmentarily and poorly transmitted body of literature, found it necessary, faced with alternate versions of a given tale, to turn to comparison and the sketching of family trees."[11]

In point of fact, the study of legends and fairy tales left its imprint on the fledgling discipline of Comparative Literature in Germany and the adjoining regions (notably the Alsace, Switzerland, and Northern Italy) and probably stifled its growth in Scandinavia. Van Tieghem commented in 1931: "Thematology is . . . strongly developed in Germany. This is true of all those countries where the folk literature is vital, where it has remained alive, and where it exercises a profound influence on the literature produced by men of letters."[12] To be sure, this statement relates to conditions which the *Geistesgeschichte* of the twenties had profoundly modified. Yet, from 1929 to 1937, Paul Merker was still active as editor of a series of themat-ological monographs. But not until after World War II, was the time ripe for Elisabeth Frenzel to set about compil-ing her dictionary of literary themes, which had been re-peatedly called for by Karl Goedeke and Petersen. The fruits of her labor, forming an indispensable platform for comparatistically oriented thematology, were published in 1962 as a collection of "longitudinal cross-sections through the history of literature."[13] Using her contribution to *Deut-sche Philologie im Aufriss* (1957) as a prop, the same author published, in 1963, a small *Realienbuch*, which was fol-lowed, three years later, by her book *Stoff- und Motivge-schichte*.[14] Concurrently with this development initiated by Frenzel, Germany witnessed a renaissance of "survival" and *topos* studies undertaken in many cases by the repre-sentatives of the "Bonn School" gathered around the editor of *Arcadia*.

Ever since Baldensperger's denunciation of *Stoffge-schichte* in the first issue of *RLC*, French scholars have been wary of thematology, as have the *geistesgeschichtlich* inclined Germans, albeit for much more pragmatic rea-sons. Baldensperger sought to prove the scientific vacuity of the thematological approach by pointing out that such studies will always be incomplete and full of *disjecta membra*, since all the links of a chain can never be flaw-lessly reconstructed. This criticism was further sharpened by Paul Hazard, who dismissed thematology because it did not confine itself to the study of *rapports de fait*.[15]

Van Tieghem, being somewhat less stringent than Haz-ard, assigned to thematology the task of determining not only "the dependence of more recent authors upon their foreign predecessors," but also "the role played by their own genius, their ideal, and their art, in the variations they have played on a common theme" (Van Tieghem, p. 89). However, he considered this type of comparatism to be properly placed within General Literature. Guyard, for his part, apologetically notes that "despite Paul Hazard, it is necessary to take account of these studies, whose authors have sincerely desired to promote the cause of Comparative Literature" (Guyard, p. 49) and concedes that "the thematological realm offers many resources to the scholar;" for "without falling into folklore or crude erudition, Comparative Literature is capable of finding there a sure opportunity for contributing to the history of ideas and feelings, of which the writers were always the most vocal and the most persuasive exponents" (p. 57).

Baldensperger's and Hazard's objections notwithstanding, thematology was never ignored in French academic circles, where the number of comparatists rejecting the "official" doctrine was always large. Methodologically, the subject was recently discussed, at some length, by the Belgian scholar Raymond Trousson, whose reputation rests primarily on the merits of his two-volume monograph on the Prometheus theme. His booklength essay, along with Elisabeth Frenzel's stated views, will serve as the basis of my subsequent discussion.

Trousson's book may occasion some shrugging of shoulders among American, German, and French literary critics and historians; but, if the latest developments may be regarded as symptomatic, it is only a question of time until its contribution to scholarship will be universally acclaimed. As the author states in his introduction, the study is a kind of personal confession or stock taking:

Why do [men] feel the need constantly to inventory their ancestral legends? It is because to study their history, to pore over the secret of their infinite mutations, is also to learn to know their own odyssey, in which there is something supremely exalted and often supremely tragic. In every mind devoted to justice, there is an Antigone. . . . These heroes are in us, and we in them; they partake of our lives, and we see ourselves reflected in

their shapes. . . . Our myths and our legendary themes are our
polyvalence; they are the indices of humanity, the ideal forms of
the tragic destiny, the human condition.[16]

To be sure, as comparatists, we could immediately raise
the objection that the phenomena spotlighted by Trousson
are not so much literary universals as Jungian archetypal
categories. This may well be true, but even so, Comparative Literature, in this case, might at least serve as the
means to a nonliterary end. Nonetheless, it should be noted
that, in thematology, the aesthetic interest declines in proportion as the emphasis is shifted from the action to its
agent, as happens, for instance, in Käte Hamburger's book
*Von Sophokles zu Sartre: Griechische Dramengestalten
antik und modern*.[17] If, following Aristotle, one defines
drama primarily as action, the wrenching of individual figures from their context is a dislocation that must, perforce,
destroy the nexus. Käte Hamburger took that risk. She also
sensed that it is precisely this wresting the part from the
whole to which, from Croce to the present, the foes of thematology have objected.[18] Hence, her note of caution:

Since I am solely concerned with the conception of the figures
and their behavior, my attention is not directed at the structure
of the plays and my gaze does not follow the details of the action.
In fact, in many instances a thorough analysis accounting for
every moment and every figure of the various ancient and modern
works discussed here must be forgone, since it would detract
from the guiding principle of this comparative study. (p. 25)

Miss Hamburger seems to have wasted no time on re-
flecting whether it is the function and purpose of thematology to prove the identity of the figures or the unity of
the theme. Her assertion that in cases where different problems are posed the identity of the figures is "merely a sign
of the immutability of the basic situations which were established by the tragedians" (p. 24), sounds slightly naive
when viewed in light of Croce's earlier observation:

If the figure and the plot have acquired new life in the poet's
mind, that new life is the true figure and the true plot. If no new

life has been instilled, that which always interests us is the
stirring, however feeble, of new life—and not the alleged
tractability or what is believed to be the ideal way in which the
theme should have been treated.[19]

For Croce, there exists no continuity of literary figures
in the sense postulated by Käte Hamburger. As he puts it,

In the series of *Sophonisbe* dramas studied by Ricci, there is no
Sophonisbe but, rather, Trissino, Mairet, Corneille, Voltaire, or
Alfieri: these men are the true protagonists, but not the daughter
of Hasdrubal, wife of Sifax and bride of Massinissa—a mere
name, or mere external facts, which the poet fills with the
proper substance.[20]

In her theoretical musings, Miss Hamburger fails to see
the logical fallacy inherent in the assumption that, simply
because the protagonists of two plays are called Electra,
both figures must be identical and, therefore, comparable.
But, in fact, such an identity can only be established via
the correspondence of essential traits and experiences. The
more these traits and experiences diverge, the more a character ceases to be "himself."

To conclude the historical survey, I briefly turn to the
views of American comparatists on thematology. As previously stated, there is in the United States no strong tradition along these lines; as yet, very few prominent scholars
in this country have made such a study the cornerstone of
their historical/critical endeavors. Woodberry, as well as
Chandler, included this branch of learning within the
province of Comparative Literature, but did so largely for
the sake of rounding off. Thanks to the efforts of A. O.
Lovejoy, the 1920's witnessed the emergence of the History of Ideas, a discipline programmatically focused on
meaning and for which *Stoff* was just as incidental as it
was for the neo-classical formalists.

The extent to which thematology was discredited in
America only two decades ago[21] is evident from the fact
that Wellek/Warren's introduction to the *Theory of Literature* does not contain a separate chapter on this subject.

Even in its index, the words "Stoff" and "theme" are missing. This noticeable gap is best explained by the book's overall structure, the authors being bent on differentiating between intrinsic and extrinsic approaches to literature. "Extrinsic," in their regard, is the study of literature in its relation to the (other) arts and sciences; while "intrinsic" study, for them, is the type of inquiry which is attuned to the purely literary aspects of a novel, play or poem. Naturally, the question arises whether thematology belongs to the first or the second category. Wellek/Warren's answer is unequivocal: *Stoff* is *extrinsic* as long as it has not been assimilated and digested by the writer; it becomes *intrinsic* as soon as that transmutation has occurred. However, the qualitative leap, mentioned in Chapter Two in connection with Guillén's notion of influence, places a gap between these two conditions. Thematology thus falls sadly between two chairs.

The only references in the *Theory of Literature* to thematology are found in the chapter entitled "Literary History," where we are told that it is wrong to speak of originality only in connection with the choice of subject matter; for, "in earlier periods there was a sounder understanding of the nature of literary creation, a recognition that the artistic merit of a merely original plot or subject was small" (W/W, p. 271). True originality, the authors assert, inheres in the shaping and treatment of the material. On the next page, *Stoffgeschichte* is dealt a mortal blow in a manner that would have pleased Croce, as well as Baldensperger and Van Tieghem:

With this type of study [the history of poetic diction] one might be expected to class the many historical studies of themes and motifs such as Hamlet or Don Juan or the Wandering Jew; but actually these are different problems. Various versions of a story have no such necessary connection or continuity as have meter and diction. To trace all the differing versions of, say, the tragedy of Mary Queen of Scots throughout literature might well be a problem of interest for the history of political sentiment, and would, of course, incidentally illustrate changes in the history of taste—even changing conceptions of tragedy. But it has itself no real coherence or dialectic. It presents no single problem and certainly no critical problem. *Stoffgeschichte* is the least literary of histories. (W/W, p. 272)

Significantly, even the journal *Comparative Literature* omits thematology from its comprehensive program. No wonder, then, that the *Bibliography of Comparative Literature*, which appeared in 1950 and devotes ample space to this subject area, was so harshly judged by some comparatists. Yet, even in the United States, time does not stand still. What, ten, or even five, years ago, was anathema to professors of literature is now well on its way to becoming once more acceptable. Thus Harry Levin places his stamp of approval on thematology in the following excerpt from his contribution to *The Disciplines of Criticism*:

If a theme itself can be so concretely pinned down, particularized into a local habitation and a name, the speculative area of thematics remains much wider and more flexible. We have seen that it embraces much of what used to be set aside as having to do with externals of literature. We are now willing to admit that a writer's choice of subject is an esthetic decision, that the conceptual outlook is a determining part of the structural pattern, that the message is somehow inherent in the medium. (p. 145)

As far as thematology is concerned, the circle has thus finally come full course, and I can proceed, with a good conscience, to offer some remarks concerning the methodology underlying this branch of Comparative Literature.

In the center of my theoretical considerations regarding *Stoff- und Motivgeschichte* I place the dialectics of *Stoff* and motif to which Elisabeth Frenzel alludes in the title of her book. As regards *Stoff*, further distinction must be made between preformed subject matter and raw material (*Rohstoff*) which is still to be shaped. *Rohstoff* is "an element external to the work of art, which becomes part of it

only in the poetic process. Such matter can be anything
which nature and history furnish to the writer" (Frenzel,
p. 21).

Even in its rawest state, however, the *Rohstoff* is often
somehow preformed—if not aesthetically, then at least as
a "simple form" (*einfache Form*), such as a news account
or an eyewitness report. A totally amorphous *Stoff* exists,
at best, in the guise of purely documentary or statistical
material. Or would undigested experience do the trick?
This is essentially a semantic problem, for one must decide
whether any kind of structured experience, prior to its
verbal expression, already constitutes *Stoff*.

It should also be remembered that many themes—most
of those treated in Greek drama, that of the *Nibelungenlied*, that of the *Chanson de Roland*, and numerous others—actually do not, or no longer, exist as *Rohstoff* but
only in a literary *Gestalt*, however primitive. Accounting
for this difficulty, Elisabeth Frenzel chose to open her survey at the point "where firm footing is gained through an
existing version," and to touch only briefly upon "the pre-
histories and meanings of individual figures belonging to
the realm of mythology," as well as on "the more or less
convincingly deducible primitive and preliminary versions" (p. xiv). *Stoff* in the "narrower sense" is, in her view,

a well delineated story line [*Fabel*] existing prior to the literary
work, a "plot," which, as an internal or external experience, as a
report on a contemporary event, as a historical, mythical, or
religious action, as a work already shaped by another writer, or
even as a product of the imagination, is treated in literary
fashion. (p. 21)

The unity of a theme lies, accordingly, "in the lowest
common denominator of all extant versions" (p. 25). But,
we ask ourselves, how can this denominator be derived
from the different treatments of a subject? The most suitable answer would seem to be that the common denominator of a *Stoff* is the combination of motifs absolutely
essential to its profile.

In the Don Juan theme, for example, the motif of seduction will hardly do as the only hallmark. The seduction must, rather, be a running motif at the very center of the hero's life. Even then the *Stoff* would be incomplete, however, without its explicitly religious overtones—the invitation extended to the dead Commander, the Don's balking at repentance, and the damnation of the *dissoluto punito*. Trousson comes to analagous conclusions with regard to the Medea and Pandora themes. It can, therefore, be assumed that the identification of *Stoff* can be accomplished only by means of breaking it down into its components (motifs).

For the sake of clarity and consistency, it would be useful, in principle, if we could replace the German word *Stoff* by "theme"; for the German *Thema* and the French *thème* obviously have the same root as their English cognate, whereas the German *Stoff* corresponds more closely to the English "subject matter" and the French *matière*. But the problem is complicated by the fact that theme or *Thema* point towards the History of Ideas and seem to imply an abstraction from *Stoff* (as in the German phrase "Er äussert sich zum Thema" [he comments on the subject]. Moreover, as Levin points out, in both English and French the word has a distinctly rhetorical-pedagogical ring:

> Our keyword *theme* may sound somewhat jejune, particularly to those who associate it with required compositions for Freshman English. The original Greco-Latin *thema* simply denoted a rhetorical proposition, the argument of a discourse, what in Jamesian parlance we now like to term the *donnée*. It could be the topic chosen by the orator or assigned to the schoolboy; through the pedagogical influence of the Jesuits the term became equated with an academic exercise; and the French soon specialized it to mean a translation of a given passage into another language. (*The Disciplines of Criticism*, p. 128)

Van Tieghem further adds to the confusion by designating as themes precisely those phenomena which I prefer to call *motifs*, namely, "the impersonal situations, the traditional motifs, the subjects, places, settings, usages, etc.," while labeling *légendes* those "events or groups of events whose protagonists are mythic, legendary, or historical heroes" (Van Tieghem, p. 90). For our present purpose, then, the word "theme" would seem to be less suitable than *Stoff*. However, in order to honor usage, I shall, in the remainder of this chapter, use *Stoff* in the singular but themes (instead of the awkward *Stoffe*) in the plural.

In this context, musical terminology could give rise to further confusion between *Stoff* and theme. Since the so-called "absolute" music has no content properly speaking, the thematic material here takes the place of the subject matter. The musical theme, however, as the starting point of an instrumental composition or as a basis for variations, is the member of a series which extends from the individual note over the motive to melody. Since the difference is largely quantitative, it is not always possible to distinguish between a long motive and a short theme, or between a long theme and a short melody.

What, then, is the relation between motif and theme in literature? For an answer to that important question we turn first to Frenzel and Trousson. In the opinion of the German scholar,

the word "motif" designates a smaller thematic (*stofflich*) unit, which does not yet encompass an entire plot or story line but in itself constitutes an element pertaining to content and situation. In literary works whose content is relatively simple, it may be rendered in condensed form through the central motif [*Kernmotiv*]; generally, however, in the pragmatic literary genres, several motifs are required to make up the content. In lyric poetry, which has no actual content and, thus, no subject matter in the sense here intended, one or several motifs constitute the sole thematic substance. (p. 26)

Trousson parallels this view:

What is a motif? We have chosen to use this term for designating a setting or large concept denoting either a certain attitude— e.g. rebellion—or a basic impersonal situation in which the actors are not yet individualized—for example, the situation of a

man between two women, of the strife between two friends or
between a father and his son, of the abandoned woman, etc.
(Trousson, p. 12)

What is striking in Trousson's treatment is the fact that
the Frenchman, who calls the theme (thème) "a specific
expression of a motif, its individualization or, if you wish,
the result of a passage from the general to the particular"
(ibid., p. 13), regards literary motifs as part of the Rohstoff.
This view, however, is unique in literary scholarship.

From the two above definitions it follows that, generally, motifs relate to situations, and themes to characters.
Themes are concretized through characters,[22] whereas motifs are derived from situations, for "we grasp them only
when we abstract them from their specific embodi-
ments."[23] (Situations, by the way, are groupings of human
views, feelings, or modes of behavior, which give rise to,
or result from, actions in which several individuals partici-
pate.) Decidedly, motifs never reach the level of abstraction proper to problems or ideas; and Trousson errs when
listing as motifs "the idea of happiness or progress" (p. 13).
Using the terminology adopted by Robert Petsch, one may,
moreover, speak of stereotyped combinations of motifs
and situations as formulae. Such formulae are, naturally,
often found in Jolles' simple forms—like fairy tales, fables,
folk tales, and legends.

The total store of motifs available to writers throughout
the world is relatively small—Paul Merker estimates their
number as amounting to about one hundred[24]—that of
themes, on the other hand, is practically unlimited. Mathe-
matically, the sum of possible thematic combinations
among motifs in groups of two, three, four, or more, is easy
enough to calculate. In addition, there are the endless variants governed by time and place and in the historical,
mythological, legendary, or fantastic trappings in which a
theme may be clothed. The total number of available situations, of course, is even smaller than that of possible
motifs, as there are relatively few characteristic modes of

human behavior capable of producing and sustaining action. (Semantically, the possibility of theatrical realization is clearly inherent in the concept of situation.) Thus Georges Polti, emulating Carlo Gozzi, sought to define pragmatically the *Thirty-Six Dramatic Situations*, convinced as he was that their number could not be increased.[25]

The situations which Polti lists—we still have to discuss their choice and grouping—are so general as not to be limited to one civilization or to one level of society. What Goethe said about the motifs fits to a "t," for according to him they are "phenomena of the human spirit, which have repeated themselves and which will continue to repeat themselves."[26] By contrast, the universality of motifs is subject to certain limitations imposed by temporal and geographical conditions and idiosyncrasies. What meaning, for example, would an African pygmy or an Australian Bushman attach to the palace-hut dichotomy? And how ridiculous the so-called Graf-von-Gleichen motif of the man between two women would be in the eyes of a Mohammedan or Mormon, or the motif of conflict between secular and divine law (*Antigone*, Reinhard Goering's *Seeschlacht*) in the eyes of a people whose King is also its High Priest? It is precisely for this reason that, with all due caution, we would like to extend the validity of Trousson's assertion that "in regard to themes, factual relations and cultural unity are indispensable conditions" (p. 70), to motifs as well.

It goes without saying that themes have a much narrower scope than motifs. This is especially true of historical subjects whose relevance is geographically limited and whose comprehension requires a specific awareness of time and place. Only where the historical peculiarities have been sloughed off and universal human traits have come to the fore, such themes may acquire a broader basis. Thus it is that the themes of Greek tragedy—which are either mythical or legendary—are well-known throughout the West, while only for a few of the more recent ones—

such as the Don Juan or the Faust *Stoff*, in both of which the historical core is already surrounded by an aura—can this stake be claimed. Even the Joan of Arc *Stoff*, for example, has a somewhat limited appeal; and with the Napoleon and Hitler themes, which are, from our perspective, much too diffuse and episodic, it may be our closeness, historically, which keeps them from acquiring the kind of cohesion which suits the thematologist's taste.

Despite Croce's blunt rejection of Ricci's attempt to explain the artistic weakness of all Sophonisbe dramas as a consequence of flaws inherent in that particular *Stoff*, it must be granted that certain themes may well carry their own weight. As Ricci puts it,

Every author is doubtless responsible for the defects of his work. But, in the case of a Corneille, Voltaire, and Alfieri, it would be rash to blame these authors for the mediocrity of their *Sophonisbes*. It is quite possible that there are more general reasons, relating to the nature of the theme. At first glance, the most intriguing subjects are not always the best and most tragic ones.[27]

I have to rest my case at this point, since, as Croce ironically notes, we are dealing here with a *circulus vitiosus*; for we know that a *Stoff* is suitable for tragedy (*tragédiable*) only because several dramatists have already used it. A great writer, however, should be capable of extracting even from a recalcitrant *Stoff* a modicum of theatrical and literary effect.

In Trousson's view, the *type*, i.e., the embodiment of a motif (or, more precisely, of a character trait) that never attains individuation intervenes between the concepts of theme and motif. Since types are, in a manner of speaking, characters in the formative stage, one may regard them as thematic modes which have not yet developed a valid symbolic prototype:

Certain motifs never develop to the point where they turn into themes. They are arrested at a stage in their evolution which one might call that of the type: thus, the motif of avarice produces

the type of the miser, which can be found in Plautus and Molière,
in Balzac and Ghelderode, but which has not established a
literary tradition epitomized by a specific personage. (Trousson,
p. 14)

Types, then, are more universal than themes and are therefore better suited for comparatively oriented analogy
studies.

In order to counter Baldensperger's and Van Tieghem's
objections that thematology slights continuity, and thus
completeness, Trousson creates two subspecialties, the one
dealing with the so-called heroic themes, and the other
with the so-called situational ones. In the first instance,
the study focuses on the character of the hero who lends
dignity to the *Stoff*; in the second, attention is centered on
the action resulting from the interplay of the figures.[28]

In the case of "heroic" figures—Prometheus, Orpheus,
Heracles, Faust, for instance—a choice of specific situations is moot, according to Trousson; for most of these
characters have outgrown the frame of reference originally
assigned to them. There is a process of accretion, in that at
different times and places the same figure may display different or even opposite, characteristics:

Supple, Protean, polyvalent and independent of narrative frames,
the heroic theme, due to the almost endless proliferation of
phenomena, is capable of integrating itself into the characteristics
of thought, manners and taste of a given century, of assuming
virtually all, even the most contradictory, meanings, of adapting
itself to all the nuances of contemporary life by embracing all the
variations: thematology is, concurrently, *Geistesgeschichte*.
(Trousson, p. 39)

Conversely, identical ideas may also be expressed by different characters acting as their *symboles condensés*. During the Romantic period, for instance, Faust, Cain, Satan,
and Manfred were all portrayed as rebels. In such cases,
the personality and the character of the hero is relatively
immaterial; in other words, the theme is subordinated to
the motif. If, in view of this fact (which refutes Käte Ham-

burger's thesis concerning the persistent identity of characters despite thematic changes), the comparatist should
attempt to compile the history of such "themes," he would
have to renounce from the outset any hope of achieving
total coverage; for a catalogue of all the references and
allusions he is likely to encounter would be both futile and
unwieldy.

According to Trousson, however, completeness can and
must be aimed at in outlining the history of situational
themes, which involve specific milieus and confrontations
within a specific framework. Trousson feels that almost all
historical themes belong to this category,

because the authors enjoy, in this respect, considerably less
freedom of choice than with regard to legendary themes,
considering the pressure of historical fact, which is exercised by
the time (Waterloo cannot be moved to the twentieth century),
the place (Cromwell cannot be executed in America), . . . and the
veracity of facts (Mary Stuart cannot be made Queen of
England). (p. 36)

This statement applies, naturally, only to a more or less
realistic treatment of such themes, since no limits can be
set to the poetic imagination, even in its use of strictly historical subjects. Brecht, for instance, has his Joan Dark
wandering around the stockyards of Chicago; and his Co-
riolanus displays character traits which differ substantially
from those traditionally ascribed to that pseudo-historical
figure.

As examples of such situational themes Trousson lists
Antigone and Oedipus, and maintains that when we hear
these names we do not so much think of their bearers as
of the events to which their fates are linked. The same
holds true, he claims, for the figures of Phaedra and Medea, whose destinies are intricately bound up with those
of Hippolytus and Jason, respectively. Moreover, Antigone and Oedipus have no true polyvalence, for the number
of possible variants in the motivation of their actions—
which is all the leeway given to the adaptor—is extremely

small. The comparatist concerned with the history of a situational theme will, thus, be typically confronted with self-contained works (rather than mere allusions), whose number is extremely limited. This is due to oversaturation, which results when no strikingly new interpretations are possible. Harry Levin shares this view and confesses that

> themes, like biological entities, seem to have their cycles, phases of growth, of heyday, and of decline, as with *Troilus and Cressida*. It is not surprising, in our latter day, that so many of them seem to have reached a state of exhaustion. Audiences get tired of hearing the same old names, and writers find it harder and harder to compete with their illustrious forerunners. But motifs seem inexhaustible. (*The Disciplines of Criticism*, p. 144).

Trousson also feels that many situational themes are prone to dramatic treatment, because in a play the story lines must be clearer and the plots more compact than in an epic or novel, while the lyric is by its nature too fragmentary and aphoristic (Trousson, p. 42). Frenzel, too, suspects that there exists a natural affinity between certain themes and specific genres, a fact she explains partly by their structural properties and partly by the simple weight of tradition.[29]

In the eyes of many readers, Trousson's distinction between heroic and situational themes may seem to be mere hair-splitting, especially since experience teaches us that pure specimens of either type are rare. Idiomatically, this removal of mythical or legendary heroes from their original setting is attested by such phrases as "he's a real Don Juan" or "his striving is truly Faustian." On the other hand, there are cases which prove that situational themes may also exist apart from the basic situation and can be transposed into a new context, as in the case of the Antigone *Stoff*, which is built into the dramatic action of Reinhard Goering's drama *Seeschlacht*.

In order to eliminate still another source of confusion, I turn once more to the question of the motif. That word derives from *movere* (to move) and thus originally carries the meaning of *movens*—that which moves something. The musical motive actually engenders a motion, since music is a linear time-art, at least in its melodic components. In the plastic and visual arts, on the other hand, motif is linked to movement only in a figurative sense. Actually, in painting, sculpture, architecture, and the decorative arts, the term denotes either the model (= *Vorlage*) of a work—i.e., Cézanne's Mont Saint-Victoire or Van Gogh's cypresses at Arles—or the use of recurrent compositional features, called in English *design* or *pattern*. The first meaning relates to a content category, and the second to a structural ingredient, which roughly corresponds to the leitmotif in music. The emphasis in literature is on content, for the literary motif is conducive to action only to the extent that it contains a situational element.[30] Those scholars, on the other hand, who proceed psychologically or psychoanalytically, rather than morphologically, are the victims of a false etymology. Thus Joseph Körner and Willy Krogmann[31] use the term *Motiv* synonymously with the English motive, rather than motif, as signifying a mental impulse or basic urge dormant in the subconscious and impinging upon the work of art *in statu nascendi*. For these scholars, motif persistence (*Motivkonstanz*) no longer means the transmission of a thematic pattern from one generation or one writer to another but the thematic unity of a poet's works (as, for example, the motif of male infidelity in the writings of the young Goethe)[32] related to a basic world view. The study of motifs thus understood, however, is not comparative, but monographic. In its search for constants of human behavior, it becomes comparative only at the universal level of Freudian complexes or Jungian archetypes. As far as literary history is concerned, it is doubly ironic that these complexes bear the respective names of the exemplary themes. Psychoanalysts "define the general motif by the particular *Stoff* which it has generated: the motif of the father-son rivalry is called the Oedipus complex, and the motif of the incestuous love between father and daughter the Electra complex" (Trousson, p. 13).

I have stated that from a literary viewpoint *situation* denotes divergent feelings or thoughts reflected in, or giving rise to, an action or conflict. Using Polti's book as an example, I would like further to clarify the meaning of this term. Unfortunately, Polti himself never arrives at a formal definition. What he means by "situation" is shown, in passing, by his observation that every dramatic situation (his study being restricted to such) arises "from a conflict between two principal directions of effort."[33] This would exclude those conflicts which rage within an individual, as well as unmotivated or one-sided actions. Thus, in connection with the twenty-sixth situation (amorous crimes of passion) Polti calls sexual assault or rape an act rather than a situation.

A "situation" also presupposes two or more persons engaged in a conflict. The actual dramatic nexus of a given play, accordingly, takes the form of a rhythmic sequence of actions and situations, the situations resulting from the actions, and triggering further actions in their turn. As Kayser notes: "It lies in the nature of situation that the motifs point towards a 'before' and an 'after.' The situation has arisen, and the tension it generates demands a resolution" (*Das sprachliche Kunstwerk*, p. 62). Levin erroneously believes that Gozzi computes a maximum of thirty-six *plots* for the stage. In fact, he knew that situations, like motifs, can be reshuffled in numerous ways to form myriad constellations.

Unfortunately, the situations which Polti lists are too diffuse to produce a coherent pattern. On the one hand, the French critic catalogues simple acts like abduction, rebellion, murder, and adultery; while on the other, he lists genuine motifs, such as enmity or jealousy, which must first be translated into the language of the stage. This patent mixture of motifs and situations is enhanced by Polti's statement that there is no situation "which may not be combined with any one of its neighbors, nay, with two, three, four, five, six of them and more" (Polti, p. 120). To prove his point, he cites the case of Oedipus, which he assigns to the eighteenth situation, while suggesting cross-references to the eleventh, sixteenth, nineteenth, and twentieth situations as well. It is easy to see, however, that only motifs can be abstractly combined, while situations are sequential.

What I have so far said suggests that, thematologically, the situation constitutes a link between the motif and the action, just as the type forms a link between the motif and the theme. An action suggests physical activity, whereas the motif is abstracted from concrete reality. The situation, however, tips the scale: "The physical situation, which . . . inspires the painter and sculptor, means little in the literary work if it lacks a spiritual dimension. It is this dimension which we must view as belonging to the literary motif."[34] If the motif is static and the action dynamic, the situation must then be the "pregnant moment from which all the motifs of the action evolve."[35] As a literary category, the situation is, accordingly, more closely linked to structure than to content and carries relatively little thematological weight.

The smaller the thematic unit in question, the less productive, from the comparatist's point of view, will be an investigation. In our field, themes are the ideal objects of study, whereas motifs, due to their endless ramifications and interlacings, are much more difficult to trace. Nevertheless, Van Tieghem highly recommends this specialty:

As regards maternal jealousy, blood vengeance, sacrifice to duty, etc., comparative studies of this sort—they are rare—might cast a vivid light on the genius and the art of different writers, as well as on the change of sensibility in their public. (p. 92)

Van Tieghem quite correctly notes that there are few comparative monographs of the kind exemplified by Kurt Wais' book *Das Vater-Sohn Motiv in der Dichtung bis 1800*.[36]

In winding up this thematological survey, I proceed to a brief discussion of the smallest thematic units, namely the *trait* (*Zug*), the *image*, and the *topos*. As long as they are not symbolically enhanced and thus shunted over to the realm of meaning, both trait and image are additive or decorative elements which become objects for thematological research only through conscious repetition or subtle linkage. The *trait* is an incidental attribute, which, taken by itself, is fairly insignificant. According to Petsch, however, it can be raised to the level of the motif by means of a *Pointe* that shows it to be characteristic or symptomatic. Through the *Pointe*, as it were, the trait is pushed into the limelight.[37]

The *image*, also, is often too inconsequential to arouse one's thematological curiosity. How many images there are in a novel, an epic, or a drama! Still, these are sometimes used as leitmotifs. And Caroline Spurgeon has written a book on Shakespeare's imagery, in which she attributes to each play a characteristic "cluster of images" which provide a clue to the author's intentions. For the comparatist as comparatist precious little is to be gained here, however. It may well befit the classical philologist to study the imagery of a Virgil within the corpus of Virgilian writings, but the comparative study of the *Bilder* used by various authors would seem to belong more properly to the province of *Kulturgeschichte*, where monographs on the flea, the rose or the nose in literature have their place.

The *leitmotif* has been defined as a "repetition of the same word sequence, at least by way of allusion or in slight variations, at different points of a poetic work," which, in this manner, "are related to each other through this attribute which they have in common" (Frenzel, p. 31). As I have already indicated, this phenomenon is meaningful only in the structure of the individual work.

Occupying roughly the same place within the hierarchy of thematological values as the trait and the image, but far more fruitful for Comparative Literature, is the literary *commonplace* or *topos*. Modest in scope, the *topos* yields

food for thought to the literary critic and historian. Derived from classical rhetoric, the *topoi* were originally arguments which served, within a given speech, to make
something palatable to the listeners, and which, in the pursuit of this goal, appealed either to the hearer's mind or
heart.[38] They also served as mnemonic aids. In late Antiquity, the *topoi* made their way into poetics and were gradually naturalized in literature. Only those readers who are
familiar with ancient and medieval usage can tell exactly
whether an image, a metaphor, or a figure of speech is
newly minted or fraught with tradition. In comparative
topos studies, the interpenetration of originality, tradition,
and imitation thus constitutes an important factor.

Literary scholarship is somewhat divided over the exact
nature and function of the *topos*. Kayser, for instance, assigns to topology the task of writing the history "of certain
concrete images, motifs, or figures of speech" (*Das sprachliche Kunstwerk*, p. 75). With regard to the latter, one
might think of expressions like *mater natura*, which Walter Veit says could well be reduced to the pure concept
natura, and of the metaphor *naturae cursus*, which Hans
Galinsky has recently analyzed from a historical perspective.[39] For the thematologically oriented comparatist, it
would be important to know exactly how a *topos* turns
into a motif (the *locus amoenus*) or a theme (the world as
a stage) and whether, besides the motifs and themes which
are extended *topoi*, there are those which have found their
final, unconsecrated home in the cliché or commonplace.

Seven ✐ The Mutual Illumination of the Arts

A question of great concern to the theorist of Comparative Literature is that of the relationship of literature to the other arts (chiefly music and painting). Remak extends our discipline, as we have seen, to include "the study of the relationships between literature on the one hand and other areas of knowledge and belief, such as the arts . . . on the other" (S/F, p. 3). He is, then, of the opinion that the comparative study of the arts constitutes a legitimate branch of Comparative Literature, as long, that is to say, as literature is used as either the point of departure or the focal point of the investigation.[1] When he registered this claim in 1961, only a handful of American scholars shared his view. Perhaps the most stalwart champion of the "Comparative Arts" approach at the time was Calvin S. Brown, the author of a methodologically significant book on *Music and Literature*,[2] who argued in a lecture delivered in 1959 and published that same year:

Comparative Literature accepts the fact that all the fine arts are similar activities, despite their differing media and techniques, and that there are not only parallels between them induced by the general spirit of differing eras, but that there are frequently direct influences of one art on another. Not all of these relationships fall in the field of the comparatist. The parallels between baroque architecture and baroque music, for example, are off his beat. But the relationships of literature with the other arts are a part of his domain and are, by general consent [sic!], usually considered as a part of comparative literature even when only one country is involved.[3]

Until very recently, it is safe to say, the study of the arts in their mutual interpenetration was a sort of academic twilight zone that was either annexed to aesthetics or, for lack of interest on the part of literary critics and historians, claimed by art history and musicology.[4] Thus, for many centuries, the critical discussion of the musico-literary *Gesamtkunstwerk* known as opera was frowned upon in literary scholarship; and emblematics, by default, fell easy prey to the iconologists. But after the appearance of works like Joseph Kerman's incisive study *Opera as Drama*, my own documentary collection of writings on *The Essence of Opera*, and the monumental handbook of sixteenth- and seventeenth-century emblematics compiled by Arthur Henkel and Albrecht Schöne, these territorial rights are being disputed. George Bluestone's booklength analysis of the ties between literature and film, based on cinemato-graphic versions of several famous novels, further confirms these proprietary rights.[5]

Within the Modern Language Association of America, the study of the mutual illumination of the arts is pursued by the members of a group designated as General Topics IX which, for the last fifteen years or so, has made a valuable bibliographical contribution to the subject.[6] Finally, it seems, the realization that the separation of the arts is an artificial one in both life and scholarship has dawned upon American scholars. Thus it was that, in the fall of 1966, at a conference of chairmen of Comparative Literature de-partments and programs in Racine, Wisconsin, three sym-posia were held in which literature was variously juxta-posed to the plastic arts and music. Similarly, at the annual MLA conference in December, 1967, one forum discussion each on the film and on literary and art history was con-ducted. Special issues of the journals *Comparative Litera-ture Studies* and *Comparative Literature* on literature and the other arts have appeared in the meantime; and the participants of the Bloomington meeting of the ACLA in April, 1968, bravely, although not altogether successfully, tackled the question of literary Impressionism.[7]

Also, a few years ago, the MLA published a collection

curiously and unidiomatically entitled *Relations of Literary Study: Essays on Interdisciplinary Contributions*, in which along with the cross fertilization of literature and history, mythology, biography, psychology, sociology, and religion, the links connecting literature and music are discussed in an essay by Bertrand H. Bronson.[8] It is symptomatic of the editorial qualms surrounding this enterprise that the term "Comparative Literature" is scrupulously avoided in the introduction by James Thorpe, who, nevertheless, admits that "the relation between literature and music is different from that of all of the others in this volume. Literature is one of the arts, along with (at least) music, painting, and sculpture" (p. xiii). Be that as it may: there is scarcely any doubt that, sooner or later, the study of literature's share in the mutual illumination of the arts will, along with the sociology of literature and the revived genology and thematology, find a prominent place in the next phase of the history of Comparative Literature.

What European comparatists think, or have thought, about the study of this interrelationship will be briefly noted in the following pages. In France, for instance, the possibility for inclusion of this special area within *littérature comparée* emerged only in the latter half of the 1960s. Although, as early as 1810, Sobry had published a *Cours de peinture et littérature comparées*, the tracing of affinities between literature and the *beaux-arts* was always considered the aim of aesthetics: "Their relations remain scarcely explored. France has made their study a branch of aesthetics and smothers it with abstractions" (P/R, p. 133). Still, even in the early twentieth century, an "outsider" occasionally tried to do justice to this phenomenon, for instance André Coeuroy, in his book *Musique et littérature: Etudes de musique et de littérature comparées*, and Paul Maury in his sketchy survey *Arts et littérature comparée: Etat présent de la question*.[9]

The patriarchs of Comparative Literature paid little or no heed to the mutual illumination of the arts. In Baldensperger's programmatic foreword to the first issue of the

Revue de littérature comparée, there is no reference to this topic; and since neither Betz's bibliography nor Baldensperger's expanded version thereof boasts of an appropriate rubric, it must be assumed that the relevant chapter in the *Bibliography of Comparative Literature* owes its existence to Friederich's initiative.[10] However, some scattered entries are also found in the now defunct bibliographical section of *RLC* under the heading "Ambiance: La Vie, les idées et les arts."

In Van Tieghem's handbook, music and the plastic arts are rarely mentioned. Their presence is briefly acknowledged in the chapter "Ideas and Feelings," which contains a subsection entitled "Aesthetic and Literary Ideas" (p. 107f.). But even here, for instance, the author is careful to avoid giving the impression that Courbet might have influenced the literary Realism of the 1850s or that there are distinct relations between the Impressionist style of Monet and certain aspects of literary Symbolism. Van Tieghem thus closes his eyes even to manifest historical data when they don't fit into his methodological straitjacket.

In Guyard, a further retrogression is noticeable, for in the chapter "Great European Currents: Ideas, Doctrines, Feelings" of his small manual, he refers only to "literary doctrines and ideas" (p. 97). The door leading to cultural history was thus nailed shut, and even the otherwise iconoclastic author of *Comparaison n'est pas raison* did not see fit to break it open. The position taken by Pichois and Rousseau, who devote four pages to this question, is therefore doubly welcome. In the relevant section of their book, the passage quoted above continues as follows:

Common sense confines itself to vague assertions: while the arts address themselves to man in general, literature, in spite of translations, [appeals] to limited groups; the former [speak] to the senses, whereas the latter [speaks] to the mind. Between these extremes, explaining a book or a literary school through their artistic context, embodying iconography and musical illustrations into literary history, studying the birth and growth of art criticism, comparing poetry with music or the theater with

architecture, shedding light on correspondences and affinities—
all these are precise and useful investigations. (P/R, p. 133)

Before turning to the situation in Germany, we ought to
cast a glance across the border at Holland, where in the
past few years several comparatists have taken positions
relevant to the present topic. A comparative outlook which
encompasses nonliterary phenomena is rejected by Cornelis de Deugd in these clear and sober terms: "Comparative Literature aims at literary study without regard to
boundaries; but what may be crossed are the boundaries
of the different nations that have produced literature, *not
the boundaries of literature itself.*"[11] Jan Brandt Corstius,
on the other hand, is more conciliatory, for he deems a
knowledge of the *ambiance* of literary works necessary for
their understanding in a cultural-historical context, but
does so without expressly condoning or advocating the
systematic study of this class of relationships.[12]

In the Netherlands, it is H. P. H. Teesing who most enthusiastically supports the *wechselseitige Erhellung*. He
does so programmatically in an essay intended as a rejoinder to the eleventh chapter of the *Theory of Literature.*[13]
In contrast to de Deugd and Brandt Corstius, Teesing does
not speak as a "professional" comparatist, however, but
rather in his capacity as Director of the Utrecht Institute
for Literary Theory. Therefore he has even less need to
mince matters. I will shortly refer to his interesting argument.

In Germany, it was Max Koch, who in his introduction
to the first volume of his *Zeitschrift für vergleichende Litteraturgeschichte*, published in 1887, defended the study of
the influence of art on literature on the following grounds:

To stress the connections between political and literary history
more than is usually done will be one of the chief tasks of this
journal, as will also be the demonstration of the interrelatedness
of literature and the plastic arts, philosophy, etc., which is
incumbent upon comparative literary history. Only recently, the
seventh volume of the *Goethe-Jahrbuch*, containing [Karl]

Dehio's identification of Early Italian Renaissance paintings as a
source for *Faust*, has offered an example of how fruitfully art
history and literary history can reinforce each other. (p. 11)

The teaming up of literary and art history (for evident
historical reasons, music history never joined the fray) has
always been popular in German academic circles. One
could set up a fullblown family tree in which the role of
the forefathers would fall to Lessing and Johann Jakob
Winckelmann. For our century, Jost Hermand has recently
offered a scholarly history of the systematic study of this
kind of interrelationship.[14]

Koch's call was subsequently heeded by the philologists
among the students of Heinrich Wöfflin. In 1915 Wölfflin
had published his *Kunstgeschichtliche Grundbegriffe*, a
book in which stylistic features of Renaissance and Baroque art are identified and then tested with the help of
selected illustrations. Oskar Walzel used this model when,
shortly afterwards, he sought to demonstrate that Shakespeare was not a Renaissance dramatist but a Baroque playwright.[15] Thus, the first, decisive step had been taken; and
as early as 1917, addressing the Berlin Kant Society, Walzel
systematically expounded the *Wechselseitige Erhellung der
Künste*.[16] As he states in a brief postscript to the printed
version of his lecture, he wavered for some time as regards
the title of his paper. Karl Woermann had suggested the
superscription "Comparative Aesthetics of the Visual and
Verbal Arts"; but Walzel decided on "Mutual Illumination
of the Arts," since the most adequate formulation he envisaged ("In the study of the artistic form of works belonging to one art, is it advisable to take into account those
pervasive typical features which have emerged from the
study of the traits characteristic of another art?") seemed
to him much too cumbersome.

In the twenties and thirties, Fritz Strich, Karl Vossler,
and Kurt Wais respectively followed in Walzel's footsteps
and ultimately gathered a following even outside of Germany, especially in the Anglo-Saxon countries. And in

1930, Fritz Medicus sketched a methodological outline—
as part of Ermatinger's handbook *Philosophie der Literaturwissenschaft*—of the problems involved in the "comparative history of the arts."[17]

One of the most prominent and fervent disciples of
Walzel in our time is the American scholar Wylie Sypher,
whose study *Four Stages of Renaissance Style* stays chronologically close to Wölfflin. His extensive survey *Rococo
to Cubism in Art and Literature* (intended as a sequel) by
contrast freely indulges in, often farfetched, analogies.[18]
(Mario Praz' recent book *Mnemosyne: The Parallel between Literature and the Arts* suffers from the same weak-
nesses.) For instance, Sypher links stylistically Pope's
mock-heroic epic *The Rape of the Lock* and Watteau's
paintings: "The rococo artist, like Pope, finds himself in an
interregnum between baroque and the oncoming romantic
pantheism. Nonetheless, Pope's verse, like Lepautre's architecture and Watteau's painting, belongs to a distinguishable style" (p. 34).

Vossler's essay, dating from 1935,[19] and the studies published by Wais in 1936 and 1937[20] temporarily exhausted
the drive launched by Walzel in the context of German
literary scholarship gauged to *Geistesgeschichte*. The subject lay dormant during the war and during the immediate postwar years. Even today, German comparatists do
not seem to make a concerted effort to improve this lamentable state of affairs. The journal *Arcadia*, for instance,
publishes very few relevant contributions in this area. It
would be a shame, however, if in the long run the Germans were to forego participation in cultivating a field in
which they have so successfully labored in the past.

Turning to the systematic portion of my survey of the
problems connected with the comparative study of literature and its sister arts, I take up Calvin S. Brown's previously cited definition, according to which even cases involving only one national culture are to be considered
meat for the comparatist. According to this view—which
the authors of the *Bibliography of Comparative Literature*

seem to share—books such as Helmut Hatzfeld's *Literature Through Art: A New Approach to French Literature* and Jean Hagstrum's *The Sister Arts: The Tradition of Literary Pictorialism and English Poetry from Dryden to Gray* would be squarely placed within our field.[21] Beginning with Volume 10 (1961), the editors of the *Yearbook of Comparative and General Literature* took exception to this view; for, in the annual bibliographical supplements to Baldensperger/Friederich, they list only studies of interrelationships in which linguistic boundaries are crossed. Thus, they record entries on the subject of "Rodin and Rilke" but not on the relationship between Debussy and Mallarmé.

As my initial definition has shown, in literature a subject is comparative only if it concerns two national literatures or works written in two different languages. Here language is the *tertium comparationis*. When, however, we use linguistic or national boundaries as criteria in the study of the interrelation between the arts, we are exercising our prerogative without accounting for the qualitative differences which prevail between the various media (words, sounds, colors) and techniques. To strike a compromise would be methodologically suspect in my opinion. Either one takes the view that Beethoven's contacts with literature and Hofmannsthal's with music are appropriate subjects for the comparatist, or one altogether cedes to musicology the task of describing and analyzing a composer's and a librettist's struggle with the subject of the opera jointly produced by them. In rare cases, the literary critic/historian may concurrently be a musicologist. But such cases are rare—and even rarer are those where joint efforts result in the total comprehension of a masterpiece straddling two different arts. The claim that Mozart's relations to German literature are the concern of bona fide Germanists but that his links with Italian letters lie within the province of Comparative Literature is patently absurd.

Once we have drawn this fundamental but necessary distinction, we are free to turn our attention to more specific problems. The first, decisive step on the path toward a clarification of the relation between aesthetics on the one hand and literary scholarship on the other demands the exclusion of the problems designated by Walzel and Wais as "comparative aesthetics" (*vergleichende Ästhetik*), that is, those questions which pertain to the common structural bases of the arts, namely, to such matters as the delimitation of space- and time-arts, surface- and depth-arts. Theodor Meyer Greene more than adequately covered this subject in his compendium *The Arts and the Art of Criticism*, and Thomas Munro authored a pragmatic companion piece entitled *The Arts and Their Interrelationships*.[22] There is little doubt that this approach can be applied to Comparative Literature, but it will always involve a potentially dangerous consideration of mere analogies. Thus Lessing's *Laokoön* offers, besides the comparison between the Roman sculpture by that name and the corresponding passage from the first book of the *Aeneid*, references to Homer, Shakespeare, and Ariosto; and Joseph Frank's essay "Spatial Form in Modern Literature," which is intended as a sequel to Lessing's treatise, freely uses examples from English, American, and French literature in describing and defining certain structural properties.[23]

The utmost care must also be exercised in the application to literature of Wölfflin's paired terms "statics" and "dynamics," "open" and "closed" form, and "unity" and "multiplicity." This is equally true of terms like "rhythm," "harmony," and "perspective," as Walzel has shown, using "rhythm" as his object of demonstration. Stated succinctly: in music and literature, "rhythm" refers to actual movement; but in the plastic arts, it is the eye of the observer which moves, while the objects under surveillance are fixed in space.

In the historical and critical study of interrelationships, one does well to proceed pragmatically, by initially focusing on *rapports de fait*. As a model for the historical delineation of a form of expression common to two different arts, Wolfgang Kayser's monograph *The Grotesque in Art and Literature* remains valid despite its gaps.[24] In presenting his case, Kayser studiously avoids giving the impression that the parallelism of art and literature rests on constants reducible to abstract concepts. In other words, he proceeds historically rather than dogmatically.

As an ambivalent example of parallelism bolstered by abstraction one could mention Hocke's study *Die Welt als Labyrinth: Manier und Manie in der europäischen Kunst*,[25] which, whatever its flaws, is a mine of valuable information. Hocke tries to follow the suggestion, made by Curtius, that, at least in literary history, the designation Baroque should be replaced by Mannerism. Curtius, that is to say, wanted "to empty [the term Mannerism] of all art-historical content and to broaden its meaning in such a way that it constitutes the common denominator for all literary trends opposed to Classicism."[26] Hocke lists six Mannerist periods of European cultural history: Alexandrian, Roman (the "silver Latinity"), an early and a late medieval, Mannerism proper [1520–1650!], Romanticism, and the current age which, according to him, stretches from 1880 to 1950 (p. 10f.). By positing a common denominator for Surrealism and the bizarreries of the Baroque, Hocke grossly violates the spirit of historicity demanding a chronological segmentation.

If one wishes to show how the arts mutually benefit and illuminate each other within a given segment of time, one does well, in principle, to study them in relation to the period or movement in which they partake. It would seem to be obvious that, in doing so, one can and must consider the artistic intentions as voiced in theoretical manifestoes. The purism displayed in this regard by the authors of the *Theory of Literature* is disconcerting to say the least, for, using Neoclassicism as an example, they maintain:

But "classicism" in music must mean something very different from its use in literature for the simple reason that no real classical music (with the exception of a few fragments) was

known and could thus shape the evolution of music as literature
was actually shaped by the precepts and practice of antiquity.
Likewise painting, before the excavation of the frescoes in
Pompeii and Herculaneum, can scarcely be described as
influenced by classical painting in spite of the frequent reference
to classical theories and Greek painters like Apelles and some
remote pictorial traditions which must have descended from
antiquity through the Middle Ages. (W/W, p. 127f.)

Teesing refutes this theory by pointing out that "Gluck
and other composers as well as the Classicist painters abstracted the structural principles of their art from literature, sculpture and architecture, thereby showing that the
organizing principle can be transplanted from one art to
another" (YCGL, 12 [1963], p. 33). That the theory and
practice characteristic of one art can be successfully transplanted to another, especially in the case of tightly knit
artistic movements, is evidenced by Surrealism, for example.

Whatever his theoretical position, the literary historian
in actual practice has no choice but to take art history and
musicology into account, because so much is to be learned
from them, particularly in stylistic matters. As we have
seen in Chapter Five, numerous literary period terms (Baroque, Rococo, Biedermeier) are after all derived from the
other arts, and presuppose for their full comprehension a
certain familiarity with extra-literary phenomena. Where
the visual arts are in the forefront of cultural developments, they must for better or worse take their place in any
literary-historical survey; whereas, when the reverse is true
—as in the case of Symbolism or Surrealism—such broad-
ening is desirable if the techniques originally borrowed
from literature have been modified and channeled back
into it.

The illusion of the purity of the arts, which neoclassical
and classicist art theory from Horace to Lessing seeks to
uphold, can be meaningfully posited only for certain periods; for it is dialectically opposed to the Baroque-Roman-
tic-Surrealistic conception (Curtius' "Mannerism"), which

regards the fusion of the arts as a step toward a higher synthesis. Literary scholarship will have to deal with these mixed forms in which the arts have entered into some kind of symbiosis. The most important conglomerates implicating literature are the opera (including the operetta, the "musical," and the *Singspiel*), the oratorio, the cantata, and the film—perhaps even the ballet; and among the smaller forms we have the *Lied*, the emblem, the picture story (à la Wilhelm Busch), and the American cartoon.[27] In the history of drama, opera plays an important role, and that not only on account of the libretto, which forms its literary backbone. Greek tragedy, for example, constituted a total work of art (*Gesamtkunstwerk*), in which music was not simply an ornamental flourish but decisively influenced word choice and word placement in strophic repetition.[28] The Baroque revival of classical drama was, rightly, though mistakenly from a historical and scholarly point of view, "staged" in the spirit of ancient music. But even after the generic split between opera and drama, music was never totally banished from the legitimate stage. Even apart from the so-called incidental music (Grieg's contribution to Ibsen's *Peer Gynt* and Bizet's music for Daudet's *L'Arlesienne*, to name two of the best-known examples), it remained an organic component in many Shakespearean plays, such as *Twelfth Night* and *The Tempest*. And it was hardly accidental that Stanislavsky "orchestrated" *Othello*, for music functions as a mood builder in many dramas (Chekhov's *Cherry Orchard*, among others).[29] Let it also be noted, in passing, that Goethe conceived the second part of the Helena act in *Faust II* in operatic terms, and that Schiller considered his verse play *Die Braut von Messina* as an attempt at revitalizing tragedy by way of opera.

It is hardly a secret that throughout history operatic texts have been from time to time regarded as literature and staged as plays, and that by no means only in neoclassical periods. Metastasio's authorial ambitions and Gluck's expressly literary treatment of his librettos come to mind. And only recently, Hofmannsthal's *Rosenkavalier* was experimentally performed in Vienna. A definitive history of the libretto, which would be, in part, a literary history, could serve to clarify such matters.[30] Conversely, the dramaturgy of alienation (*Verfremdung*), evolved by Brecht in his notes to the play *Die Dreigroschenoper* and to the opera *Mahagonny*, found its purest and least adulterated expression in a musico-literary context.

For the literary scholar concerned with artistic interpenetration, the phenomenon of the double talent (*Doppelbegabung*), whose existence is regarded by Wais as constituting proof of the original unity of the arts (*Symbiose der Künste*, p. 14f.), will also be of considerable interest; for, in cases of an artistic union achieved within a single person, the question arises as to how the various arts are linked when they are practiced alternately, or concurrently, by one individual.[31] What ties exist, for instance, between the sculptor and the poet in Michelangelo? How plastic are Ernst Barlach's dramas, how musical certain of E. T. A. Hoffmann's novellas, and how pictorial or "graphic" is Kubin's novel *Die andere Seite*?

In evaluating and judging this rare phenomenon, Wais and the authors of the *Theory of Literature* have conflicting views. For while Wellek and Warren discern obvious qualitative differences in the pictorial and poetic efforts of Blake, Thackeray, and Rossetti—which they take to be proof that the means of expression as well as the underlying traditions obstruct the mutual enrichment of the arts[32]—Wais considers it "indisputable that Blake's watercolors, for all their dependence on Fuseli's school, obey a similar, nay the same, stylistic law as his dreamlike poetry" (p. 29) and goes on to maintain that Thackeray's drawings "with their sanctimoniously correct and vulgar lines," express what is also branded by his writing: "the mask of pious innocuousness donned by predatory hypocrites." A poet's critical discussion of an art which he himself does not practice may also be considered as an activity similar to *Doppelbegabung*, insofar as it bridges several artistic realms: we might cite, as examples, the *salons* of

Diderot, Baudelaire, and Zola, as well as the music criticism of E. T. A. Hoffmann and Shaw.

Like the mixed forms mentioned above, the many transitional genres which link literature with music or the plastic arts offer a challenge to the scholar interested in the mutual illumination of the arts. As an acoustic phenomenon, verbal expression naturally points in the direction of music; and as the vehicle of images and symbols it waxes pictorial. These innate tendencies of language are sometimes willfully exaggerated and played off against the meaning. In lyric poetry, with its patently onomatopoeic overtones, the sense of hearing comes even more fully into play. Whenever this aspect of the spoken language is stressed at the expense of the other elements, paraliterary products such as Detlev von Liliencron's poem "Die Musik kommt" or Verlaine's "Art Poétique" (in which the programmatic lines "De la musique avant toute chose" and "Tout le reste est littérature" constitute an epistemological frame of reference) may result. In the Symbolist art of a Baudelaire, Mallarmé or Valéry, on the other hand, sense seeks to re-enter by way of an admittedly subjectivized symbolism. Even more radical than the poetic Impressionists or Symbolists are the Expressionist and Dadaist makers of sound-poems, a Rudolf Blümner or Hans (Jean) Arp, whose syllabically or rhythmically ordered sound sequences ("Ango Laina" and "Elefantenkarawane") pass themselves off as either pure expression or pure nonsense —which, superficially, turn out to be much the same thing. These poems do not really exist on paper but come to life only in actual recitation.

In the study of structural parallels between literature and music, the greatest care must always be taken. Where poems are consciously modelled on musical forms, good intention on the part of the poet must naturally be assumed. This applies, as Calvin S. Brown has persuasively argued, in the case of Thomas de Quincey's "Dream-Fugue," but also in that of Paul Celan's moving "Todes-Fuge." The more extended and complex the works under scrutiny, the more difficult is the comparison. The many disparate interpretations of Eliot's "Four Quartets" are cogent proof of this contention. Sometimes a search for parallels is unproductive even though the poet himself condones or provokes it. Concerning *Der Steppenwolf*, for instance, Hermann Hesse said that it was "structured as tightly and securely as a sonata around the intermezzo of the tract." On this remark, as on a cornerstone, Theodore Ziolkowski builds his interpretation of the novel as a prose sonata.[33] Similarly, even when a novel—such as Heinrich Mann's *Die kleine Stadt*—bears overtly melodramatic traits, some of its personages being singers involved in an operatic production, the mutual illumination of the arts can easily lead to their confusion.

Especially in lyric poetry, there is no dearth of borderline cases spanning literature and the plastic arts. Basically, it makes no difference whether such "thing poems" (*Dinggedichte*) linguistically reproduce real or imaginary pictures or sculptures. Keats' "Ode to a Grecian Urn" thus merits the same attention as Rilke's "Griechischer Torso Apolls" or Gottfried Benn's "Karyatide." The fact that description is not identical with imitation is clearly spelled out by Wellek and Warren, who remind us that "the term *sculpturesque* applied to poetry, even to that of Landor or Gautier or Hérédia, is merely a vague metaphor, meaning that poetry conveys an impression somehow similar to the effects of Greek sculpture" (W/W, p. 125). In the case of Gautier and Hérédia, one is, of course, dealing with so-called Parnassians, whose goal it was to create finely chiselled, hard and jewel-like poetry. The poetics of Imagism is particularly enlightening, insofar as these poets were concerned with reproducing the exact moment in which a visual impression is translated into its verbal equivalent. Their métier was "the casting of images upon the visual imagination," whereby they hoped to succeed in blurring the outlines of poetry and the plastic arts.[34] Pound's haiku-like poem "In a Station of the Metro" is a lyric manifesto of this movement:

> The apparition of these faces in the crowd;
> Petals on a wet, black bough.

The so-called "pattern poem," too is a curiously hybrid phenomenon. Its tradition is older than is usually thought and goes back beyond the age of the Metaphysicals—whom Dylan Thomas successfully imitated—to the Middle Ages, and even to Antiquity. Among its more recent practitioners, Guillaume Apollinaire, above all, has made use of this pseudoemblematic art, whose humorous possibilities Morgenstern exploited in his nonpoem "Fisches Nachtgesang." Now in the ascendant, "concrete poetry"—indebted to Dadaistic practices and modelled, in part, on Expressionist typography—also may be said to fall under this general heading.

A chapter on the literary imitation of the conventional or experimental techniques employed in the plastic arts might also include the study of works like Katherine Mansfield's story "Her First Ball," where pictorial Impressionism is so well transposed that thoughts and feelings pass before our mind's eye as if in the flow of life itself. A similar task, but within a larger framework, was tackled by Virginia Woolf in *To the Lighthouse*, one of whose principal characters is the painter Lily Briscoe, whose goal it is to secure, through complete fidelity in the reproduction of her impressions, some permanence for the landscapes used as models. Seen from the viewpoint of art history, the goal which she achieves at the end of the novel might be called "Cézanne's conquest of Impressionism."

Without in the least intending to exhaust the topic, I would like in closing to touch upon two other subjects for the study of which the comparatist who reaches beyond literature might qualify. To be sure, the first phenomenon I have in mind does not readily lend itself to scholarly observation—I mean artistic inspiration, which has come to our attention in Chapter Two, where the discussion focused on melodic-rhythmic incitation. Equally profitable would be an investigation of literary "influences" on music. Here I think not only of tone-poems like Hector Berlioz' "Harold in Italy" (which may be termed a musical paraphrase) but also of the last movement of Beethoven's String Quartet in F, op. 135, whose major theme evolved from the question "Muss es sein?" and the answer "Es muss sein."[35] (Beethoven's musical ideas often evolved from a verbal core.) This is the exact reverse of the situation which Valéry describes in his account of the genesis of his "Cimetière Marin."

The second class of phenomena constitutes a rough parallel to the situation described in Dyserinck's essay on *image* and *mirage* studies. We remember that Dyserinck expressed the view that such studies are truly literary (and therefore congenial to comparatists) when the national myths and legends are expressly dealt with in the works to be scrutinized. If one were to apply this yardstick to the study of the mutual illumination of the arts, one would fasten on novels or dramas, as well as epic or lyric poems, which are thematically concerned with questions of art and artistry, such as E. T. A. Hoffmann's *Kreisleriana*, Emile Zola's *L'Oeuvre*, Romain Rolland's *Jean Christophe*, Thomas Mann's *Doktor Faustus*, and Max Frisch's *Stiller*. The literary use of musical leitmotifs—such as the return of a theme from Vinteuil's violin sonata in Proust's *A la Recherche du temps perdu*—also falls into this category.

Appendix One
✍ History

Within the limited framework of this survey, the earliest stages, or the *prehistory*, of Comparative Literature as a discipline cannot be considered at sufficient length. By *prehistory* I mean primarily that early stage of the development which saw the publication of critical essays in which parallels between individual writers and works were noted but no factual links or verifiable influences were systematically established.

1. *France*

Within the Romance-language world, such an approach is found as early as Dante, who, in the ninth chapter of his treatise *De vulgari eloquentia,* contrasts Old French literature (the *langue d'oc*) with its Provençal equivalent (the *langue d'oïl*). In Germany, this prehistorical phase stretches from Johann Elias Schlegel's *Vergleichung Shakespeares und Andreas Gryphs* (1742) and Lessing's *Hamburgische Dramaturgie* (1769) to A. W. Schlegel's comparison, in French, of the *Phaedras* of Euripides and Racine (1807). In France, the comparative method grew out of the age-old tension between conservatives and progressives and the resulting dialectic of imitation and originality. The controversy opened with the eighth chapter of Joachim du Bellay's *Défense et illustration de la langue française* (1549) and was more or less vociferously continued in Corneille's *Discours sur les trois unités* (1660) and the famous quarrel between the Ancients and the Moderns (1687–1716). In the theater, the resistance to foreign (espe-

cially Italian) influences was particularly strong during
the War of the Bouffons (1751–1754) and the quarrel between the Gluckists and the Piccinnists (1770–1774). Foreign models were more favorably judged in Voltaire's *Lettres philosophiques* (1734), Diderot's "Euloge de Richardson" (1761; a comparison with Racine), and Stendhal's
essay *Racine et Shakespeare* (1822).

The prehistory of Comparative Literature enters its second phase with the gradual emergence of the concept of
world literature and of the—biologically and sociologically
slanted—view accepting the artistic products of different
countries, ages, and regions as being equally meaningful.
Already Boileau's opponents in the *Querelle*, especially
Saint-Evremond, had insisted "that the ideal of beauty is
not constant throughout the ages and common to all countries, but must necessarily vary according to place and
time."[1] The same conception, historically tinged and
linked with the notion of progression (but not "progress"),
is found in Herder's *Briefwechsel über Ossian und die
Lieder alter Völker*:

> Woe betide the philosopher reflecting on people and customs
> who takes his native scene to be the only one and who always
> mistakes the earliest efforts for the worst. As all scenes belong to
> the whole of a continuous drama, a new and remarkable aspect
> of humanity is revealed in each.[2]

In Herder's case, we cannot yet speak of a focus on genuine interrelationships and their critical analysis; we can
do so, however, in the case of Madame de Staël's palimp-
sest of Comparative Literature, her famous book *De
l'Allemagne* (1810), where we read—seventeen years before Goethe's remarks on the subject of *Weltliteratur*: "The
nations must serve each other as guides. . . . Every country
would do well, then, to welcome foreign thoughts; for, in
such matters, hospitality makes the fortune of the host."[3]
However, Madame de Staël did not draw scholarly conclusions from this insight: "She scarcely studied the bonds
which unite the two literatures [German and French] and

the influences which they exercised upon each other"
(Van Tieghem, p. 25). As is shown by the foreword to her
study *De la Littérature considéré dans ses rapports avec
les institutions sociales*, her interest was, indeed, of a more
sociological cast:

I have set out to examine the influences of religion, customs, and
laws on literature and the reciprocal influence of literature on
religion, customs, and laws. In French there are certain treatises
on the art of writing and the principles of taste which leave
nothing to be desired; but it seems to me that one has not yet
considered how the human faculties have gradually developed by
means of the famous works which have been composed, in every
genre, from Homer to the present day.[4]

For many decades to come, this sociological interest,
fanned by Saint-Simon, was to overshadow French Comparative Literature in its initial stages. The man chiefly responsible for this development was Hippolyte Taine,
whose dogmatic insistence on the significance of *race*,
milieu, and *moment* did not lose its magic until the end
of the nineteenth century. Van Tieghem shrewdly realized that Taine's conception violates the spirit of French
comparatism, which was consolidating itself after World
War I, when he noted that the concept of literary influence cannot be fitted into these three coordinates:

[Taine] showed that every work of art is the product of race, of a
milieu which modifies the race, and of a moment which causes
the expression of certain attitudes to dominate at a given time.
The notion of influence was absent from this imposing structure
—unless one subsumes it under the more general concept of
moment—an interpretation which is sometimes, but not always,
legitimate, but was never, it seems, even implicitly suggested by
Taine ... [who] seems to have been convinced that literature,
like painting, is the necessary expression of the ideal and the
temperament of a given race under specific temporal and local
circumstances, and that the more significant and perfect the
works of art are, the better they reveal that ideal and that
temperament without the admixture of foreign elements. But
how could the eloquent logician have been able to see in the

most justly admired masterpieces the result of a perpetual
collaboration between an author's genius and diverse literary
influences? (p. 29)

Whereas, for all the shortcomings of her method,
Madame de Staël knew how to separate the aesthetic
moment from the nonaesthetic, a number of French
scholars who may be regarded as the actual forerunners
of Comparative Literature freely mixed artistic with philosophical and sociological factors. This was the case with
Philarète Chasles, who summarized the content of his
1835 lecture on "foreign literature compared" (littérature
étrangère comparée) as follows: "the study of the remote
influence of mind on minds; the magnetic effect of
thought on thought; the fertility of thought which, at the
heart of an often obscure life, bursts forth to conquer distant peoples or future ages." Chasles, in other words, was
more concerned with intellectual than with literary history.[5]

As a scholarly discipline, littérature comparée matured
in France only in the third and fourth decades of the nineteenth century.[6] It was preceded by the publication of
comparative studies in physiology (Cuvier's Anatomie
comparée, Blainville's Physiologie comparée, and Coste's
Embryogénie comparée), mythology (the Abbé Tressan's
Mythologie comparée à l'histoire), philosophy (Degeran-
do's Histoire comparée des systèmes de philosophie), eroti-
cism (de Villers' Erotique comparée), and aesthetics (Sobry's
Cours de peinture et de littérature comparée), and especially in Indo-Germanic philology.[7] The first volume of
Jean-Jacques Ampère's Histoire de la littérature française
au moyen âge comparée aux littératures étrangères (1841),
for example, is devoted to the development of the French
language, as is also the case with the second edition of
Ampère's Cours de littérature française (1846), the first
volume of which offers a "tableau of Medieval literature
in France, Italy, Spain, and England." Comparative literary
studies thus struggled long and hard on their way to becoming Comparative Literature in the current sense.

Reference should also be made to Sismonde de Sismondi's book *La Littérature du midi de l'Europe* (1813), whose author "wanted to show, primarily, the reciprocal influence of a people's political and religious history on their literature, and of their literature on their character; to clarify the relation between the laws of justice and honesty and those of beauty; and, lastly, the link between virtue and morality on the one hand, and sensibility and imagination on the other."[8] The honor of being the first scholars to use the term *littérature comparée* falls to Messrs. Noël and Laplace, who, as Wellek informs us, published in 1816 "a series of anthologies from French, classical and English literature with the otherwise unused and unexplained title: *Cours de littérature comparée*."[9] Needless to say, their action had no immediate or long-range consequences.

Thus either Ampère or Abel François Villemain must be regarded as the true father of a systematically conceived Comparative Literature in France—or anywhere, for that matter. In 1829, Villemain delivered a lecture at the Sorbonne entitled "Examination of the influence exerted by French eighteenth-century writers on foreign literatures and on the European mind." In the foreword to his *Cours de littérature française*, we find the characteristic sentence: "For the first time at a French university a comparative analysis of several modern literatures which, deriving from the same source, have not ceased to communicate with each other and have been commingled at various epochs, is being undertaken."[10] In one of his *Nouveaux Lundis* (1865), Sainte-Beuve hailed Ampère as the true Columbus of Comparative Literature, especially on the basis of his intimate knowledge of several foreign languages in his extensive travels which had permitted him to gather firsthand information.[11] At the age of nineteen, the budding scholar had visited Goethe in Weimar (1819) and had returned to France deeply impressed; and in 1832, substituting for Villemain, he had given his widely acclaimed lecture on the "comparative history of literatures."

However great the progress made by French comparatism in the second quarter of the nineteenth century, Comparative Literature did not become an academic discipline until after 1890, when the Realist-Naturalist period in art and literature had come to an end. As we shall see, this is somewhat paradoxical. In 1880, following the example of Claude Bernard's *Introduction à la médecine expérimentale* (1865), Emile Zola had published his manifesto *Le Roman experimental*, which he supplemented by several programmatic essays on the Naturalist theater. But in 1884 the Impressionists were already holding their first exhibition; two years later, Jean Moréas wrote his Symbolist manifesto for *Le Figaro*; and in 1887 five of Zola's literary disciples broke with their master in a public protest over moral and aesthetic issues. Around 1890, the effect of literary Naturalism had dissipated in the other European countries as well, and Hermann Bahr loudly proclaimed the imminent death of this international movement. Neo-Romanticism, as well as literary Impressionism and Symbolism, quickly supplanted the shortlived scientific *verismo*.

In view of these facts, it seems rather anachronistic that a positivistically and sociologically oriented school of Comparative Literature should have been founded in the 1890s with Joseph Texte's monograph *Jean Jacques Rousseau et les origines du cosmopolitisme littéraire*. The actual birthday of our discipline as an academic subject occurred in 1897, when a chair of Comparative Literature was established in Lyon; not until 1910 was it followed by a second chair (at the Sorbonne). Texte, the first incumbent at Lyon, initially lectured on the influence of the Germanic literatures on French letters since the Renaissance. In 1893 he offered some theoretical comments on the new specialty,[12] and five years later he published a methodologically important definitional essay. We shall not scrutinize Texte's opinions, since they more or less closely resemble Van Tieghem's views, which were treated in Chapter One. Let it only be said that Texte, for all his scientific precision, did not wish to see Comparative Literature regarded as a discipline comparable to the natural sciences:

I do in no way intend to attach literary history to the
experimental sciences: like all the other kinds of history, the
history of literatures is no *science* in the proper sense of the word.
But, like every other kind of history, it can legitimately be called
scientific once it has met two conditions: 1) that of aspiring to an
end higher than being the simple pastime of the historian or his
audience; and 2) that of exhausting *all* the means for obtaining
knowledge of the kind of truth which constitutes its proper goal.[13]

This feeble compromise with science is based on Texte's
doubtful assumption that it is the proper task of Comparative Literature to lay the foundations for a "psychology of
races and men." Thus, we already find ourselves in the
midst of the controversy over the views of Carré and
Guyard which was to surface fifty years later.

Like certain of his successors, Texte (crowning his exposition, and misinterpreting Goethe's notion of *Weltliteratur*) voiced the hope that national literatures might,
in the not too distant future, relinquish their individual
characteristics and merge into one truly European literature. Comparative Literature was to serve as catalyst in this
process:

Finally, because it was in the logic of things that, after having
sufficiently compared, approached, and, shall we say, scrambled
works of varying [national] origins, the European [reading]
public, constantly increasing, will formulate a kind of common
ideal, namely that of a literature whose advent we can hope for
—or fear—and which will no longer be specifically English,
German, French, or Italian, but simply European.[14]

With one laughing and one weeping eye, Frédéric Loliée
offered the same prognosis in the final chapter of his *Histoire des littératures comparées des origines au XXᵉ siècle*
(1903), which is otherwise irrelevant to our survey since
its perspective was obsolete even at the time:

Intellectual cosmopolitanism will spread, in order to level them,
over the national differences. Civilization pursues its path,
inexorably destructive of local variants. Types are disappearing,
idiosyncrasies are fading, and everywhere each man is beginning
to resemble his fellow; travelers now touring the world are

finding fewer contrasts and piquant details in social customs than
do the scholars exploring past ages.[15]

When, in 1900, Louis-Paul Betz published the first version of his *Bibliographie de littérature comparée* in book
form, it was Texte he asked to write the preface. In the
second section of this introduction, the latter interestingly
enough subdivided the province of Comparative Literature into the following areas: 1) theoretical questions and
general problems; 2) comparative folklore; 3) the comparative study of modern literatures; and 4) universal literary
history (corresponding to Van Tieghem's *littérature générale*). Texte was, thus, far indeed from developing a systematic approach along the lines followed by his twentieth-century successors.

This is also true of Betz, who, born in the United States
in 1861, the son of an Alsatian emigrant, grew up in Switzerland, studied law at Strasbourg and Jena, worked in his
uncle's business in New York for seven years, returned to
Zurich around 1890, became a student of modern literature, and was accorded the *venia legendi* in 1896.[16] Betz
made outstanding contributions to Comparative Literature in his bibliography (the basis for Baldensperger-Fried-
erich's *Bibliography of Comparative Literature*), as well as
in a significant methodological essay we shall discuss in
the section devoted to the history of Comparative Literature in Germany. Although his publications were bilingual,
he was actually conversant with three languages.[17]

Before turning to the godfather of Comparative Literature in France, Fernand Baldensperger, who was Texte's
successor in Lyon and edited an expanded version of
Betz's bibliography, it would be well to consider an event
that took place in 1900 and acquired some significance
for the history of our discipline. During the hot summer
days of that year, historians from all over the world convened in Paris. The sixth section of their international
congress concerned itself with the "comparative history of
literatures," and its participants, from both France and

abroad, called (as it turned out, for the time being, in vain) for the founding of an "International Society of Comparative Literary History."[18] This dream was not to come true until nearly half a century later.

The official hosts for this particular conference, which was attended by guests from Italy, Sweden, Holland, England, Luxemburg, Switzerland, Greece, and the United States, were two famous scholars, Gaston Paris and Ferdinand Brunetière. In his opening address, Paris assigned to Comparative Literature the dual task of studying both literary and folkloristic parallels. For him, Comparative Literature was "a new science which touches on folklore, mythography, and comparative mythology, and is strongly interested in the history of the human mind. It transcends the realm of literature proper."[19]

Brunetière, the other main speaker, lectured on "European Literature." His ideas strongly impressed the audience and, after their publication, the educated public in France and the rest of Europe. Seen from today's vantage point, Brunetière's conception is far more modern than that of his illustrious colleague, and was later shared by Baldensperger in many essential points. Thus Brunetière states: "What has come to be called *literary*, is it not uniquely that which has been intended as such, or, to state it more precisely, is it not something which has tended, on the part and in the mind of the author, whether he be unknown or famous, toward a conscious and willed realization of a certain idea of grace and beauty?"[20]

For Brunetière, then, conscious artistic intention was the yardstick by which literature was to be measured. At the same time, he declared European literature to be a province of world literature (which for him, however, was identical with *littérature comparée*), and a small and rather insignificant one at that.[21] For practical reasons, this restriction of the definition to one geographical segment of literature was necessary, he felt, because true influences and reciprocal effects are possible only within a single culture. If one transgresses these limits, he argued,

one begins to deal with casual encounters and coinci-
dences the study of which is scientifically unproductive.

As has been shown in Chapter Five, the value of Brunetière's contribution to the development and consolidation of Comparative Literature in France is considerably
diminished by virtue of the fact that, as a follower of
Taine, he unwaveringly adhered to the belief in the principle of evolution as applied to art and literature. In this
vein, but with a curious idiosyncratic twist, he concluded
his essay "European Literature" with an outline of European letters since the Renaissance, viewed as a chronological succession of dominant national literatures: those
of Italy, Spain, France, England, and Germany, in that
order.

With the founding of three French chairs of Comparative Literature (Strasbourg having followed Lyon and Paris
in 1918), the first major phase of the history of our discipline in the country of its origin came to an end. Its stan-
dard-bearer in the second phase was Fernand Baldensperger, who was born in 1871 in Alsace, succeeded Texte at
Lyon in 1901, arranged and introduced the new, expanded
edition of Betz's bibliography in 1902, and taught at the
Sorbonne from 1910 onward. Working alone at first, and
subsequently with Hazard and Van Tieghem, he established at the Sorbonne the Institute of Modern and Comparative Literatures, which, for a quarter of a century or
so, was the Mecca of comparatists.[22] The pre-eminence of
its tenets and methods was practically undisputed in the
Balkan countries as well as in the Near and Far East; and
only in the last two decades have the efforts of the "American" school begun to pave the way for a loosening up of
orthodox rigidity in the pedagogy of our field.

In 1925, by the way, a place for Comparative Literature
studies was created at the Collège de France, where the
chair of Latin philology was transformed into one entitled
"History of Mediterranean and Latin American Literatures." Its holder, until his recent retirement, was the
Hispanist Marcel Bataillon, who also serves as Director

of the *Revue de littérature comparée*, founded in 1921 and edited, after Basil Munteano's resignation, by a committee of nine specialists. In 1935, Baldensperger accepted an invitation to America and was replaced by Jean-Marie Carré.[23] For several years he taught at Harvard University, but subsequently moved to the University of California at Los Angeles. During his stay in the United States, he gave Comparative Literature in this country both a personal and a professional incentive whose historical significance must not be underrated.

Baldensperger's creed—and the gospel of the Paris School until the appearance of Van Tieghem's handbook in 1931 —was stated in his programmatic introduction to the first issue of the *Revue de littérature comparée*, entitled "Comparative Literature: The Word and the Thing." Here, the French scholar disposes, point by point, of what he considers to be the outmoded perspectives of Texte, Paris, and Brunetière. In dealing with Brunetière's theory of evolution, he rejects the teleological point of view which presupposes a historical development that proceeds from cause to effect almost mechanically and leaves no room for creative spontaneity: "In assigning to literary *genres* a sort of *necessity*, in attributing to them an independent existence, this imperious mind created entities to which the past was subordinate in a manner so absolute that no reality could justify it" (*RLC*, I, 24).

Thematological studies were rejected by Baldensperger, because, for one thing, they are invariably fragmentary— that is, all the links in the chain of adaptations of a theme can hardly ever be identified: "The many broken contacts would leave incomplete the chain which is to be reconstituted, so that the thematological attempts at reconstruction, ignoring the oral and otherwise undetermined intermediaries would, all too frequently, leave the historical mind, i.e., the mind which is concerned with continuous series, dissatisfied" (ibid., p. 23).

Baldensperger also considered Taine's influence on Comparative Literature to be dangerous because the exclu-

sive stress on the milieu automatically leads to a denigra-
tion of nonenvironmental factors: "His favored principle
of convergences, of the concordance of forces and effects,
the work of art determined by a mixture which is a combination of the general state of mind and the manners
surrounding it, the 'internal structure' which he detects
both in a poem and in a race—all these growing demands
of his theories prevent a more fruitful application of comparative methods" (ibid., p. 16).

In ridding Comparative Literature of thematology, the
hunt and the craze for sources (the "small pleasure of
searching for sources, not in order to extrapolate originality, but in order to reduce initiative and denounce plagiarism" [ibid., p. 10f]), as well as of the sociological-evolu-
tionary method espoused by Taine and Brunetière,
Baldensperger made room for what he regarded as more
relevant approaches and methods within the budding discipline. His own preference was for what he called genetics
or artistic morphology (ibid., p. 6).

In the affirmative portion of his essay, the editor of the
Revue de littérature comparée underscores the significance of mobility in international cultural life: "Instead
of considering great reputations as stars whose rise and
orbit within a fixed heaven can be scanned, we should take
into account the mobility of the planes from which the
stars whose light will reach into the future have detached
themselves" (ibid., p. 26). In the comparatists' work yet to
be done, the stress was to be laid on the second-rate writers
and works including, one supposes, Trivialliteratur and
the details hitherto neglected—to be uncovered only
through extremely patient and painstaking labor:

It would be important to recapture the dynamism which
impelled not only the distinguished works which we have always
held in regard, but also the great mass of creations which
sustained them and which are now unknown. We must also
recapture the favorable or unfavorable opinion of the public, now
considered more or less trustworthy "witnesses," who received
them, and the social trends guided by similar attitudes. (ibid.,
p. 25)

It was in this "sociological" sense that Baldensperger probably wanted to have understood his journal's Cartesian motto—"The nature of things is more easily understood when one sees them grow, step by step, and when they are not viewed as being ready-made."[24]

As to the contents of the *Revue*, and the scholarly outlook which they reflect, an overall impression can be gained by a quick glance at the three book-length tables of contents now available. My synoptic view of the *Troisième Table de la 'Revue de littérature comparée' 1951–1960*[25] may serve in lieu of a detailed critique, which would exceed the limits imposed upon this survey. It also reflects a recent, but very modest, change in editorial outlook.

Tables of contents such as the one to be reviewed here are involuntary confessions which reveal to what extent the editors of a journal have fulfilled their self-assigned task. The fact that the *Revue de littérature comparée* . . . is a truly French publication is hardly surprising. Literary interrelations in which France has no part, either as emitter, transmitter or receiver, are scarcely dealt with here; and the comparatist whose operational basis lies outside of French literary territory has, in many cases, only very limited use for the *Revue*. Such "provincialism" (if the reader will pardon the expression) is fortunately unknown to its American sibling, the . . . quarterly periodical *Comparative Literature*. In the timespan covered by the *Table*, the interrelations between Occident and Orient, the influence of Antiquity on the Modern Age, and Medieval literature were handled rather perfunctorily in accordance with the spirit of the definitions handed down by Van Tieghem and Guyard. Also, there is a lack of weighty contributions relating to twentieth-century literature. Emphasis is placed on the inter-European tradition of the Enlightenment, Classicism, and Romanticism. From 1951 to 1960, therefore, the *Revue* scarcely knew how to account for the three thousand years [of European cultural history] surveyed by Goethe. It is equally regrettable that relatively few foreign scholars were brought in as contributors. However, in the last few years, the picture has slightly changed for the better. For example, according to our *Table*, eighteen essays are devoted to Victor Hugo, twelve each to Goethe, Shakespeare, and Rousseau, but not a single piece to Chaucer, Strindberg, Dostoevsky, and the Schlegels.[26]

In connection with the *Revue de littérature comparée*, we might also mention the "Bibliothèque de littérature comparée" (1921 ff.) and its successor, the "Etudes de littérature étrangère et comparée," whose close ties with the Institute at the Sorbonne are self-explanatory.

A contemporary of Baldensperger, who was the "grand old man" of Comparative Literature in France, Van Tieghem also rendered extremely great services to our discipline. His name will go down in the history of the field primarily because it is linked with the first systematically conceived and methodologically consistent survey, the volume *La littérature comparée,* which I have so frequently mentioned. Beginning in 1911, Van Tieghem was a collaborator of the *Revue de synthèse historique,* wherein he periodically reported on new publications relevant to Comparative Literature. In 1921 (the year in which the *Revue de littérature comparée* was founded), he published the important essay "La Synthèse en histoire littéraire: Littérature comparée et littérature générale."[27] In France, General Literature found eloquent expression in the broad syntheses of Paul Hazard, particularly in that scholar's *magnum opus,* the book *La Crise de la conscience européenne* (1925).[28]

With the German occupation of France in 1940, the development of Comparative Literature in that country came to a sudden halt. For the time being even the *Revue de littérature comparée* ceased publication, and, from 1942 to 1946, it was replaced after a fashion by the University of Cardiff's *Comparative Literature Studies*—not to be confused with the American journal by that name, which was originally based at the University of Maryland but is now published at the University of Illinois.

The slow growth of French comparatism after the war, which—with the creation of chairs in Mainz and Saarbrücken—also spread to French-occupied Germany, was not accelerated until around 1950, as full academic chairs or *maîtrises de conférences* began to be established, in rapid succession, at various provincial universities. This

happened in 1949 at Dijon, in 1951 at Bordeaux and Toulouse, in 1952 at Clermont-Ferrand, Lille, and Rennes, and
shortly afterward also in Grenoble and Aix. After 1966,
Comparative Literature prospered, at least temporarily,
even in the Francophone part of North Africa, where the
Cahiers algériens de littérature comparée ran its brief
course.[29] In 1954, the French comparatists founded the extremely active *Société Française de littérature comparée*,
which convenes each year at a different regional center
and regularly publishes its *Proceedings*.[30]

Hand in hand with this expansion of academically pursued and increasingly decentralized comparative literature
studies in France went a conceptual liberalization, which
—despite a certain reluctance on the part of the more conservative Paris School—gradually spread to the Sorbonne,
where professors like Charles Dédéyan had remained so
unflinchingly loyal to *Stoffgeschichte*. This welcome
change would hardly have occurred, had it not been for
the American precedent and example; and even as late as
1951, Guyard was still able to market his eclectic survey,
which breathes the spirit of Van Tieghem's work. However, even in France the Guyard manual was poorly received, and, as we have seen, in the revised edition (1961),
its author felt obliged to make certain concessions to the
new trend.[31]

One of the boldest attacks against the inordinately narrow limits placed on Comparative Literature by the found-
ers of the Paris School was launched by René Etiemble,
who is now a professor of Comparative Literature at the
Sorbonne. The way had been paved by a number of "out-
siders," such as Pierre Maury, whose booklet *Arts et littérature comparées: Etat présent de la question* had appeared
as early as 1934.[32] More substantial and far-reaching in its
consequences was the view expressed by the medievalist
Jean Frappier, who took issue with the fact that the work
of his comparatist colleagues was limited "to coordinating
and developing studies dealing with Comparative Literature from the Renaissance to the present." In the paper

"Littérature médiévale et littérature comparée," which he presented at the Second Congress of the ICLA, he explained why Medieval studies are especially well suited to the comparative approach and what factual and methodological difficulties must be met before they can succeed. Frappier's apologetic tone demonstrates how well this internationally known scholar knew that he was moving on what was still a largely untrodden path:

> The subject which I shall briefly treat has no need of lengthy justifications. At least, I imagine that no one today seriously wishes to contest the legitimacy of applying the principles of Comparative Literature to the Middle Ages as well as to more recent times. It must be admitted, however, that this enlarged conception of literary comparatism is not very old, that (with rare exceptions) it dates back only about fifteen or twenty years, and that there is still considerable progress to be made. (*Proceedings II*, Vol. I, p. 25).

Frappier's view has gradually prevailed, even in France, as shown by the fact that "international literary exchanges in the Middle Ages" served as the central topic for the Seventh National Congress of the French Comparative Literature Association.

Embracing a still more "progressive" view, a French comparatist teaching at the University of Bordeaux, and at present director of a center for mass communication research, gave further impetus to a redefinition and re-orientation of our discipline beyond strictly aesthetic-literary bounds. In 1958, Robert Escarpit published a concise survey of the state of research and the future tasks of literary sociology, such as had previously been practiced with scientifically cruder means by Professor Levin Schücking in Germany.[33] Escarpit's field of specialization is linked with Van Tieghem's and Guyard's conception of Comparative Literature through the terms *transmission* and *reception*, which reappear, transposed into the economic sphere, as *distribution* and *consumption*, respectively. At the Sixth Congress of the ICLA in Bordeaux (1970), which was organized by Escarpit, the topic "literature and sociology" was rightfully accorded the status due it in our technological age, although, both qualitatively and quantitatively, the contributions under this rubric were rather disappointing.

The revaluation of all the values dear for so long to the French comparatists was considerably hastened—although by no means completed—by the publication in 1963 of Etiemble's polemical essay *Comparaison n'est pas raison: La Crise de la littérature comparée*.[34] In this book, the author, whose appointment to the Sorbonne is to be seen as a semi-official recognition of his stance, advocates the expansion of comparative studies to the extra-European (especially the Far Eastern) countries. In addition, he supports the comparative study of metrics, stylistics, metaphorics, and poetics, as well as a comparatistically oriented approach to problems of structure and translation. Etiemble's program, which is in part utopian (especially as regards the sections "The Teaching of Comparative Literature Must Be Centralized," "For a Bibliography . . . ," "A Universal Working Language?" and "The Ideal Comparatist") yields ample food for thought and, for some time to come, will remain an important reservoir of ideas.

Claude Pichois and André-M. Rousseau's handbook, the first truly "enlightened" French manual of Comparative Literature, appeared in 1967. A product of joint labor, it naturally runs the risk of offering a double perspective. The scholarly contributions made by each of the two authors are not specifically identified; but the preface includes the statement:

It so happens that, of the two authors of the present work, the one leans toward history, the other toward philosophy. Each has, therefore, devoutly followed his interest, which is the best way of being truthful. But since the philosopher does not despise history, and the historian is sympathetic to all new trends, insofar as history no longer limits itself to the mechanical study of causes and effects, and philosophy goes beyond the pure game of abstractions, their expositions, through the dialectic alternation of the two methods, result in a continuous movement. Accordingly, the following pages tend to reflect a vital law of all literary criticism. (P/R, p. 8f.)

When the table of contents of Van Tieghem's book is compared with that of the Pichois/Rousseau volume, it is at once apparent that the structural differences between the two works are minimal. In both, the history of the discipline is exhaustively reviewed in the first part or chapter. The second chapter ("International Literary Exchanges") of the more recent survey roughly corresponds to the fifth, sixth, and seventh chapters of Part Two of Van Tieghem's *La Littérature comparée*, whereas the third chapter (corresponding exactly to the third part of its antecedent) concerns *littérature générale* and *littérature universelle* and presupposes a basically outmoded viewpoint or, at least, an outmoded terminology.

In Chapter Four, Pichois and Rousseau discuss the History of Ideas, as does Van Tieghem in Part Two, Chapter Four, of his book. An apparent innovation is constituted by the material treated in Chapter Five and presented under the heading of "Literary Structuralism," a label suggesting that Pichois/Rousseau were riding the crest of a current fashion in French literary criticism. Actually, the two scholars deal mostly with such conventional topics as thematology (the equivalent of Van Tieghem's Part Two, Chapter Three) and the "aesthetics of translation." Inserted between these sections is a brief sketch of what the authors term "literary morphology"; but they do not manage to offer a clear profile of this subject, which, in their treatment, impinges upon the theory of genres and, by way of phenomenology, upon the so-called analogy studies.

May we assume that the contents of the Pichois/Rousseau book conveys a faithful picture of the present state of Comparative Literature as pursued at French universities? Aside from the more radical views expressed by Escarpit and Etiemble, nothing stands in the way of our drawing this conclusion. That no real progress is being made was recently demonstrated by the publication of Simon Jeune's "essai d'orientation," *Littérature générale et littérature comparée*, which, offered as a methodological overview charting a middle course between Guyard and Etiemble, pays little more than lip service to the broader views of the "American" school.

2. Germany

Just as in France, Comparative Literature in Germany was, at first, a branch of literary *history* rather than literary *criticism* or *theory*. In this sense, Kasper Daniel Morhof may be considered as the actual founder of the discipline labeled General Literary History (*Allgemeine Literatur-geschichte*) until well into the last century.[35] Prior to Friedrich and August Wilhelm Schlegels' famous and enthusiastically received lectures in Vienna,[36] Morhof was emulated by two Göttingen professors, Friedrich Bouterwek and Johann Gottfried Eichhorn, who were members of a "Learned Society" and who at the beginning of the nineteenth century produced, within the context of a projected General History of the Arts and Sciences, a *Geschichte der Poesie und Beredsamkeit* (1801–19) and a *Geschichte der Literatur von ihren Anfängen bis auf die neueste Zeit* (1805–1811), respectively.

Bouterwek, who was more farsighted than Eichhorn, was tempted by the thought of a "continuation of this history . . . as a synchronic treatment of the progress of the aesthetic spirit and taste in the different languages of modern Europe," but ultimately confined himself to the "more natural and equally instructive" presentation of the "history of the belles lettres of each nation . . . uninterruptedly to its conclusion." In so doing, he anticipated, in his own way, the theory of the literary change of guard which Brunetière was to propagate over half-a-century later and which is now so firmly linked to his name. Bouterwek argued: "The path taken by recent European art leads, clearly, to this goal and to the natural transition from one literature to another."[37] It led, as Bouterwek sought to show, from Italy to Spain, Portugal, France, England, and Germany.

As in most European countries, the conditions in Germany were such that the systematically pursued comparative study of literature swam into view only after the study of that country's national literature had been philologically secured. This stage was reached with Gervinus' *Geschichte der poetischen Nationalliteratur der Deutschen* (1835–1842) and Karl Goedeke's *Grundriss der Geschichte der deutschen Dichtung aus den Quellen* [Volumes 1 and 2 (1856–1859)]. However, the academic study of German literature did not achieve equal status with classical philology until the days of Wilhelm Scherer and Erich Schmidt. While Schmidt persistently wanted to see the study of phenomena external to German literature approached from the German perspective, Scherer moved in the direction of Comparative Literature proper.

The opening sentences of Schmidt's inaugural lecture at the University of Vienna in 1880 declare: "The history of literature should be part of the history of a people's spiritual and intellectual development, with comparative glances thrown at other national literatures." A few pages later Schmidt asserts:

The concept of national literature does not tolerate a stiff protective tariff; in intellectual life we are all free agents. But can we [the Germans] determine the self-sufficiency or dependence, the share of receptivity and productivity, and true and false assimilation, as well as how German literature has gradually acquired a universal role? First and foremost there arises the question concerning its relation to Antiquity, which has been viewed through so many different glasses.[38]

Scherer shows an even greater understanding of the comparative approach; for already in the first volume of his *Kleine Schriften*, edited by Konrad Burdach and Erich Schmidt,[39] we encounter several references to "comparative poetics." Dating from the years 1870–1876, they relate throughout to the work of Moriz Haupt, whom Scherer celebrates as a true pioneer. In his inaugural address before the Berlin Academy of Sciences, delivered on July 6, 1854, Haupt proclaimed his comparatist faith:

The linking of classical philology with the study of German literature has, for him who is only moderately equipped, the disadvantage of dissipating his strength and not letting him attain in both areas what he could perhaps achieve in one; but it has advantages which compensate for that drawback. From classical philology, which has prospered much longer as an academic discipline, German philology can glean both rules and methods; and German antiquity, through contrasts and analogies, permits the world of the Greeks and Romans to be seen in a clearer and more lifelike perspective. Chiefly through the scrutiny of parallel phenomena I have tried to interpret the nature and history of the epic, which are hidden from the one-sided view—more in teaching, it is true, than through publications.[40]

In 1870, in a review of three volumes of the *Zeitschrift für deutsche Philologie*, Scherer voiced the hope that an "aesthetics based on a historical foundation" might be created, "which, by the inductive method, and proceeding from the spiritual condition of primitive peoples . . . would try to trace . . . the origin of the . . . poetic genres." It would not be difficult, he continued, to treat the drama, or the epic, in this manner; it is in regard to the natural science of the epic that the basis has been most successfully laid."[41] Scherer, then, would have liked to see the anthropological approach combined with the scientific doctrine of evolution.

In his obituary on Haupt (1874), Scherer praised his colleague's endeavors in an area which he himself called the "natural history of the epic," i.e., "observations regarding the analogous developments of epic poesy among the Greeks, the Germans, the French, the Serbs, the Finns, among others." He also pointed out that Haupt had given parallel courses on Homer and the *Nibelungenlied* and had thereby initiated Comparative Literature, "just as, since Aristotle, there exists a comparative politics and a natural science of political systems."[42] Thus, the decisive word had been uttered.

It was in the context of an 1835 review of an "announcement" ascribed to Haupt, however, that Scherer most deeply reflected on "comparative poetics." He even developed his own system, which is still of interest, since it shows that the founding fathers of German philology and literary historiography were incapable of working their way toward a genuinely comparative history of *literature*. According to Scherer, comparative poetics, like comparative philology, deals with three kinds of relations: those that rest on a fundamental likeness, those that involve reciprocal influence, and those that are innately literary. Comparative mythology investigates thematic parallels within the Indo-Germanic (Scherer says "Aryan") sphere, whereas the second branch treats the themes common to novellas and fairy tales, and the third deals with genetically unrelated "non-Aryan parallels."[43] For Scherer, then, "comparative poetics" was scarcely more than a glorified thematology with a home base in folklore or mythology.

Roughly contemporary with Haupt, his Munich colleague Moriz Carrière evolved a theory of literature based on principles of aesthetics and comparative literary history. As early as 1854, in the appendix of his book *Das Wesen und die Formen der Poesie*, this scholar had promulgated "ideas for a comparative presentation of the Aryan folk-epic among Indians, Persians, Greeks, and Germans."[44] (This kind of approach was clearly in the air at that time.) He cultivated the field more systematically when, thirty years later, he published a book called *Die Poesie, ihr Wesen und ihre Formen, mit Grundzügen der vergleichenden Literaturgeschichte*. In his foreword, he advocated the creation of more solid bases for this scholarly pursuit:

Our national literature . . . has finally been accepted as one of the academic disciplines, and separate departments have been created. The students should now turn their attention to Comparative Literature, where diligence and learning, as well as aesthetic judgment, are required. To study themes such as Prometheus, Medea, Romeo and Juliet, Don Juan, and Faust, according to their interpretation among different peoples, to compare works by Lope [de Vega] and Calderón with those of

Shakespeare and Goethe, seems to me a worthwhile task, whose accomplishment will provide excellent tools for building the new discipline, which, like every other subject, can grow and flourish only when many forces are joined.[45]

What Carrière advocated, then, to begin with, was the thematological approach, which, according to his own stated intentions, was to have been expanded into a comparative history of poetic forms. Unfortunately, the main portion of Carrière's book is devoid of any reference to comparative studies. Only in the nearly two hundred pages of the final chapter does the author offer "Characteristics of and Suggestions about the Comparative Literary History of the Drama" from its religious origins up to *Faust*. For all his enthusiasm, then, Carrière, like so many of his contemporaries, lacked methodological rigor in his attempt to introduce Comparative Literature into the German academic scene.

The crystallization of the German efforts to effect a breakthrough for Comparative Literature did not come until 1887, when Max Koch founded his *Zeitschrift für vergleichende Litteraturgeschichte*. One year earlier, Karl von Reinhardstoettner had published a book on modern adaptations of Plautus' comedies. In his preface, he justified the gaps in his survey by stating that he had made "concessions to comparative literature."[46] In other words, he did not wish to present a "catalogue of all the imitations of Plautus which have appeared" but, rather, wanted to show "which of the playwright's comedies have been most heartily welcomed in the modern age."

Koch's preface to the first issue of his journal marks a turning point in the history of Comparative Literature in Germany.[47] It consists essentially of two parts: a concise survey of German comparative literary criticism and historiography from Morhof to Benfey and Goedeke (pp. 1–10), and a tally of the areas of specialization which constitute the program of this journal and its sister organ, the *Studien zur vergleichenden Litteraturgeschichte* (pp.

10–12). This list embraces 1) the art of translation; 2) the history of literary forms and themes, and the study of supranational influences; 3) the history of ideas (Rudolf Unger's *Problemgeschichte*); 4) the "ties between political and literary history"; 5) the "ties between literature and the plastic arts, between philosophical and literary developments, etc."; and 6) the "science of folklore, which has finally come of age after having been neglected until recently." Lastly, Koch designates German literature as the point of departure and central focus for the scholarly efforts enjoined by him, and allocates a place to the "most recent literature, insofar as it may be viewed in the context of the historical development."

If one leafs through the *Zeitschrift für vergleichende Litteraturgeschichte* and the *Studien zur vergleichenden Litteraturgeschichte*, one notes that Koch, their editor, loyally carried out his program. For there is no dearth of comparative studies of myths and fairy tales, of thematological essays and folkloristic investigations relating to both the European and non-European sphere (India, Africa, and China). Considerable space is also accorded to political and religious history; and there is a surfeit of contributions focusing on international literary influences (Dante in Germany, Lessing in Hungary, Heine on Burns, Goethe on Ugo Foscolo). In line with Ludwig Geiger's, the co-editor's, interests, the Renaissance and Humanism (Hans Sachs, Conrad Celtis) receive inordinate attention, whereas the links between literature and the plastic arts are treated only in scattered articles. Among those specialties not included in Koch's program but represented in both publications I mention especially poetic theory. Oddly enough, several essays in the *Zeitschrift* are solely concerned with the German classics (especially Heinrich von Kleist). Koch himself would hardly have termed these pieces comparative but seems to have made concessions to certain of his collaborators.

An overly sharp line of demarcation between philology and criticism was drawn by Wilhelm Wetz in his study

*Shakespeare vom Standpunkt der vergleichenden Littera-
turgeschichte* (1890).[48] Wetz distinguished between "aesthetic" and comparative literary history, and condemned
the former for proceeding deductively "from certain fi
aesthetic axioms" and for looking at literature only in order to see to what extent it bears out those assumptions:
"It sees its primary task . . . in the determination of the
absolute value ascribable to a work."[49] In his view, Comparative Literature, on the other hand, does greater justice
to the immanent values:

Aiming always at identifying characteristic traits, it will, in
studying an entire literature, primarily stress its national
character; in the case of the various literary genres, it will
emphasize chiefly that in which they differ from the same forms
as they are used in other countries. It will not be satisfied,
however, with ascertaining facts, but will also trace their causes,
which are to be found in the intellectual and spiritual make-up
of the different nations. It thus turns psychological and becomes
capable of extracting from literature valuable information about
the national character.[50]

As we have seen in Chapter One, this psychologically
oriented brand of Comparative Literature is now in ill re-
pute, and many comparatists tend to dismiss it altogether.

While thus in the late 1880's and early 1890's, the name
and the (still disputed) method of Comparative Literature
gradually took hold in Germany, the academic position of
this youngest branch of philology was called into question
in the course of a debate carried on in several literary journals—especially the *Litterarisches Echo*—around the turn
of the century. At the outset, Goethe's *Weltliteratur* was
once more seized upon and discussed, with Ernst Martin's
lecture "Goethe über *Weltliteratur* und Dialektdichtung"
(1899) apparently serving as a springboard. The debate involved many misapprehensions and misinterpretations of
the kind we have already dwelt upon.

In 1899, the Danish scholar Georg Brandes published
the essay "Weltliteratur," in which—without directly re-

ferring to Goethe—he used that term in the sense of
"Great Books." Moreover, he included within the canon of
great literature the outstanding scientific and historio-
graphical works and even travelogues.[51] Brandes was followed by R. M. Meyer, who contributed an essay on contemporary world literature to the *Deutsche Rundschau*.[52]
Meyer saw *Weltliteratur* as the totality "of the greatest
poetic products of individual geniuses" and, like Brandes,
wanted to include scientific and philosophic works under
this heading. Meyer's permissive conception was emphatically rejected by Ernst Elster, who demonstrated that by
Weltliteratur Goethe meant simply the "extension of literary interest beyond national boundaries" and, concomi-
tantly, the "expansion of the literary market."[53] Yet, despite this refutation, Meyer's ideas continue to haunt the
academic scene.[54]

The links between *Weltliteratur* and Comparative Literature were further studied by Elster with reference to an
article by Betz originally published in *Litterarisches Echo*.
It is worthy of our immediate attention. Betz was inspired
by Brunetière's address at the Paris Congress to present an
outline of the history of comparativist scholarship in the
German-speaking and non-German-speaking countries. At
the conclusion of his essay, he expressed the hope that,
following the French and American example, chairs of
comparative literary history would soon be established in
Germany as well:

Precisely because in Germany, which justly prides itself on its
broad literary culture (the Germany which gave us a Herder and
which, through Goethe, coined the word *Weltliteratur*), the
words of the unforgettable Strasbourg professor Ten Brink ("the
branching off of a new discipline from the trunk of academic
scholarship is usually followed by the creation of a new academic
chair at our institutions of higher learning") have not yet come
true, it might be wise to listen to a "literary echo" which is
reaching us from abroad. Basically, this echo is the reverberation
of a call which was first sounded in German lands.[55]

In his pointed rejoinder to Betz, the Göttingen scholar Hans Daffis called the creation of such chairs at German universities premature:

We should, therefore, before contemplating the institution of chairs of Comparative Literature at our universities, make room for additional representation of our own literature. Moreover, at each university, there should be someone who integrates literary history by treating it as a component of a general "cultural history" combining the history of German politics, economics, literature, music, and the plastic arts to offer a composite history of German life and art (*Art und Kunst*), much as the venerable Riehl has done in Munich.[56]

Elster supported Daffis' views, but for different reasons. To him, the term Comparative Literature seemed misleading insofar as the comparative method (which, like Wetz, he played off against the philological approach) was appropriate within a national literature as well. What Betz had in mind, according to Elster, was "international literary history," which, as it were, was already practiced by those professors occupying chairs devoted to the study of the various national literatures. In his opinion, the term Comparative Literature was coined, in analogy to Comparative Philology, in order to make universal literary historiography more palatable to university administrators. This parallel, however, Elster maintained, was based on false premises, since scholarly research uncovers "through the comparative study of the historical monuments of a language those of prehistorical and nonhistorical times as well," and since it is only from these that "the development of the individual languages [can be] fully gauged and properly evaluated." To his mind it was meaningful only when applied to the "folk traditions of olden times" and in the case of "myth, legend, fairy tale, and folk tale."[57]

Just how much Elster's and Daffis' attacks on Comparative Literature helped to prevent it from becoming an academic discipline is hard to tell. It is a fact, however, that,

prior to World War I, no German university heeded Betz's
call. Nonetheless, the excitement over Comparative Literature as a subject and a body of techniques subsided
slowly. In 1903, Jellinek published his *Bibliographie der
vergleichenden Literaturgeschichte* (to be discussed in Appendix II), and in the following year a collection of essays
by Karl Federn, entitled *Essays zur vergleichenden Literaturgeschichte*, made its appearance. In the preface, the author stated: "I first heard the term which I have chosen to
grace the title of this book from a prominent Austrian
scholar [probably Jellinek], who applied it to my essays."[58]
Federn made no attempt, however, to define this accepted
term.

When the *Studien zur vergleichenden Litteraturgeschichte* and the *Zeitschrift für vergleichende Litteraturgeschichte* ceased publication in 1909 and 1910, respectively,
the low point in the history of Comparative Literature in
Germany was reached. "The entire movement, which exhausted itself in unproblematic thematology, . . . seems
now to have bogged down and ground to a halt,"—thus
the cold, clear retrospective judgment of Julius Petersen, a
representative of the incipient *Geistesgeschichte*, which
was quickly draining the strength of Comparative Literature.[59] One of its most vociferous precursors was Eugen
Kühnemann, who as early as 1900, in a review of Betz's
bibliography, condemned the "current literary-historical
'business' with its one-sided emphasis on *Stoff*." Kühnemann went on to call Comparative Literature "an eminently philological problem, but only in the true meaning
of that word, according to which philology is identical
with a sound sense of reality" by its effort "to trace things
to their roots and [discern] in the wealth of phenomena
the permanent law and the uniform task."[60]

Kühnemann's essay was the clarion call of an age concerned with essences, and which, in the intellectual
sphere, embraced the ideal of a literary history without
names, and a cultural history free of politico-geographical
boundaries and strictly chronological limits. The climate

of these "Expressionist" decades was all the more unfavorable to Comparative Literature as both during and immediately following World War I two opposing camps ruled German intellectual life: the Nationalists, who hoped to restore the study of the national literature to prominence; and the Pacifists, who dreamed of a United States of Europe.

In the 1930's, the reconstitution of Comparative Literature in Germany seemed possible only around a Franco-German axis, for the Romance language scholars were the only ones to use the comparative method extensively on their academic home ground. But, whereas in France a firm and lasting foundation for our discipline was being created through the founding of the *Revue de littérature comparée* in 1921, German scholars like Karl Vossler, Viktor Klemperer, and Ernst Merian-Genast, were still indulging in more or less abstract reflections on the concept of *Weltliteratur*.[61] Administratively, German comparatism lagged so far behind that Julius Petersen could say in 1928:

At many [foreign] universities, institutes of Comparative Literature have been established. Between them, an international organization is being planned on the model of the League of Nations; and as an instrument of mutual understanding, cultural rapport, and universal peace . . . Germany is by no means excluded from cooperation. She is an important object of comparative study, but only passively so—the impression is unavoidable that, as a country, she has lost the position of leadership in a discipline to which she herself gave birth, and that she has lost it in the same degree that she has yielded her position in world politics.[62]

Not until the latter part of the 1920's was the existence of Comparative Literature as a discipline formally acknowledged by some German universities. In Leipzig (Viktor Klemperer) as well as in Würzburg (Eduard von Jan), part-time teaching positions in our field were opened to a handful of Romanists. Von Jan's inaugural speech (delivered on February 1, 1927, and subsequently published in the *Germanisch-Romanische Monatsschrift*) bears the characteristic title "Französische Literaturgeschichte und vergleichende Literaturbetrachtung."[63] Without throwing off the shackles of *littérature comparée* as preached and practiced by the French, the German scholar opted for an expansion of the discipline in the direction of *littérature générale* and, beyond that, to *Geistesgeschichte*. The term *vergleichende Literaturwissenschaft* was now firmly entrenched in Germany, one imagines in analogy to *Geisteswissenschaft*, although an eminent comparatist like Kurt Wais still seems to prefer the oldfashioned term (witness the title of the recent *Festschrift* published in his honor). In von Jan's opinion, Comparative Literature,

> using individual authors and works as points of orientation, [should] trace the changes which certain ideas and genres have experienced. Consequently, [Comparative Literature] must not limit itself to studying the works themselves but must expand its investigations to cover the effects they have produced. That is to say, it must consider in equal measure the literary works and the reading public, i.e., objects as well as subjects. . . . In particular, this task includes [the study of] the fortunes of literary works abroad.[64]

Von Jan also expected Comparative Literature "to reconstruct the ideological context from which the author and his work have emerged." This context was not to be geographically limited but was to encompass the entire contemporary world. On September 29, 1927—half a year after this inaugural lecture—Petersen delivered a well-received and in every respect remarkable speech on the topic "Nationale oder vergleichende Literaturgeschichte?", on the occasion of the fifty-sixth meeting of the German *Philologen* in Göttingen. In this lecture, he sealed the fate of thematology narrowly conceived and positivistically executed. Positivism, in his view, was an alien, mechanical mode of thought which ran counter to the inwardness [*Innerlichkeit*] of the German mind" (*DVLG*, 6 [1928], p. 41). This formulation, which required only a slight ideological intensification to make a perfect nationalistic slogan, recalls the rejection, on the part of Goethe and his "Storm and Stress" friends in Strasbourg, of the spirit of French Encyclopaedism as voiced retrospectively in *Dichtung und Wahrheit.*

Petersen paid homage to the spirit of the age by urging that the territory hitherto occupied by Comparative Literature be distributed among *Geistesgeschichte,* national literary history, and general literature, respectively. As to the autonomy of the various national literatures, he held that there are "international buffer zones, constituting joint protectorates" (p. 45), which might be treated from either angle. The study of international literary relations, on the other hand, was to be pursued from the perspective of the receiving country:

In the case of movements, which invariably lead from a productive to a receptive factor, the interest, on the part of the observer, should focus on the recipient. The productive factor is known and will hardly reveal any significant features through the analysis of its effects; but the kind and extent of the effect it produces will lead to characteristic disclosures concerning the nature of the receiving element. (p. 46)

According to this view, Friedrich Gundolf's book *Shakespeare und der deutsche Geist,* for instance, would squarely belong to German literary historiography. When it is a matter of presenting an overview of a poet's international impact, however, its history, says Petersen, may be "grasped in its entirety only from the standpoint of the producing agent" (p. 47). Petersen calls this method "not so much comparative as summarizing" and wonders "whether the result does not make more bibliographical than literary-historical sense."

Turning to *Geistesgeschichte,* a path "on which German literary scholarship has embarked" (p. 51), Petersen maintains that both *littérature générale* and thematology fall under its sway. Thus, instead of postulating "reciprocal influence," one should, from now on, try to show the "internal regularity of parallel processes linked by destiny." But

that approach presupposes, for Petersen, the replacement
of the "perspective of national trends of evolution" by the
"horizontal linking of contemporaries, coevals, and of the
spirit of the age [*Zeitgeist*]" (p. 51). This, in his view, was
precisely the course charted by the *Deutsche Vierteljahrsschrift für Literatur- und Geistesgeschichte*.

Referring to the evolutionary trends within a given national literature, Petersen also pointed out that the comparative method was just as appropriate in their case as it
was in the case of international phenomena: "[National
literary history] turns comparative in its own domain . . .
if it does not restrict itself to letting the literature and the
spirit of entire periods—such as the German Enlightenment, the Storm and Stress, German Classicism, and German Romanticism—evolve, chronologically, from each
other but instead juxtaposes them synthetically as self-
contained units" (p. 48).

At the end of his lecture, Petersen states—as, for much
more practical reasons, Hans Daffis had done a quarter of
a century earlier—that it would be premature to establish
chairs in Comparative Literature at German universities.
Instead, he proposes the creation of centers for international literary research as being more appropriate to the
current state of scholarship.

The grave danger incurred by *Geistesgeschichte*,
through its favorite game of abstracting such standardized
categories as Gothic, Baroque, Classicism, and Romanticism from the plethora of cultural phenomena, was
pointed up by Werner Milch in his essay *Über Aufgaben
und Grenzen der Literaturgeschichte*.[65] Milch notes that
this danger inevitably arises in the course of striving for
absolutes and as a necessary consequence of the growing
detachment from the live historical process. The final upshot of this process is the formation of pseudo-concepts
such as Hellenistic Romanticism or Expressionist Gothic,
which, in extreme cases such as that exemplified by Herbert Cysarz in literal application, may result in the trans-

fer of stylistic concepts to the human sphere, so that a
Gothic or Baroque man ultimately emerges. It was this
type of excess that Milch wanted to expose in his essay.

A second strain of historical absolutes resulting from a
false conception of the nature of *Geisteswissenschaft* was
introduced by Kurt Wais (since 1934 a lecturer, and subsequently professor, of Romance languages and Comparative
Literature at the University of Tübingen) in his essay
"Zeitgeist und Volksgeist in der vergleichenden Literaturgeschichte" (*GRM*, 22 [1934], pp. 291–307). Like Petersen,
Wais uses the "methodologically indispensable principle
of synchronism" as a yardstick for the "sound, scientifically meaningful comparison between national idiosyncrasies" (p. 301). As an entity polar to this *Zeitgeist*, but
dialectically linked with it, he identifies the *Volksgeist*.
Both are "a thorn in the flesh . . . of the strict positivist,
. . . because both derive from permanently inexplicable,
irrational sources, which cannot be biologically and sociologically explained or anthropomorphized, and whose
roots lie in the religious sphere" (p. 305).

How, then, according to Wais, does Comparative Literature relate to these "spirits"? In his view, the *Zeitgeist*
"creates with ceaseless motion a constantly aging and self-
renewing body of thought that can be conceptualized and
defined, that is binding for all, may be discussed among
peoples and can possibly be transferred from one people
to another" (p. 306). A comparative European *Geistesgeschichte*, therefore, would seem to lie within the realm of
possibility. The *Volksgeist*, however, which is the true
source of genuine *Dichtung*, must be reflected in the spiritual history, the essential core, of a national community,
which no two peoples share, and which is, therefore, neither interchangeable nor comparable. Wais, then, considers Comparative Literature meaningful only in relation to
intellectual, rationally comprehensible phenomena. But
where the irrational, spiritual essence is to be grasped, only
the Anglicist, Germanist or Romanist is a competent judge.

Thus Comparative Literature is ultimately reduced to an "auxiliary discipline" (p. 307), which must be content with a place in the shadow of true literary scholarship.

The tendency to exalt *Volksgeist* at the expense of *Zeitgeist* grew into outright chauvinism during the years immediately preceding World War II and, naturally, during the War itself. How could Comparative Literature flourish in a country in which the plays of Shakespeare, Molière, and Eugene O'Neill were banned from the stage, and where the novels of the great French and Russian writers were no longer accessible? It is certainly true that, as Richard Alewyn stated in 1945, "the new masters have not for a moment indulged in isolationism, as the world has become painfully aware. On the contrary, they have skillfully used all the cultural links with the world outside, and they have forged new ones of their own."[66] This was done, however, within the frame of an expansionist cultural policy which wanted to prove that although the world had not yet been cured by the German spirit, it would be saved by it in the next few decades. Here, then, influence would be measured by the productive, but not by the receptive, factor.

"But there are no chairs of world or comparative literature at the universities in German-speaking countries," Alewyn regretfully concluded. Thus, a new beginning had to be made after the holocaust of 1945. The premature deaths of Max Kommerell and Werner Milch, and the emigration of eminent Romance scholars like Erich Auerbach, Helmut Hatzfeld, and Leo Spitzer, had produced a vacuum which could not readily be filled. Only in the French sector of occupied Germany was new life stirring. Of all the victorious allies, France, in fact, pursued the most dexterous and successful cultural policy in ravaged and sadly partitioned Germany.

Wais resumed his work in Tübingen, and, in 1950 and 1958, respectively, organized two international congresses at which the present state and the future tasks of Comparative Literature in Europe and overseas were discussed.[67] And at the Johannes-Gutenberg-Universität in Mainz, which was re-opened after a long hiatus, a chair of Comparative Literature—the first in Germany—was instituted on the Parisian model. Its first occupant was the Heine scholar Friedrich Hirth, to whom we are indebted for providing the first comprehensive historical and methodological survey of the goals of Comparative Literature in postwar Germany, a document with a function similar to that of Koch's foreword to the first issue of the *Zeitschrift für vergleichende Litteraturgeschichte*.[68] The essay, which in many particulars is based on statements made by Elster, Koch, and others, is somewhat diffuse, however, and evidences some terminological uncertainty.

At the outset, Hirth follows the example of Petersen in trying to exclude, or at least contain, the historical element: "All that Comparative Literature has in common with literary history is its subject matter. The method, however, is different, for Comparative Literature does not pursue historical ends. By comparing analogous phenomena, it tries to penetrate to their innermost core, and to ascertain the laws which are responsible for their similarities and differences."[69] Hirth also delimits Comparative Literature against cultural history and the History of Ideas, since, in his view, it excludes everything "which cannot be viewed aesthetically."[70]

Since, according to Hirth, Comparative Literature is solely concerned with belles-lettres, and specifically with "written products" (p. 1313), it need not become involved in the comparative study of folksongs or legends (even in their fixed, literary form). Thus Hirth blocks Carrière's and Scherer's entry into the comparativist pantheon. Hirth's methodological purism is not all that pure, however, since he asks, like Petersen, that one should not insist on the condition "that Comparative Literature be always and exclusively international" (p. 1307); for, methodologically, the study of the relation between Gryphius and Lohenstein is in no way different from that of the links between Shakespeare and Goethe. And at the conclusion of his survey, once more contradicting himself, Hirth asserts that Comparative Literature has "not only an aesthetic, but also a philosophical, political, [and] sociological dimension" (p. 1315). However great his share in reviving Comparative Literature in Germany after the zero point, the contradictory nature and the inconsistency of his theoretical views were, ultimately, more of a hindrance than a help in its postwar development.

After Hirth's death, the inheritance of newly orphaned German comparatism fell first to Walter Höllerer, lecturer at Erlangen and Frankfurt and, for many years now, a professor of German at the Technical University of Berlin. Höllerer discussed the subject in several German and foreign literary periodicals. In 1951, for instance, he published an essay entitled "Methoden und Probleme der vergleichenden Literaturwissenschaft," in which he followed the example of Milch and Curtius by declaring himself in favor of limiting comparative studies to the Occident (i.e., essentially Europe).[71] In contrast to the "utopian" discipline of World Literature, Comparative Literature was to remain eminently practicable. Comparative Literature in the narrower sense, however, was not greatly served by Höllerer, who summarily asked that the discipline he had circumscribed should set itself the task of making visible, through comparison, the internal links and the minutest changes effected in Western Literature.[72] Höllerer's jargon, unfortunately, obscures the real issues.

In an essay published two years later and entitled "La Littérature comparée en Allemagne depuis la fin de la guerre,"[73] Höllerer stated that the Germans reject both littérature comparée in the narrow sense ("there is no such thing as a science of encounters and travels, of 'emitters', 'receivers', and 'transmitters'") and littérature générale ("which, by means of comparison, seeks to establish an extratemporal aesthetic system based on factors common to literary genres, formal properties, etc."),[74] and that an effort was being made to replace them with a truly "comparative history of European literature."

Hermann Schneider's attempt to apply the comparative method to medieval studies[75] and Wais's continuing efforts on behalf of the theory and practice of Comparative Literature notwithstanding, there is no doubt that Horst Rüdiger, Hirth's successor in the Mainz chair and currently a professor of German and Comparative Literature at Bonn University, is now the leading spokesman for comparatists in the German-speaking world. Through his essays in the *Schweizer Monatshefte*,[76] his participation in international congresses, and his editorship of the journal *Arcadia*, which he himself founded in 1966, he regained for German comparatism a voice in the world. The scholarly program of *Arcadia* reveals Rüdiger's conception of Comparative Literature as that of a classical philologist, schooled in Greek and Latin, whose literary interests are centered not so much on literary criticism as on the survival of ancient thought and art throughout the Middle Ages and into the present.

Insofar as can be judged from the first six years of publication, the editor of *Arcadia* tends to give decided preference to essays on the survival of Antiquity as well as to *topos* studies, although, more recently, essays pertaining to the interrelation of the arts have also found their way into the journal. The articles concerning the interaction of national literatures in the nineteenth and twentieth centuries, on the other hand, are frequently shorter and do not consistently attain the same high level. It is to be hoped that the second part of *Arcadia*'s program ("the study of the reciprocal relations between Slavic and Western literatures, as well as between European and non-European literatures") will soon be carried out.

In the most thorough and lucid exposition which Comparative Literature in postwar Germany has, so far, produced (it, too, was published in the *Schweizer Monatshefte*), Rüdiger makes a comparatist's confession of faith. For him, this brand of literary scholarship is confined to European literature "in the broadest sense of the word," albeit with the inclusion of ancient as well as Near and

Far Eastern influences and taking into account the "European-American literary unity" of most recent times.[77]

Rüdiger excludes the study of the "images of other nations" (Guyard's *images* and *mirages*) and positivistic thematology. He would also like to see the term "influence" replaced by "effect" or "survival" (*Wirkung*), which presupposes the existence of "vital forces." In developing his own high-minded program, he stresses the relevance of the following subject areas: the study of the survival of ancient and Biblical literature (whether on the order of magnitude represented by myth or on that represented by the *topos*), the occupation with the transmitters of literary values (with special emphasis on Renaissance Humanism), and the concern with the theory and practice of translation. As might be expected, Rüdiger sets very high standards for the comparatist's linguistic equipment, making mandatory the knowledge of Greek and Latin (Rüdiger himself is a co-editor of the collection *Die Überlieferung der antiken Literatur*)[78] and of the most important modern foreign languages.

Hopefully, this conception of Comparative Literature—which is conservative by American standards—will soon make proselytes in Germany. The future looks relatively rosy, at least in the German Federal Republic, as is demonstrated by the creation of chairs in Darmstadt, Berlin, Aachen and Bielefeld. The Deutsche Gesellschaft für Allgemeine und Vergleichende Literaturwissenschaft was founded in 1969. A branch of the ICLA, it has met twice so far (Mainz, 1970, and Regensburg, 1972). The Proceedings of the first congress have already been published under the title *Zur Theorie der Vergleichenden Literaturwissenschaft* (Berlin: de Gruyter, 1971). Those of the second congress, devoted to the question of literary genres, will appear shortly under the same imprint. However, in the deaths of Fritz Strich and Peter Szondi, who taught Comparative Literature at the University of Zurich and the Free University of Berlin respectively, German comparatism has suffered a grievous loss which will be hard to recoup.

In the German Democratic Republic as well, there have recently been signs of a growing interest in the comparative approach, emulating the Russian example. In a brief note attached to his previously mentioned survey of the state of Comparative Literature in the two Germanies, Walter Höllerer ruefully concluded that, with the exception of studies in the mutual relations between German and Slavic literature, no efforts were being made in East Germany.[79] This situation, he continued, was aggravated by the fact that, since 1951, students in the GDR had to concentrate their studies in one major subject; thus they were, in actual fact, denied the chance to expand their knowledge beyond the realm of a single national literature. As to the existence of professional chairs of Comparative Literature, Höllerer stated, there was nothing positive to report, although Halle, Jena, and Greifswald—partly because of their library holdings—"offer possibilities for work." The professor of Romance Languages in Jena at that time was Eduard von Jan, whose Würzburg inaugural lecture we have already mentioned; but, as Höllerer reports, he had not engaged in comparative work for years, and the last dissertation written along those lines had been completed in 1944.

Höllerer's remarks could be supplemented with a reference to the work done by the Romanists Fritz Neubert (until 1949), Viktor Klemperer, and Werner Krauss, as well as the former professor of German at the University of Leipzig, Hans Mayer (now at the Technical University of Hanover). Mayer participated in the Utrecht Congress of the ICLA as the sole representative of the GDR, whereas no East German delegation had attended the earlier congresses held in Venice and Chapel Hill.

In the early 1960s, a gentle wind began to fan the interests of Comparative Literature in East Germany. Several scholars from the GDR participated in the congress of East European comparatists held at Budapest in 1962; and, in the same year, Werner Krauss presented to the Plenary Session of the German Academy of Sciences in Berlin the paper mentioned in Chapter One.[80]

Krauss justified the choice of his topic (*Probleme der vergleichenden Literaturgeschichte*) by stating that, in view of recent American and French initiatives, it was inevitable "that the demands of this plucky young discipline should be considered by us as well, and that its potential be weighed and scrutinized" (p. 3). The model of a truly Marxist, synchronically oriented Comparative Literature, according to him, was to be found in the work of A. N. Veselovsky, who, in his "comparative poetics," had sought to explain "the evolution of all literatures" on the basis of one principle (p. 13). According to the dean of German Romanists, in the use of this method "even temporally and spatially unconnected phenomena are linked with each other because of an inner necessity that is ultimately explained by common social presuppositions." In this way, the basic tenor of all recent contributions to Comparative Literature east of the Elbe was established.

In the concluding portion of his paper, whose "facts," by the way, are not always reliable,[81] Krauss strongly objects to the unsystematic and unprincipled linking of historically unrelated phenomena, i.e., to the so-called analogy studies:

Whereas Comparative Literature in France is still willing to keep in mind the great themes of French literature, the methodological sloppiness evidenced in the leading journal of the American comparatists, Werner Friedrich's [sic!!] *Comparative Literature* is incredible, for it seems that [in its pages] relations can be established between any two points in space and time. . . . Not all the articles in Friedrich's journal err in this direction. Alongside the many trifling pieces, one also encounters more relevant approaches. The chaos of perspectives and the total lack of selectivity will certainly be excused as the price that has to be paid for scholarly freedom. (p. 15f.)

Krauss' lecture was a call for the revival of Comparative Literature in the German Democratic Republic, and the Fribourg Congress was promptly attended by a number of East German representatives. The chief editor of *Weimarer Beiträge* at that time, Evamaria Nahke, subsequently discussed it in her journal. With reference to Etiemble's paper entitled "Is It Necessary to Revise the Concept of Welt-literatur?" she argued, like Krauss, that the literatures of the world should be studied "before the rise of any direct relations between them."[82] As with Veselovsky's Stadial-ism, stress was now to be placed on synchronic phenom-ena. In this way, folklore would also come into its own, after having been banished from Comparative Literature for so many decades.

At the end of her report, Ms. Nahke clearly states the future requirements:

> Given the present state of scholarship, the first item of business should be the coordination of all the worthwhile individual efforts in comparative and world literature made so far. We should set up new collectives, to proceed without delay toward the creation of a purposeful and elitist cadre at our universities in this area of specialization ... and uncover the wealth of factual source material at our disposal and capable of opening new vistas for comparative literary study. ... Only when these prerequisites are met, shall we succeed in following the example of the Soviet Union by establishing an Institute for World Literature and in gaining a stronger voice in future international congresses. (p. 262)

At the Belgrade and Bordeaux congresses of the ICLA, the GDR was represented by a large delegation comprised of university professors and members of the literary sec-tion of the German Academy of Sciences in East Berlin. In the last few years, the Academy has, in fact, made con-certed efforts to identify and document the abundant sources available to it. In December 1966, moreover, it sponsored an international colloquium (to which no par-ticipants from the West were invited, however).[83] Thus in the mid-sixties, the academic future of Comparative Lit-erature in East Germany did not seem to look quite as bleak as it had a few years earlier. And, on the initiative of the Germanist Walter Dietze, Leipzig University was in the process of founding an institute for comparative studies, a move which was ultimately to result in the crea-tion of a chair. However, little progress has been made

between 1968 and the present (1973). To be sure, scholars
like Klaus Träger and Dietze have recently published volumes of essays offered as studies in German and Comparative Literature; but the only visible sign of a change of
attitude and cultural policy is the reorganization of the
literary section of the East Berlin Academy of Sciences and
the assignment of Robert Weimann to a place of responsibility within the framework of this institution.

3. *The United States*

The history of Comparative Literature in the United
States begins, nominally, in the last third of the nineteenth
century. But the cosmopolitanism represented both academically and nonacademically by Ralph Waldo Emerson,
Henry Wadsworth Longfellow, and James Russell Lowell,
(roughly comparable to the views of Matthew Arnold in
England) may be regarded as a trend which was to culminate in the formal institution of Comparative Literature.
To all appearances, the first course devoted expressly to
the study of "general or comparative literature" was given
in 1871 at Cornell University by the Reverend Charles
Chauncey Shackford, who did not establish any sort of
tradition, however; for, after he retired in 1886, no successor was named until 1902.[84] At that time, the Aristote-
lian scholar Lane Cooper was appointed to the faculty of
Cornell, where he headed a department of Comparative
Literature from 1927 to 1943. In his autobiography, *Experiments in Education*, he discusses this aspect of his work.[85]

Another early champion of Comparative Literature in
America was Charles M. Gayley, who conducted a seminar on comparative literary criticism at the University of
Michigan from 1887 to 1889, and subsequently taught at
the University of California. There in 1912, he succeeded
in establishing a department of Comparative Literature,
which, four years later, was re-united with the English department. In a letter dated July 20, 1894, and addressed to
the editor of *The Dial*—probably the first contribution to

the public discussion of Comparative Literature on this continent—Gayley urged the founding of an American Society of Comparative Literature. It is symptomatic that he also pondered the name Society of Literary Evolution, thus showing himself to be a brother in spirit to Brunetière.

"Each member," Gayley's letter proclaims, "should devote himself to the study of a given type or movement in a literature with which he is especially, and at first hand, familiar. Thus, gradually, wherever the type or movement has existed, its evolution and characteristics may be observed and recorded."[86] The society, whose task it was to have been to define the nature of literary genres through teamwork, was to fill a glaring gap in literary historiography, for "the work is not yet undertaken by any English or American organization, or by any periodical or series of publications in the English language." Despite this prophetic voice in the wilderness of philological specialization, roughly six decades were to pass before the actual founding of the American Comparative Literature Association (ACLA).

The first American chair of Comparative Literature was instituted at Harvard University during the academic year 1890/91; its first occupant was Professor Arthur Richmond Marsh, who promised to give four courses (partly for graduates and partly for undergraduates) in medieval literature. Modern literature, on the other hand, seems not to have been treated along comparative lines at American universities until after the turn of the century.

Professor Marsh described his work in a paper read to the members of the Modern Language Association at its meeting in Boston in 1896. He referred to the new discipline as "yet undeveloped in theory" and "still extremely limited in practice." Marsh envisaged the scope of comparative literature much more generously than we (burned by experience) do today: comparative literature was to "examine . . . the phenomena of literature as a whole, to compare them, to group them, to classify them, to enquire into the causes of them, to determine the results of them."[87] At the conclusion of his essay, Marsh gives a scholarly cast to his definition by assigning to Comparative Literature the study of "literary origins," "literary developments" ("the process by which is gradually elaborated the material out of which literary masterpieces are made"), and "literary diffusion" (p. 167). Gayley's skepticism regarding original genius and concerning the work of art as a personal or unique creation ("I do indeed believe that no literary masterpiece . . . can be properly regarded as the peculiar and individual creation of the man that brings it to birth" [p. 169]) today strikes us as being largely unwarranted, because it refers back to Taine, whose methodology is suspect.

It was not until 1904 that an actual department of Comparative Literature was established at Harvard. It was chaired for fifteen years by H. C. Schofield, whose illustrious colleague was Irving Babbitt, head of the conservative school (later known as "Neo-Humanism") and author of the anti-Romantic books *The New Laocoön* and *Rousseau and Romanticism*.[88] In 1910, Schofield founded the "Harvard Studies in Comparative Literature," a series of monographs which made its debut with George Santayana's book *Three Philosophical Poets: Lucretius, Dante, Goethe*, and as part of which Albert Lord's widely acclaimed study on the principles of epic narration, *The Singer of Tales*, appeared in 1960.[89] In 1946, the department was reorganized by Harry Levin, who headed it, once again, following the death of the Slavist Renato Poggioli. Its present chairman is Walter Kaiser.

The oldest American department of Comparative Literature is the one founded in 1899 at Columbia University. It was originally headed by George E. Woodberry, assisted by the Neo-Humanist Joël E. Spingarn, and subsequently by J. B. Fletcher. However, by 1910 it was reintegrated with Columbia's English department, with which it continues to be fused.[90] The year 1903 may be called the *annus mirabilis* of American Comparative Literature, for it was then that the first specialized English-language periodical, the *Journal of Comparative Literature*, was launched. It, unfortunately, ceased publication within the year (four issues). Among the contributors to the first and only volume, we find Baldensperger and Croce ("L'umorismo," pp. 200–228). The latter took the occasion of the founding of the *Journal* to discuss Comparative Literature in his own periodical, *La Critica*.

Woodberry's *credo* is found in the preface to the first issue of his magazine, whose legitimate heir, *Comparative Literature*, was not to appear until forty-five years later.[91] Methodologically, Woodberry's outline lacks precision, as it covers, among other things, the study of literary works "within the limits of a single literature." As the chief concerns of the discipline he sought to define, Woodberry listed the study of "sources . . . themes . . . forms . . . environments . . . [and] artistic parallels." Thus, the traditional triad of relevant subjects is linked with the sociological perspective. Woodberry's reference to artistic parallels was somewhat premature for the United States, but found an echo in the voice of G. Gregory Smith, an Englishman whose contribution to *Blackwood's Edinburgh Magazine* will be discussed shortly.

Just how genteelly the humanist Woodberry went about his business is demonstrated by the following excerpt from his editorial:

It appears to me . . . that the study of forms should result in a canon of criticism, which would mean a new and greater classicism, having in its own evolution refining and ennobling influences upon the work of original genius, and also upon public taste as turned to the masters of the past; and that the study of themes should reveal temperamentally, as form does structurally, the nature of the soul, and it is in temperament, in moods, that romanticism, which is the life of all literature, has its dwelling place. To disclose the necessary forms, the vital moods of the beautiful soul is the far goal of our efforts.[92]

Originality, the beautiful soul (Goethe's *schöne Seele*), Classicism, and Romanticism, as used here by a "gentleman critic," turn into rather woolly concepts which have no precise meaning and do not lend themselves as cornerstones in the theoretical foundation of the new discipline.

The facts adduced so far make it evident that the decline of American comparative studies after World War I, lamented by Friederich in his plea "The Case of Comparative Literature" (1945), had already begun around 1900, i.e. before the creation of a methodological framework: "The teaching of and graduate work in comparative literature during the past years' has been declining so deplorably in our American universities that it seems imperative to investigate the causes of the decline and to take a stand against it with a solid and vigorous program that will restore this important branch of our Humanities to the respected place it so richly deserves."[93] Statistically, Friederich's case is strengthened by the fact that, in the first decade of our century, only two new Comparative Literature departments were founded in the United States. They were joined, in the following decade, by short-lived departments at the Universities of California (1912–1916) and Texas (1919–1926).[94]

Aside from Woodberry's program, the most important comparativist document of the prewar era was the inaugural lecture of Frank W. Chandler, who was installed in 1910 as the Ropes Professor of Comparative Literature at the University of Cincinnati. These remarks, like those of his predecessor, are now largely of historical interest because Chandler did not want to restrict Comparative Literature to belles-lettres, but assigned it an ancillary role in what might be called "comparative sociology" or "comparative psychology":

But the notion of literature as a whole is by no means incompatible with the notion of the separate literatures as national. Indeed, it is only as we think of the whole body of literary work that we may truly perceive national differentiae. And in discovering such differentiae will lie part of the duty of the student of comparative literature. . . . Practically, the sources of national differentiae must be sought in racial, geographical and historical conditions; and the operation of such conditions upon art must be analyzed.[95]

Chandler, then, was propounding the kind of literary sociology preached by Hutcheson Macaulay Posnett at the end of the nineteenth century but not systematically practiced until the twentieth. His concern with "national differentiae," moreover, anticipates the type of "*image-mirage*" studies advocated by Carré and Guyard.

As the real goal of Comparative Literature Chandler designates the study of "themes . . . types . . . environments . . . origins . . . influences [and] diffusion," that is, a syncretic mixture of the formulas used by Marsh and Woodberry. In addition, he names the study of literature "by periods or movements, the examination of it with a view to ascertaining its genetic laws," the consideration of problems of literary aesthetics, and the detection of the laws of "literary growth" within national literatures (p. 15f.). The study of literature thus collided with aesthetics on one hand and the natural sciences on the other (although, in the latter case, Chandler advises the use of caution).

For all the good will it presupposes, Chandler's view of Comparative Literature was much too broad and, on the whole, for the coming generation of scholars, an example which was by his own admission more of a deterrent than an inspiration: "But not only is this field difficult by reason of its newness and immensity: it is peculiarly difficult also by reason of its diversity. A knowledge of history and aesthetics, anthropology and folklore, is to be presumed of those who would here speak with authority" (p. 22).

The academic decline of Comparative Literature in the United States is clearly evident in a report written in 1925 by Professor Frank L. Schall,[96] who knew from firsthand experience that the term "Comparative Literature" meant little enough to the American student of the 1920s. Thus it was, for example, that the study of Ibsen—probably as a writer representative of a relatively small country—was naively spoken of as being "comparative," and that "comparative" was mistakenly identified with "contemporary."[97]

In the twenties, Comparative Literature, then, was more

or less arbitrarily lumped together with "General Literature," "World Literature," "Great Books," and "Humanities." Thus Schall had ample reason for stating: "The
distinction between *littérature comparée* and *littérature
générale* is not always precise in the United States. It often
happens that in certain curricula the latter term is substituted for the former, while the subject matter of the course
is not noticeably changed" (p. 53). Nor did it escape
Schall's attention, that, at that time, Comparative Literature was often pursued within the framework of the individual philologies, without being accorded its proper
name. After all, Albert Guérard at Stanford, whom Schall
describes as an authority on Comparative Literature, called
himself "Professor of General Literature."[98]

Even in the 1920s and 1930s, however, amid all the confusion of terms and feelings, lonely voices were calling for
a restoration of Comparative Literature as a discipline with
its own distinct profile. In 1926, for instance, Oscar J.
Campbell wrote an essay entitled "What is Comparative
Literature?" It contains the statement:

The term "comparative literature" provokes emotion. The
dilettante greets it effusively. A study with so ample a descriptive
title will provide him, he expects, with a short and easy road to
an appreciative understanding of all the important modern
literatures. The scholar is likely to regard the term with
disapproval. He suspects that the profession of an interest in
comparative literature is a form of intellectual presumption; and
he believes the peculiar virtues claimed for its methods and its
aims to be identical with those inherent in all scientific
studies of literature.[99]

Unfortunately, Campbell showed himself unable to un-
dermine this view, for his own definition as well was lacking in clarity. To be sure, he did refute Woodberry's notion
that it is possible to work comparatively within a national
literature (p. 27), but his reference to the two "roots" of
the discipline, "the investigation of origins of poetry" (p.
29) and "the study of folklore, mythography, and compar-

ative mythology" (p. 31), is disconcerting, to say the least. Campbell seems to revert to Gaston Paris and sides with Brunetière, when he states: "One need not assert with Taine that a work of modern literature is a sort of automatic register of 'race, milieu, and moment' to believe that no man of letters can emancipate himself from the influence of his social environment and the spirit of his age."

Even if one admits that Campbell himself called these viewpoints, which were indispensable to his conception of Comparative Literature, "in a sense preliminary to the main and central study of comparative literature" (p. 33), the damage to methodology had been done. One is, however, somehow reconciled by the fact that, in concluding, Campbell lists the signalling of similarities (rather than differences) and the study of artistic originality as the ultimate goals of our discipline.

But the lowest point in the American debate on Comparative Literature was not reached until 1936, when several learned specialists had their say in two issues of the journal *Books Abroad*. Their rather fruitless debate concerned, among other things, the question as to who was the real father of Comparative Literature.[100]

As so often in the history of Comparative Literature, a war, along with the pacifist tendencies sparked by it, gave new impetus to the by now lingering discipline. In 1942, thanks to the efforts of Arthur E. Christy, the National Council of Teachers of English created a "Comparative Literature Committee," which was charged with the task of promoting the study of world literature in general and "comparative" literature in particular at American high schools, colleges, and universities. This was the urgently needed first step toward a consolidation of the efforts of those scholars who were skeptical about studying national literatures in isolation.

Christy was born in China, the son of an American missionary, spent his youth in Asia, and after completing his academic studies, held the position of Professor of English and Comparative Literature at Columbia University from

1930 to 1945.[101] In 1942, he founded the *Comparative Lit-erature Newsletter*, which was designed as an organ of the above-mentioned committee. Political viewpoints also played their part, as is evidenced by President Roosevelt's letter (referring to the so-called liberal arts colleges as a "mainspring of liberal thought throughout the country"), in the first issue of the new journal, which also included Pearl Buck's remarks on "The Values of Literature."

Christy's journal ran for four years (1942–1946) and thirty issues, but never really developed into a vital outlet in spite of the interest evinced by its academic readers.[102] Besides short monographic contributions on the history of Comparative Literature in America and commentaries on its present state and future prospects, the *Newsletter*'s hec-tographed pages also contain articles laying the foundation for the editor's grandly conceived bibliographical hand-book, described as follows by one of Christy's associates:

The following notes represent the beginning of our attempt to plan a guide to comparative and 'world' literature. We believe that this guide should first of all be of use to college teachers whose teaching or study must cross national boundaries. Supposing a person trained to teach one body of literature who now needs to explore another literary region, these notes suggest the first serious guides to the new study. I present in each case 1) the name of a standard study of the specific literature or literary region; 2) the name of a standard work of bibliographical reference to translations of the literature into English; 3) the names of current surveys of scholarship in the literature, the number of which seems to increase steadily. The various literatures are classified by countries, by periods, by international relationships.[103]

In the first issue of the third volume (pp. 1–10) of the *Newsletter*, a detailed plan for the organization and struc-ture of this joint undertaking was presented, along with a provisional list of the associates. This plan was not carried out at the time; in fact, until very recently a guide to world literature for use by high school teachers was the only project completed on behalf of the committee of the National Council of Teachers of English.[104] Since 1967, three volumes of a five-volume set of bibliographies entitled "The Literatures of the World in English Translation" have appeared under the general editorship of G. B. Parks: *The Greek and Latin Literatures*, *The Slavic Literatures*, and *The Romance Literatures* (all published by Frederick Ungar in New York).

With Christy's death in 1946, the *Comparative Literature Newsletter* ceased publication; in the meantime, however, a stalwart champion of Comparative Literature arose in the person of Werner Paul Friederich, a native Swiss who had settled in America and taken his doctorate at Harvard University. Since 1936, Friederich, now retired, taught at the University of North Carolina, where a department of Comparative Literature has existed since 1925, though without a faculty of its own.[105] In 1945, he published the essay "The Case of Comparative Literature," previously referred to, which offers a detailed plan for the reform of academic curricula. In the years to come, this article frequently was to serve as a basis for discussion.[106]

Friederich's plans for reform were by no means exclusively gauged to the University of North Carolina, but were relevant to the entire academic community. The author was far-sighted enough to recognize the necessity of creating a broad organizational framework. Thanks to Friederich's initiative, in 1948 the seven existing "Comparative Literature Groups" of the Modern Language Association (Prose Fiction, Popular Literature, Arthurian Literature, Renaissance, Anglo-French, Anglo-German, and Franco-German) were placed under the umbrella of a section.[107] Friederich also developed a four-point program, which was realized, in quick succession, within the course of a decade. Only when these obligations had been met did he yield the reins in order to make room for the next generation.

In 1949, the first issue of the journal *Comparative Literature* was published at the University of Oregon; in 1950 the Baldensperger–Friederich *Bibliography of Comparative*

Literature appeared at the University of North Carolina; and in 1952 the first volume of the *Yearbook of Comparative and General Literature,* "an organ in which the practical aspects of our calling could be analyzed and constantly re-examined," was issued. The initial program of this yearbook was outlined in the following terms by its founder and editor:

The present Yearbook, . . . while not accepting research articles on literary problems per se, opens its pages wide to all comparatists who wish to discuss such problems as the scope and the task of Comparative Literature, the teaching of Great Books courses, the difficulties encountered in achieving interdepartmental collaboration or in choosing the most suitable texts or the best available translations, the delineation (if any) of Comparative, General, and World Literature, the administrative technical problems involved in setting up the necessary curricula for an international study of literature, and so forth.[108]

The year 1954 saw the publication of Friederich's *Outline of Comparative Literature from Dante to O'Neill,* co-authored with David H. Malone; and in the same year the International Comparative Literature Association was founded in Oxford. Its second congress was appropriately held in Chapel Hill, the seat of the University of North Carolina.

As already indicated, the late 1950's witnessed an important development in the history of American Comparative Literature. Haskell M. Block (trained at the Sorbonne) had suggested the creation of a national association, the ACLA, which was founded in 1960 as a branch of the ICLA. Today the American branch has three hundred members, who can proudly look back on the four triennial conventions which have been held to date (New York in 1962; Cambridge, Massachusetts, in 1965; Bloomington, Indiana, in 1968; and New Haven, Connecticut, in 1971).[109] Its official organ is a newsletter entitled ACLAN, which, founded in 1965, has appeared somewhat sporadically. It was temporarily revived by W. B. Fleischmann and is now edited by

Herbert Weisinger and by the Secretariat of the ACLA at the State University of New York in Binghamton.

After Yale University (1948) and Indiana University (1952) had started the postwar boom, a six-year interval ensued, after which Comparative Literature began to flourish anew. Almost every prestigious graduate school, including Stanford and Princeton, has, by now, acknowledged the trend; and each academic year brings good tidings about the founding of new Comparative Literature departments and programs. According to a survey published in Volume Twenty (1971) of the *Yearbook of Comparative and General Literature*, there are at present over seventy degree-granting programs in the United States, with, roughly, 2500 students pursuing Bachelor's degrees, Master's degrees or Doctorates in our field. Numerically, the University of California (Berkeley) leads the fray with 175 graduate majors, followed by New York University with 165 and Indiana University with 120.

There is also, at present, no dearth of scholarly journals in our field. In 1963, the quarterly *Comparative Literature Studies* was founded at the University of Maryland; since 1967, it has been published at the University of Illinois. In the editor's brief preface to a special advance issue of this magazine, we encounter the statement: "*Comparative Literature Studies* . . . will feature articles on literary history and the history of ideas, with particular emphasis on European literary relations with both North and South America." The first five volumes of the journal reveal, however, that by no means all of the articles accepted for publication represent *littérature comparée* in the proper sense. For instance, one entire issue surveys the present state of literary criticism in the nations of Europe and America, while another explores the interrelationship between literature and religion, and a third the mutual illumination of the arts. *CLS*'s orientation toward *Geistesgeschichte*, one assumes, may be partly due to the fact that it was at Johns Hopkins University in Baltimore (Maryland) that A. O. Lovejoy introduced the "History of Ideas."

For about five years now, the journal *Comparative Drama* has been published by Western Michigan University; but, qualitatively, its content leaves something to be desired. Also, at the end of 1967, *Genre*, a magazine, which, for obvious reasons, is mainly concerned with genological questions, made its debut in Chicago. At the December, 1967, meeting of the Modern Language Association, its editors sponsored a symposium, to which I have referred in Chapter Five. Attention should also be drawn to the recently founded journal *New Literary History*, which is edited by Professor Ralph Cohen at the University of Virginia. It promises to become one of the leading periodicals in the field of literary theory and historiography.

In 1962, the first English-language collection of essays on Comparative Literature was published. A second, revised and expanded edition appeared in 1971 under the title *Comparative Literature: Method and Perspective*.[110] The book contains a series of articles on pedagogy and methodology, whose authors, with one exception, teach or taught at Indiana University and have contributed lectures to an introductory course for graduate students in the field. At the close of 1967, a companion piece to the books of Van Tieghem and Guyard, Jan Brandt Corstius' *Introduction to the Comparative Study of Literature*, made its appearance. Unfortunately, this otherwise useful survey does not really meet the strict demands to be placed on such a manual; for its emphasis lies primarily on the history of literature and literary criticism, and its treatment of our specialty revolves primarily around the concepts of tradition and convention. Questions of method, which are neither directly nor indirectly related to this approach, are briefly touched upon in his Chapter Six, entitled "Some Concepts Basic to the Study of Comparative Literature." *Comparative Literature: Matter and Method* (University of Illinois Press, 1969), on the other hand, is a collection of essays originally published in *CLS*, rather than a comprehensively systematic introduction to our field. *Comparatists at Work,* edited by Stephen G. Nichols, Jr., and R. B. Vowles (Waltham, Mass.: Blaisdell, 1968), contains an assortment of essays, only one of which—Wellek's "The Name and Nature of Comparative Literature"—directly relates to the theory or history of Comparative Literature.

4. *England*

In England, according to F. C. Roe, systematic literary historiography was initiated, at the beginning of Queen Victoria's reign, with Henry Hallam's *Introduction to the Literature of Europe in the 15th, 16th and 17th Centuries.*[111] In the preface to the first edition of his book, the author offers a brief survey of the history of such undertakings, which, as did Max Koch, he traces back to Daniel Georg Morhof. Hallam weighs the advantages of the method he has chosen and arrives at the conclusion:

The advantages of such a synoptical view of literature as displays its various departments in their simultaneous condition through an extensive period and in their mutual dependency seem too manifest to be disputed. And since we possess little of this kind in our own language, I have been induced to undertake that to which I am, in some respects at least, very unequal, but which no more capable person, so far as I could judge, was likely to perform.[112]

Adhering to polyhistorical custom, Hallam did not at all restrict himself to belletristic literature, but discussed philosophical, legal, medical, and even theological writings, as well.[113]

The term "comparative literature," an adaptation of the French *littérature comparée,* was apparently coined by Matthew Arnold a decade after the publication of Hallam's *Introduction.* Arnold persistently pleaded for the untrammeled study of literature, and thus became a veritable midwife to our discipline in England. L. A. Willoughby reports

that Arnold took the expression from his unfinished translation of Jean-Jacques Ampère's *Histoire comparative*, but
I have not succeeded in substantiating this claim.[114] As far
as I know, Ampère wrote no work of that name: and Willoughby's remarks are suspect to the Arnold specialists I
have consulted. Yet, in May, 1848, Arnold wrote to his
sister: "How plain it is now, though an attention to the
comparative literatures for the last fifty years might have
instructed any one of it, that England is in a certain sense
far behind the continent."[115]

The strongest impulse yet for Comparative Literature in
England was furnished by a book published in 1886 by a
lawyer turned professor of classical philology and English
literature at the University College in Auckland, New
Zealand: *Comparative Literature*, written by Hutcheson
Macaulay Posnett, was the first comprehensive methodological survey of the field, so labeled, in any language.
Symptomatically, the work appeared as Volume 54 of the
International Scientific Series, which included, among
other books, Herbert Spencer's *The Study of Sociology* and
Théodoule Ribot's *Diseases of Memory* in an English version. Posnett's monographic study was directly preceded
by Robert Hartmann's *Anthropoid Apes* (Volume 52) and
Otto Schmidt's *The Mammalia in Their Relation to Pri-
meval Times*.[116]

Posnett, who introduces himself as a disciple of the ju-
rist Sir Henry Maine, regarded literary history as a branch
of sociology, which is hardly surprising for a child of the
age of positivism.[117] He described his method as an "application of historical science to literature" and condemned
(in a retrospective essay written fifteen years later) the
"unhistorical" trend, represented by literary criticism and
theory. He declared war on the "literary specialists, champions of the old and unhistorical criticism, and many ama-
teur critics who are content to echo the sentiments of the
old school without inquiry" (p. 856), and loudly proclaimed: "While fully recognizing the hopeful prospects
of Comparative Literature, especially in Germany, France,

and America, I must confess a desire to see the study less exclusively in the hands of literary men" (p. 866).

One is sorely tempted to blame Posnett for broadcasting views which, in the meantime, have been corrected by history itself; but one must not forget that, in spite of his plea for accuracy and objectivity, the author of *Comparative Literature* did not wish the discipline he had adumbrated to be mistaken for an offshoot of natural science rigidly conceived. In this way, he differed from Zola, who had stubbornly maintained that even in products of the human mind and the human imagination the iron law of causality is at work: "Once it has been proved that the human body is a machine whose cogs can be dismantled and reassembled as the scientist sees fit, it will be time to pass on to Man's emotional and intellectual acts."[118]

In an essay published in 1901, Posnett expressly warned against a mechanical application of scientific laws, which he regarded as no more than "a brief summary of a vast number of observed and recorded facts" (p. 857). When speaking of "social evolution, individual evolution, and the influence of environment" as the most important factors in the comparative study of literature, he alleged, one must not imply "that these 'laws' possess some mysterious authority over the literary world."

Comparative Literature as conceived and defined by Posnett relies less on the influence of "climate, soil, animal and plant life" than on the study of social development "from communal to individual life" (*Comparative Literature*, p. 20). Its special task is the reconstruction of the development leading from the ordering principle of the clan to those of the municipal, national, and universal culture: "We therefore adopt, with a modification hereafter to be noticed, the gradual expansion of social life, from clan to city, from city to nation, from both of these to cosmopolitan humanity, as the proper order of our studies in comparative literature" (Ibid., p. 86).

Today we regard Posnett's views as untenable, if only for the reason that for him Comparative Literature was

not necessarily supranational. The British scholar even
went so far as to call the study of international literary
relations a mere border area of Comparative Literature,
because he felt that in pursuing foreign influences gradual
evolution within a given cultural sphere would be ignored:
"The cases of Rome and Russia are enough to prove that
external influences, carried beyond a certain point, may
convert literature from the growth of the group to which
it belongs into a mere exotic, deserving of scientific study
only as an artificial production indirectly dependent on
social life" (*Comparative Literature*, p. 83). Here, the ghost
of Taine is walking abroad, destroying one's faith in Comparative Literature; for the stranglehold of *race, milieu,*
and *moment* "firmly anchors its victim in national waters
and does not permit him to drift out into the more international seas."[119] Taine's followers apparently did not realize that pearls are foreign bodies within the oyster.

The comparatist's real concern, Posnett maintained, is
pinned to the internal development of the various national
literatures as an expression of their social progress: "National literature has been developed from within as well
as influenced from without; and the comparative study of
this internal development is of far greater interest than
that of the external, because the former is less a matter of
imitation and more an evolution directly dependent on
social and physical causes" (p. 81). The study of this phenomenon is comparative, in Posnett's view, only to the
extent that different stages of a development can be simultaneously observed in a cross-section of the contemporary
life of a nation. The comparative study of national and
international phenomena thus basically involves the drawing of parallels between normally progressing, temporarily
interrupted, and retrogressive historical processes.

In his essay "The Science of Comparative Literature,"
Posnett once more emphasized that, as far as he was concerned, "comparative" was synonymous with "historical,"
but that the former term had the advantage of being applicable to spatially as well as temporally separated levels:

What, then, is the method of Comparative Literature? What is
the method of studying literary facts which leads us to recognize
a literary science? It is a method for which no single name as yet
exists. From the standpoint of time we call it 'historical,' from
other standpoints we call it 'comparative.' The name
'comparative' is, on the whole, the better name; because we often
find existing at the same time, and even in the same country,
types of social and individual life ranging from very low to very
high degrees of evolution. (p. 864)

Posnett was not particularly pleased with the term "comparative literature," which Arnold had put into circulation
and which he himself was the first to systematically apply.
Since there was no English word corresponding to the
German *Literaturwissenschaft,* he found himself compelled "to make the name of the subject-matter do duty
for the uncoined name of the study of the subject-matter"
(p. 856). Saintsbury overlooks this self-imposed stricture
when accusing Posnett of using "a very awkward phrase,
neither really representing *littérature comparée* nor really
analogous to 'Comparative Anatomy.' 'Comparative Study
of Literature' would be better; otherwise, 'Comparative
Criticism' or 'Rhetoric' is wanted."[120] This objection has
often been raised by friends and foes of our discipline; but
it is clear by now that we must live with the awkward term
as an ineradicable *fait accompli.*

Saintsbury himself, who—"for the usual reasons," most
likely because it was not critically oriented—bluntly refused to treat Posnett's book in his history of literary criticism, willingly opted for "Comparative Literature": "I have
never myself, since I began to study literature seriously
almost forty years ago, had the slightest doubt about its
being not only the *vita prima* but also the *vita sola* of
literary safety."[121] On the basis of both his three-volume
A History of Criticism and the projected twelve-volume
series of monographs on *Periods of European Literature,*
Saintsbury must undoubtedly be regarded as one of the
ranking European comparatists of his age; among his contemporaries, only Georg Brandes approaches him in stat-

ure.[122] Posnett, by the way, was one of the first scholars to express the need for a large-scale synoptic study of European literature—conceived along his own lines, of course —such as is currently being prepared under the auspices of the ICLA.[123]

The period of comparative literary historiography ushered in by Hallam ended with Sir Sidney Lee's book *The French Renaissance in England: An Account of the Literary Relations of England and France in the Sixteenth Century*, which had been preceded by an English version of Loliée's previously mentioned *Historie comparative* . . . . [124] In his preface, Lee states that he hopes "to have succeeded in bringing home . . . the interest attaching to that comparative study of European literature, on which I have sought to lift a corner of the curtain" (p. v), and confirms that the comparative study of literature "has been pursued in this country on a smaller scale and less systematically than abroad. Yet the comparative study of literature is to my thinking a needful complement of those philological and aesthetic studies which chiefly occupy the attention of English scholars."

Before turning to the academic side of Comparative Literature studies on John Bull's Island—a task facilitated by various recent developments—a brief comment is due on two unusually interesting essays by G. Gregory Smith. In the first, published anonymously, "The Foible of Comparative Literature" (1901), that author reviewed the results of the previously mentioned Paris Congress of Historians. After rejecting the viewpoints represented by Brunetière and Gaston Paris, which he later denounced as "bibliographical," he offered what at that time was a bold conception of Comparative Literature, and which remained unsurpassed in some of its radical implications until the appearance of Etiemble's book. Among other things, Gregory Smith wished to see Comparative Literature applied to a horizontal, rather than a vertical, cross-section of European or world literature: "Is not [Brunetière's] analysis exclusively 'perpendicular' in effect, whereas, if there is any general value in the term 'comparative,' it should be horizontal'?" (p. 43).[125] This was an important step away from pure nineteenth-century historicism.

Smith went so far as to bypass historical positivism and to expand his definition of Comparative Literature to the point of including the study of parallelisms. In doing so, he dismissed, from the outset, the "classic" views subsequently espoused by Van Tieghem and Guyard: "May there not be a comparative interest in things whose only connection is from analogy, or even in forms and motives, between which there may be not only no admitted or known connection, but not even an obvious hint of likeness?" (p. 45). Lastly, the English critic—fifteen years before Oskar Walzel!!—pondered the inclusion of the study of the mutual illumination of the arts: "Whether the different arts have, or do not have, a common aesthetic basis, is a question which need not prevent our discovering certain analogies or using one art as a touchstone for the others; and we may do so without being convicted of the quackery of the symphony-in-blue journalism." All of these calls went, naturally, unheeded.

In an essay published four years later and entitled "Some Notes on the Comparative Study of Literature," Gregory Smith returned to the subject of the Paris Congress and advocated the replacement of orthodox comparative studies by literary criticism: "If instead of the connexion between individual books or phases we substitute the connexion and development of critical ideas, we have at once greater possibilities for the comparative student" (p. 4).[126] By means of this shift, he hoped to bring about a reorientation of Comparative Literature, with emphasis to be placed on "the unity of literature rather than the differences, or, let us say, the unity in the differences" (p. 5).

As for the academic viability of Comparative Literature in England, it should be stated that, for reasons still to be

elucidated, internal and external obstacles were constantly
being placed in its way. As R. A. Sayce has recently noted:
". . . It must be admitted that comparative literature meets
with resistance, and the slowness of British universities (in
contrast to American and continental universities) in taking up the subject is one instance."[127] Sayce singles out
two circumstances as being chiefly responsible for this de-
plorable state of affairs: the positivistic rigor of the French
comparatists, on the one hand, and the presence of linguistic barriers, such as are immaterial to the art or music
historian, on the other. In the academic sphere, these walls
are symbolized by the departmentalization of the various
philologies, as at Oxford, for example, "where barriers between faculties are fairly rigid."

English skepticism toward Comparative Literature has
still other, far more deeply ingrained causes, however. For
one, I would consider it significant that—at least in the
nineteenth century—the English student of *humaniores
litterae* was a comparatist by implication, since he was
versed in ancient letters and knew how to measure his
native literature by the standards which Antiquity provided. As a separate discipline, however, Comparative Literature flourishes only where a knowledge of Greek and
Latin is no longer taken for granted, such as in places
where the classics are no longer a basic part of education.

Chairs of modern languages, primarily English, were not
instituted in England until the latter part of the nineteenth
century, and were originally considered to be stepchildren
of classical philology. Henry Gifford, for example, reports
that "not long since, at Oxford a moratorium used to fall
after the year 1830," which is to say that only those literary
works written prior to that relatively distant date were
deemed worthy of scholarly inquiry.[128] Only after the turn
of the century were departments specializing in the study
of the modern foreign languages (German, French, Italian,
etc.) created, and the basis for comparative studies within
the context of academic life established. "Until the opening years of the century," says Roe (*YCGL*, 3, [1954], p. 7),

comparative literature did not find a place among subjects recognized in the Faculties of Arts. At that time, when several university institutions in the United Kingdom received their charters as universities, some chairs of Modern Languages were created; before the end of World War I these numbered thirty-one, nearly all of them Chairs of French or German.

Willoughby, who confesses that he first heard the term "comparative literature" in 1904 from the lips of J. G. Robertson, reports that the latter served from 1896 to 1903 as an Associate Professor at Strasbourg (where Betz was teaching), and that if Robertson had decided to remain on the continent, he would probably have become Betz's successor (*Forschungsprobleme*, I, p. 2). In England, such a career was not open to him at the time; for Comparative Literature was not "officially" recognized there until 1921—the year in which the *Revue de littérature comparée* was founded—when Fernand Baldensperger gave eight lectures on eighteenth-century European literature at the University College of Aberystwyth in Wales. At the time Eric Partridge published his *Critical Medley: Essays, Studies and Notes in Comparative Literature* in 1926, he was living in Paris. Like Posnett and Betz before him, he, too, vainly called for the creation of chairs in Comparative Literature in his homeland.

The most recent phase in the history of Comparative Literature in England is slightly more exhilarating. During the years 1942–1946, for instance, twenty-four issues of a journal entitled *Comparative Literature Studies* were published at the University of Cardiff. This magazine was intended as a temporary substitute for the *Révue de littérature comparée*, which had ceased publication during the German occupation, and functioned under the aegis of the French government in exile. Willoughby (*Forschungsprobleme*, I, p. 28) considers it fitting "that precisely . . . at the hem of the Celtic world, under the auspices of the French Consul for West England and of the authors Walter de la Mare and Hugh Walpole, a new undertaking was begun: *Comparative Literature Studies*, directed by Marcel

Chicoteau and Kenneth Unwin." The editors outlined the
following goals:

This new series of studies embodies the work and research of
British scholars interested in the interrelationship of European
language and literature. Published in book form, these studies are
available from time to time, and all centres of intellectual
understanding in this country are earnestly asked to give their
whole-hearted support to this war-time literary endeavor. No
such publication has previously existed in Britain.

In the sixteenth issue, following a declaration issued by
the French Cultural Mission to England, the journal announced its intention of staying alive, even though the
Revue de littérature comparée had already resumed publication. However, this plan was unfortunately abandoned
after only one year.

From 1948 to 1951, students at the University of Aber-
deen (Scotland) operated a Society for Comparative Literature; and in 1953, Britain's first lectureship in Comparative
Literature was instituted at Manchester. This brave action
was followed by the creation of a chair at the University
of Essex, a step which illustrated the tendency of those
English brick universities established in the sixties to set
up interdisciplinary programs in an effort to break with
the autonomous "Oxbridge" tradition, much as the universities at Constance and Bochum are breaking with
many hallowed German academic traditions. In the Com-
monwealth countries (with the sole exception of Canada),
similar tendencies are scarcely discernible.[129]

In the fall of 1964, the Faculty of Medieval and Modern
Languages at Oxford University finally took the initiative
and approved a "course in general and comparative literature."[130] Candidates for the Bachelor of Philology degree
are asked to specialize in two or three national literatures
and have to present a thesis of roughly eighty pages, as
well as three seminar papers (one each on literary theory
and criticism, on questions of methodology, and on one of
twenty selected comparative topics). The first Doctorate in

Comparative Literature at Oxford was awarded in 1968. The ice thus apparently has been broken even at the tradition-bound universities; and it is to be hoped that England will finally emerge from its splendid isolation and play a more active role in the ICLA, in which to date it has been represented by such outstanding individuals as Roger A. Shackleton and A. M. Boase. In the last few years, however, Comparative Literature seems to have bogged down academically, since British scholars adamantly refuse to commit themselves as to matters of method. Thus neither Henry Gifford's *Comparative Literature* nor C. L. Wrenn's *The Idea of Comparative Literature* can be regarded as scientifically viable introductions to the discipline, for both pamphlets—they are little more than that —are much too "impressionistic" to be useful. And as of 1972, the Chair of Comparative Literature at the University of Manchester is vacant, the incumbent having left the British Isles for academically greener shores.

5. *Italy*

In his essay "La letteratura mondiale" (1946), the Italian scholar L. F. Benedetto sadly concluded that his and his contemporaries' childhood dream of the future blossoming of Comparative Literature in their homeland had not come true: "Reality has not lived up to our childhood dreams, as we had hoped, for the urgently desired synthesis has not been achieved. Comparative Literature has not attained—in view of the traditional disciplines and, generally, in the eyes of the public, especially in Italy—that high and unquestionable respect which it merits in our opinion."[131] The fact that, so far, Italian scholars have devoted themselves only sporadically and without much enthusiasm to Comparative Literature is attributable above all to the pervasive influence of Croce, who at the beginning of the twentieth century denied it the right to establish itself as an independent, methodologically sound academic discipline.

In point of fact, even today Italy cannot boast of any separate, autonomous chairs of Comparative Literature; yet "comparative" scholarship—primarily directed at the interaction between Italian and Anglo-Saxon literature— is by no means dead.[132] One need only recall the extensive historico-critical output of the Roman anglicist Mario Praz, now retired.[133] The contemporary Italian scholar Benedetto described the state of affairs quite accurately when he wrote:

Even if chairs were not increased to the extent desired, at least within the individual philological specialties chairs for the most important foreign literatures have been established. They may be regarded as adequate substitutes. The teachers of foreign languages and literatures, especially at the Italian universities, have therefore been, almost without exception, excellent comparatists. (p. 133)

A high point in these efforts on the part of the modern philologies represented at Italian universities was reached with the publication of the volume *Letterature comparate*, edited by Attilio Momigliano. This work offers a systematic survey covering the history of the relationships between Italian literature on one hand and Provençal, French, Spanish, German, Scandinavian, and Greco-Roman (as well as Italian dialect) literature, on the other. However, it does not specifically concern itself with the current state and the tasks of Comparative Literature. The book is the final volume in a series of studies devoted to the history of Italian literature and seeks to determine the latter's international ambience. Momigliano's brief introduction closes with the remark that it is the aim of this collective effort not only to broaden the perspective of university students, but also to afford high-school teachers the possibility of introducing world literature to their pupils.[134] (We might mention, in passing, that only in France and Italy—and recently in the United States and Germany— have academically affiliated comparatists paid attention to secondary school education. Antonio Porta, for instance, devotes an entire chapter of his monograph *La letteratura comparata nella storia e nella critica* to the "teaching of Comparative Literature" at Italian high schools.[135]

The history of Comparative Literature in Italy is rather erratic and hard to reduce to a simple pattern; but let us, nonetheless, briefly review it. Just as Goethe's concept of *Weltliteratur* stands at the beginning of modern Franco-German attempts aimed at establishing a supranational conception of European literature, Giuseppi Mazzini's advocacy of a *letteratura europea* or *letteratura dei popoli* lies at the root of similar efforts in Italy. Mazzini broached his views in the essay "Concerning a European Literature," which appeared in 1829 in the Florentine journal *Antologia*. Here we read: "In Europe there prevails a unity of desires and needs, a common thought, a universal soul, which will lead the nations along similar paths to the same goal. Accordingly, literary scholarship, if it does not wish to become sterile, must embrace this trend, express it, and support it: the study of literature must become European."

Mazzini's essentially Romantic ideal of a European literature resting on a national basis, and of an appropriate pan-European historiography, fell far short of being realized; for, following the triumph of positivism in the second quarter of the century, the idealism of the preceding generation quickly waned. During that period an awakening Italian journalism also surfaced, whose fervor increased and thus delayed the birth of pan-Europeanism by many decades. Franco Simone depicts the Italian situation after 1848 as follows:

> Following the crisis of 1848, Italian culture no longer afforded to the aspirations of the Risorgimento the resources, which formerly, on the path toward national unity and regeneration, had moved the thought and directed the action of so many

worthy men. Having attained by way of reaction a crude sort of positivism, and repudiating the leading ideas of the past, the new Italian culture proceeded to form a naturalistic vision of reality and to study, accordingly, only material facts.[136]

In Comparative Literature, this emphasis on "facts" produced a phenomenon corresponding to the thematological approach of a Max Koch or Gaston Paris in the so-called Turin School, founded and initially headed by Arturo Graf.[137] It is no accident that a product of this school provoked Croce's massive attack on comparative thematology.

Academically, the bell for Comparative Literature in Italy was sounded in 1861, when, in his capacity as Minister of Public Instruction, the leading historian of the second half of the century, Francesco De Sanctis, created a chair of comparative literary history at the University of Naples. Its first occupant was to have been the young German writer Georg Herwegh, who did not accept this honorable appointment, however. The chair thus remained vacant until De Sanctis himself occupied it from 1871 to 1875; after a long interval he was succeeded but not replaced by his chief assistant, Francesco Torraca. Torraca's appointment was confirmed in the same year in which Croce, in his newly founded journal, La Critica, was preparing to throttle the life out of "old style" Comparative Literature.

But what about De Sanctis' views concerning Comparative Literature? Unfortunately, this question cannot be satisfactorily answered, partly because De Sanctis (like many another Italian literary historian)[138] neither was, nor wanted to be, a systematic thinker. Although he was strongly influenced by Hegel, he abhorred all systems and repeatedly called himself a pragmatist.[139] This did not prevent him, however, from making theoretical pronouncements on literary matters.

From today's standpoint, it seems paradoxical that the "father" of Comparative Literature in Italy devoted his main work (the Storia della letteratura italiana) solely to a survey of his native literature. For him, it was an indisputable fact that one could grasp the spirit of a national literature only by deeply immersing oneself in its historical, geographical, sociological, and cultural context: "It is one of my duties to record what happens to the Italian mind, for literature lives only when it is grounded in a vital spirit" (quoted from Porta, p. 66).

There is a surfeit of paradoxes in the life and work of De Sanctis. For example, he insisted, on the one hand, on the self-sufficiency of the work of art, but was constantly referring to historical-sociological phenomena, on the other. One can easily see how profoundly indebted Croce's theory of pure expression was to De Sanctis' example when one comes across the following observation: "A work can resemble another work in this point or that, but it is, first and foremost, its own model." Elsewhere De Sanctis wrote: "The common features will never furnish any insight into the specific character of a work, since that character is not expressed in those things which the work shares with the century, the school or its predecessors, but is solely expressed in its uniqueness and in that which cannot be transferred."[140]

These views originate with the same man whose working hypothesis has been defined thus: "It is frequently said, that De Sanctis was a moralist who suppressed the objective study of Italian history; actually De Sanctis always envisaged his goal: namely, that the history of a literature can be nothing other than the moral history of the nation that has produced that literature."[141]

If we apply to Comparative Literature De Sanctis' general theory—pieced together from his scattered remarks— we discover that the Italian scholar believed that comparisons were meaningful only within a national tradition (for example, between Dante and Boccaccio, or between Tasso and Ariosto), because only here a unified frame of reference is present. He sharply condemned, on the other hand, the study of mere parallels (analogies), whether thematic or relating to literary characters, both within a single lit-

erature (as with Saint-Marc Girardin's comparison of Corneille's Horace and Victor Hugo's Triboulet) and on an
international scope (as with Schlegel's treatise on the two
Phaedras).[142] He despised "the art of rebaptizing an individual by giving him the name of another" and warned
his colleagues:

You must examine things as they are in themselves,
individually, and not with the aid of more or less distant, external
relations. This kind of criticism based on relations and parallels
has the same effect as antitheses and conceits: it impresses us,
surprises us, and may please us as well; but not for long, for we
soon discover its hollowness.[143]

In the history of Comparative Literature, then, the role
of De Sanctis fluctuates, for this scholar, abhorring the
polar extremes of analogy studies and thematological positivism, at the same time scorned the golden mean—the
study of reciprocal supranational influences. Italian comparatism, had it followed his example, would unquestion-
ably have reached a dead end. The representatives of the
Turin School, however, were little concerned by the critique levelled against them by their Neapolitan colleague,
and continued to pay tribute to the spirit of historiographic
positivism. Arturo Graf, for instance, considered it his
most urgent task to discover "not variants and mutations,
but conformities and constants." He was emulated by
Simone Pucci in Genoa, who, in 1880, expounded the
Principi di letteratura generale italiana e comparata, as
well as by Cesare de Lollis, Pietro Toldo, the young Arturo
Farinelli, and Torraca.

It was left to Benedetto Croce to replace the inconsis-
tent, and at times contradictory views of his predecessor
De Sanctis, with a monolithic conception that was openly
hostile to the institution of Comparative Literature. On
various occasions and in different ways, Croce dealt our
discipline such decisive blows that he almost completely
atomized it in the process. To do him justice, however,
one must consider that in principle his rejection, based on

a solid theoretical foundation, by no means excluded the practical use of comparative methods—at any rate, not as early as the 1890's. Indeed, one of the leading experts on Croce, Gian N. Orsini, argues persuasively: "[Croce] was a comparatist all his life. He started early, evidently inspired by the nineteenth-century interest in comparative studies, and in his twenties (1892–1894) investigated the literary, intellectual, and social relations between Italy and Spain from the Middle Ages to the end of the eighteenth century."[144]

By 1894, however, Croce was beset by doubts. In an essay dating from that year, he stated that the search for parallels "is not a self-sufficient activity but only one of the forms which the interpretation and evaluation of literary works may take from time to time."[145] And at the age of twenty-seven he called the comparative method "a simple instrument of historical research" aimed at "establishing larger contexts" by integrating transmitted evidence with the aid of similar or parallel, but more perfect, examples.[146]

Croce's first direct confrontation with Comparative Literature took place shortly after 1900, in connection with Woodberry's *Journal of Comparative Literature* and Koch's *Studien zur vergleichenden Litteraturgeschichte*. On August 27, 1902, the young historian wrote to Vossler:

You may have learned from [Joel] Spingarn that a journal for Comparative Literature will be published in New York. Spingarn has written me to request an article. I cannot understand how a specialty can be made out of comparative literature. The journal, edited by Max Koch, should serve as a warning. Any serious literary investigation, any exhaustive critical study needs to be comparative, that is, it presupposes the knowledge of the work's historical context within world literature.[147]

The crucial point here is the recognition that comparison is not only a common and convenient but also an indispensable instrument of literary study and can, therefore, never be the cornerstone of a separate discipline. This issue also crops up in a brief article published in the first volume of *La Critica*, entitled "La letteratura comparata," where Croce discusses Koch's definition of the subject.[148] At the outset, he vigorously asserts: "Comparative Literature uses the *comparative method*. By its very nature as a simple research tool, the comparative method cannot lay claim to delimiting an entire field of specialization" (p. 77).

As for the research methods praised by Koch, they were, in Croce's view, "only the hallmarks of erudition and unsuited for organic interpretation." They do not aim, he continued, "at allowing us to understand a literary work, they do not permit us to get to the heart of the artistic creation." Nor can it be their intention to determine "the aesthetic genesis of a literary work" or the truly "creative moment."[149] Instead, Croce maintains, this method focuses on "the external history of the finished work (scandals, translations, imitations, etc.), or on a segment of the *Stoff* which contributed to its genesis (literary tradition). . . ." Comparative Literature, in his view, was desirable only when—as Spingarn had urged in his brief contribution to the Paris Congress—it aimed at an historical-aesthetic analysis (say, in the form of a history of world literature) (p. 80).

In the following year, Croce fixed his sights on an aspect of Comparative Literature that was particularly dear to the positivists: thematology or *Stoffgeschichte*.[150] The comparison of different treatments of the same subject, he felt, proceeded from a false premise, for Voltaire's *Sophonisbe* had actually nothing in common with Trissino's or Alfieri's. Insofar as each writer makes the theme he has chosen his own and assimilates it to himself, one cannot speak of influences in the narrow sense:

When criticism, for its part, uses Sophonisbe as the basis from which to proceed in the examination of those works, it only repeats the error of those poets who sang *invita Minerva*. . . . When the persons and the theme have received new life through the writer's imagination, that new life is the true character and the true plot; if they have not, what may be of interest is the—

perhaps sterile—attempt to inspire new life, but not an alleged
skill or the presumably ideal way in which the theme could have
been treated. (p. 486)

"The lion is assimilated lamb," said Paul Valéry; and
Goethe had something similar in mind when he told Ek-
kermann: "One might just as well ask a stout man about
the cows, the sheep, and the pigs he has eaten and which
have given him his strength."[151] Croce wholeheartedly endorsed this view. When speaking of influences, he felt, one
was referring to literature (letteratura), and not to "poesy"
(poesia); only ideas, however—the raw material of "poesy"
—can be transplanted from one work, country, or language
to another.[152] For this reason, he also assigned no value to
translations, since these are bound to be defective.

Even with the total rejection of thematology and all literary and historical studies operating with the notion of
influence, Croce's arsenal of weapons leveled against Comparative Literature as a scholarly discipline was by no
means exhausted. Reference should also be made to his
negative assessment of genology, an antipathy already
clearly evident in De Sanctis. Seen in light of Croce's plea
for autonomy, the setting of individual works into the
frame of a firm tradition of preformed literary models must
seem an exercise in futility. For in this way no decisive
statements can be made about the value of a drama, a
novel, an epic, or a poem. And, finally, according to Croce's repeatedly expressed opinion, "the influence of a
writer on a foreign literature is properly a part of the latter
and not of the history of the former."[153] This was a view
shared, as we have seen, by Julius Petersen.

It would be foolish, however, to assert that Croce consistently refused to compare the artistic monads whose
self-sufficiency he so emphatically stressed, for around
1920, he concluded, surprisingly enough, that the only true
literary history was that of the literary personality, the living core of creative dynamism. The historian Croce thus
struck a compromise with the aesthetician: "The true logi-

cal form of literary and art history," we read in an essay, "The Reform of Literary and Art History," cited by Orsini "is the characterization of the single artist and his work and the corresponding expository form is the essay or the monograph."[154] As Franco Simone confirms in his survey of Comparative Literature in Italy, this view gave rise subsequently to a series of monographic studies initiated by Croce's book on Goethe (1918).

In turning to what happened in Croce's wake in Italian literary scholarship, I think it proper to mention the "conversion" of Arturo Farinelli, the most important Italian comparatist in the first half of the twentieth century—a man whose name is equally well known in the German-speaking world. Farinelli taught at Innsbruck from 1896 to 1904 and published such studies as *Deutschlands und Spaniens literarische Beziehungen* (1892–1895) and *Grillparzer und Lope de Vega* (1894). In 1904, he accepted an appointment at the University of Turin, where he began to devote himself increasingly to the study of *littérature générale*. In 1916, he published a monograph on the theme *La vita e un sogno*, followed, in 1924, by a study called *Byron e il Byronismo*. Farinelli steeped himself in the Romantic literature of Germany, Spain, Italy, and France. His turn to studies on individual authors occurred rather abruptly, around 1925. In an essay entitled "Il sogno di una letteratura mondiale," he stated that "for a literature which is not intent on cheap effects and catch-phrases, the broadest world, the only world, is the heart of the individual."[155] And five years later, in his contribution to the *Festschrift* for Baldensperger, he proclaimed his new message of scholarly salvation:

In every judgment or evaluation we make, we will have to confine ourselves to the innermost realm rather than attribute excessive significance to influences as determining or even revolutionizing forces, since we are convinced that only the psyche and the secret harmonies of the soul are decisive in determining the fate of poesy and art.[156]

Farinelli himself practiced what he preached by writing monographs on Shakespeare, Michelangelo, Petrarch, Leopardi, Goethe, and Mozart.

After Farinelli's death, Comparative Literature ceased to make much headway in Italy, even though scholars like Praz, Orsini, Simone, and Pellegrini frequently crossed the borders of national literature in pursuing their professional interests.[157]

In 1946, Pellegrini, in association with Vittorio Santoli, founded the *Rivista di letterature moderne*, which, in its eighth year of publication (1955), without explanation changed its title to *Rivista di letterature moderne e comparate*. The professed aim of this journal was to study literature from a European perspective:

> Out of a desire for clarity, we have named our publication *Rivista di letterature moderne*; actually, it could just as well have been called *Rivista di letteratura*, since we are convinced that there is only one literature—namely world literature—which finds expression in various languages and forms, but which is basically a single literature. . . . Europe presupposes the existence of one culture, one mentality, one ethos, as well as certain specific forms of art and expression. . . . For this reason, artificial categories and divisions are excluded from our journal.

In 1948, while the process of scientific reconstruction was under way in postwar Italy, L. F. Benedetto issued a plea not only for a reintegration of the study of national literatures but also for a joining of the literary-historical method with that of literary criticism: "In order for Comparative Literature to flourish, in order for a general history of literature to become possible, misunderstandings must be cleared up; we must all become aware that literary criticism and literary history are two different but equally legitimate disciplines.[158]

In the winter semester 1949/1950, Antonio Porta organized the first manifestly comparative course ever to be offered in Italy, comprising four lectures on European literature at the Università Bocconi in Milan. A critical description of this series is found in the printed version of the introductory lecture, which appeared under the title *La letteratura comparata nella storia e nella critica*.[159] But Porta's well-meaning attempt did little to change the status quo; and once more Italian comparative scholarship went into hibernation, from which it awoke but temporarily in 1956, when the first Congress of the ICLA convened in Venice. All papers read at that congress dealt with the topic "Venice in Literature," which signified a methodological regression and provided no opportunity, either directly or indirectly, for assessing the new trends which had made themselves felt in the meantime. The brief inaugural address delivered by the Rector of the University of Venice, Italo Siciliano, demonstrates, both in its tone and outlook, the unlikelihood of a renascence of Comparative Literature in Italy.[160] In contrast to their French, American, and Japanese colleagues, Italian scholars seem thus to have heeded the warning which Croce had sounded in 1907:

> The solemnity with which the label "comparative" is usually applied to more or less organic branches of knowledge whose scientific basis is questionable has not yet gone out of style, and its disappearance will not come about for some time yet. When, one day, a cultural history of this century is written, its author may well devote one of the most amusing chapters to the search for new sciences, which, ultimately, are neither new nor sciences.[161]

6. The Other Countries

Among the Scandinavian countries, only Denmark, on account of the outstanding role played by Georg Brandes, can claim to have a comparatist tradition; this has in recent years, though with less distinction, been cultivated by the late Paul Krüger of Aarhus University, who edited the correspondence of his great compatriot.[162] Today's leading Danish exponent of Comparative Literature is Professor Billeskov Jansen of Copenhagen (where the journal *Orbis*

Litterarum, which is internationally, though not comparatistically, oriented, is also published). While Norway and Finland can scarcely be found on the world map of Comparative Literature, there is no dearth of comparatists in Sweden, where S. N. Tigerstedt (Stockholm) and Sven Linnér (Uppsala) are active, although no chairs of Comparative Literature exist at their respective universities.

In the Benelux nations, Holland plays a more important role in organizational and administrative matters than its bilingual neighbor Belgium. The Institute of Comparative Literature at the University of Utrecht (founded in 1948 by W. A. P. Smit and Hendrik Sparnaay and now directed by Jan Brandt Corstius), is an academic center of international significance, especially in the symbiotically related Institute for Literary Theory (headed by H. P. H. Teesing), which has distinguished itself by sponsoring the *Utrechtse Publikaties voor Algemene Literatuurwetenschap*,[163] the *Regesten*, which they replaced, and a serial bibliography (discontinued in 1961) of comparative studies within the Flemish- and Dutch-speaking area. Comparative studies are also pursued at the Universities of Amsterdam and Groningen. At present, the holder of the Amsterdam Chair of Comparative Literature is Jan Kamerbeek, Jr., a former associate of Brandt Corstius. The actual pioneer of Comparative Literature in the Netherlands was William de Clerq (1795–1844), who, in 1824, published a study concerned with the influence of foreign literatures on Dutch letters.[164]

In the Flemish part of Belgium, Comparative Literature was elevated to a science in 1922 when, before the Leiden Congress of Philologists, Frank Baur delivered a speech (not published until 1927) on the methodology of the discipline. Baur divided Comparative Literature into four segments—krenology, doxology, genology, and thematology—a practice subsequently sanctioned by Van Tieghem. There is at present only one chair of Comparative Literature in Belgium, occupied by Professor Gobbers at the newly founded University of Antwerp; but Walter Thys

(Ghent) and, in the French-speaking sector, Roland Mortier, Jean Weisgerber and Raymond Trousson (Brussels), are also true comparatists in spirit as well as letter.[165]

As an academic subject, Comparative Literature is still practically unknown on the Iberian peninsula and in Central and South America. Historically, this may be explained by the fact that the modern philological disciplines were not officially recognized in Spain until the 1920s, and that they are still treated in a somewhat perfunctory manner. Thus, the number of Spanish and Portuguese journals devoted to literary history and criticism has been inordinately small. Nor are major developments apparently in the offing, even though a number of younger Latin American scholars are strongly interested in the comparative approach. As a curricular discipline, then, Comparative Literature is practically nonexistent, such isolated cases as that of the University of Cali (Colombia) notwithstanding.

As far as I know, the earliest discussion of the methodology of Comparative Literature on the Iberian Peninsula dates from the year 1912, when Fidelino de Figueiredo published his book *A Critica litteraria como sciencia*. In the subsection "Comparative Literature and Criticism of Sources," the Portuguese scholar broaches the pertinent issue. It comes as no surprise that he believes, with Croce, in comparison as a technique intrinsic to all literary criticism and feels that a separate discipline cannot be founded upon this method. But Figueiredo recommends the extension of literary studies to include the general history of literature and the history of ideas.[166] Two decades later, he voiced pretty much the same opinion in his study *Pyrene: Ponto de vista para uma introducão á História Comparada das Literaturas Portuguesa e Espanhola*,[167] where we read on page 12:

Comparative Literature—and I repeat what I stated in 1912—does not have its own method, for it uses the common method of literary history, which is aleatory in itself. It merely spreads its investigation to a wider field, crossing national boundaries in its search for the causes of phenomena and for external influences. It is merely an extension of the limits of scholarship.

More recently, the influence of Wolfgang Kayser has made itself felt within the Portuguese-speaking world. Since Kayser, who taught for a number of years at the University of Lisbon, exalted the virtues of *Werkimmanenz*, however, his impact was more strongly felt in literary theory and criticism than in the incipient field of Comparative Literature.

Apart from several scholars of Spanish origin who are now teaching at American universities—especially Claudio Guillén at the University of California in San Diego, and Bernardo Gicovate at Stanford University[168]—Figueiredo has found few successors, although institutes for Comparative Literature exist, nominally, in Mexico (Antonio Alatorre) and in Chile, and even though Guillermo de Torre remains active in Argentina. But at the Centro de Investigaciones de Literatura Comparada in Santiago de Chile, (directed by Roque Esteban Scarpa), for instance, the scope of the discipline is so broadly conceived that monographs on individual poets and writers (Thomas Mann, T. S. Eliot, Eugenio Montale, among others) are apparently viewed as being comparative. Just how little thought is commonly given in South America to questions of methodology is evident from an essay in *CLS* authored by Estuardo Nuñez and mislabeled "Comparative Literature in Latin America."[169] Spain, Portugal, and their American "provinces" are, then, in a professional and academic sense, virgin territory for Comparative Literature. This was confirmed by a bibliographical survey recently undertaken by Aurora Ilárraz, a graduate student at Indiana University.

Though an attempt to outline the rich and complex history of Comparative Literature in Eastern Europe, with its many short circuits due to political developments, must be a lost labor of love in the present context, the attempt needs nevertheless to be made. To begin with, it should be pointed out that, given the great number of interrelated but independent Slavic languages even within the vast territory of the Soviet Union, an application of the comparative method is, naturally, called for. Accordingly, Roman Jakobson and Dmitrii Čiževskij and others have endeavored to examine the Slavic literatures as an integrated whole.[170]

However, the study of the relationship between Slavic and Western literatures has frequently run into governmental opposition, primarily because the so-called influences present in that relationship were, for the most part, one-directional (i.e., flowing from West to East), as far as literature prior to the middle of the nineteenth century is concerned. Either the existence of such influences was denied on principle, or reference was made to the sociologically and anthropologically tinged doctrine of Stadialism, which replaces "influences" by historically conditioned "parallels":

The idea of "development" as a circle or a series of self-repeating circles has led Veselovsky's followers to the theory of so-called stadialism, according to which literary facts are considered regardless of their genesis, their historical environment, their chronology, and their locale, but merely with reference to their "analogousness." Stadialism as applied to literature implies parallel cyclical development without borrowing.[171]

Although the Gorky Institute for World Literature in Moscow and the Pushkin Institute in Leningrad remained active throughout and organized several conferences in the late fifties, Comparative Literature in the Western sense did not flourish in the Soviet Union even after the death of Stalin. Around 1960 a new chapter began to unfold, due in part to Hungarian initiative. For in the year following the Utrecht Congress, the Budapest Institute of Comparative Literature hosted a conference whose principal topic was the comparative study of the Slavic literatures, and to which several Western scholars were invited. The papers read at this meeting were collected and edited by Istvan Sötér of the Hungarian Academy of Sciences, and published in a volume whose contents attracted considerable attention in the West.[172]

Hungary's organizational feat did not remain without

consequences. On the occasion of the Fribourg Congress of the ICLA, for instance, the Hungarian delegation presented a collection entitled *Littérature hongroise, littérature européenne*[173]; and at the close of 1966, the German Academy of Sciences in East Berlin, following suit, convoked the congress previously referred to. In spite of a few slightly embarrassing incidents, the Belgrade Congress held in 1967 resulted in the formation of a kind of *entente cordiale* between East and West. The presence of a sizable Soviet delegation under the leadership of Viktor Zhirmunsky and M. P. Alexeyev was truly epoch-making. The plan, drafted in Belgrade, of a comprehensive History of Literature in European Languages is now being co-ordinated by members of the Hungarian Academy. An international colloquium dealing with the issues likely to be encountered in the preparations for this enterprise was held in Budapest (November 17 and 18, 1971). Its participants addressed themselves primarily to the problem of periodization. The texts of all communications have been reproduced in the first issue of the new magazine *Neohelicon*, which is intended as a mouthpiece of the Coordinating Committee of that international venture.

In proceeding from the general to the particular, I should like to glance briefly at the history of Comparative Literature in the Soviet Union and Hungary; as for the other East European countries (Yugoslavia, Rumania, Poland, Bulgaria, and Czechoslovakia), we must confine ourselves to bibliographical data.[174] The "father" of Comparative Literature in Russia is Alexander Veselovsky (1838–1906), who, from 1870 until his death, occupied a chair for General Literature in St. Petersburg.[175] Werner Krauss summarizes his scholarly accomplishments in the following terms:

In his *Comparative Poetics*, Veselovsky wanted to encompass the development of all literatures. In the process, even temporally and spatially unconnected phenomena move close together because of the inherent law, which is an outgrowth of common

social postulates. Thus, Veselovsky juxtaposes Old High German
poetry with the archaic poetry of the Greeks and the American
Indians. The *Iliad* and the *Kalevala*, *Beowulf* and the old
Abyssinian Balay Song are placed on the same level. For the
execution of his vast plan, Veselovsky had to form some idea
concerning typical phases in the social development of the
human race, and for these individual stages (*Stadien*) he garnered
the appropriate typical works and genres.[176]

The theory of Stadialism postulated by Veselovsky's students—primarily by Zhirmunsky—was, like Formalism,
tacitly sanctioned during the first, experimental phase of
Soviet history, but came under heavy fire in the 1930s.
Zhirmunsky, who, in his book on Byron and Pushkin, as
well as in his study of Goethe and Russian literature, had
described Russia's passive role in the literary interchange,
was now ostracized, and the stadialists were accused of
espousing a theory which was deterministic and pessimis-
tic, presupposed a certain uniformity in the historical development, and could explain neither national idiosyncrasies nor the historical progress of mankind as a whole.

In a series of articles published in the *Yearbook of Comparative and General Literature*, Gleb Struve has attempted
to show in considerable detail what fate befell Comparative Literature in recent decades. He discerns four distinct
stages in the development of the official Soviet attitude
toward the discipline:

1) a period of relative freedom, approximately from 1917 through
1929, when it was not necessary for a literary scholar to be a
Marxist. . . . 2) the second period, which covered the thirties and,
on the whole, lasted through the war years . . . and which was
characterized by so-called Socialist Realism in literature . . . and
by the growing insistence on compliance with the strict Marxist
doctrine where literary scholarship was concerned. . . . 3) the
third period, which was inaugurated by the famous resolution of
the Central Committee of the Communist Party in 1946, which
emphasized the necessity of rooting out the relics of bourgeois
mentality in Soviet Literature, and more particularly the spirit of
"servility before the capitalistic West."[177]

As Struve observes in the first sequel to his survey, the fourth phase was initiated by the so-called thaw of 1955. In the years immediately following, Veselovsky and Zhirmunsky were rehabilitated, and, at a conference sponsored by the Gorky Institute for World Literature in 1959, basic questions relating to the comparative study of literature were publicly aired from seven different viewpoints.[178] This conference acted as a stimulus in various other People's Republics. The pace of this development, however, was markedly different in each of the countries concerned. Only Yugoslavia has created a sizable number of chairs of Comparative Literature, while elsewhere things are lagging behind—less so in Rumania than in Bulgaria, Poland, and Czechoslovakia.[179] Reference has already been made to the situation in the German Democratic Republic. Hungary occupies a very special place, since for centuries it was culturally closer to the West than to the East.[180] Thus, it is not surprising that as early as 1877 a comparative journal was created in Klausenburg (now Cluj). This journal ceased publication in 1888—two years after the founding of Koch's *Zeitschrift für vergleichende Litteraturgeschichte*.[181]

The founder and editor of the polyglot *Acta Comparationis Litterarum Universarum* was Hugo Meltzl de Lomnitz (1846–1908), a native of Transylvania, who as a child spoke German, Hungarian, and Rumanian, and who subsequently acquired a knowledge of classical, Slavic, and Germanic languages as well. He studied in Leipzig and Heidelberg, and in 1873 was appointed Professor of German at the University of Klausenburg. His journal was founded upon the belief that "any race, however politically insignificant, is and always will remain, from the standpoint of Comparative Literature, as important as the greatest nation" (I, 311). In literary terms, this meant that "from the comparative point of view the importance of one literature should not prevail at the expense of another; whether they be European or non-European, they are all equally important" (II, 496). Small wonder, that, with a tradition extending back to the nineteenth century, Hungary's name is promient on today's world map of Comparative Literature, and that it possesses in the Budapest Institute—an affiliate of the Hungarian Academy of Sciences presently under the direction of Györgyi Vajda—one of the most vigorous institutions of its kind. Its members are both effective organizers and productive scholars.

Of the continents not yet surveyed, Asia is the only one meriting close attention. In the Far East it is Japan above all whose scientific contribution concerns us in the present context, although South Korea now also has its own association and magazine. In fact, it has recently hosted the first international conference in our field devoted to the study of the literary relations between West and East.[182] As Saburo Ota, chairman of the Japanese Society for Comparative Literature (Nihon Hikaku Bungaku Kai), indicates, the study of that country's national literature has always been comparative, since its classic writers are invariably studied in light of their Chinese models: "This was a primitive stage of comparative study in Japan, as [the Japanese scholars] had no systematic method or academic principles and did not distinguish between comparison and parallelism."[183]

Japan was introduced to the methodology of French-style *littérature comparée* in 1943 through the translation of Van Tieghem's book, although Posnett's and Loliée's books had been available for decades, and even though the term "Comparative Literature" had come into use as early as the 1930s. The end of World War II witnessed a revival of this scholarly approach, and in 1948 the above-mentioned association, which has approximately six hundred members, was called into being. It issues a yearbook entitled *Hikaku Bungaku* (Comparative Literature). In addition, there are *Hikaku Bungaku Nenshi* (published at Waseda University) and *Hikaku Bungaku Kenkyu*. Academically, however, Comparative Literature is represented only at the University of Tokyo, and the number of graduate students majoring in that subject is relatively small.[184]

As long as Comparative Literature in Japan emulated the positivism of the orthodox Paris School, it dealt almost exclusively with the Western influences to which the indigenous literature of the Meiji era (1868–1912) had been subjected. The numerous translations from the Western languages which were published during that period, and the relevant statistical surveys, were the focus of its attention. It also emphasized source and reception studies. A nationalistic reaction, parallel to that which almost concurrently swept the Soviet Union, was thus predictable:

There is good reason for such antipathy to comparative literature among scholars of Japanese literature. Some students of comparative literature are inclined to emphasize Western influences so much that they end in saying that modern Japanese literature is nothing but a sheer imitation of Western literature. Such opinions have caused serious disputes among scholars and have given a bad reputation to comparative literature in Japan.[185]

More recently, the less orthodox American views on Comparative Literature have begun to circulate in Japan; and it is to be hoped that in the future the perspectives suggested by Etiemble will also receive attention in the Land of the Rising Sun.

In India, comparative scholarship is still in its infancy. Until about six years ago, it was academically confined to Jadavpur University in Calcutta, where a Department of Comparative Literature had been founded in 1956. It was originally under the directorship of Buddhadeva Bose.[186] On the initiative of R. K. Das Gupta, the chairman of the Department of Indian Languages and Literatures at the University of New Delhi, who made a fact-finding tour through Europe and the United States in 1969, special attention is now being lavished on the interrelation between works written in the major literary languages such as Hindi, Bengali, and Tamil. For the last two years, Professor Das Gupta has taught at the University of Alberta in Edmonton (Canada).

In the Arab states, too, it was after World War II that

significant progress was made with regard to Comparative
Literature as an academic discipline. To be sure, for decades there have been Egyptian and, lately, Algerian scholars, who took their degree at the Sorbonne; but the auspicious moment for instituting chairs of Comparative
Literature seems only now to have arrived.[187] Here, too, a
change in perspective is desirable, since until recently the
stress was almost exclusively on the influence of West
European books on Arabic letters (and therefore primarily
on the last fifty or seventy-five years). Only when the significant Arab contribution to ancient, medieval and Renaissance occidental literature forms an essential part of the
research program at Arab universities will Comparative
Literature take firm hold in that part of the world as well.

In conclusion to the historical part of this study, it is to
be noted that Israel, too, has made a modest beginning
both in Jerusalem and in Tel-Aviv, where Benjamin Hru-
shovski is chairman of a Department of Poetics and Comparative Literature.

Appendix Two
✍ Bibliographical Problems

To grasp the bibliographical situation in Comparative Literature, one should proceed historically, paying attention to the early stages and slow evolution (extending over several generations) of that still indispensable standard reference work, the *Bibliography of Comparative Literature* compiled by Werner Paul Friederich and Fernand Baldensperger.[1] It should be kept in mind, however, that the actual pioneering was done by Louis-Paul Betz, who in 1896 published in the *Revue de Philologie française et de Littérature* a list entitled "Essai de bibliographie des questions de littérature comparée," which catalogues some three thousand entries.[2]

Betz's bibliography is divided into ten chapters, which —arranged according to nations—consider not only the mutual relations between the modern, i.e., post-medieval, literatures, but also the effect (Rüdiger's *Wirkung*) on Western literature of the works of classical antiquity and the Orient. In this regard, Betz was more "prophetic" than Van Tieghem, whose handbook, following the practice at the Sorbonne, admits only in theory such geographic and temporal extensions of the field. The fact that the list of studies on literary theory in Chapter One is not strictly limited to comparative items also attests to the unorthodox views of the Swiss scholar, but concurrently betrays a certain lack of methodological rigor.

Objections might also be raised to the sections on linguistic and philological interactions which are appended to the various chapters of this oldest version of B/F; for here Betz definitely made concessions to the *Zeitgeist*.

Moreover, precisely by demonstrating the compiler's progressiveness, the following remark, placed at the head of
the section on Franco-German literary relations of the
eighteenth and nineteenth centuries demonstrates the essentially positivistic outlook of the age: "Throughout this
bibliography, *literary parallels* are recorded as well" (p.
263, Betz's emphasis).

One is pleasantly surprised to discover, among other
things, that Betz, in contrast to his successors, rejected the
one-sided stress on the role of the emitter. Thus, besides a
section on Molière in Germany (III B 1) he has another on
Goethe and French literature (III B 2), as well as a listing
of studies "regarding the influences exercised on Dante's
work" (VI A 5), which adopts the perspective of the receiver. In the booklength version of the bibliography, the
sections on French, German, English, Italian, Portuguese
and Provençal literature have been supplemented by chapters on the Scandinavian and Slavic, to which sections on
North American and Hungarian letters were added in the
expanded and revised edition of 1904.

In 1900, Betz's compilation was published in book form
under the title *La Littérature comparée: Essai bibliographique*, with a foreword by Joseph Texte, who then occupied the chair of Comparative Literature at the University
of Lyon.[3] In this format, it contains more than four thousand entries, offers an index of names, and is further distinguished from the earlier version by the fact that, within
each individual chapter, the chronological order has replaced the alphabetical arrangement. As Betz notes in the
introduction, "Firstly, this 'second' edition numbers almost a thousand titles more than the first; and, secondly,
following the advice of my colleagues, I have substituted
the chronological arrangement for the alphabetical order
used in the first edition" (p. xi). Traces of this reorientation
are still visible in the first two chapters of Part One of the
B/F *Bibliography*, where the titles published before 1900
are listed in order of their appearance, while all other items
are arranged alphabetically according to author.

Betz's choice of French as the vehicle for a comparative bibliography published in the, then, German city of Strasbourg and gathered by a scholar residing in the German-speaking part of Switzerland is pragmatically explained by the fact that the original compilation had appeared in a French journal. In explicitly referring to this circumstance, Betz probably wished to stave off a chauvinistic interpretation of his intentions:

> The chapter titles, the notes, the references, in short, all that is
> not text, is written in French. I could let it be understood that the
> use of that language was a tribute to France—and there would
> be a grain of truth in this. But the full truth, as always, is much
> simpler. This bibliography is, in fact, only a second edition:
> it appeared two years ago in the *Revue de Philologie Française
> et de Littérature*. (p. xi)

At the end of his brief preface, Betz expressed his gratitude not only to Joseph Texte, but also to Arturo Farinelli and Arthur L. Jellinek, a "man of letters in Vienna" who was then working on a similar bibliography, which saw print shortly before the untimely death of the Zurich *Ordinarius*, but the first installment of which had been serially published in the *Studien zur vergleichenden Litteraturgeschichte*. In 1903, Jellinek published the first and only volume of what was intended as a periodic *Bibliographie der vergleichenden Literaturgeschichte*,[4] listing the pertinent items for 1902.[5] As is evident from his brief preface to the slender volume, which comprises no more than nineteen pages totalling 281 entries, the author conceived it as being preliminary to the "dictionary of thematology" proposed by Goedeke. He was, therefore, primarily concerned with finding "a definite and unified nomenclature for the individual themes, motifs, formulae, and types" (p. 1). Thus, the chapter "Themes and Motifs" of the bibliography covers nearly two hundred titles, that is, three-fourths of the total number. By contrast, only seventy entries on the subject of "Literary Relations and Interrelations" and eighteen "general and theoretical" studies are accounted for. The folkloristic orientation of Jellinek's catalogue (which heavily relies on the "Reinhold Köhler-Johannes Bolte terminology") explains why no attempt at differentiating comparative from noncomparative titles is made in the main portion of the work. For this reason, as well, Jellinek's opus is little more than a historical curiosity.

Shortly after Betz's death, a new edition of *La Littérature comparée* was issued, twice the original size (5700 titles) and edited by Baldensperger, Texte's successor at Lyon. Outwardly, the new edition differs from the original insofar as the entries are now consecutively numbered; and its use is greatly facilitated by the addition of an *index méthodique* which covers both subjects and authors.[6] For the rest, the editor piously stuck to his model, even in regard to the philological-linguistic appendices, whose relevance he himself questioned:

In one point only the present repertory has not profited from the four years separating it from the original publication. I mean the appendices attached to the chapters on literary relations between two nations and devoted to philological and linguistic studies. The abortive state in which they have remained is the best rebuke to their presence here. They should either have been given more prominence by not being relegated to the position of postscripts, or they should have been altogether ceded to philology. In the latter case, one could have retained those works which deal with questions such as the limits of a language or the linguistic signs of intellectual intercourse. I could not bring myself to take either of these paths, even though some time ago, in an article published in the *Revue critique*, I demanded the suppression, pure and simple, of these appendices. If Betz has allowed them to stand, he wished, no doubt, to assign to them, at the very least, the role of pointers and enticements. (p. xiii)

As Baldensperger subsequently notes, Betz originally wanted to incorporate into the second edition of his book an expanded version of the bibliography on Christianity in literature which he had published in the *Studien zur vergleichenden Litteraturgeschichte*. The new editor thought it inappropriate, however, to execute the will of his predecessor; as he put it, "Such an ambition has something immoderate about it, something perilous, and illegitimate" primarily, one assumes, because here literary elements are fused with nonliterary ones: "For," he continued, "if Comparative Literature can rightfully concern itself with the fate of religious books . . . considered as literary monuments, would we serve it like an inconsiderate friend by ascribing to it a domain extending to questions of dogma and doctrine?" (p. xii). This argument reminds one of the distinction which Van Tieghem was later to draw between the history of literature and that of ideas. For the chapter planned by Betz, Baldensperger substituted a thematological section entitled "Motifs, Themes, and Literary Types, of Religious, Legendary, or Traditional Origin," subdivided into two sections ("Of a Religious Nature" and "Of a Secular Nature"). Unfortunately, the titles listed in that portion of the bibliography are chronologically arranged, and thus go against the grain of thematological classification.

The fact that Baldensperger did not fully endorse Betz's system of classification and his principles of selection can also be inferred from a remark which pertains, literally, to the completeness, but implicitly to the organization, of his material: "Betz's effort at nomenclature tended perhaps not so much to give the list completeness with regard to studies devoted to one or the other subject . . . as to reveal the great variety of subjects and the complexity of intellectual ties which make Western civilization so closely knit" (p. xi f.). Fifty years later, Wellek was to refer in similar terms to B/F.[7]

The final redaction of the bibliographical material collected by Baldensperger was a long time in coming. In the interim, comparatists had to resort in bibliographical matters to the lists which appeared from 1921 onward in the *Revue de littérature comparée*. When in 1940 Baldensperger relinquished his chair at Harvard and moved to California, he bequeathed his card-file, with its 15,000 titles, to the Widener Library. Five years later—and shortly before his return to Europe—he further decided to fuse his collection with the one assembled by Friederich. The latter then took on the Herculean task of editing the material, which by that time had swelled to almost 33,000 entries, but decided to retain the system of classification developed by his senior colleague: "It became immediately apparent that the division into Books and Chapters proposed by Professor Baldensperger was superior to my own, always rather unsatisfying, system; as every reader can see, it is also far better than the arrangement made by Betz almost fifty years ago" (B/F, p. xii).

In the context of this cursory description of the bibliographical tools available to practitioners of our discipline, I can only allude to the many and varied difficulties in store for the user of B/F. In many particulars, my critique has been anticipated by several scholarly reviewers, of whose arguments I shall avail myself without specific reference.[8] Let us keep in mind to begin with that complexity and sophistication in bibliographical matters are not necessarily desirable, for the usefulness of such compilations grows in direct proportion as the length of time required to locate the needed information decreases. Subtle bibliographies require skilled readers—that is, experts—who are willing and able to savor subtleties. In raising this point, Munteano aptly remarks: "In multiplying the categories so happily, in our opinion, M. Baldensperger has simultaneously multiplied the difficulties of classification."[9]

Even a cursory glance at the *Bibliography of Comparative Literature* will alert the reader to the fact that the hefty volume has no author or subject index and that, despite the (sporadic) cross-references, the otherwise innocuous failure to number the titles consecutively further complicates the search for entries hard to classify. Only if they had refrained from orienting themselves solely towards emitters, the authors would have been justified in omitting this feature. If, for example, one wishes to study the influence of various English authors on a specific German writer, one is forced to consult eleven different sections in the Eighth Part of Book Four ("English Contributions"); as major emitters, Byron, Carlyle, Defoe, Milton, Richardson, Scott, Shakespeare, Shelley, and Sterne, are each accorded a separate chapter, while chapters on "English Influences upon Germany" and "English Influences upon Individual Authors" round out the picture.

Further aggravation results from the fact that, in the items recorded by him, Friederich was not always able to determine whether an author had functioned as an emitter or receiver. The solution he found was not exactly Solomonic:

Another problem which often defied accurate interpretation dealt with the possibility that two authors may merely have been compared and that no tracings of influences were intended. Articles with the title "Boccaccio and Cervantes" I placed under Boccaccio, unless they stated expressly that they were a mere comparison (in which case I filed them in the Fifth Part of Book One, dealing with Similarities and Contrasts). But how about two contemporaries—e.g., "Dickens and Balzac" or "Leopardi and Espronceda"? Unless I knew of actual influences, I was inclined to place such cards about two contemporaries also in the chapter on Comparisons, for I could not be too sure whether Leopardi had influenced Espronceda or Espronceda Leopardi. Here again it may pay to turn to the chapter on Comparisons if the reader does not find what he wants in Book Four. (B/F, p. xvi)

Since, on the one hand, Friederich embraces an outmoded methodology, while, on the other, he expands the territorial claims of Comparative Literature in tacitly rejecting the restrictive dogmas of Carré, his bibliography rests on a compromise. Old-style Comparative Literature survives, for instance, in the strong emphasis on thematology—a subject which occupies, roughly, 140 out of a total of 700 pages. Friederich also emulates the example set by Jellinek and Betz-Baldensperger in failing to distinguish between the treatment of motifs and themes on a national and an international level. Hence, the listing of studies on "Molière and Physicians," "Liliencron and War," "Wordsworth and Nature," and "Tolstoi and Divorce." In order not to get bogged down in the morass of thematology, Friederich felt the need for limiting himself: "I therefore restricted myself to only a few examples of such treatments which, I hope, will not be criticized as being either too much or too little" (p. xvii).

Friederich's "conservative" view of Comparative Literature is further demonstrated by his retention of such philologically oriented chapters as "The English Language," or "The Italian Language." In apologetically noting, "At times it was also hard to keep away from Philology, as the various chapters on the Greek, Latin, French, German or English languages will prove, where I had to include language teachers and language boundaries, without, however, becoming involved in vowel gradations or weak adjective endings" (p. xvii), the compiler brushes aside the views which Baldensperger had broached as early as 1904. The insertion of a chapter on "Similarities and Contrasts" (I, 5, i)—which must be regarded as another stopgap measure—is one more sign of his methodological inconsistency, since it smuggles outmoded *littérature générale* into a partly old-fashioned *Bibliography of Comparative Literature*.

Baldensperger/Friederich's bibliography shows itself as rather more "progressive"—in the sense of Remak's definition of Comparative Literature, which I accepted with some reservations—in its inclusion of chapters on the relationship between literature and politics on the one hand, and those prevailing between literature and the "Arts and Sciences" (I, 3) on the other. These chapters, however, occupy a mere twenty pages between them, and are thus woefully inadequate. Friederich himself was not satisfied with this choice, hence his prefatorial remark: "Other borderline cases where I have tried to find a happy middleground between too much and too little have to do with Literature and Politics . . . Literature and Science . . . and, above all, Literature and Philosophy . . . or Literature and Religion" (p. xviii). In matters bibliographical, however, the Golden Mean is hardly the ideal yardstick.

Of the many strictures against the *Bibliography of Comparative Literature* by Munteano, Skard, Trousson, and Wellek, the following should perhaps also be mentioned, if only for the sake of completeness: 1) its methodologically untenable division between individual and collective motifs, themes, and genres; 2) its skimpy presentation of works dealing with literary theory and criticism as well as genre studies; and 3) its glaring lacunae in the area of Slavic and Oriental studies. The inclusion of special chapters on the Alsace (I, 4, i) and Switzerland (IV, 9)—where Rousseau and Madame de Staël are located—is pardonable insofar as Baldensperger was Alsatian and Friederich is Swiss, but it must be emphatically rejected from the standpoint of the cosmopolitanism of our discipline. Just how much partisanship is involved here is evident from the fact that, in his preface, Friederich explicitly states that in principle he has combined "related countries under one heading."

In spite of the numerous objections which, for more or less cogent reasons, were raised against the *Bibliography of Comparative Literature,* the book retains its value as a reference work with which we must learn to live. With the founding of the *Yearbook of Comparative and General Literature* in 1952, Friederich opened an outlet through which the bibliographical listing of comparative studies could be brought up to date in annual supplements. The organizational pattern of the *Bibliography* was retained for nine years (as long, that is to say, as Friederich remained the chief editor of the *Yearbook*), but modified in such a way that not all the chapters were updated annually. Instead, the catching up was done only for those chapters for which sufficient material had accrued in any given year or number of years. Particulars concerning the distribution of topics among the supplements are given in Volume Eight (p. 87).

In Volume Six of the *Yearbook,* the editorial responsibility for the bibliographical supplement was assumed by Hugh Chapman, Jr.—assisted by W. B. Fleischmann in

Volume Eight and by Friederich himself in Volume Nine. But the picture changed completely in 1960, when the editorial duties for the entire *Yearbook* were assumed by a group of comparatists at Indiana University, who decided to change the mode of classification, chiefly with the aim of simplifying the whole apparatus and limiting the contents of the bibliography to belles-lettres.[10]

In the course of reorganization, the chapters devoted to the interrelation between literature and politics, religion, and science, as well as the purely philological sections, were cancelled, and the special role of the chapter on the mutual illumination of the arts was eliminated. Through the alphabetical arrangement of titles in the seventh and eighth sections of the revised annual bibliographies ("Individual Countries" and "Individual Authors"), the location of approximately three-fourths of the entries was greatly facilitated. The very same intention is also served by the rejection of the unilateral approach and the substitution of the "dual" perspective suggested by Battailon.[11] Thus, anyone using the bibliographies for the years 1960 to 1969 need not worry about whether, in a given instance, Dickens influenced Balzac, or Balzac Dickens; for the relevant entries automatically appear under both B(alzac) and D(ickens). In this way, the index of names, called for by many critics of B/F was dispensable. Further simplification through the adoption of the bibliographical practices prevailing in the other modern philologies is achieved by the use of standard PMLA abbreviations for approximately 1,200 professional journals.

But all the changes wrought by the editors of the *Year-book* have done precious little to solve the basic question; for now the comparatist has to cope with two conflicting patterns which cannot be fully reconciled. A gathering of the supplements and their integration with the parent volume (which should be pruned and relieved of excess baggage) is highly desirable but economically unfeasible.[12] Thus, the previously mentioned index volume is the best we can hope for under the circumstances. In fact, the bibliographical situation in our field has further deteriorated because the editors of the *Yearbook* have reluctantly decided to discontinue the supplements beginning with Volume Twenty (1971). By way of partial recompense, they promise to publish, in the future, specialized annotated bibliographies alongside the regularly featured reviews of research.

An indirect consequence of the organizational changes in the *Yearbook* supplements was the disappearance of two serially published continental bibliographies. The *Comparatistische Bibliografie*, issued since 1955 by the Institute for Comparative Literature at Utrecht, was of limited value in that it confined itself to items couched in Dutch, Flemish and Afrikaans; but the loss of the quarterly compilation in the *Revue de Littérature comparée* is still sorely felt. To be sure, this serial listing suffered from the fact that it, too, was emitter-oriented and did not strictly limit itself to bona fide comparative studies; but, if only for the scope of its coverage, it was an extremely useful tool. Moreover, since 1950, eight installments of this publication have been gathered, biennially, in the *Bibliographie générale de littérature comparée*, without any attempt at integrating the quarterly listings.[13] The appended name and subject matter indices help to make at least partial amends for this failure, however.

In the section "For a Bibliography" of his book *Comparaison n'est pas raison*, Etiemble comments on the paucity of currently available bibliographical sources, especially in view of the vast global scope of Comparative Literature.[14] An inveterate optimist, this maverick calls a truly international cooperation in this area a prerequisite for the eventual creation of an analytical—if not the ultimately desired critical—bibliography. Etiemble would like to see this world-wide listing supplemented by a central catalogue of all relevant works-in-progress, something like the "Research in Progress" section published for several years in PMLA.

Etiemble's plan is admirable but impracticable. A more

practical solution, in my view, would be a partial reorganization of the PMLA Bibliography, which for well over a decade has provided the most comprehensive coverage of secondary literature (now over 20,000 titles a year). For the comparatist, the present arrangements of the subjects in this compilation are far from ideal. The numerical cross-references, for example, are not systematically carried forward from one section to another, and the section "General and Miscellaneous" is so arbitrarily subdivided that one must scan all the titles listed under that heading if one wishes to find what one is looking for. The subsection "Literature, General and Comparative," for instance, lists 150 items for 1966; but only twenty of these are formally described as comparative. By "General Literature," on the other hand, the editors apparently mean the same thing as Van Tieghem's *littérature générale*, a concept which, as we have seen, is hardly viable in Comparative Literature.

Shortly before the manuscript of the original German version of this book was completed, a new development along the lines indicated above became visible. As Harrison T. Meserole pointed out in a paper read at the Bloomington conference of the ACLA, if all goes well, within the next five years or so the electronic brain of the computer should be able to do the work so inadequately performed by the human mind.[15] Thanks to the automatization of manual labor, it may soon be possible by simply pressing a button to assemble bibliographical data of every conceivable manner in whatever form desired. Etiemble's bibliographical pipedream thus seems on the verge of coming true; yet even as the printer reaches for this page no spectacular progress has been made along the lines suggested by Professor Meserole, and the bibliographical situation in Comparative Literature has temporarily reached a zero point.

᎙ Selected Bibliography of Secondary Literature

For additional references, consult the relevant sections of Balden-sperger/Friederich's *Bibliography of Comparative Literature* (including the annual supplements in vols. 1–9 of the *Yearbook of Comparative and General Literature*), and sections I ("Comparative, World, and General Literature"), II ("Translations, Translators, Correspondents, Travellers, and Other Intermediaries"), III ("Themes and Motifs"), IV ("Literary Genres, Types, Forms and Techniques") and V ("Epochs, Currents, and Movements") of the supplements in vols. 10–19 of the *Yearbook*. Abbreviations as in the annual MLA Bibliography.

1. *Comparative Literature and General Literature*

Abe, Jiro. *Hikaku Bungaku* (Comparative Literature). Tokyo, 1932/33. 2 vols.

Aldridge, A. Owen, ed. *Comparative Literature: Matter and Method* (Urbana, Ill.: U. of Illinois Press, 1969). A collection of essays from *CLS*.

Backer, F. de. "Littérature comparée: Questions de méthode," *Bulletin de l'Académie Royale de Belgique*, classe des lettres, fifth series, 45 (1959), 209 ff.

Baldensperger, Fernand. "Littérature comparée: Le mot et la chose," *RLC* 1 (1921), 5–29.

Bauer, Gerhard. "Theorie der Literatur in der allgemeinen und vergleichenden Literaturwissenschaft" in *Zur Theorie der vergleichenden Literaturwissenschaft*, ed. H. Rüdiger (Berlin, 1971), 15–40. Of little methodological value.

Baur, Frank. "De vergelijkende methode in de literatuurweten-schap," *Album Vercouille* I (Brussels, 1927), 33–45.

———. "De Philologie van het letterkundig Comparatisme" in *Handelingen van het XXIIe Vlaamse Filologencongres*, 1957.

Bémol, Maurice. "Goethe et Valéry: Leurs vues comparées sur la comparaison littéraire," *RLC* 21 (1947), 382–403.

Betz, Louis-Paul. "Kritische Betrachtungen über Wesen, Aufgabe und Bedeutung der vergleichenden Literaturgeschichte," *Zeitschrift für französische Sprache und Literatur* 18 (1896), 141–156.

———. "Literaturvergleichung" in *Studien zur vergleichenden Literaturgeschichte der neueren Zeit* (Frankfurt, 1902), 1–15.

Block, Haskell M. *Nouvelles Tendances en littérature comparée* (Paris, 1970).

Brandt Corstius, Jan. *Introduction to the Comparative Study of Literature* (New York: Random House, 1967).

Brown, Calvin, S. "Comparative Literature," *The Georgia Review* 13 (1959), 167–189.

Brunetière, Ferdinand. "La Littérature européenne" in *Variétés littéraires* (Paris, 1904), 1–51. Text of lecture given in September, 1900, and first published in the *Revue des deux mondes*.

Campbell, Oscar J. "What is Comparative Literature" in *Essays in Memory of Barrett Wendell*, ed. W. R. Castle, Jr., and P. Kaufman (Harvard University Press, 1926), 23–40.

Chandler, Frank W. "The Comparative Study of Literature" in *University* [of Cincinnati] *Studies*, second series, VI/4 (1910), 1–26. Reprinted in *YCGL* 15 (1966), 50–62.

Chasles, Philarète. "Littérature étrangère comparée," *Revue de Paris* 13 (1835), 238–262.

Cioranescu, Alexandru. *Principios de literatura comparada* (La Laguna, Teneriffa: Universidad de La Laguna, 1964).

Conrad, N. I. "Problems of Comparative Literature in Our Day" (in Russian). *Izvestija Akademii Nauk*, Class of Languages and Literatures, 18 (1959), 315–333. See the essay by R. Triomphe in *RLC* 34 (1960), 304–310.

Croce, Benedetto. "La letteratura comparata," *La Critica* 1 (1903), 77–80.

———. Review of Charles Ricci, *Sophonisbe dans la tragédie classique italienne et française* in *La Critica* 2 (1904), 483–486.

Curtius, Ernst Robert. "Antike Rhetorik und vergleichende Literaturwissenschaft," *CL* 1 (1949), 24–43.

Deugd, Cornelis de. *De Eenheid van het Comparatisme* (Utrecht, 1962). Offers a fine bibliography of Dutch contributions to the field.

Dima, Alexandru. *Principii de literaturǎ comparatǎ* (Bucharest, 1969). Reviewed in *Arcadia* 5 (1970), 198–199. Second ed. 1972.

Ďurišin, Dionýz. *Problémy literárnej komparatistiky* (Bratislava, 1967). Engl., French and Russ. summary on pp. 182–193.

———. "Some General Questions of Comparative Literature" in *O Medziliterárnych Vzťahoch: Sborník Venovany VI. Medzinárodnému Kongresu Slavistov* (Bratislava, 1968), 11–24. English, with Slovak summary.

———. *Vergleichende Literaturforschung* (Berlin: Akademie-1972). German version, slightly modified, of *Problemy*. . . .

———. *Z dejín a teórie literárnej komparatistiky* [From the History and Theory of Comparative Literature] (Bratislava, 1970). A collection of essays. English summary on pp. 367–376.

Dyserinck, Hugo. "Crisis in de vergelijkend literatuurwetenschap," *Spiegel der Letteren* 4 (1960), 175–193.

Elster, Ernst. "Weltliteratur und Literaturvergleichung," *Archiv* 107 (1901), 33–47.

Elwert, W. Th. "L'Emploi de langues étrangères comme procédé stylistique," *RLC* 34 (1960), 409–437.

Etiemble, René. *Comparaison n'est pas raison: La Crise de la littérature comparée* (Paris: Gallimard, 1963). A shortened version appeared in *Savoir et Goût*, the third volume of E.'s *Hygiène des Lettres* (Paris, 1958), 154–173. English version: *The Crisis in Comparative Literature*, tr. G. Joyaux and H. Weisinger (Michigan State University Press, 1966).

Faj, A. "Considerazioni sulla letteratura comparata," *Forum Italicum* 3 (1969), 337–354.

Figueiredo, Fidelino de. "Litteratura comparada e critica de fontes" in *A Critica litteraria como sciencia* (Lisbon, 1914), 63–67.

———. "Da critica comparativa" in *Pyrene: Ponto de vista para uma introduccão á história comparada das literaturas Portuguesa e Espanhola* (Lisbon, 1935), 10–15.

Fokkema, D. W. "Cultureel relativisme en vergelijkende literatuurwetenschap," *Maatstaf* 19 (1971), 1–15. Slightly enlarged as a special pamphlet (Amsterdam, 1971). Engl. version in *Tamkang Review* 3 (1972), 59–71.

Fransen, J. *Iets over vergelijkende literatuurstudie, 'perioden' en 'invloeden'* (Groningen, 1936).

Friederich, Werner P. "The Case of Comparative Literature," *AAUP Bulletin*, 31 (1945), 208–219.

————. *The Challenge of Comparative Literature and other Addresses*, ed. W. deSua (Chapel Hill: U. of North Carolina Press, 1970).

Gayley, C. M. "A Society of Comparative Literature," *The Dial*, August 1, 1894.

Gicovate, Bernardo. *Conceptos fundamentales de literatura comparada: Iniciacion de la poesia modernista* (San Juan, Puerto Rico, 1962). See esp. the introduction, pp. 7–12.

Gifford, Henry. *Comparative Literature* (London: Routledge, Kegan Paul, 1969).

Gsteiger, Manfred. "Theorie und Praxis der vergleichenden Literaturwissenschaft," *Schweizer Monatshefte* 48 (1968), 1127–1133.

————. "Zum Begriff und über das Studium der Literatur in vergleichender Sicht" in *Zur Theorie der vergleichenden Literaturwissenschaft*, ed. H. Rüdiger (Berlin, 1971), 65–87. Of little methodological value.

Guillén, Claudio. "Literatura como sistema," *Filologia romanza* 4 (1957), 1–29.

————. "Perspectivas de la literatura comparada," *Boletin informativo del Seminario de Derecho Politico* (Princeton, N.J.) 8 (1962), 57–70.

————. *Literature as System: Essays Toward the Theory of Literary History* (Princeton University Press, 1970). A number of essays, partly revised and bearing on literary history and theory.

Guyard, Marius-François. *La Littérature comparée* (Paris: Presses Universitaires de France, 1951). Third ed., 1961.

Hankiss, Janos. "Theorie de la littérature et littérature comparée" in *Proceedings II*, Vol. One, 98–112.

Hergešić, Ivo. *Poredbena ili komparativna književnost* (Zagreb, 1932). 97 pp.

Hilal, Muhammad Ghunaymi. *Comparative Literature in Contemporary Arabic Literature* (in Arabic) (Cairo, 1962). Reviewed by G. Tutungi in *YCGL* 13 (1964), 64–67.

Hirth, Friedrich. "Vom Geiste vergleichender Literaturwissenschaft," *Universitas* 2 (1947), 1301–1320.

Höllerer, Walter. "Methoden und Probleme der vergleichenden Literaturwissenschaft," *GRM*, N.F. 2 (1952), 116–131.

Holmes, Urban T. "Comparative Literature, Past and Future" in *Studies in Language and Literature*, ed. G. R. Coffman (Chapel Hill: U. of North Carolina Press, 1945), 62–75.

Jan, Eduard von. "Französische Literaturgeschichte und vergleichende Literaturbetrachtung," *GRM* 15 (1927), 305–317.

Jechová, H. "L'Importance des analyses stylistiques dans les études de littérature comparée" in *La Littérature comparée en Europe orientale*, ed. I. Sötér (Budapest, 1963), 223–228.

Jeune, Simon. *Littérature générale et littérature comparée: Essai d'orientation* (Paris: Les Lettres Modernes, 1968).

Jintāro, Kataoka. *An Analytical Approach to Comparative Literature* (Tokyo, 1971).

Jost, François. *Essais de Littérature comparée.* Vol. 1: *Helvetica* (Fribourg, 1964); vol. 2: *Europeana*, first series (Urbana, Ill., 1968).

———. "Komparatistik oder Absolutistik?" *Arcadia* 3 (1968), 229–234.

———. "La Littérature comparée, une philosophie des lettres" in *Essais de Littérature comparée, Europeana*, first series, 313–341.

Kobayashi, Tadashi. *Hikaku Bungaku nyumon* (Introduction to Comp. Lit.) (Tokyo, 1950).

Koch, Max. "Zur Einführung," *Zeitschrift für vergleichende Litteraturgeschichte* 1 (1886), 1–12.

Krauss, Werner. *Probleme der vergleichenden Literaturgeschichte.* Sitzungsberichte der Deutschen Akademie der Wissenschaften zu Berlin (Berlin, 1965).

———. "Nationale und vergleichende Literaturgeschichte" in *Zur Interpretation literarischer Werke* (Hamburg: Rowohlt, 1968).

Kühnemann, Eugen. "Zur Aufgabe der vergleichenden Literaturgeschichte," *Centralblatt für Bibliothekswesen* 18 (1901), 1–11.

La Drière, Craig. "The Comparative Method in the Study of Prosody" in *Proceedings II*, Vol. One, 160–175.

Leo, Ulrich. "Literaturvergleichung und Monographie: Bemerkungen zu *Forschungsprobleme der vergleichenden Literaturgeschichte*," *Romanische Forschungen* 64 (1952), 421–432. Included in *Romanistische Aufsätze aus drei Jahrzehnten* (Cologne, 1966), 30–45.

Levin, Harry. "Comparing the Literature," *YCGL* 17 (1968), 5–16.

Linnér, Sven. "Om den litteraturhistoriska komparationen," *Samlaren* 80 (1960), 75–88. Enlarged version in Linnér's book *Litteraturhistoriska argument* (Stockholm, 1964), 1–27.

———. "The Structure and Functions of Literary Comparisons," *JAAC* 26 (1967), 169–179.

Malone, David H. "The 'Comparative' in Comparative Literature," *YCGL* 2 (1954), 13–20.

Markiewicz, H. "Forschungsbereich und Systematik der vergleichenden Literaturwissenschaft," *Weimarer Beiträge*, 1968, 1320–1330.

Marsh, A. R. "The Comparative Study of Literature," *PMLA* 11 (1896), 151–170.

Mayo, Robert S. *Herder and the Beginnings of Comparative Literature* (Chapel Hill: U. of North Carolina Press, 1969).

Moriarty, Michael E. "The Uses of Analogy: An Essay in the Methodology of Comparative Literature." Diss. Indiana University, 1971.

———. "H. M. Posnett and Two American Comparatists," *YCGL* 21 (1972), 15–22. Francis Gummere and A. M. Mackenzie.

Munteano, Basil. "Situation de la littérature comparée: Sa portée humaine et sa legitimité" in *Proceedings II*, Vol. One, 124–142. Enlarged version in Munteano's book *Constantes dialectiques en littérature et en histoire* (Paris, 1967), 85–135.

———. "Conclusion provisoire," *RLC* 27 (1953), 50–58.

Nahke, Evamaria. "IV. Kongress der Internationalen Vereinigung für vergleichende Literatur," *Weimarer Beiträge*, 1965, 252–262.

Nakajima, Kenzo and Yoshio Nakano. *Hikaku Bungaku josetsu* (Preface to Comparative Lit.) (Tokyo, 1951).

Neri, Ferdinando. "La tavola dei valori del comparatista" in *Letteratura e leggenda* (Torino, 1951), 289–299. Originally in *Giornale storico della letteratura italiana*, 1937.

Neupokoéva, I. G. "Methodological Questions of Studying Literatures in their Connection and Cooperation" (in Russian) in *Littérature comparée en Europe orientale*, 25–39.

Nyirö, L. "Problèmes de littérature comparée et théorie de littérature" in *Littérature hongroise, Littérature européenne*, ed. I. Sötér and O. Süpek (Budapest, 1964), 505–524.

Ocvirk, Anton. *Teorija primerjalne literarne zgodovine* (Introduction to the Theory of Comp. Lit.) (Ljubljana, 1936). In Slovenian. 203 pp. French summary, pp. 183–190.

Ota, Saburo. *Hikaku Bungaku* (Comparative Literature) (Tokyo, 1958).

———. "The Statistical Method of Investigation in Comparative Literature" in *Proceedings II*, Vol. One, 88–97.

Partridge, Eric. "The Comparative Study of Literature" in *A Critical Medley* (Paris: Champion, 1926), 159–226.

Petersen, Julius. "Nationale oder vergleichende Literaturgeschichte?", *DVLG* 6 (1928), 36-61.

Petrus, Pavel. "Zu einigen theoretisch-methodologischen Problemen der vergleichenden Literaturforschung" in *Sborník Ševčenkovsky* (Bratislava, 1965), 83–97. In Czech, with German summary.

Pichois, Claude and André Rousseau. *La Littérature comparée* (Paris: Colin, 1967). Trans. into Dutch, German and Spanish.

Poggioli, Renato. *The Theory of the Avant-Garde* (Harvard University Press, 1968). From the Italian.

Posnett, Hutcheson Macaulay. *Comparative Literature* (New York, 1886). Reprint New York: Johnson, 1970.

————. "The Science of Comparative Literature," *Contemporary Review* 79 (1901), 855–872.

Remak, Henry H. H. "Comparative Literature: Its Definition and Function" in S/F, 3–37. Brought up-to-date in the second edition (1971), pp. 17–24.

————. "Comparative Literature at the Crossroads: Diagnosis, Therapy and Prognosis," *YCGL* 9 (1960), 1–28.

Rod, Edouard. *De la Littérature comparée*. Inaugural lecture at the University of Geneva. (Geneva, 1886).

Roddier, Henri. "De l'Emploi de la méthode génétique en littérature comparée" in *Proceedings II*, Vol. One, 113–124.

————. "Littérature comparée et Histoire des idées," *RLC* 27 (1953), 43–49.

Rüdiger, Horst. "Nationalliteraturen und europäische Literatur: Methoden und Ziele der vergleichenden Literaturwissenschaft," *Schweizer Monatshefte* 42 (1962), 195–211.

————. "Grenzen und Aufgaben der vergleichenden Literaturwissenschaft" in *Zur Theorie der vergleichenden Literaturwissenschaft*, ed. H. Rüdiger (Berlin, 1971), 1–14.

Samarin, R. M. "Vom gegenwärtigen Stand des vergleichenden Literaturstudiums in der ausländischen Wissenschaft" (transl. from the Russian), *Kunst und Literatur in der Sowjetunion* 9 (1961), 11–34.

Schirmunsky, Victor M. "Les Problèmes de stylistique comparée" in *Littérature comparée en Europe orientale*, 77–82.

————. "On the Study of Comparative Literature," *Oxford Slavonic Papers* 13 (1968), 1–13.

Schulz, Hans-Joachim. "Max Koch and Germany's First Journals of Comparative Literature," *YCGL* 21 (1972), 23–30.

Schwarz, Egon. "Fragen und Gedanken zur vergleichenden Literaturwissenschaft vom Standpunkt eines Germanisten," *GQ* 38 (1965), 318–324.

Siciliano, Italo. "Quelques Remarques sur la littérature comparée," *Lettere Italiane* 8 (1956), 3–8. Opening speech of the first ICLA Congress, held in Venice.

Smith, G. Gregory. "The Foible of Comparative Literature," *Blackwood's Edinburgh Magazine* 169 (1901), 38–48. Published anonymously. Reprinted in *YCGL* 19 (1970), 58–66.

———. "Some Notes on the Comparative Study of Literature," *MLR* 1 (1905), 1–8.

Sötér, Istvan. "Les Recherches comparatives complexes" in *Aspects et parallélismes de la littérature hongroise* (Budapest, 1966), 101–114.

Stallknecht, Newton P. and Horst Frenz, eds. *Comparative Literature: Method and Perspective* (U. of Southern Illinois Press, 1961). Second, enlarged and modified ed., 1971.

Strelka, Joseph. *Vergleichende Literaturkritik: Drei Aufsätze* (Berne: Francke, 1970). Three methodological essays.

Strich, Fritz. "Weltliteratur und vergleichende Literaturgeschichte" in *Philosophie der Literaturwissenschaft*, ed. E. Ermatinger (Berlin, 1930), 422–441.

Sziklay, L. "Einige methodologische Fragen zur vergleichenden Literaturgeschichte," *Studia Slavica* (Budapest) 9 (1963), 311–335.

Texte, Joseph. "L'Histoire comparée des littératures" in *Etudes de littérature européenne* (Paris, 1898), 1–23.

Thompson, Stith. "Literature for the Unlettered" in *S/F*, 171–188.

———. "Comparative Problems in Oral Literature," *YCGL* 7 (1958), 6–16.

Thorlby, Anthony. "Comparative Literature," *TLS*, July 25, 1968, 793–794. Reprinted in *YCGL* 18 (1969), 75–81.

Thys, Walter. "De vergelijkende literatuurwetenschap," *Spiegel der Letteren* 1 (1957), 251–266.

Träger, Claus. "Zum Gegenstand und Integrationsbereich der Allgemeinen und Vergleichenden Literaturwissenschaft," *Weimarer Beiträge*, 1969, 90–102.

Vajda, Györgyi M. "Rapport relatif au projet d'une Histoire de la littérature européenne" in *Proceedings V*, 775–794.

Van Tieghem, Paul. *La Littérature Comparée* (Paris: Colin, 1931). Third ed., 1946.

———. "La Synthèse en histoire littéraire: Littérature comparée et littérature générale," *Revue de synthèse historique* 31 (1921), 1–27.

Vries, D. de. "De vergelijkende literatuurstudie," *Neophilologus* 20 (1935) 170–175, 300–310.

Wais, Kurt. "Vergleichende Literaturbetrachtung" in *Forschungsprobleme* I, 7–12.

———. "Zeitgeist und Volksgeist in der vergleichenden Literaturgeschichte," *GRM* 22 (1934), 291–307.

Wehrli, Max. "Weltliteratur und vergleichende Literaturwissenschaft" in W.'s book *Allgemeine Literaturwissenschaft* (Berne, 1951), 153–156.

Weisstein, Ulrich. "Dialect as a Barrier to Translation: The Case of German Literature," *Monatshefte* 54 (1962), 233–243.

———. "Influences and Parallels: The Place and Function of Analogy Studies in Comparative Literature" in *Festschrift* for Horst Rüdiger (Berlin: de Gruyter). In press.

Wellek, René. "The Concept of Comparative Literature," *YCGL* 2 (1953), 1–5.

———. "The Crisis of Comparative Literature" in *Proceedings II*, Vol. One, 149–159.

———. "Comparative Literature Today," *CL* 17 (1965), 325–337.

———. "The Name and Nature of Comparative Literature" in *Comparatists at Work*, ed. S. Nichols, Jr. and R. Vowles (Waltham, Mass.: Blaisdell, 1968), 3–27. Reprinted in W.'s *Discriminations: Further Concepts of Criticism* (New Haven: Yale U. Press, 1970), 1–36.

Wellek, René and Austin Warren. *Theory of Literature* (New York: Harcourt Brace, 1949). Chapter Four: "General, Comparative and National Literature."

Weselowsky, Alexander. "On the Methods and Aims of Literary History as a Science," tr. by H. Weber, *YCGL* 16 (1967), 33–43. Inaugural lecture at St. Petersburg University, 1870.

Wetz, Wilhelm. "Über Begriff und Wesen der vergleichenden Litteraturgeschichte" in W's book *Shakespeare vom Standpunkt der vergleichenden Litteraturgeschichte* (Worms, 1890), 3–43.

Will, J. S. "Comparative Literature: Its Meaning and Scope," *UTQ* 8 (1959), 165–179.

Woodberry, George. Editorial in the first issue of the *Journal of Comparative Literature*, 1903. Reprinted in *YCGL* 11 (1962), 5–7.

Wrenn, C. L. *The Idea of Comparative Literature* (Cambridge, Engld., 1968).

Yano, Hojin. *Hikaku Bungaku* (Comparative Literature) (Tokyo, 1956).

2. Literary Comparison within the Slavic Literatures

Czičevsky, Dimitri. *Outline of Comparative Slavic Literatures* (Boston: American Academy of Sciences, 1952).

Dolansky, Julius. "Das vergleichend-historische Studium der Literaturen Osteuropas" in *La Littérature comparée en Europe orientale*, 101–114.

Gáldi, Laszlo. "Littérature comparée et métrique comparée en Europe orientale" in *La Littérature comparée en Europe orientale*, 207–213.

Jakobson, Roman. "The Kernel of Comparative Slavic Literature," *Harvard Slavic Studies* 1 (1953), 1–72.

———. "Comparative Slavic Studies," *Review of Politics* 16 (1954), 67–90.

Klaniczay, Tibor. "La Possibilité d'une littérature comparée de l'Europe orientale" in *La Littérature comparée en Europe orientale*, 115–128.

Kravčov, N. I. "Voprosy sravnitel 'no-istoričeskogo izučenija slavjanskix literatur," *Vestnik Moskovskogo Universitet*, seventh series (1964), 16–30.

Markovitch, M. "Introduction à l'histoire comparée des littératures slaves" in *Literary History and Literary Criticism*, ed. L. Edel (New York, 1965), 165–176.

Sijavušgil, S. "Osnovi na edna sravnitelna literatura na balkanskite strani," *Literaturna Mišl* (Sofia), Nr. 5 (1966), 53–64.

"Slavistics and Comparative Literature," *YCGL* 9 (1960), 104–110. A symposium edited by Z. Folejewski.

Smal-Stocki, R. *J. S. C. de Radius, an Unknown Forerunner of Comparative Slavic Literature* (Washington, D.C.: Shevchenko Scientific Society Study Center, 1960).

Sziklay, L. "Literarhistorische Slawistik oder vergleichende ostund südosteuropäische Literaturgeschichtsschreibung?", *Ost und West*, 1967, 715–723.

Winter, Eduard. "Eine Propagandistin der vergleichenden slawischen Literatur: Therese Jacob (Talvj)" in *La Littérature comparée en Europe orientale*, 313–319.

Wollman, Frank. *K methodologii srovnávaci slovesnosti slovanske* (Brno, 1936).

———. "Zur Frage der vergleichenden slawischen Literaturwissenschaft," *Zeitschrift für Slawistik* 6 (1961), 211–216.

Additional items by Wollman in *Slavia* 36 (1967). Further bibl. information in Durišin's *Problémy*. . . .

3. Comparative Literature and Medieval Letters

Curtius, Ernst Robert. *Lateinische Literatur und europäisches Mittelalter* (Berne: Francke, 1948). English version: *Latin Literature and the European Middle Ages*, tr. W. R. Trask (New York: Pantheon, 1953).

Frappier, Jean. "Littératures médiévales et littérature comparée: Problèmes de recherche et de méthode" in *Proceedings II*, Vol. One, 25–35.

Graf, Arturo. *Storia letteraria e comparazione: Prolusione al corso di storia comparata delle letterature neolatine* (Torino, 1877).

Schneider, Hermann. "Weltliteratur und Nationalliteratur im Mittelalter," *Euphorion* 45 (1950), 131–139.

Ullman, B. L. "Medieval Latin and Comparative Literature" in *Proceedings II*, Vol. One, 16–25.

4. World Literature and Cosmopolitanism

Auerbach, Erich. "Philologie der Weltliteratur" in *Weltliteratur: Festgabe für Fritz Strich zum 70. Geburtstag*, ed. W. Muschg and E. Staiger (Berne, 1952), 39–50.

Beil, Else. *Zur Entwicklung des Begriffs der Weltliteratur* (Leipzig, 1915).

Bender, Helmut and Ulrich Melzer. "Zur Geschichte des Begriffs 'Weltliteratur'," *Saeculum* 9 (1958), 113–122.

Benedetto, L. F. "La letteratura mondiale," *Il Ponte* 2 (1946), 120–134.

Brandes, Georg. "Weltlitteratur," *Das litterarische Echo* 2 (1899), col. 1–5.

Brandt Corstius, Jan. "Wereldliteratuur" in *De muze en het morgenlicht* (Zeist, 1957), 149–170. Originally under the title "De ontwikkeling van het begrip wereldliteratuur" in *De vlaamse Gids* 41 (1957), 582–600.

———. "Writing Histories of World Literature," *YCGL* 12 (1963), 5–14.

———. "The Impact of Cosmopolitanism and Nationalism on Comparative Literature from the Beginning to 1880" in *Proceedings IV*, Vol. One, 380–389.

Carlsson, Anni. "Die Entfaltung der Weltliteratur als Prozess" in *Weltliteratur: Festgabe für Fritz Strich* . . . , 51–66.

Einsiedel, Wolfgang von. "Die Weltliteratur und ihre Provinzen," *Merkur* 22 (1968), 85–100.

Etiemble, René. "Faut-il reviser la notion de 'Weltliteratur'?", *Proceedings IV*, Vol. One, 5–16.

Gillet, J. "Cosmopolitisme et littérature comparée" in *Les Flandres dans les mouvements romantique et symboliste* (Paris, 1958), 45–51.

Gillies, Alexander. "Herder and the Preparation of Goethe's Idea of World Literature," *Publications of the English Goethe Society,* n. s. 9 (1933), 46–67.

Guerard, Albert. "What is World Literature?" in *Preface to World Literature* (New York, 1940), 3–16.

Hankiss, Janos. "Littérature universelle?", *Helicon* 1 (1938), 156–171.

Hazard, Paul. "Cosmopolite" in *Mélanges . . . offerts à Fernand Baldensperger* (Paris, 1930), I, 354–364.

Klemperer, Viktor. "Weltliteratur und europäische Literatur," *Logos* 18 (1930), 362–418.

Krehayn, J. "Zum Begriff der Weltliteratur als literaturwissenschaftliche Kategorie," *Philologica Pragensia* 9 (1966), 225–235.

Merian-Genast, Ernst W. *Voltaires "Essai sur la poésie épique" und die Entwicklung der Idee der Weltliteratur* (Leipzig, 1926), Vol. 40 of Romanische Forschungen.

Meyer, R. M. "Die Weltliteratur der Gegenwart," *Deutsche Rundschau* 104 (1900), 269–291.

Proceedings IV, Vol. One. Contains numerous contributions to the topic of cosmopolitanism.

Remak, Henry H.H. "The Impact of Cosmopolitanism and Nationalism on Comparative Literature from the 1880s to the Post-World War II Period," *Proceedings IV*, Vol. One, 390–397.

Remenyi, Joseph. "The Meaning of World Literature," *JAAC* 9 (1951), 244–251.

Schrimpf, Hans-Joachim. *Goethes Begriff der Weltliteratur* (Stuttgart: Metzler, 1968).

Strich, Fritz. "Weltliteratur und vergleichende Literaturgeschichte" in *Philosophie der Literaturwissenschaft*, ed. E. Ermatinger (Berlin, 1930), 422–441.

———. *Goethe und die Weltliteratur* (Berne: Francke, 1946). English *Goethe and World Literature*, tr. C. A. M. Sym (New York: Hafner, 1949).

Texte, Joseph. *Jean-Jacques Rousseau et les origines du cosmopolitisme littéraire: Etudes sur les relations littéraires de la France et de l'Angleterre au XVIIIe siècle* (Paris, 1895).

Vossler, Karl. "Nationalliteratur und Weltliteratur," *Zeitwende* 4 (1928), 193–204.

Wais, Kurt. "Le Cosmopolitisme littéraire à travers les âges" in *Proceedings IV*, Vol. One, 17–29.

5. Periodicals and Yearbooks

ACLAN (*American Comparative Literature Association Newsletter*), ed. by A. Renoir (Vol. One, Nos. 1 and 2), W. B. Fleischmann (Vols. Two through Five) and H. Weisinger (Vol. Six). 1965ff.

Acta Comparationis Litterarum Universarum (Klausenburg-Cluj), ed. Hugo Meltzl de Lomnitz. 12 vols. (1877–1888). See the essay by G. M. Vajda in *YCGL* 14 (1965), 37–45, and the account by C. Ijac in *RLC* 14 (1934), 733–745.

Arcadia, Zeitschrift für vergleichende Literaturwissenschaft, ed. H. Rüdiger. 1966ff.

Cahiers Algériens de Littérature comparée, ed. J. E. Bencheikh. 1966-Annual publication, now discontinued.

Comparative Literature, ed. C. H. Beall (vols. 1–23) and T. R. Hart (vol. 24ff.). Published at the University of Oregon. 1949ff.

Comparative Literature Newsletter, ed. A. O. Christy for the National Council of Teachers of English. 4 vols. (1942–1946).

Comparative Literature Studies (Cardiff), ed. M. Chicoteau and K. Unwin. 24 issues (1941–1946). Temporarily replaced *RLC*.

Comparative Literature Studies, ed. A. O. Aldridge. Special Advance Issue (1963) and 1964ff. Originally published at the

University of Maryland (vols. 1–3), now at the University of Illinois.

Helicon, Revue Internationale des problèmes générales de la littérature, ed. J. Hankiss. 5 vols. (1938–1942). See the account by K. Bór in *La Littérature comparée en Europe orientale,* 294–297 (in Russian).

Hikaku Bungaku (Comparative Literature), ed. K. Nakajima. Organ of the Japanese Comparative Literature Association. 1958ff. Annual publication.

Hikaku Bungaku Kenkyu (Comparative Literature Studies), ed. S. Ota at the University of Tokyo. Semi-annual publication.

Hikaku Bungaku Nenshi (Comparative Literature Yearbook), published by Waseda University. Annual publication.

Jadavpur Journal of Comparative Literature, ed. N. Guha and B. Bose (Nos. 1–3). 8 issues (1961ff.)

Journal of Comparative Literature, ed. G. Woodberry. 1 vol. (1903). Published at Columbia University.

Littérature comparée en Canada, Comparative Literature in Canada. Newsletter of the Canadian Comparative Literature Association, ed. by M. V. Dimić. 1969ff. Two issues per year.

Neohelicon (Budapest), ed. by M. Szabólcsi and G. M. Vajda for the Coordinating Committee of the International History of Literature in European Languages. 1973ff.

Revue de littérature comparée, ed. M. Bataillon with the help of an editorial committee. Founded by F. Baldensperger, edited first by him, then by P. Hazard and J.-M. Carré, and finally by B. Munteano. 1921ff. Vol. 20 comprises the years 1940–1946 (3 issues).

Rivista di letterature italiane e comparate, ed. C. Pellegrini. 1948ff. Originally *Rivista di letterature italiane.*

Studien zur vergleichenden Litteraturgeschichte, ed. M. Koch. 7 vols. (1901–1907).

Tamkang Review: A Journal Mainly Devoted to Comparative Studies between Chinese and Foreign Literature (Taipei, Taiwan). 1970ff.

Yearbook of Comparative and General Literature, ed. H. Frenz, H. H. Remak and U. Weisstein at Indiana University. Founded and edited (vols. 1–9) by W. P. Friederich at the University of North Carolina. Now published at Indiana University.

Yearbook of Comparative Criticism, ed. J. Strelka. 5 vols. 1968ff.
Published at Pennsylvania State University.
Zeitschrift für vergleichende Litteraturgeschichte, ed. M. Koch.
17 vols. (1887–1906). L. Geiger coeditor beginning with vol.
3. Vols. 15 and 16 edited by W. Wetz and J. Collin. See the
essay by H. J. Schulz in *YCGL* 21 (1972), 23–30.

6. Proceedings and Festschriften

A. Proceedings
  1. AILC/ACLA
     a) Venice, 1955: *Venezia nelle letterature moderne,* ed.
        C. Pellegrini (Venice/Rome; Istituto per la collabora-
        zione culturale, 1961).
     b) Chapel Hill, 1958: *Comparative Literature: Proceedings
        of the Second Congress of the ICLA,* ed. W. P. Friede-
        rich (Chapel Hill: University of North Carolina Press,
        1959). 2 vols.
     c) Utrecht, 1961: *Actes du IIIᵉ Congrès de l'AILC,* ed. W. P.
        Smit (The Hague: Mouton, 1962). Contains only the
        main papers and summaries of the shorter contribu-
        tions. See the account by Horst Rüdiger in the
        Schweizer Monatshefte 41 (1961), 806–810.
     d) Fribourg, 1964: *Actes du IVᵉ Congrès de l'AILC,* ed.
        François Jost (The Hague: Mouton, 1967). 2 vols. See
        the account by E. Koppen in the *Schweizer Monat-
        shefte* 44 (1964), 971–974.
     e) Belgrade, 1967: *Actes du Vᵉ Congrès de l'AILC,* ed.
        N. Banašević (Amsterdam: Swets & Zeitlinger, 1969).
        Not altogether complete, insofar as several papers and
        the transcripts of the two symposia are missing. See the
        review by Milan Dimić in *YCGL* 20 (1971), 121–125.
     f) Bordeaux, 1970: Proceedings to be published in 1973 by
        the Verlag Kunst und Wissen in Stuttgart, Germany.
  2. Proceedings of the meetings held by the French Compara-
     tive Literature Association.
     a) Bordeaux, 1956: *Littérature générale et histoire des
        idées* (Paris, 1956).
     b) Lille, 1957: *Les Flandres dans les mouvements roman-
        tique et symboliste* (Paris, 1958).

c) Dijon, 1959: *La France, la Bourgogne et la Suisse au XVIIIe siècle* (Paris, 1960).

d) Toulouse, 1960: *Espagne et littérature française* (Paris, 1961).

e) Lyon, 1962: *Imprimerie, commerce et littérature* (Paris, 1965).

f) Rennes, 1963: *Littérature savante et littérature populaire: Bardes, conteurs, écrivains* (Paris, 1965).

g) Poitiers, 1965: *Le Moyen Age* (Paris, 1967).

h) Grenoble, 1966: *L'Italianisme en France au XVIIe siècle* (Torino, 1968).

3. Proceedings of the triennial ACLA meetings.

a) New York, 1962: *CLS*, Special Advance Issue, 1963.

b) Cambridge, Mass., 1965: *CL* 17 (1965), 325–345, and *ACLAN* 1 (1965), 32–44.

c) Bloomington, Indiana, 1968: *YCGL* 17 (1968).

d) New Haven, Conn., 1971: Lectures by René Wellek and Horst Rüdiger, as well as the symposium on translation in *YCGL* 20 (1971), 5–36; Steven P. Scher on Literature and Music in *YCGL* 21 (1972), 52–56.

4. Proceedings of the meetings of the German Comparative Literature Association.

a) Mainz, 1970: *Zur Theorie der Vergleichenden Literaturwissenschaft*, ed. H. Rüdiger (Berlin: de Gruyter, 1971). Papers by G. Bauer, E. Koppen and M. Gsteiger.

b) Regensburg, 1972: to be published by de Gruyter (Berlin, 1973).

5. Commission Internationale d'Histoire Moderne (since 1948: Fédération Internationale des Langues et Littératures Modernes [FILLM]).

a) Budapest, 1931: "Les Méthodes en histoire littéraire," *Bulletin of the International Committee of Historical Sciences*, No. 14 (1932).

b) Amsterdam, 1935: "Les Périodes de l'histoire littéraire de l'Europe depuis la Renaissance," ibid., No. 36 (1937), pp. 225–398.

c) Lyon, 1939: "Les Genres littéraires," *Helicon* 2 (1939), 115–224.

d) Paris, 1948: *La Littérature dans ses rapports avec les mouvements sociaux et politiques* (Paris, 1950).

e) Florence, 1951: *Les Langues et littératures modernes dans leurs rapports avec les beaux-arts*, ed. C. Pellegrini (Florence, 1955).

f) Oxford, 1954: *Literature and Science* (Oxford, 1955).

g) Heidelberg, 1957: *Stil- und Formprobleme der Literatur*, ed. P. Böckmann (Heidelberg, 1958).

h) Liège, 1960: *Langues et littératures* (Paris, 1961). Vol. 161 der Publications de la Faculté de Philosophie of the University of Liège.

i) New York, 1963: *Literary History and Literary Criticism*, ed. Leon Edel (New York: New York University Press, 1965).

j) Strasbourg, 1966: *Le Réel dans la littérature et dans la langue*, ed. Paul Vernois (Paris: Klincksieck, 1967).

k) Islamabad (Pakistan), 1969: unpublished.

l) Cambridge, England, 1972: unpublished.

6. Indiana Conference on Oriental-Western Literary Relations (Indiana University, Bloomington, Ind.)

a) June, 1954: *Proceedings* ed. by Horst Frenz and G. L. Anderson (Chapel Hill: U. of North Carolina Press, 1955).

b) June, 1958: *Asia and the Humanities*, ed. H. Frenz (Bloomington, Ind., 1959).

c) June, 1962: "Third Conference on Oriental-Western Literary and Cultural Relations," *YCGL* 11 (1962), 121–236.

d) June, 1966: "Fourth Conference on Oriental-Western Literary and Cultural Relations," *YCGL* 15 (1966), 159–224.

e) June, 1970: "Islam in World Literature," *YCGL* 20 (1971), 57–88.

7. Other Conferences

Aktuelle Probleme der vergleichenden Literaturforschung, ed. G. Ziegengeist (Berlin: Akademie-Verlag, 1968). Papers read at a conference held in East Berlin from December 6 to 8, 1966.

Annales internationales d'histoire: Congrès de Paris, 1900. VIe section: Histoire comparée des littératures (Paris, 1901).

Budapest Colloquium, Colloque méthodologique de littérature comparée, Budapest, November 17 and 18,

1971. Proceedings in *Neohelicon*, Nos. 1/2 (1973), pp. 21–337. Three major topics: 1) Histoire littéraire —Valeur esthétique; 2) La Zone littéraire; 3) Courants littéraires—Epoques littéraires.

Forschungsprobleme der vergleichenden Literaturgeschichte, ed. K. Wais and F. Ernst. 2 vols. (Tübingen: Niemeyer, 1951, 1958).

International Comparative Literature Conference on East-West Relations, held at Tamkang College in Taipei (Taiwan) between July 18 and 24, 1971. Proceedings published in a double issue of the *Tamkang Review* (vols. II/2 and III/1). See the account by A. Owen Aldridge in *YCGL* 21 (1972), 65–70.

La Littérature comparée en Europe orientale, ed. I. Sötér (Budapest, 1963). Papers read at a conference held in Budapest between October 26 and 29, 1962. Reviewed by D. McCutchion in *Jadavpur Journal* . . . 5 (1965), 88–100, and R. Matlaw in *YCGL* 13 (1964), 53–55.

Littérature hongroise, littérature européenne: Etudes de littérature comparée. Published by the Hungarian Academy of Sciences on the occasion of the fourth ICLA congress. Edited by I. Sötér (Budapest, 1964).

Problemy mezhdunarodnykh literaturnykh sujazej (Leningrad: Leningrad University Press, 1962). Papers delivered at a conference organized by the Gorky Institute of World Literature in Moscow during 1960. See the reports by E. Matlaw in *YCGL* 13 (1964), 49–53, and by O. Egorov in *Zeitschrift für Slawistik* 7 (1962), 151–163.

Vzaimosvjazi i vzaimodejstvie nationalnykh literatur (Moscow: Academy of Sciences, 1961). Proceedings of a meeting, held in 1957 at the Gorky Institute for World Literature. See the report by R. Matlaw in *YCGL* 13 (1964), 49–53.

B. *Festschriften*

Beiträge zur vergleichenden Literaturgeschichte: Festschrift für Kurt Wais zum 65. Geburtstag, ed. J. Hösle (Tübingen, 1972).

Connaissance de l'Etranger: Mélanges offerts à la mémoire de Jean-Marie Carré (Paris, 1964).

The *Disciplines of Criticism*, ed. P. Demetz, T. Greene and
L. Nelson, Jr. (New Haven: Yale University Press,
1968). *Festschrift* for René Wellek.
Festschrift for Horst Rüdiger, ed. B. Allemann and E. Kop-
pen (Berlin: de Gruyter). In press.
*Mélanges de littérature comparée et de philologie offerts à
Mieczyslaw Brahmer* (Warsaw: PWN, 1967).
*Mélanges d'histoire littéraire générale et comparée offerts à
Fernand Baldensperger* (Paris, 1930). 2 vols.
Studi in onore di Carlo Pellegrini (Torino, 1963).
Weltliteratur: Festgabe für Fritz Strich zum 70. Geburtstag,
ed. W. Muschg and E. Staiger (Berne, 1962).

7. Book Series

Bibliothèque de la Revue de Littérature Comparée, ed. F. Balden-
sperger and P. Hazard. 113 vols. (1920–1937).
Columbia University Studies in English and Comparative Litera-
ture. 168 vols. (1899–1955).
Etudes de Littérature étrangère et comparée. 62 vols. (Paris,
1938ff.).
Harvard Studies in Comparative Literature. 32 vols. (Cambridge,
Mass., 1910ff.).
Komparatistische Studien, ed. Horst Rüdiger. 1 vol. (Berlin, 1971).
University of North Carolina Studies in Comparative Literature.
53 vols. (Chapel Hill, 1950ff.).
Princeton Essays in European and Comparative Literature. 6 vols.
(1969ff.). Not particularly relevant to our discipline.
Proceedings of the Comparative Literature Symposium of the
Texas Technological College, ed. W. T. Zyla. 3 vols. (Lub-
bock, Texas, 1968ff.).
Studia litteraria Rheno-Traiectina. 6 vols. (Utrecht, 1950–1959).
Studien zum Fortwirken der Antike, ed. Horst Rüdiger. 5 vols.
(Heidelberg: Winter, 1968ff.).
University of Southern California Studies in Comparative Litera-
ture, ed. D. H. Malone (Los Angeles, 1968ff.). Includes the
proceedings of the annual University of Southern California
conference in Comp. Lit. Not all volumes are relevant to our
discipline.
Utrechtse publikaties voor Allgemene Literatuurwetenschap. 8
vols. (Utrecht, 1962ff.).

Zürcher Beiträge zur vergleichenden Literaturgeschichte. 5 vols.
    (1952ff.).

8. *History and Present State of Comparative Literature*
    Studies in Various Countries

a) *Australia*
    Friederich, W. P. "The 1955 Meeting of the Australasian Uni-
        versities' Modern Language Association," *RLC* 30 (1956),
        237–239.
b) *Belgium*
    Thys, Walter. "A Glance at Comparative Literature in Bel-
        gium," *YCGL* 9 (1960), 31–43.
c) *Bulgaria*
    Valčev, G. "Entwicklungstendenzen der vergleichenden Li-
        teraturforschung in Bulgarien" in *Aktuelle Probleme der
        Vergleichenden Literaturforschung*, ed. G. Ziegengeist
        (Berlin: Akademie-Verlag, 1968), 140–144.
d) *Canada*
    "Canadian Programmes in Comparative Literature," *Compar-
        ative Literature in Canada* 3 (1971), No. 1, pp. 15–31.
e) *Czechoslovakia*
    Rosenbaum, K. "Entwicklungslinien der slowakischen ver-
        gleichenden Literaturforschung" in *Aktuelle Probleme
        . . . , *118–127.
    Wollman, F. "Les Comparatistes de Prague et leur école,"
        Slovešná Veda 1 (1951), 51–54. In Czech.
    Wollman, S. "Überblick über die Entwicklung der tschechi-
        schen vergleichenden Literaturforschung" in *Aktuelle
        Probleme . . . , *100–117.
f) *England*
    McCutchion, David. "Comparative Literature in England,"
        Jadavpur Journal of Comparative Literature 6 (1966),
        145–149.
    "Not so Odious," *Times Literary Supplement*, March 12, 1964.
        Reprinted in *YCGL* 14 (1965), 72–73.
    Roe, Frederick C. "Comparative Literature in the United
        Kingdom," *YCGL* 3 (1956), 1–13.
    Sayce, R. A. "Comparative Literature," *Times Educational
        Supplement*, March 26, 1965. Reprinted in *YCGL* 15
        (1966), 63–65.

Wilkinson, Elizabeth. "Neuere Strömungen der angelsächsischen Ästhetik in ihrer Beziehung zur vergleichenden Literaturwissenschaft" in *Forschungsprobleme I*, 141–158.

Willoughby, L. A. "Stand und Aufgaben der vergleichenden Literaturgeschichte in England," ibid., 21–28.

g) *France*

Body, Jacques. "Les Comparatismes vus de France," *Neohelicon*, Nos. 1/2 (1973), pp. 354–359.

Carré, Jean-Marie. "L'Institut de Littérature Comparée de l'Université de Paris," *YCGL* 1 (1952), 46–49.

Escarpit, Robert. "La Littérature comparée dans les universités françaises de province," *YCGL* 5 (1956), 8–12.

Texte, Joseph. "Les Etudes de littérature comparée à l'étranger et en France," *Revue internationale de l'Enseignement* 25 (1893), 253–269.

Voisine, Jacques. "Les Etudes de littérature comparée," *Revue de l'Enseignement superieur* 3 (1957), 61–67.

———. "L'Enseignement de la littérature comparée dans une université française" in *Proceedings II*, Vol. One, 216–222. Lille.

Additional material can be found in the manuals by Guyard, Pichois/Rousseau and Van Tieghem, as well as *passim* in *RLC*.

h) *Germany*

Alewyn, Richard. "Comparative Literature in Germany," *Comparative Literature Newsletter* 1 (1943), No. 4, pp. 1–2.

Höllerer, Walter. "La Littérature comparée en Allemagne depuis la fin de guerre," *RLC* 27 (1953), 27–42. An Italian version appeared in the *Rivista di letterature moderne e comparate* 3 (1952), 285–299.

Oppel, Horst. "A Glance at Comparative Literature in Germany," *YCGL* 7 (1958), 16–23.

Rüdiger, Horst. "Comparative Literature in Germany," *YCGL* 20 (1971), 15–20.

Wuthenow, Ralph-Rainer. "Vergleichende Literaturwissenschaft in Deutschland," *Hikaku Bungaku* 11 (1966), 6–22.

i) *Holland*

Eupen, M. D. van. "The Growth of Comparative Literature in the Netherlands," *YCGL* 4 (1955), 21–26.

Lee, A. van der. "Zur Komparatistik im niederländischen Sprachraum" in *Forschungsprobleme II*, 173–177. Additional information in Cornelis de Deugd's book *De Eenheid van het Comparatisme.*

j) *Hungary*

Vajda, György M. "Hauptzüge der Geschichte der vergleichenden Literaturforschung in Ungarn" in *Littérature comparée en Europe orientale*, pp. 306–313.

———. "Stand, Aufgaben und methodologische Position der vergleichenden Literaturforschung in Ungarn" in *Aktuelle Probleme* . . . , pp. 89–99.

———. "Essai d'une histoire de la littérature comparée en Hongrie" in *Littérature hongroise, littérature européenne*, pp. 525–588. With a bibliography prepared by K. Bór.

k) *India*

Bose, Buddhadeva. "Comparative Literature in India," *YCGL* 8 (1959), 1–10.

l) *Italy*

Simone, Franco. "Benedetto Croce et la littérature comparée en Italie," *RLC* 27 (1953), 1–16.

m) *Japan*

Aldridge, A. Owen and Shunsuke Kamei. "Problems and Vistas of Comparative Literature in Japan and the United States: A Dialogue," *Mosaic: A Journal for the Comparative Study of Literature and Ideas* 5 (1972), 149–163.

Ota, Saburo. "The First Decade of the Japan Society of Comparative Literature," *YCGL* 6 (1957), 1–6.

———. "Comparative Literature in Japan," *Jadavpur Journal of Comparative Literature* 3 (1963), 1–10.

Yamagiwa, Joseph K. "Comparative, General and World Literature in Japan," *YCGL* 2 (1953), 28–39.

n) *Poland*

Brahmer, Mieczislav. "Etudes polonaises de littérature comparée," *Bulletin de l'Académie Polonaise* (Paris), April, 1952.

Markiewicz, Henri. "Entwicklungsprobleme und Ergebnisse der vergleichenden Literaturforschung in Polen" in *Aktuelle Probleme* . . . , 128–139. Original Polish version in *Slavia* 36 (1967), 291–299.

Zaleski, Z. L. "La Litterature comparée en Pologne," *YCGL* 2 (1953), 14–19.

o) *Romania*

Cornea, Paul. "La Troisiéme Conference roumaine de littérature comparée." *Neohelicon*, Nos. 1/2 (1973), pp. 383–386.

Dima, A. and O. Papadima, eds. *Istoria si teoria comparatismului în România* (Bucharest, 1972). Nine essays. Summaries in English, French, German and Russian.

Munteano, Basil. "La Littérature comparée en Roumanie," *RLC* 11 (1931), 515–535.

──────. "La Littérature comparée chez les Roumains," *YCGL* 2 (1953), 19–27.

p) *Russia and the Soviet Union*

Lukács, Borbála H. "Recent Comparative Research in the Soviet Union," *Neohelicon*, Nos. 1/2 (1973), pp. 359–367.

Struve, Gleb. "Comparative Literature in the Soviet Union, Today and Yesterday," *YCGL* 4 (1955), 1–21.

──────. "Comparative Literature in the Soviet Union: Two Postscripts," *YCGL* 6 (1957), 7–10.

──────. "More About Comparative Literature Studies in the Soviet Union," *YCGL* 8 (1959), 13–18.

See also the reviews by R. E. Matlaw in *YCGL* 13 (1964), 49–55, R. Triomphe in *RLC* 34 (1960), 304–310, and D. McCutchion in *Jadavpur Journal* . . . 5 (1965), 88–100, as well as the essay by E. Bojtar in *Helikon* (Budapest), 10 (1964), 62–72.

q) *South and Central America*

Nuñez, Estuardo. "Literatura comparada en Hispanoamerica," *CLS* 1 (1964), 41–45.

r) *Switzerland*

Jost, François. "La Littérature comparée en Suisse" in *Proceedings II*, Vol. One, 62–70.

s) *Taiwan*

Chu, Limin. "Comparative Literature Studies in Taiwan," *Tamkang Review* October, 1971/April, 1972 (double issue), 509–516.

Deeney, John J. "Comparative Literature Studies in Taiwan," *Tamkang Review* 1 (1970), 119–145.

t) *United Arab Republic*

Hilal, G. M. "Les Etudes de littérature comparée dans la Republique arabe," *YCGL* 8 (1959), 10–13.

Tutungi, Gilbert V. "Comparative Literature in the Arab World," *YCGL* 13 (1964), 64–67. Review of a book by G. M. Hilal.

u) *United States*

Baldensperger, Fernand. "La Littérature comparée aux Etats-Unis," *RLC* 21 (1947), 446–449.

Chambers, Leland H. "Survey of Comparative Literature Programs," *YCGL* 16 (1967), 60–78; and 17 (1968), 203–208.

———. "Comparative Literature Programs in the United States and Canada," *YCGL* 20 (1971), 89–109.

Friederich, W. P. "L'Organisation des 'Comparatistes' aux Etats-Unis," *RLC* 22 (1948), 115–121.

———. "Zur vergleichenden Literaturgeschichte in den Vereinigten Staaten" in *Forschungsprobleme II*, 179–192.

Lange, Victor. "Stand und Aufgaben der vergleichenden Literaturgeschichte in den USA" in *Forschungsprobleme I*, 21–28.

Levin, Harry. "La Littérature comparée: Point de vue d'outre-Atlantique," *RLC* 27 (1953), 17–26.

Moriarity, Michael. "Comparatism in the United States: an Impression." *Neohelicon*, Nos. 1/2 (1973), pp. 359–367.

Peyre, Henri. "A Glance at Comparative Literature in America," *YCGL* 1 (1952), 1–8.

———. "Seventy-Five Years of Comparative Literature: A Backward and a Forward Glance," *YCGL* 8 (1959), 18–26.

Schall, Frank L. "Littérature comparée et littérature générale aux Etats-Unis," *Etudes Françaises* 6 (1925), 43–60.

Pedagogical Aspects:

Frenz, Horst. "Comparative Literature for Undergraduates?", *YCGL* 4 (1955), 52–55.

Frenz, Horst and Ulrich Weisstein. "Teaching the Comparative Arts: A Challenge," *CE* 18 (1956), 67–71.

Remak, Henry H. H. "The Organization of an Introductory Survey" in *Proceedings II*, Vol. One, 222–229. Part of a symposium in which A. Balakian and R. Clements participated along with H. Oppel and H. Roddier.

A Syllabus of Comparative Literature, compiled by the Faculty of Comparative Literature, The Graduate School, Rutgers University (New York, 1964). Second ed. 1972.

"Symposium on Graduate Study in Comparative Literature,"

CLS Special Advance Issue (1963), 135–142. From the proceedings of the first meeting of the ACLA.

The Teaching of World Literature, ed. H. M. Block (Chapel Hill: U. of North Carolina Press, 1960). Proceedings of a meeting held at the University of Wisconsin.

"Undergraduate and Graduate Curricula, a Symposium," YCGL 17 (1968), 112–121. Proceedings of the second triennial meeting of the ACLA, D. H. Malone, W. deSua, V. Hall, R. H. Byrnes and R. J. Clements participating.

Bio-bibliographical sketches of leading American comparatists are scattered throughout the first nine volumes of YCGL.

v) Yugoslavia

Deanović, Mirko. "La Littérature comparée et les pays slaves" in Proceedings II, Vol. One, 70–79.

Kogoj-Kapetanić, Breda. "Komparativna istraživanja u Hrvatskoj književnosti" in Jugoslavenska Akademija Znąnosti i Umjetnosti (Odjel za suvremenu književnost), vol. 350 (Zagreb, 1968), pp. 305–404. A history of Comparative Literature in Croatia with bibliography (pp. 402–404).

Tartalja, Ivo, "Les Premiers Travaux sur l'Histoire de la Littérature Générale chez les Serbes" (in Serbo-Croatian) in Monographies de l'Académie Serbe des Sciences et des Arts, Classe de Littérature et de Langue, vol. 379, No. 13 (Belgrade, 1964). 135 pp. Summary in French on pp. 122–124.

Vujicsics, D. "A szerb összehasonlitó irodalomtudomány 1945-ig," Helikon 16 (1970), 218–226. Comp. Lit. in Serbia.

9. Influence, Imitation, Reception

Balakian, Anna. "Influence and Literary Fortune: The Equivocal Junction of Two Methods," YCGL 11 (1962), 24–31.

Block, Haskell M. "The Concept of Influence in Comparative Literature," YCGL 7 (1958), 30–37.

Clemen, Wolfgang. "Was ist literarischer Einfluss?", Neusprachliche Mitteilungen aus Wissenschaft und Praxis 22 (1969), 139ff.

"The Concept of Influence: A Symposium," CLS, Special Advance Issue (1963), 143–152. From the second triennial meeting of the ACLA.

Dyserinck, Hugo. "Zum Problem der *images* und *mirages* und ihrer Untersuchung im Rahmen der vergleichenden Literaturwissenschaft," *Arcadia* 1 (1966), 107–120.

Escarpit, Robert. "Les Méthodes de la sociologie littéraire" in *Proceedings II*, Vol. One, 142–148.

————. *Sociologie de la littérature* (Paris: Presses Universitaires de France, 1960). No. 777 in the series "Que sais-je?"

————. "Creative Treason as a Key to Literature," *YCGL* 10 (1961), 16–21.

Farinelli, Arturo. "Gli influssi letterari e l'insuperbire delle nazioni" in *Mélanges d'histoire littéraire générale et comparée, offerts à Fernand Baldensperger* (Paris, 1930), I, 271–290.

Fransen, J. *Iets over vergelijkende literatuurstudie, "perioden" en "invloeden"* (Groningen, 1936).

Gobbers, W. "Over de problematiek van de invloedenstudie" in *Handelingen van het 26. Vlaams Filologencongres* (Ghent, 1967), 628–641.

Guillén, Claudio. "Literatura como sistema: Sobre fuentes, influencias y valores literarios," *Filologia romanza* 4 (1957), 1–29.

————. "The Aesthetics of Influence Studies in Comparative Literature" in *Proceedings II*, Vol. One, 175–192. A slightly expanded version appears in G.'s book *Literature as System*, pp. 17–52.

————. "A Note on Influences and Conventions" in *Literature as System*, pp. 53–68. A longer version of Guillén's contribution to the *CLS* symposium.

Hassan, Ihab H. "The Problem of Influence in Literary History: Notes Toward a Definition," *JAAC* 14 (1955), 66–76.

Koppen, Erwin. "Hat die Vergleichende Literaturwissenschaft eine eigene Theorie? Ein Exempel: Der literarische Einfluss" in *Zur Theorie der Vergleichenden Literaturwissenschaft*, ed. Horst Rüdiger (Berlin: de Gruyter, 1971), 41–64.

Lubbers, Klaus. "Aufgaben und Möglichkeiten der Rezeptionsforschung," *GRM*, N.F. 14 (1964), 292–302.

Schücking, Levin L. *Soziologie der literarischen Geschmacksbildung*, third ed. (Berne/Munich: Francke, 1961). English version: *The Sociology of Literary Taste*, tr. B. Battershaw (University of Chicago Press, 1966).

Shaw, Joseph T. "Literary Indebtedness and Comparative Literature" in *S/F*, 58–71.

"Termes et notions littéraires: Imitation, influence, originalité" in *Proceedings IV*, Vol. Two, 697–1362.

10. Problems of Translation

Arrowsmith, William and Roger Shattuck, eds., *The Craft and Context of Translation* (New York: Doubleday Anchor Books, 1964). A symposium with sixteen contributions.

Brower, Reuben A., ed. *On Translation* (New York: Oxford University Press, 1959). Sixteen contributions and a bibliography compiled by B. Q. Morgan (pp. 271–293).

Frenz, Horst. "The Art of Translation" in S/F, 72–95.

Italiander, Rolf, ed. *Übersetzen: Vorträge und Beiträge vom internationalen Kongress literarischer Übersetzer in Hamburg 1965* (Frankfurt/Bonn: Athenäum, 1965).

Levý, Jiří. *Die literarische Übersetzung: Theorie einer Kunstgattung*, tr. W. Schamschula (Frankfurt/Bonn: Athenäum, 1969). From the Czech. Bibliography pp. 291–298.

Mounin, Georges. *Die Übersetzung: Geschichte, Theorie, Anwendung* (Munich, 1967).

Störig, H. J., ed. *Das Problem des Übersetzens* (Darmstadt, 1963).

11. Periodization

Analyse de la périodisation littéraire, ed. Ch. Bouazis (Paris: Editions universitaires, 1972). Proceedings of a conference held in Bordeaux.

Baldensperger, Fernand. "The Decreasing Length of Some Literary Periods," *Bulletin of the International Committee of Historical Sciences*, No. 36 (1937), 307–313.

"Courants littéraires—Epoques littéraires." *Neohelicon*, Nos. 1/2 (1973), pp. 177–325. Proceedings of the Budapest Colloquium, Nov., 1971.

Cysarz, Herbert. "Das Periodenprinzip in der Literaturwissenschaft" in *Philosophie der Literaturwissenschaft*, ed. E. Ermatinger (Berlin, 1930), 92–129.

Foerster, Max. "The Psychological Basis of Literary Periods" in *Studies for William A. Read* (Baton Rouge, La.: Louisiana State University Press, 1940), 254–268.

Guillén, Claudio. "Second Thoughts on Literary Periods" in *The*

Disciplines of Criticism (New Haven, 1968), pp. 477–510. Reprinted in G.'s book *Literature as System: Essays toward the Theory of Literary History* (Princeton University Press, 1971), 420–469.

Meyer, R.M. "Prinzipien der wissenschaftlichen Periodenbildung, mit besonderer Rücksicht auf die Literaturgeschichte," *Euphorion* 8 (1901), 1–42.

Panofsky, Erwin. "Renaissance and Renascences," *Kenyon Review* 6 (1944), 201–236. Expanded in Panofsky's book *Renaissance and Renascences in Western Art* (Stockholm: Almquist and Wiksell, 1965), 1–113.

"Les Périodes de l'histoire littéraire de l'Europe depuis la Renaissance" in *Bulletin of the International Committee of Historical Sciences No.* 36 (1937), 225–398. Proceedings of Third Congress of the *Commission*.

Petersen, Julius. "Die literarischen Generationen" in *Philosophie der Literaturwissenschaft*, ed. E. Ermatinger (Berlin, 1930), 130–187.

Peyre, Henri. *Les Générations littéraires* (Paris: Boivin, 1948).

Pinder, Wilhelm. *Das Problem der Generation in der Kunstgeschichte Europas* (Cologne, fourth ed., 1949).

Poggioli, Renato. *The Theory of the Avant-Garde,* tr. G. Fitzgerald (Harvard University Press, 1968). Originally published in 1962 under the title *Teoria dell'arte d'avanguardia*.

"A Symposium on Periods" in *New Literary History: A Journal of Theory and Interpretation* 1 (1970),

Teesing, H.P.H. *Das Problem der Perioden in der Literaturgeschichte* (Groningen: Wolters, 1948). Exhaustive bibliography on pp. 140–145.

———. "Die Bedeutung der vergleichende Literaturgeschichte für die literarhistorische Periodisierung" in *Forschungsprobleme* I, 13–20.

———. "Die Magie der Zahlen: Das Generationsprinzip in der vergleichenden Literaturgeschichte" in *Miscellanea Litteraria*, ed. H. Sparnaay and W.P.A. Smit (Groningen, 1959), 147–173.

Wechssler, Eduard. *Die Generation als Jugendreihe und ihr Kampf um die Denkform* (Leipzig, 1930).

Wellek, René. "Periods and Movements in Literary History," *English Institute Annual for 1940* (New York: Columbia University Press, 1941), 73–93.

Wiese, Benno von. "Zur Kritik des geistesgeschichtlichen Epochenbegriffs," *DVLG* 11 (1933), 130–144.

12. *Genology*

Behrens, Irene. *Die Lehre von der Einteilung der Dichtkunst, vornehmlich vom 16. bis 19. Jahrhundert.* (Halle, 1940). Bibliography on pp. 240–252.

Brandt Corstius, Jan. "Oude en nieuwe genres" in *De muze in het morgenlicht* (Zeist, 1957), 99–123.

Brunetière, Ferdinand. *L'Evolution des genres dans l'histoire de la littérature* (Paris, 1890).

Burke, Kenneth. "Poetic Categories" in *Attitudes Toward History* (New York, 1937), Vol. One, pp. 41–119.

Diaz-Plaja, Guillermo. *Teoria y historia de los géneros literarios* (Barcelona, sec. ed., 1941).

Donohue, James J. *The Theory of Literary Kinds: Ancient Classifications of Literature* (Dubuque, Iowa, 1943).

Ehrenpreis, Irwin. *The "Types" Approach to Literature* (New York: King's Crown Press, 1945). Opening section contains a summary of Irene Behrens' book. Good bibliography.

Etiemble, René. "Histoire des genres et littérature comparée" in *Littérature comparée en Europe orientale*, 203–207.

Fubini, Mario. "Genesi e storia dei generi letterari" in *Critica e poesia* (Bari, 1956), 143–274. German version: *Entstehung und Geschichte der literarischen Gattungen*, tr. U. Vogt (Tübingen: Niemeyer, 1971).

Genre. A literary periodical published by members of the English Department, U. of Illinois, Chicago Circle. Vol. 1 (1968) ff.

"Les Genres littéraires," *Helicon* 2 (1939), 115–224. Proceedings of the Third Congress of the *Commission internationale d'histoire moderne.*

Ghiano, Juan Carlos. *Los géneros literarios* (Buenos Aires, 1951).

Guillén, Claudio. "On the Uses of Literary Genre" in *Literature as System: Essays toward a Theory of Literary History* (Princeton University Press, 1971), 107–134.

Hardison, O. B., Jr. "*Poetics*, Chapter I: 'The Way of Nature' ", *YCGL* 16 (1967), 5–15.

Hernadi, Paul. *Beyond Genre: New Directions in Literary Classification* (Ithaca: Cornell University Press, 1972).

Jolles, André. *Einfache Formen* (Tübingen: Niemeyer, third ed., 1963).

Kayser, Wolfgang. *O problema dos géneros literarios* (Coimbra, 1944).

Moisés, Massaud. *A Criacão literária: Introducão à problemática da literatura* (Sao Paulo, 1967).

Müller, Günther. "Bemerkumgen zur Gattungspoetik," *Philosophischer Anzeiger* 3 (1929), 129–147.

Pearson, N. H. "Literary Forms and Types" in *English Institute Annual for 1940* (New York: Columbia University Press, 1941), 61–72.

Petersen, Julius. "Zur Lehre von den Dichtungsgattungen" in *Festschrift für August Sauer* (Stuttgart, 1925), 72–116.

Prang, Helmut. *Formgeschichte der Dichtkunst* (Stuttgart: Kohlhammer, 1968).

Ruttkowski, Wolfgang. *Die literarischen Gattungen: Reflexionen über eine modifizierte Fundamentalpoetik* (Berne/Munich: Francke, 1968). Based on the Staigerian notion of *Stimmung.* Excellent bibliography.

———. "Gattungspoetik im Literaturunterricht: Grundsätzliches und Praktisches über einen Kurs in Vergleichender Literaturwissenschaft," *Die Unterrichtspraxis* 4 (1971), 103–116.

Staiger, Emil. *Grundbegriffe der Poetik* (Zurich: Artemis, 1946).

Valentin, Veit. "Poetische Gattungen," *Zeitschrift für vergleichende Litteraturgeschichte* 5 (1892), 35–51.

Viëtor, Karl. "Probleme der literarischen Gattungsgeschichte," *DVLG* 9 (1931), 425–447.

Vincent, Abbé C. *Théorie des genres littéraires* (Paris, twentieth ed., 1948).

Wellek, René. "Genre Theory, the Lyric and *Erlebnis*" in *Festschrift für Richard Alewyn* (Cologne: Böhlau, 1967), 392–412. Now in W.'s book *Discriminations: Further Concepts of Criticism* (New Haven: Yale University Press, 1970), 225–252.

Wellek/Warren, *Theory of Literature* (New York, 1949), Chapter Seventeen.

Zagadnienia Rodzajów Literackich (Problems of Literary Genres). Periodical published since 1958 by the Societas Lodziensis of the University of Lodz (Poland).

13. Thematology

Beiss, Adolf. "Nexus und Motive: Beitrag zur Theorie des Dramas," *DVLG* 36 (1962), 248–276.

Beller, Manfred. "Von der Stoffgeschichte zur Thematologie: Ein Beitrag zur komparatistischen Methodenlehre," *Arcadia* 5 (1970), 1–38.

Croce, Benedetto. Review of Charles Ricci's book *Sophonisbe dans la tragédie classique italienne et française* in *La Critica* 2 (1904), 483–486.

Czerny, Z. "Contribution à une théorie comparé du motif dans les arts" in *Stil- und Formprobleme in der Literatur,* ed. P. Böckmann (Heidelberg, 1959), 38–50.

Frenzel, Elisabeth. *Stoffe der Weltliteratur: Ein Lexikon dichtungsgeschichtlicher Längsschnitte* (Stuttgart: Kröner, 1962).

———. *Stoff-, Motiv- und Symbolforschung* (Stuttgart: Metzler, 1965).

———. *Stoff- und Motivgeschichte* (Berlin: Schmidt, 1966). Detailed bibliography on pp. 159–172.

Körner, Josef. "Erlebnis, Motiv, Stoff" in *Vom Geiste neuer Literaturforschung* (Festschrift für Oskar Walzel), ed. J. Wahle and V. Klemperer (Berlin, 1924), 80–90.

———. "Motiv" in *Reallexikon der deutschen Literaturgeschichte,* ed. P. Merker and W. Stammler, Vol. Two (1926/28), 412–415.

Krogmannm Willy. "Motivübertragung und ihre Bedeutung für die literarhistorische Forschung," *Neophilologus* 17 (1932), 17–32.

———. "Motiv" in *Reallexikon der deutschen Literaturgeschichte,* ed. W. Mohr and W. Kohlschmidt, vol. 2 (1965), 427–432.

Levin, Harry. "Thematics and Criticism" in *The Disciplines of Criticism: Essays in Literary Theory, Interpretation and History,* eds. P. Demetz, T. Greene and L. Nelson, Jr. (Yale University Press, 1968), 125–146.

Merker, Paul. "Stoff, Stoffgeschichte" in *Reallexikon der deutschen Literaturgeschichte,* ed. P. Merker and W. Stammler, vol. 3 (1928/29), 305–310.

Petersen, Julius. *Die Wissenschaft von der Dichtung: System und Methodenlehre der Literaturwissenschaft* (Berlin, secd. ed., 1944), 169–180.

Polti, Georges. *Les trente-six situations dramatiques* (Paris, sec. ed., 1912). English version by Lucille Ray (Ridgewood, N.J., 1917).

Sauer, Eberhard. "Die Verwertung stoffgeschichtlicher Methoden in der Literaturforschung," *Euphorion* 29 (1928), 222–229.

Trousson, Raymond. "Plaidoyer pour la *Stoffgeschichte*," *RLC* 38 (1964), 101–114.

———. *Un Problème de littérature comparée: Les études de thèmes. Essai de méthodologie* (Paris: Les Lettres Modernes, 1965).

Veit, Walter. "Toposforschung: Ein Forschungsbericht," *DVLG* 37 (1963), 120–163.

———. " 'Topics' in Comparative Literature," *Jadavpur Journal of Comparative Literature* 5 (1966), 39–55.

Venezia nelle letterature moderne, ed. C. Pellegrini (Venice/ Rome: Istituto per la collaborazione culturale, 1961). Proceedings of the first ICLA Congress.

14. Mutual Illumination of the Arts

A Bibliography on the Relations of Literature and the Other Arts 1952–1967 (New York: AMS Press, 1969).

Bluestone, George. *Novels into Film* (Baltimore: Johns Hopkins Press, 1957). Paperback ed. U. of California Press, 1961.

Brown, Calvin S. *Music and Literature: A Comparison of the Arts* (Athens: U. of Georgia Press, 1948).

———. "Musico-Literary Research in the Last Two Decades," *YCGL* 19 (1970), 5–27.

———. "The Relations Between Music and Literature as a Field of Study," *CL* 22 (1970), 97–107. Part of a special issue devoted to Music and Literature.

Coeuroy, André. *Musique et littérature: Etudes de musique et de littérature comparée* (Paris, 1923).

Frenz, Horst and Ulrich Weisstein. "Teaching the Comparative Arts: A Challenge," *CE* 18 (1956), 67–71.

Gaither, Mary. "Literature and the Arts" in *S/F*, 153–170.

Greene, Theodore M. *The Arts and the Art of Criticism* (Princeton University Press, second ed., 1947).

Günther, Herbert. *Künstlerische Doppelbegabungen* (Munich, second ed., 1960).

Hagstrum, Jean H. *The Sister Arts: The Tradition of Literary Pictorialism in English Poetry from Dryden to Gray* (University of Chicago Press, 1958).

Hatzfeld, Helmut. *Literature Through Art: A New Approach to French Literature* (New York: Oxford University Press, 1952).

Hauser, Arnold. *The Social History of Art* (N.Y.: Knopf, 1951). German edition: *Sozialgeschichte der Kunst* (Munich: Beck, 1953) in 2 vols.

Henkel, Arthur and Albrecht Schöne, eds. *Emblemata* (Stuttgart: Metzler, 1967).

Hermand, Jost. *Literaturwissenschaft und Kunstwissenschaft: Methodische Wechselbeziehungen seit 1900* (Stuttgart: Metzler, 1965). Second ed. 1970.

Hocke, Gustav René. *Die Welt als Labyrinth: Manie und Manier in der europäischen Kunst* (Hamburg: Rowohlt, 1957). 2 vols.

Kayser, Wolfgang. *Das Groteske in Literatur und Kunst* (Oldenburg: Stalling, 1960). English version: *The Grotesque in Art and Literature*, tr. U. Weisstein (Bloomington, Ind.: Indiana University Press, 1963), Paperback: New York (McGraw Hill, 1966).

Kerman, Joseph. *Opera as Drama* (New York: Knopf, 1956).

Les Langues et littératures modernes dans leurs relations avec les beaux-arts, ed. C. Pellegrini (Florence, 1955). Proceedings of the fifth FILM Congress.

Maury, Paul. *Arts et littérature comparés: Etat présent de la question* (Paris, 1934).

Medicus, Fritz. "Das Problem der vergleichenden Geschichte der Künste" in *Philosophie der Literaturwissenschaft*, ed. E. Ermatinger (Berlin, 1930), 188–239.

Müller-Blattau, Joseph. *Das Verhältnis von Wort und Ton in der Geschichte der Musik: Grundzüge und Probleme* (Stuttgart: Metzler, 1952).

Munro, Thomas. *The Arts and their Interrelations* (New York: Philosophical Library, 1951).

Praz, Mario. *Mnemosyne: The Parallel between Literature and the Visual Arts* (Princeton University Press, 1970). For the Bollingen Foundation.

Relations of Literary Study: Essays on Interdisciplinary Contributions, ed. J. Thorpe (New York: MLA, 1967). On pp. 127–150, an essay by B. H. Bronson concerning literature and music.

Scher, Steven Paul. "Notes Toward a Theory of Verbal Music," *CL* 22 (1970), 147–156.

Smith, Patrick. *The Tenth Muse* (New York: Knopf, 1970). A history of the libretto.

Sypher, Wylie. *Four Stages of Renaissance Style: Transformations in Art and Literature 1400–1700* (New York: Doubleday Anchor Books, 1955).

———. *Rococo to Cubism in Art and Literature* (New York: Knopf, 1960).

Teesing, H.P.H. "Literature and the Other Arts: Some Remarks," *YCGL* 12 (1963), 27–35.

Vossler, Karl. "Über gegenseitige Erhellung der Künste" in *Heinrich Wölfflin-Festschrift* (Dresden, 1935), 160–167.

Wais, Kurt. *Symbiose der Künste* (Stuttgart: Metzler, 1937).

———. "Vom Gleichlauf der Künste" in *Bulletin of the International Committee of the Historical Sciences* No. 37 (1937), 295–304.

Walzel, Oskar. *Gehalt und Gestalt im Kunstwerk des Dichters* (Berlin: Athenaion, n.d.). Chapters 11, 12 and 14.

———. *Wechselseitige Erhellung der Künste* (Berlin, 1917).

Weisstein, Ulrich. "The Libretto as Literature," *BA* 35 (1961), 14–22.

———. *The Essence of Opera* (New York: The Free Press, 1964). Paperback ed. New York (Norton, 1970).

Wellek, René. "The Parallelism between Literature and the Arts" in *English Institute Annual for 1941* (New York: Columbia University Press, 1942), 29–63.

Wellek/Warren, *Theory of Literature* (New York, 1949). Chapter Eleven: "Literature and the other Arts" (pp. 124–135).

15. Bibliography

Baldensperger, Fernand and Werner P. Friederich, *Bibliography of Comparative Literature* (Chapel Hill: U. of North Carolina Press, 1950). Reprinted by Russell & Russell (New York, 1960). Continued in the annual supplements of the *Yearbook of Comparative and General Literature*, vols. 1–9 (1952–1960). Reviewed by B. Munteano in *RLC* 26 (1952), 273–286, S. Skard in *JEGP* 52 (1953), 229–242, and R. Wellek in *CL* 3 (1951), 90–92.

Bataillon, Marcel. "Pour une Bibliographie internationale de littérature comparée," *RLC* 30 (1956), 136–144.

Betz, Louis-Paul. "Essai de bibliographie des questions de littérature comparée," *Revue de Philologie française et de littérature* 10 (1896), 247–274, and 11 (1897), 22–61, 81–108, 241–274.

————. *La Littérature comparée: Essai bibliographique* (Strasbourg, 1900).

————. *La Littérature comparée: Essai bibliographique*, ed. F. Baldensperger (Strasbourg, 1904). Reprint AMS Press (New York, 1969).

Bibliographie générale de littérature comparée. Contains eight installments each of the quarterly bibliographies published in *RLC*. Vol. 1 (1949/50) ff.

A Bibliography on the Relations of Literature and the Other Arts 1952–1967. Published for the General Topics IX Group of the MLA (New York: AMS Press, 1969).

Comparatistische Bibliografie. Published, between 1955 and 1960, by the Institute of Comparative Literature at the University of Utrecht (Holland). On file cards. Lists publications in Dutch, Flemish and Afrikaans.

Etiemble, René. "Pour une bibliographie . . ." in *Comparaison n'est pas raison*, pp. 30–35 (pp. 14–17 of the English version).

Fisher, John H. "Serial Bibliographies in the Modern Languages and Literatures," *PMLA* 66 (1951), 138–156.

Jellinek, Arthur L. *Bibliographie der vergleichenden Literaturgeschichte* (Berlin, 1903). Preceded by lists in Koch's *Studien zur vergleichenden Litteraturgeschichte.*

Malclès, L. N. "Histoire universelle et européenne: Littérature comparée" in *Les Sources du travail bibliographique*, vol. 2 (Geneva, 1952), 418–433.

Meserole, Harrison T. et al. "Bibliographical Problems in Comparative Literature: A Symposium," *YCGL* 17 (1968), 99–111.

Revue de Littérature Comparée. Quarterly bibliographies from vol. 1 (1921) through vol. 34 (1960).

Rosenberg, Ralph. "Bibliographies," *CL* 2 (1950), 189–190. "A check list of regular American bibliographies which contain material pertaining . . . to comparative literature."

Yearbook of Comparative and General Literature, vols. 10 (1961) through vol. 19 (1969). Annual supplements to B/F according to a new system of classification.

✑ Notes

1. "Littérature comparée: Le mot et la chose," in *RLC*, 1 (1921), p. 12.

2. The special problems which arise with the inclusion of medieval studies in comparative literature were discussed by Jean Frappier in his highly informative essay "Littérature médiévale et littérature comparée: Problèmes de recherche et de méthode," in *Proceedings II*, vol. I, pp. 25–35. See also Horst Rüdiger's programmatic remarks in the first issue of *Arcadia*.

3. However, Guyard states (p. 13): "The press plays its role in stressing the good or bad qualities of a given country, but the task of the comparatist begins with the literary transpositions, which have been, in part, suggested by this information and by the conduct of diplomats and journalists."

4. "The Concept of Comparative Literature," *YCGL*, 2 (1953), p. 4.

5. "It had then (in 1951), and still does have, something seductive for young scholars. But there are other perspectives, either new or rejuvenated, which are available today (1961): for one, the comparative study of forms and styles is again open to them; for another, they are urged to create a sociology of literature" (Guyard, p. 22).

6. *De F. T. Graindorge à A. O. Barnabooth: Les Types américains dans le roman et le théâtre français (1861–1917)* (Paris, 1963). See my review of this book in *Arcadia*, 2 (1967), pp. 113–116.

7. The quote is taken from the essay "Comparative Literature: Its Definition and Function," *S/F*, pp. 3–37.

8. *RLC*, 1 (1921), p. 7.

9. On the relationship between Ibsen and George Sand, Van Tieghem remarks (p. 136f.): "They moved within the same current, but they were not indebted to each other: there was no influence. The other example is that of Daudet, who was considered . . . an imitator of Dickens. But he persistently denied having read him. However strange it may seem, there was no influence, but only a common current."

10. Both Makoto Ueda's *Zeami, Basho, Yeats, Pound: A Study in Japanese and English Poetics* (reviewed by Earl Miner in *CL*, 18 [1966], p. 176f.) and Amiya Kumar Dev's essay "Catharsis and Rasa" (*YCGL*, 15 [1966], pp. 192–197) move in the direction of aesthetics.

11. *Arcadia*, 1 (1966), p. 3f.

12. *Probleme der vergleichenden Literaturgeschichte.* Sitzungsberichte der Deutschen Akademie der Wissenschaften zu Berlin, Klasse für Philosophie, Geschichte, Staats-, Rechts- und Wirtschaftswissenschaften, Jahrgang 1963, No. 1, Berlin, 1963.

13. *Weimarer Beiträge,* 11 (1965), pp. 252–262.

14. "The Science of Comparative Literature," *The Contemporary Review,* 79 (1901), p. 856.

15. On p. 7 of his expository remarks in the first issue of *RLC,* Baldensperger states that Littré, in his *Dictionnaire,* objected to the use of the participle "comparée," noting that: "*Anatomie comparée* sounds worse than *anatomie comparative.*"

16. Concerning the journal *Comparative Literature,* its editors state that it is intended to be a forum "for those scholars and critics who are engaged in the study of literature from an international point of view." "Its editors," they continue, "define comparative literature in the broadest possible manner, and accept articles dealing with the manifold interrelations of literatures, with the theory of literature, movements, genres, periods, and authors—from the earliest times to the present. *Comparative Literature* particularly welcomes longer studies on comprehensive topics and on problems of literary criticism."

17. Regarding Stendhal's treatise on Racine and Shakespeare, Guyard observes disdainfully: "It is either criticism or eloquence" (p. 7), and Carré pokes fun at the rhetorical practices of literary critics (Ibid., p. 6).

18. *Die Literaturen der Welt in ihrer mündlichen und schriftlichen Überlieferung: Beiträge zu einer Gesamtdarstellung* (Zurich, 1964), p. v.

19. Ibid., p. xix.

20. See his essay "Y a-t-il une littérature suisse?" in *Essais de littérature comparée,* vol. I (Fribourg: Editions Universitaires, 1964), pp. 315–338.

21. Thus, it is evident why Professor R. K. Das Gupta, the director of the Department of Indian Languages at the University of New Delhi, calls himself, *ex officio,* a comparatist.

22. The possible effects of this problem on the study of Comparative Literature are treated in my essay "Dialect as a Barrier to Translation," *Monatshefte,* 54 (1962), pp. 233–243.

23. See also Van Tieghem's article "La Synthèse en histoire littéraire: Littérature comparée et littérature générale," *Revue de Synthèse historique,* 31 (1921), pp. 1–27.

24. On the relationship between Comparative Literature and the History of Ideas, see Henri Roddier's essay "La Littérature comparée et l'histoire des idées," *RLC,* 27 (1953), pp. 43–49. *A Dictionary of the History of Ideas* in four volumes, ed. Ph. Wiener, has just been published by Scribner's in New York.

25. We refer the reader to the bibliographical portion of our survey, where the most important contributions to the historical and system-

atic study of the concept of *Weltliteratur* are listed. In recent years, comparatists, especially in the Eastern part of Europe, have begun to operate with the concept of literary zones as intervening between those of national literature and world literature. See the relevant portion of the proceedings of the Budapest Colloquim (November, 1971) in *Neohelicon*, Nos. 1/2 (1973), pp. 115–173.

26. The following quotes are taken from the appendix of Fritz Strich's *Goethe und die Weltliteratur* (Berne, 1957). An English version of this book, *Goethe and World Literature*, was published in 1949 (New York: Hafner).

27. The title of one section of Van Tieghem's book (pp. 23–28) reads "Romantic Cosmopolitanism and the First Attempts in Comparative Literature," and the third chapter of Guyard's book is called "Agents of Literary Cosmopolitanism." Pichois and Rousseau, however, do not focus on this phenomenon.

28. Worthy of note in this connection are J. Gillet's expository remarks on the subject of "Cosmopolitanisme et littérature comparée" in *Les Flandres dans les mouvements romantique et symboliste* (Paris, 1958), pp. 45–51.

29. The relevant communications fill one volume of the two-volume *Proceedings*. Especially informative is Kurt Wais's presentation "Le cosmopolitanisme littéraire à travers les âges" (pp. 17–28).

30. This complex is pedagogically treated in the symposium *The Teaching of World Literature*, ed. Haskell M. Block (Chapel Hill: The University of North Carolina Press, 1960).

31. *YCGL*, 12 (1963), pp. 5–14.

32. Chapel Hill: The University of North Carolina Press, 1954.

33. *YCGL*, 12 (1963), p. 14. Brandt Corstius and Wellek (in the first volume of his *History of Modern Literary Criticism*) falsely accuse Goethe of having advanced the cause of cosmopolitanism (*Weltbürgertum*).

34. The best source of information for this enterprise is the bilingual *Rapport relatif au projet d'une histoire de la littérature européenne* (Budapest, 1967), which was made available at the Belgrade Congress. Several participants at the Bloomington Conference of the ACLA voiced their opinions on the project (see *YCGL*, 17 [1968], pp. 86–98). In the meantime, the first volume in the series, *Expressionism as an International Literary Phenomenon* (edited U. Weisstein) has been published jointly by the Publishing House of the Hungarian Academy of Sciences in Budapest and by Didier in Paris. Volumes concerning Renaissance literature (Ottawa/Tours Center), the literature of the *fin des lumières* (Budapest/Paris Center) and the use of folklore in Romantic literature (Alberta Center) are in active preparation.

35. Van Tieghem briefly touches on this topic in the chapter "Ideas and Feelings" of his book, which is echoed in Chapter Seven of Guyard's manual.

36. *Die Literaturen der Welt*, p. vii.

37. Robert Escarpit, *La Définition du terme "littéraire"* (Bordeaux: Centre de Sociologie des faits littéraires, 1961). Now also in *Le Littéraire et le Social: Eléments pour une sociologie de la littérature* (Paris: Flammarion, 1970), pp. 259–272. See now also René Wellek, "The Attack On Literature," *The American Scholar* 42 (1972/73), 27–42, esp. 37–41.

38. See Anna Balakian's comments on "Influence and Literary Fortune: The Equivocal Junction of Two Methods," *YCGL*, 11 (1962), pp. 24–31, especially p. 28.

39. Stith Thompson's essay "Literature for the Unlettered" (S/F, pp. 201–217) is particularly illuminating in this respect.

40. See Michael J. Moriarty, "The Uses of Analogy: An Essay in the Methodology of Comparative Literature," Diss., Indiana University, 1971, and my essay "Influences and Parallels: The Place and Function of Analogy Studies in Comparative Literature" in *Festschrift* for Horst Rüdiger, ed. B. Allemann and E. Koppen (Berlin: de Gruyter). In press.

41. The reader is referred to Craig La Drière's essay "The Comparative Method in the Study of Prosody," *Proceedings II*, vol. I, pp. 160–175, as well as to the contributions made by V. M. Zhirmunsky, L. Galdi, and H. Jechová to *La Littérature comparée en Europe orientale*, ed. I. Sötér (Budapest, 1963).

CHAPTER TWO

1. "The Problem of Influence in Literary History: Notes Toward a Definition," *American Journal of Aesthetics and Art Criticism*, 14 (1955), p. 67.

2. Anna Balakian, "Influence and Literary Fortune: The Equivocal Junction of Two Methods," *YCGL*, 11 (1962), pp. 24–31; Haskell Block, "The Concept of Influence in Comparative Literature," *YCGL*, 7 (1958), pp. 30–37; Claudio Guillén, "The Aesthetics of Influence Studies in Comparative Literature," *Proceedings II*, vol. I, pp. 175–193; J. T. Shaw, "Literary Indebtedness and Comparative Literature," *S/F*, pp. 84–97.

3. "The Concept of Influence in Comparative Literature," *CLS*, Special Advance Issue, pp. 143–152.

4. *W/W*, p. 271. Cf. Shaw's observation: "The *original* author is not necessarily the innovator or the most inventive but rather the one who succeeds in making all his own," *S/F*, p. 86.

5. One of the two main topics treated at the Fourth Congress of the ICLA was the "Definition and Illustration of Literary Terms Related to the Notions of Imitation, Originality, and Influence." I refer the reader, once and for all, to the second volume of *Proceedings IV*.

6. The poem in question is "A Lyric," in which Eliot imitates the

style of Ben Jonson. See Germer's book *T.S. Eliots Anfänge als Lyriker (1905–1915)* (Heidelberg: Winter, 1966), p. 26.

7. Regarding the definition of terms for the various subspecies of literary parody, see my article "Parody, Travesty, and Burlesque: Imitations with a Vengeance," *Proceedings IV*, vol. II, pp. 802–811.

8. Cf. Shaw's assertion (*S/F*, p. 92): "Literary influence appears to be most frequent and most fruitful at the times of emergence of national literatures and of radical change of direction of a particular literary tradition in a given literature."

9. Stuttgart, 1962. English version: *The Poetics of Quotation*, tr. T. and J. Ziolkowski (Princeton, 1968).

10. *Sociologie de la littérature* (Paris: Presses Universitaires de France, 1960). One should also note Escarpit's essay " 'Creative Treason' as a Key to Literature," *YCGL*, 10 (1961), pp. 16–21.

11. "Literature como sistema: Sobro fuentes, influencias, y valores literarios," *Filologia Romanza*, 4 (1957), p. 11, note 2. On the whole question of influences vs. "parallelisms and other synchronic groupings," see Guillén's essay "A Note on Influences and Conventions" in his book *Literature as System*.

12. For Guillén, influence, as understood by the "old" school of Comparative Literature, represents a sort of source in retrospect: "Traditional comparativism . . . takes it for granted that it is merely the perspective which differentiates the study of sources and influences. A source would be an influence in reverse, that is to say, in the direction which proceeds from the reception factor to the emission factor" (ibid., p. 8). Guillén seeks to discredit this notion.

13. Quoted by Guillén, p. 10.

14. Zurich, 1955, p. 9f.

15. The essay, "Spatial Form in Modern Literature," originally appeared in three installments in the *Sewanee Review*, was frequently anthologized, and is now found, in slightly revised form, in the volume of essays *The Widening Gyre* (New Brunswick, N.J.: Rutgers University Press, 1965), a paperback edition of which was published by the Indiana University Press in 1968.

16. Quoted by Guillén in "Perspectivas de la Litteratura Comparada," p. 65.

17. In her essay "Influence and Literary Fortune: The Equivocal Junction of Two Methods," Anna Balakian touches on the subject of Freud and Surrealism, and concludes: "As for the so-called influence of Freud, it is more 'reception' and 'mutation' than true influence. . . . The intentions of the Surrealists were entirely different from those of Freud. The aberrations of the mind, deemed pathological by Freud, were sought out by the Surrealists as manifestations of intellectual caliber and flexibility, which could enrich the domain of art" (*YCGL*, 11 [1962], p. 28).

CHAPTER THREE

1. "The study of influences will apparently do no longer. If we use, instead, the expression 'Survival' (*Wirkung*), we are not merely pouring new wine into old bottles, but mean something basically different. Effects generate from forces—*living* forces—which have the ability to bring about a transformation," *Schweizer Monatshefte*, 42 (1962), p. 306.

2. Frenzel, p. 47.

3. See my essay "Heinrich Mann, Montaigne and *Henri Quatre*," *RLC*, 35 (1961), pp. 71–83.

4. "Kafka's Sources for 'The Metamorphosis,' " *CL*, 11 (1959), pp. 289–307.

5. *Tagebücher* (New York, 1948), p. 311.

6. "The people that were scattered round about gathered on that spot . . . and they built the city over those dead bones, and from her who first chose the place called it Mantua, without other augury. . . . I charge thee, therefore, that if ever thou hear of another origin of my city thou let no false tale pervert the truth." *Inferno*, XX, 88–99. John D. Sinclair's translation.

7. René Etiemble has worked for over a decade on a study of the Rimbaud myth, but frankly admits: "I shall never pretend that my writings on the *Mythe de Rimbaud* represent the ideal of our discipline. Essays in sociology, even the sociology of religion, rarely border on Comparative Literature" (Etiemble, p. 81).

8. *Anfänge Heinrich Manns: Zu den Grundlagen seines Gesamtwerks* (Stuttgart, 1965), p. 147.

9. For example, Hölderlin translates verse 569 of the original as "Von anderen gefallen auch die Weiber" (There are other pleasing women, too), whereas Brecht—using a more literal translation—writes " 's gibt mehr als einen Acker, wo man pflügen kann" (There's more than one field where one can plow). See Wolfgang Schadewaldt, "Hölderlin's Übersetzung des Sophokles" in *Hellas und Hesperien* (Zurich: Artemis Verlag, 1960), pp. 767–824, esp. 777–778, and my essay "Imitation and Adaptation: Bertolt Brecht's *Antigone* in its Relation to Hölderlin's Version of Sophocles" *GQ* 46 (November, 1973).

10. Cf. my essay "Heinrich Mann und Gustave Flaubert: Ein Kapitel in der Geschichte der literarischen Wechselbeziehungen zwischen Frankreich und Deutschland," *Euphorion*, 57 (1963), pp. 132–155.

11. *GRM*, N.F. 14 (1964), pp. 292–302. The clearest and most incisive exposition of the various aspects of *Rezeptionsästhetik* is found in Hans Robert Jauss' book *Literaturgeschichte als Provokation* (Frankfurt, 1970).

12. As an example of the untranslatability of *Ulysses*, we might mention the sequence A E I O U, which, in his German version of the

book, Georg Goyert simply reproduces, without realizing that Joyce was playing with the meaning "A. E., I owe you."

13. From a selection of Trakl's poems in English translation, published in 1961 by the Sixties Press in Madison, Minnesota.

14. Levin L. Schücking alludes to this motto in his *Soziologie der literarischen Geschmacksbildung* (Berne, 1961), p. 95.

15. *The Blue Angel*, tr. Wirt Williams (New York, 1959). See my review in *YCGL*, 9 (1960), pp. 122–125.

16. New York: King's Crown Press, 1947. The appropriate reference is found on pp. 37–39.

17. See my essay "Brecht in America: A Preliminary Survey," *Modern Language Notes*, 78 (1963), pp. 373–396.

18. *German Criticism of Zola 1875–1893* (New York: Columbia University Press, 1931) and *French Realism: The Critical Reaction 1830–1870* (New York, 1937).

19. Frankfurt: S. Fischer, 1956, p. 76.

20. *Franz Kafka Today*, ed. Angel Flores and Homer Swander (Madison: University of Wisconsin Press, 1962), p. 113.

21. Cf. note 6 to the Chapter One.

22. The passage referred to is found on page 469 of Jeune's book.

23. "Zum Problem der 'images' und 'mirages' und ihrer Untersuchung im Rahmen der vergleichenden Literaturwissenschaft," *Arcadia*, 1 (1966), pp. 107–120.

CHAPTER FOUR

1. "Periods and Movements in Literary History," *English Institute Annual for 1940* (New York: Columbia University Press, 1941), p. 77.

2. In his book *Zur Theorie und Geschichte der Historiographie* (German edition, 1915), Croce places the value of periodization at zero. However, as Teesing notes in his study *Das Problem der Perioden in der Literaturgeschichte* (Groningen, 1948), uniqueness is also a historical category (p. 23).

3. "Prinzipien der wissenschaftlichen Periodenbildung: Mit besonderer Rücksicht auf die Literaturgeschichte," *Euphorion*, 8 (1901), p. 1.

4. See also Herbert Cysarz' essay "Das Periodenprinzip in der Literaturwissenschaft" in the handbook *Philosophie der Literaturwissenschaft*, ed. Emil Ermatinger (Berlin, 1930), p. 93.

5. Cf. the Biblical allegory with the figure of the Old Man of Crete, in Canto XIV of Dante's *Inferno*.

6. Benno von Wiese, "Zur Kritik des geistesgeschichtlichen Epochenbegriffs," *DVLG*, 11 (1933), pp. 130–144. In German literary historiography, the terms "period" and "epoch" are often used synonymously, as in Jost Hermand's recent article "Über Nutzen und Nachteil literarischer Epochenbegriffe," *Monatshefte*, 58 (1966), pp. 289–309.

7. W/W, p. 89. As Guillén points out in his essay "Second Thoughts on Literary Periods" (*Literature as System*, p. 437), Wellek must be corrected insofar as periods do not actually "compose a class of chronology" but exist "somewhere between the order of chronology and that of an atemporal typology."

8. See, e.g., Miner's paper "Japanese and Western Images of Courtly Love," YCGL, 15 (1966), pp. 174–179.

9. *Europäische Literatur und lateinisches Mittelalter* (Berne, 1954), pp. 256–259.

10. Fritz Martini attempts to define the term "modern" in his contribution to the *Reallexikon der deutschen Literaturgeschichte*, II (1965), pp. 391–415. See also R. Poggioli, *The Theory of the Avant-Garde*, pp. 216–220.

11. Teesing, p. 111. Cf. the otherwise undistinguished lecture by F. Baldensperger, "The Decreasing Length of Some Literary Periods," *Bulletin of the International Committee of Historical Science*, vol. IX, Part 3 (Paris-Washington, 1937), pp. 307–313.

12. A very informative collection of material is found in Paul Pörtner's *Literatur-Revolution 1910–1925* (Neuwied, 1960), 2 vols. Similar collections in English include *Paths to the Present: Aspects of European Thought from Romanticism to Existentialism*, ed. Eugen Weber (New York: Dodd, Mead, 1960) and *The Modern Tradition: Backgrounds of Modern Literature*, ed. R. Ellmann and C. Feidelson, Jr. (New York: Oxford University Press, 1965).

13. *Die Generation als Jugendreihe und ihr Kampf um die Denkform* (Leipzig, 1930), p. 19.

14. "Renaissance and Renascences," *Kenyon Review*, 6 (1944), pp. 201–236.

15. New York, 1953.

16. New York, 1955 (Vol. II: *Italian, French, Spanish, German and Russian Literature since 1300*); Paris, 1949; Stuttgart, 1960.

17. Teesing, in his article on the problem of literary periodization in the *Reallexikon der deutschen Literaturgeschichte*, III (1966), p. 77.

18. Curtius recommends the use of the term "Mannerism" in reference to an ideal type: "To this end we must, of course, rid the word of all art-historical connotations and expand its meaning in such a way that it will be the common denominator for all literary trends opposed to Classicism, be they pre-Classicist, post-Classicist, or contemporary with a Classicist period" (*Europäische Literatur*, p. 277). Hocke's monograph *Die Welt als Labyrinth: Manier und Manie in der europäischen Kunst* appeared in 1957; it was followed by *Manierismus in der Literatur*.

19. *Die literarische Formenwelt des Biedermeiers* (Giessen, 1958). Most recently, the concept of literary Biedermeier is again in the ascendant (vide Friedrich Sengle's monumental survey of this period).

308 Notes

20. *The Victorian Age of German Literature* (University Park: Pennsylvania State University Press, 1966), p. 5.

21. This topic was discussed by the participants in a symposium during the ACLA meeting held in Bloomington, Indiana, in April, 1968. The texts of the communications presented on this occasion are contained in vol. 17 (1966) of *YCGL*.

22. Paul Van Tieghem (ed.), *Répertoire chronologique des littératures modernes* (Paris, 1935); Adolf Spemann, *Vergleichende Zeittafel der Weltliteratur* (Stuttgart, 1951); *Dizionario letterario Bompiani*, vol. 9 (Milan, 1950). As has been mentioned, Van Tieghem's *Répertoire*, which covers the years 1455–1900, is to be updated under the aegis of the ICLA.

23. *American Literature in Germany 1861–1872* (Chapel Hill: University of North Carolina Press, 1964).

24. H. Hewett-Thayer, *American Literature as Viewed in Germany, 1818–1861* (Chapel Hill: University of North Carolina Press, 1958), and Clement Vollmer, "The American Novel in Germany, 1871–1913," *German-American Annals*, 1917.

25. In *DVLG*, 41 (1967), 202–232.

26. *Das Problem der Generation in der Kunstgeschichte Europas* (Cologne, 1949). The provocative book was first published in 1928.

27. Teesing, in *Reallexikon . . .* , p. 77.

28. Petersen, in *Die Wissenschaft von der Dichtung* (Berlin, 1944), p. 577.

29. *Four Stages of Renaissance Style: Transformation in Art and Literature 1400–1700* (New York, 1955), p. 18. Cf. also ibid., p. 200.

30. Teesing discusses this problem in his study "Die Magie der Zahlen: Das Generationsprinzip in der vergleichenden Literaturgeschichte," *Miscellanea Litteraria*, ed. H. Sparnaay and W. A. P. Smit (Groningen, 1959), pp. 147–173.

31. *Les Générations littéraires* (Paris, 1948).

32. From the preface to Brunetière's *Manuel de l'histoire de la littérature française* (1898).

33. New Haven: Yale University Press, 1963. The volume contains essays on the Baroque, on Romanticism, and on Realism. Similar essays on Classicism and Symbolism are found in Wellek's *Discriminations: Further Concepts of Criticism* (New Haven, 1970).

34. Anna Balakian, *The Symbolist Movement: A Critical Appraisal* (New York, 1967); Manuel Grossman, *Dada: Paradox, Mystification and Ambiguity in European Literature* (Indianapolis, 1970); Anna Balakian, *The Literary Origins of Surrealism* (New York, 1947); Herbert S. Gershman, *A Bibliography of the Surrealist Revolution in France* (Ann Arbor, Mich., 1969); Lillian Furst, *Romanticism* (London: Methuen, 1969).

35. Von Wiese, p. 144. On the whole question of Romanticism as a

pan-European phenomenon, see now *'Romantic'—A Word and its Cognates,* ed. H. Eichner (Toronto: U. of Toronto Press, 1972).

36. *Expressionism as an International Literary Phenomenon,* ed. U. Weisstein (Budapest/Paris, 1973).

CHAPTER FIVE

1. In order to avoid terminological confusion, *kind* will be used in the sense of *major kind* (drama, epic, fiction, lyric poetry) and *genre, form,* or *type* to designate all other classes of literary phenomena.

2. The appropriate quotations are found in Irene Behrens, *Die Lehre von der Einteilung der Dichtkunst, vornehmlich vom 16. bis 19. Jahrhundert* (Halle, 1940). A summary of that author's findings and conclusions is given by Irwin Ehrenpreis in his book *The 'Types' Approach to Literature* (New York, 1945), pp. 9–16.

3. Lines 23 and 92 respectively.

4. Letter of December 29, 1797.

5. See the opening lecture of Brunetière's course *L'Evolution des genres dans l'histoire de la littérature* (Paris, 1890), where reference is made to the way in which "a genre is born, grows, reaches perfection, declines and finally dies" (p. 13).

6. The Proceedings of this congress were published in *Helicon: Revue internationale des problèmes généraux de la littérature,* 2 (1940), 113–226.

7. Germaine Brée, "The Ambiguous Voyage: Mode or Genre"; Eliseo Vivas, "Literary Classes: Some Problems"; and Sheldon Sacks, "The Psychological Implications of Generic Distinctions" in *Genre,* 1 (1968), 87–123.

8. The term *mode,* popularized by Northrop Frye in his *Anatomy of Criticism* (Princeton, N.J., 1957), ought to be discarded since it is not primarily a generic category but a synonym for technique (point of view) with strong thematological overtones.

9. The evidence is found in Croce's *Estetica* as well as in his *Nuovi saggi di estetica.* The whole question is dealt with at some length by Gian N. Orsini, *Benedetto Croce: Philosopher of Art and Literary Critic* (Carbondale, Ill., 1961). Joel Spingarn, one of the editors of the short-lived *Journal of Comparative Literature,* shared Croce's views on this matter.

10. *Revue de Synthèse historique,* 31 (1921), 16.

11. English and American readers can now be directed to René Wellek's essay "Genre Theory, the Lyric and *Erlebnis*," *Festschrift für Richard Alewyn,* ed. H. Singer and B. von Wiese (Cologne and Graz, 1967), and *Discriminations,* pp. 225–252.

12. Ed. Alex Preminger et al. (Princeton, N.J., 1965).

13. See Behrens, pp. 22, 35. Whether *tota nostra* implies originality

or perfection is not entirely certain. The point has, once again, been raised by E. N. Tigerstedt in his contribution to *The Disciplines of Criticism: Essays in Literary Theory, Interpretation and History*, ed. P. Demetz et al. (New Haven, 1968), pp. 593–613.

14. Paget Toynbee translation, as found in his edition of the letters, *Dantis Alagherii Epistolae*, 2nd ed. (Oxford, 1966), p. 201.

15. *Theory of Literature* (New York, 1949), p. 242.

16. *La Littérature comparée*, 3rd ed. (Paris, 1961), p. 18f.

17. "The pages which follow first advance a critical proposition, that satire is a distinct genre with a number of marked characteristics, and then make use of this proposition to describe the complex and seemingly disparate mass of prose, poetry and drama which is English satire of the late Renaissance" (*The Cankered Muse: Satire of the English Renaissance* [New Haven, 1959], p. 7). Germaine Brée seems to share this view in her contribution to the MLA forum referred to above.

18. See my essay "Parody, Travesty, and Burlesque: Imitations with a Vengeance" in *Proceedings IV*, vol. 2, p. 803–808.

19. *Comparaison n'est pas raison: La Crise de la littérature comparée.* (Paris, 1963), p. 97f. The translation is that of George Joyaux and Herbert Weisinger as found in René Etiemble, *The Crisis in Comparative Literature* (East Lansing, Michigan, 1966), p. 52f.

20. "On the Methods and Aims of Literary History as a Science," trans. Harry Weber, *YCGL*, 16 (1967), 39.

21. *Poetics* 26. 1462[a], in S. H. Butcher's translation.

22. This is the title of a book by Ralph Freedman (Princeton, N.J., 1963).

23. *Poetics* 1. 1447[b].

24. See Roy Pascal, *Design and Truth in Autobiography* (London, 1960); Leon Edel, *Literary Biography* (Toronto; 1957), Franz H. Mautner, "Maxim(e)s, Sentences, Fragmente, Aphorismen" in *Proceedings IV*, Vol. II, 812–819; Peter Boerner, *Tagebuch* (Stuttgart, 1969); Gerhard Haas, *Essay* (Stuttgart, 1969).

25. See the author's essay "The Libretto as Literature," *Books Abroad*, 35 (1961), 15–22, and his anthology *The Essence of Opera* (New York, 1964); Karl-Ludwig Selig's bibliographical survey "Emblem Literature: Directions in Recent Scholarship," *YCGL*, 12 (1963), 36–41; as well as R. Schenda, "Stand und Aufgaben der Exemplaforschung," *Fabula*, 10 (1969), 69–85. Most of the recent book-length studies of the essay and the radio play come from Germany.

26. *Poetics* 1. 1447[a].

27. See Hardison's perceptive analysis "*Poetics*, Chapter I: The Way of Nature," *YCGL*, 16 (1967), 5–15.

28. See Douglas Feaver, "Words and Music in Ancient Greek Drama," *The Essence of Opera*, ed. U. Weisstein (New York, 1964), pp. 10–17.

This is an adaptation of the more scholarly article "The Musical Setting of Euripides' *Orestes*" in the *American Journal of Philology*, 81 (1960), 1–15.

29. *Lexikon der alten Welt* (Zurich, 1965), col. 1798.

30. *Sämmtliche Werke*, ed. B. Suphan, 32 (Berlin, 1883), 80.

31. Second edition (Berlin, 1944), p. 144 ff.

32. *Grundbegriffe der Poetik* (Zurich, 1946), p. 10.

33. Ibid., p. 7. The view expressed in the next-to-last sentence of the quotation is a critique, in anticipation, of an opinion voiced by René Etiemble on p. 99 of *Comparaison n'est pas raison*, whereas the last sentence finds an echo in T. S. Eliot's notions regarding the nature of the relationship between tradition and the individual talent.

34. Second edition (Berne, 1954), p. 334.

35. A third edition of Jolles' book was recently (1963) published by Niemeyer in Tübingen.

36. This formulation stems from Wolfgang Mohr's discussion of Jolles' theory in the *Reallexikon der deutschen Literaturgeschichte*, 1, 2nd ed. (Berlin, 1962), p. 321.

37. The order is alphabetical in the original German.

38. *Das sprachliche Kunstwerk*, p. 330.

39. The quotations from Goethe are taken from Ernst Beutler's edition of the *Werke und Briefe* 3 (Zurich, 1948), 480f.

40. Column 1797.

41. The quotations are taken from G. Fricke's edition of Schiller's works (Munich, 1962), 5, 694, 710.

42. Aristotle's arguments, as presented in *Poetics* 14. 1453^b, are not entirely convincing; for few plots are so constructed that "even without the aid of the eye, anyone who is told the incidents, will thrill with horror and pity at the turn of events."

43. Norfolk, Conn., 1963, p. 212.

44. *A Portrait of the Artist as a Young Man*, Signet Books 664 (New York, 1948), p. 163.

45. B. Jowett's translation, with slight emendations.

46. See Melvin Friedman, *Stream of Consciousness: A Study in Literary Method* (New Haven, 1955); Robert Humphrey, *Stream of Consciousness in the Modern Novel* (Berkeley, Calif., 1955); Shiv Kumar, *Bergson and the Stream of Consciousness Novel* (New York, 1963); Dorrit Cohn, "Narrated Monologue: Definition of a Fictional Style," *Comparative Literature*, 18 (1966), 97–112.

47. W/W, p. 241.

48. Lines 73 and 83f.

49. W/W, p. 241.

50. Irving Howe wrote a book entitled *Politics and the Novel* (New York, 1957) but wisely states in the introduction that he has "no am-

bition of setting up still another rigid category" and is solely "concerned with perspectives of observation" (p. 16).

51. From the rich literature on this genre we mention only Claudio Guillén's contribution to the Utrecht meeting of the ICLA (*Proceedings III*, 252–266) and W. M. Frohock's essay in the *YCGL*, 16 (1967), 43–52.

52. Georg Lukács, *The Historical Novel*, trans. H. and S. Mitchell (Boston, 1963); Lion Feuchtwanger, *The House of Desdemona*, trans. H. Basilius (Detroit, 1963).

53. W/W, p. 242.

54. The piece is found in *The Creative Vision: Modern European Writers on their Art*, ed. H. M. Block and H. Salinger (New York, 1960), pp. 29–39. See also Herman Meyer's extremely subtle essay "On the Spirit of Verse" in *The Disciplines of Criticism*, pp. 331–348.

CHAPTER SIX

1. For instance, in W/W, p. 250, and in B/F.

2. "If ever a word was set up to be knocked down, it is that forbidding expression, which no dictionary has yet been broad-minded enough to admit." *The Disciplines of Criticism* (New Haven, 1968), p. 128.

3. From the *Noten und Abhandlungen zum West-Östlichen Divan*, as quoted by Elisabeth Frenzel.

4. Ernst Robert Curtius, "Hermann Hesse," *Kritische Essays zur europäischen Literatur* (Berne, 1954), p. 165.

5. With reference to his novel *Mein Name sei Gantenbein* (*A Wilderness of Mirrors*), Max Frisch coined the apt term *Erlebnismuster* (experiential pattern).

6. The problem of style in general, and literary style in particular, was dealt with, at length, in two symposia. Their published proceedings appeared under the titles *Style as Language*, ed. Thomas Sebeok (New York 1960) and *Literary Style*, ed. Seymour Chatman (New York, 1971) respectively.

7. *Die Wissenschaft von der Dichtung*, p. 136.

8. From Paul Merker's article "Stoff, Stoffgeschichte," *Reallexikon der deutschen Literaturgeschichte*, vol. III (1928/29), p. 306.

9. "Thematics and Criticism," op. cit., pp. 140 and 144 respectively.

10. *Stoff-, Motiv- und Symbolforschung* (Stuttgart, 1963), p. 21. I also recommend Manfred Beller's thoughtful review of this book in *Arcadia*, 2 (1967), pp. 320–323.

11. Ibid., p. 4.

12. *La littérature comparée*, p. 87.

13. *Stoffe der Weltliteratur: Ein Lexikon dichtungsgeschichtlicher Längsschnitte* (Stuttgart, 1962).

14. Berlin, 1966.

15. "Paul Hazard almost goes so far as to omit thematology from Comparative Literature, because it does not involve literary influences." Quoted by Van Tieghem, p. 88.

16. *Un Problème de littérature comparée: Les Etudes de thèmes* (Paris, 1965), p. 6f. In its subtitle, the volume is called an "essay in methodology."

17. Stuttgart, 1965. English version: *From Sophocles to Sartre: Figures from Greek Tragedy, Classical and Modern*, tr. H. Sebba (New York, 1969).

18. "Wolfgang Kayser recently raised the objection that in thematological studies the poet's creation is no longer viewed as an independent, self-contained work of art but is seen only in terms of its component parts. His criticism applies precisely to the *Geistesgeschichte*-oriented studies, whose longitudinal sections and cross-sections are produced by a method of 'motif-unravelling', such as was used by Julius Wiegand in his *Geschichte der deutschen Dichtung* (1922)," Frenzel *Stoffe der Weltliteratur*, p. xiii.

19. *La Critica*, 2 (1904), p. 486.

20. Ibid., p. 484.

21. Erich Auerbach's attempt to illumine the various literary representations of reality in his book *Mimesis* can scarcely be termed thematological in the narrow sense, since *reality* is not a *Stoff*, but only the name for a complex of views and data.

22. In the order of magnitude, motifs are the smaller units, and themes the larger. Trousson muddles the issue when he calls the Hundred Years War a motif but the Joan of Arc *Stoff* a theme (p. 15, note).

23. Kayser, *Das sprachliche Kunstwerk*, p. 62.

24. *Reallexikon, III* (1928/29), p. 303.

25. I have consulted the English version by Lucille Ray (Boston, 1916). The second edition of the original French text appeared in Paris (Mercure de France, 1912).

26. From *Maximen und Reflexionen*, Weimar edition, 1st Section, vol. 42, p. 250.

27. Quoted by Croce in *La Critica*, 2 (1904), p. 484.

28. Elisabeth Frenzel uses this distinction (*Stoff- und Motivgeschichte*, p. 27) without giving due credit to Trousson.

29. In the chapter "Gattungsaffinität und Struktur von Stoffen und Motiven," *Stoff- und Motivgeschichte*, p. 94f.

30. Ernst Robert Curtius, in "Hermann Hesse," (see footnote 4 above).

31. "Erlebnis-Motiv-Stoff," *Vom Geiste neuer Literaturforschung, Festschrift für Oskar Walzel*, ed. J. Wahle und V. Klemperer (Potsdam, 1924), pp. 80–90.

32. Especially in the article "Motiv" in the *Reallexikon*, II (1961), pp. 427–432.

33. *The Thirty-Six Dramatic Situations*, p. 120.

34. *Die Wissenschaft von der Dichtung*, p. 169. Speaking in a similar vein, Walter Veit states: "The motif has to be defined as the verbal abstract of a repeated typical and important situation in life; the scheme of this situation represents the motivity or moving forces of a drama, novel, or even poem," *Jadavpur Journal of Comparative Literature*, 5 (1965), p. 46.

35. *Die Wissenschaft von der Dichtung*, p. 132.

36. Berlin-Leipzig, 1931.

37. *Deutsche Literaturwissenschaft* (Berlin, 1940), p. 139.

38. The scholarly impetus for reviving *topos*-studies originated with Ernst Robert Curtius. Their present state is surveyed by Walter Veit in his research report in *DVLG*, 37 (1963), pp. 120–163.

39. Veit's essay "Topics in Comparative Literature" appeared in the *Jadavpur Journal of Comparative Literature*, 5 (1965), pp. 39–55. Hans Galinsky's monograph was published, in three parts by *Arcadia*. It has since appeared in book form (Heidelberg, 1968).

CHAPTER SEVEN

1. Remak's definition is bolstered by the fact that, since 1952, at Indiana University, where he teaches, the interrelations between literature, art, and music have been studied historically and critically within the framework of the Comparative Literature program. Some pedagogical aspects of the academic pursuit of this subject are mentioned by Horst Frenz and Ulrich Weisstein in their essay "Teaching the Comparative Arts: A Challenge," *College English*, 18 (1956), pp. 67–71.

2. Athens: The University of Georgia Press, 1948.

3. "Comparative Literature," *The Georgia Review*, 13 (1959), p. 174f.

4. For example, in America by the *American Journal of Aesthetics and Art Criticism*, in France by the *Revue d'Esthétique*, in England by the *British Journal of Aesthetics*, and in Germany, from 1906 to 1943, by Max Dessoir's *Zeitschrift für Ästhetik und allgemeine Kunstwissenschaft*.

5. *Opera as Drama* (New York, 1956); *The Essence of Opera* (New York, 1964; paperback ed. New York, 1969); *Emblemata* (Stuttgart, 1967); *Novels into Film* (Baltimore, 1957).

6. See now *A Bibliography on the Relations of Literature and the Other Arts 1952–1967* (New York, 1968).

7. The papers read during that symposium are reprinted in vol. 17 (1968) of *YCGL*. The Spring, 1970, issue of *CL* was devoted to "Music and Literature," and Volume 4, No. 4 (1967) of *CLS* to "Art and Literature."

8. New York: The Modern Language Association of America, 1967.

9. Coeuroy's book appeared in 1923, Maury's study in 1934.

10. See especially Part 3 of Book I ("Literature and Arts and Sciences") and Part 1, Section 3, of Book I ("Semi-Literary Genres").

11. *De Eenheid van het Comparatisme*, p. 56.

12. "The Nonliterary Background and Textual Interpretation," *Introduction to the Comparative Study of Literature*, pp. 165–172.

13. "Literature and the Other Arts: Some Remarks," *YCGL*, 12 (1963), pp. 27–34.

14. *Literaturwissenschaft und Kunstwissenschaft* (Stuttgart, 1965).

15. "Shakespeares dramatische Baukunst," *Jahrbuch der Shakespeare-Gesellschaft*, 52 (1916), pp. 3–35.

16. Berlin, 1917.

17. Berlin, 1930, pp. 188–239.

18. New York, 1955; New York, 1960.

19. "Über wechselseitige Erhellung der Künste," *Heinrich Wölfflin: Festschrift zum 70. Geburtstag* (Dresden, 1935), pp. 160–167.

20. *Symbiose der Künste* (Stuttgart, 1936) and "Vom Gleichlauf der Künste," *Bulletin of the International Commission of the Historical Sciences*, 9 (1937), pp. 295–304. On p. 5 of *Symbiose der Künste*, Wais states: "For twenty years now, similar views have been broached in books and newspapers. These contain a grain of truth and a lot of speculation, and are based on the assumption of an ideological consistency, to which poetry, painting, and music subscribe in equal measure."

21. New York: Oxford University Press, 1952; Chicago: University of Chicago Press, 1958.

22. Princeton University Press, third ed., 1947, and New York, 1951.

23. See Frank's volume of essays *The Widening Gyre* (New Brunswick, N.J.: Rutgers University Press, 1965; paperback ed. Bloomington, Ind., 1969).

24. *Das Groteske in Malerei und Dichtung*, original edition Oldenburg, 1957; English translation Bloomington, Ind., 1963.

25. Two volumes, published by the Rowohlt-Verlag (Hamburg, 1959).

26. *Europäische Literatur und lateinisches Mittelalter*, p. 277.

27. A "primitive" form of symbiosis is synesthesia, which plays a major role in Romantic and Symbolist aesthetics, and which we encounter in writers like E.T.A. Hoffmann, Baudelaire (*Correspondances*), and Joris-Karl Huysmans (*A Rebours*).

28. See especially Douglas Feaver's essay "Words and Music in Ancient Greek Drama," *The Essence of Opera*, pp. 10–17.

29. I recommend, in addition to Stanislavsky's book on the staging of *Othello*, John Hollander's essay "Musica Mundana and *Twelfth Night*," *Sound and Poetry: English Institute Essays 1956* (New York: Columbia University Press, 1957), pp. 55–82.

30. Patrick Smith's book *The Tenth Muse* (New York, 1970) must be regarded as an unsatisfactory attempt to fill this gap.

31. On this point, see Herbert Günther's monograph *Künstlerische Doppelbegabungen* (Munich, 1960).

32. W/W, p. 128.

33. The essay "Hermann Hesse's *Der Steppenwolf*: A Sonata in Prose," *Modern Language Quarterly*, 19 (1958), pp. 115–133, appeared in slightly revised form as a chapter of Ziolkowski's study *The Novels of Hermann Hesse* (Princeton University Press, 1965).

34. The quotes are taken from my essay on Vorticism (*YCGL*, 13 [1964], pp. 28–40). They are derived from Pound's essay "How to Read" and from his book on Henri Gaudier-Brzeska.

35. The case is completely different with Schering's analyses of Beethoven's instrumental compositions as literary "program music" based on Goethe, Schiller, and Shakespeare.

APPENDIX ONE

1. Particularly characteristic are the views expressed by Saint-Evremond in his treatises *Sur les Anciens* and *Sur le Merveilleux*.

2. Johann Gottfried Herder, *Werke* in two volumes, ed. K. G. Gerold (Munich, 1953), I, p. 839. In Herder's "Einwurf gegen die Schätzung auswärtiger Nationen und das den Deutschen zugebilligte Lob" (Ibid., II, p. 489ff.), we read: "Human nature tends to comprise a universe in itself, whose motto is 'None for himself, each for all; thus you will all like one another and be happy.' A vast difference, striving for a unity which lies in all and requires all. It is called (I repeat it over and over) Reason, Justice, Goodness, Universality."

3. *Oeuvres complètes* (Paris, 1820), vol. 11, p. 145.

4. Translated from the edition published by Charpentier in 1887.

5. "Cours de M. Philarète Chasles à l'Athénée," *Revue de Paris*, 70 (1835), pp. 243 and 258.

6. An extensive survey of "The Comparative Study of Literature with Especial Reference to Anglo-French Relations and to French and English Critics" was made by Eric Partridge in his book *A Critical Medley* (Paris, 1926), pp. 159–226.

7. Cf. Baldensperger in *RLC*, 1 (1921), p. 8f., where reference is also made to the methodological difference between comparison as used in the natural sciences and in the Humanities. Baldensperger also quotes from the February, 1880, issue of the *Mercure de France*: "A comparative study of writers through whom the nations which have a literature have distinguished themselves is undoubtedly the best way of stimulating and multiplying talent."

8. Translated from the third edition (Paris, 1829), vol. 1, p. ii.

9. "The Name and Nature of Comparative Literature" in *Comparatists at Work* (Waltham, Mass., 1968), p. 7.

10. In vol 11 (1936) of the journal *Books Abroad*, several American

scholars raised the question of priority. Samuel Putnam (p. 182) opted for Villemain, a choice to which Harold S. Jantz objected (p. 401f.).

11. The essay on Ampère is found in the *Nouveaux Lundis* (Paris, 1884), pp. 183–265. It is unlikely that Edgar Quinet occupied a chair of Comparative Literature as early as 1838, as has been variously asserted. However, L. Benloew's *Introduction à l'histoire comparée des littératures* (1849), which was inaccessible to me, was delivered as an inaugural lecture at the University of Dijon. Concerning Sainte-Beuve himself, see Guyard's essay "Sainte-Beuve comparatiste?" in the *Festschrift* for Kurt Wais (Tübingen, 1972), 159–168.

12. "Les Etudes de littérature comparée à l'étranger et en France," *Revue internationale de l'Enseignement*, 25 (1893), pp. 253–269. Here literature is defined, in terms which accord with the views of Posnett, as "the expression of a certain social condition, i.e., tribe, clan, or nation, whose traditions, genius, and hopes it expresses" (p. 254f.).

13. "L'Histoire comparée des littératures," *Etudes de Littérature européenne* (Paris, 1898), pp. 1-23. See H. P. Thieme's remarks on Texte in *Modern Language Notes*, 15 (1901), pp. 396–403.

14. Betz, p. 13.

15. Paris, p. 461. The work was translated into English in 1906.

16. The facts adduced here are taken from the brief assessment by Fritz Ernst in *YCGL*, 1 (1952), pp. 36–37. See also Daniel Bodmer's essay "Louis Paul Betz—Zürichs erster Komparatist," *Forschungsprobleme II*, pp. 155–172.

17. A survey of Comparative Literature in Switzerland as a whole by François Jost appeared in *Proceedings II*, vol. I, pp. 62–70.

18. See the *Annales internationales d'Histoire: Congrès de Paris 1900, 6th Section: Comparative History of Literatures* (Paris, 1901), p. 4, where we are told: "The Sixth Section, before dispersing, asked the secretary to study the means of organizing an international society of comparative literature, whose principal goal it would be to facilitate the research which foreigners often conduct in France or which French scholars pursue abroad, with a view towards clarifying philological or literary problems of this kind."

19. From the summary of Gaston Paris' talk, ibid., pp. 39–41.

20. "La Littérature européenne," in *Variétés littéraires* (Paris, 1905), p. 4.

21. "European literature is only one province of Comparative Literature, and, within the limits of the present definition, a very narrow province at that" (ibid., p. 4).

22. Concerning Baldensperger's life and work, see W. P. Friederich's comments in *YCGL*, 1 (1952), pp. 40–41 as well as those of Marcel Bataillon in *RLC*, 32 (1958), p. 161ff. The history and function of Comparative Literature at the Sorbonne are treated by Jean-Marie Carré in *YCGL*, 1 (1952), pp. 46–48.

23. On Carré, see the remarks by Charles Dédéyan in *YCGL*, 5 (1956), pp. 38–40, and by Marcel Bataillon in *RLC*, 32 (1958), p. 5f.

24. On the genetic method, see Henri Roddier's paper "De l'emploi de la méthode génétique en littérature comparée," *Proceedings II*, vol. I, pp. 113–124.

25. Paris, 1962. The first two indices (published by Boivin) cover the years 1921–1930 and 1931–1950.

26. *Germanistik*, 4 (1963), pp. 625–626.

27. Van Tieghem's career is discussed by René Bray in *YCGL*, 1 (1952), pp. 39–40, and by Baldensperger in *RLC*, 22 (1948), p. 572f.

28. On Hazard, see Baldensperger's comments in *YCGL*, 2 (1953), pp. 44–45, and in vol. 20 (1946) of *RLC*, which was dedicated to his memory.

29. The development of Comparative Literature at the French provincial universities was discussed by Robert Escarpit in *YCGL*, 5 (1956), pp. 8–12.

30. Exact data will be found in the bibliographical appendix of this book.

31. Paris: Presses Universitaires de France, 1961.

32. Paris: Société d'Edition Les Belles Lettres, 1934.

33. *Sociologie de la littérature* (Paris: Presses Universitaires de France, 1958), in the collection "Que sais-je?" Schücking's *Soziologie der literarischen Geschmacksbildung* first appeared in 1931. A third, revised edition was published in 1961. An English version of this book, *The Sociology of Literary Taste*, was published by the University of Chicago Press.

34. A first version is found in vol. 3 of Etiemble's *Hygiène des lettres* (Paris, 1958), pp. 154-173. The Michigan State University Press published an English translation in 1966.

35. In 1682, Morhof's *Unterricht von der teutschen Sprache und Poesie, deren Uhrsprung, Fortgang und Lehrsätzen: Wobei auch von der reymenden Poeterey der Ausländer . . . gehandelt wird* was printed in Kiel. Between 1688 and 1692, his famous *Polyhistor* appeared in Lübeck.

36. A. W. Schlegel lectured in 1808 on "Dramatic Art and Literature," and his brother Friedrich four years later on the "History of Ancient and Modern Literature." In the present context we cannot afford to discuss the contributions, among others, of Johann Elias Schlegel, Johann Jacob Bodmer and Johann Breitinger, or Lessing's *Hamburgische Dramaturgie*.

37. From the introduction (p. vi) of the volume, published in 1801 by Römer in Göttingen.

38. *Charakteristiken*, first series (Berlin, 1902), pp. 466, 468.

39. Berlin, 1893.

40. *Opuscula* (Leipzig, 1876), vol. 3, p. 2.

41. *Kleine Schriften*, p. 190f.

42. Ibid., p. 120. The obituary originally appeared in the *Deutsche Zeitung* of February 18 and 21, 1874.

43. Ibid., p. 704. From the *Anzeiger für deutsches Althertum und deutsche Litteratur*, 2 (1876).

44. Leipzig, second edition, 1884, p. v.

45. Ibid., p. vi.

46. *Spätere Bearbeitungen plautinischer Lustspiele: Ein Beitrag zur vergleichenden Litteraturgeschichte* (Leipzig, 1886), p. vi. A catalogue of the kind referred to was published by H. Ullrich in 1898 under the title *Robinson und Robinsonaden*.

47. Seventeen volumes of the *Zeitschrift* appeared between 1887 and 1906. Beginning with the third volume, Ludwig Geiger served as editor, with volumes 16 and 17 being presided over by Wilhelm Wetz and J. Collin. Seven volumes of the *Studien* appeared between 1901 and 1907. In *YCGL*, vol. 21 (1972), Hans-Joachim Schulz has published an essay entitled "Max Koch and Germany's First Journals of Comparative Literature" (pp. 23–30).

48. Worms, 1890. A review by Georg Geil appeared in the fourth volume (p. 494f.) of the *Zeitschrift für vergleichenden Litteraturgeschichte*.

49. Wetz, p. 8.

50. Ibid.

51. *Das litterarische Echo*, 2 (1899), pp. 1–5.

52. *Deutsche Rundschau*, 104 (1900), pp. 269–291.

53. "Weltliteratur und Litteraturvergleichung," *Archiv für das Studium der neueren Sprachen*, 107 (1901), pp. 33–47.

54. Meyer's book *Die Weltliteratur im zwanzigsten Jahrhundert, vom deutschen Standpunkt aus betrachtet* appeared in 1915 in Stuttgart. See Arturo Farinelli's discussion of this study in his *Aufsätze, Reden und Charakteristiken zur Weltliteratur* (Bonn-Leipzig, 1925), pp. 405–421.

55. "Litteraturvergleichung," *Das litterarische Echo*, 3 (1900/1901), pp. 657–665. Reprinted in *Studien zur vergleichenden Litteraturgeschichte der neueren Zeit* (Frankfurt, 1902), pp. 1–15 and a note on p. 350.

56. "Litteratur und Universität," *Das litterarische Echo*, 3 (1900/1901), pp. 807–810.

57. *Archiv für das Studium der neueren Sprachen*, 107 (1901), pp. 40–42, 44f.

58. Munich-Leipzig, 1904.

59. "Nationale oder vergleichende Literaturgeschichte?", *DVLG*, 6 (1928), p. 39f.

60. "Zur Aufgabe der vergleichenden Litteraturgeschichte," *Centralblatt für das deutsche Bibliothekswesen*, 18 (1901), p. 10f.

61. Karl Vossler, "Nationalliteratur und Weltliteratur," *Die Zeitwende*, 4 (1928), pp. 193–204; Viktor Klemperer, "Weltliteratur und

europäische Literatur," *Logos*, 18 (1930), pp. 362–418; E. W. Merian-Genast, *Voltaires "Essai sur la poésie épique" und die Entwicklung der Idee der Weltliteratur* (Leipzig, 1926). The significance of the contribution made by the "comparatists" Erich Auerbach and Ernst Robert Curtius will be pointed up shortly.

62. *DVLG*, 6 (1928), p. 41f.

63. *GRM*, 15 (1927), pp. 305–317.

64. Ibid., p. 308.

65. Akademie der Wissenschaft und Literatur in Mainz, Abhandlungen der Klasse der Literatur, Series 1950, no. 2 (Wiesbaden, 1950). See especially the fourth and fifth sections (pp. 60–64).

66. "Comparative Literature in Germany," *Comparative Literature Newsletter*, I/4 (1945), p. 1f.

67. *Forschungsprobleme der vergleichenden Literaturgeschichte* (Tübingen, Niemeyer), vol. I (1950), vol. II (1958).

68. "Vom Geiste vergleichender Literaturwissenschaft," *Universitas*, 2 (1947), pp. 1301–1319.

69. Ibid., p. 1315. In striking contrast to this view, Hirth simultaneously propagated the kind of narrow-minded factualism fostered by Carré (see p. 1305).

70. P. 1304. However, Hirth also considers the possibility of assigning the study of the mutual illumination of the arts to Comparative Literature.

71. *GRM*, N.F. 2 (1951/1952), pp. 116–131.

72. ". . . das Unsägliche, das in der Dichtung jeweils gewagt wird, auszuschreiten, durch Vergleich innere Zusammenhänge und feinste Veränderungen der abendländischen Literatur sichtbar zu machen." Ibid., p. 130. What Höllerer had in mind can be gauged from his contribution to the Second Congress of the ICLA: "Deutsche Lyrik in der Mitte des zwanzigsten Jahrhunderts und einige Verbindungslinien zur französischen und englischen Lyrik," *Proceedings II*, vol. 2, pp. 707–724.

73. *RLC*, 27 (1953), pp. 27–42. See also Höllerer's remarks in the *Rivista di letterature italiane e comparate*, 3 (1952), pp. 285–299.

74. *RLC*, 27 (1953), p. 28.

75. "Weltliteratur und Nationalliteratur im Mittelalter," *Euphorion*, 45 (1950), pp. 131–139.

76. "Möglichkeiten und Grenzen der literarischen Begriffsbildung," *Schweizer Monatshefte*, 41 (1961), pp. 806–810, and "Nationalliteraturen und europäische Literatur: Methoden und Ziele der vergleichenden Literaturwissenschaft," ibid., 42 (1962), pp. 195–211.

77. *Schweizer Monatshefte*, 42 (1962), p. 201.

78. *Geschichte der Textüberlieferung der antiken und mittelalterlichen Literatur*, vol. I (Zurich, 1961).

79. *RLC*, 27 (1953), p. 42.

80. A shortened version of the report appeared in *La Littérature comparée et l'Europe orientale*, ed. I. Sötér (Budapest, 1963).

81. Posnett, for example, is called an American scholar (p. 6), and the journal *Comparative Literature* is denounced as W. P. Friederich's mouthpiece (*Organ*).

82. *Weimarer Beiträge*, 1965/2, pp. 252–262. The quoted passage is found on p. 255.

83. Published under the title *Aktuelle Probleme der vergleichenden Literaturforschung*, ed. G. Ziegengeist (Berlin, 1968).

84. The early stage of the academic branch of Comparative Literature in America was reviewed by Edna Hays in two contributions to the *Comparative Literature Newsletter* ("Comparative Literature in American Universities," II/1 [1943], pp. 2–4; and "Comparative Literature in State Universities," III [1944], pp. 13–16). General surveys of the current state of "comparative" scholarship were made by W. P. Friederich, F. Baldensperger, H. Levin, and H. Peyre. (See the attached bibliography.)

85. Ithaca: Cornell University Press, 1943, pp. 73–75. A bibliographical sketch of Lane Cooper by James Hutton appeared in *YCGL*, 5 (1956), pp. 42–44.

86. *The Dial*, August 1, 1894, p. 57: "A Society of Comparative Literature." See also Gayley's report "English in the University of California," in the issue of July 16, 1894.

87. "The Comparative Study of Literature," *PMLA*, 11 (1896), pp. 151–170. On the history of Comparative Literature at Harvard, see Urban T. Holmes' survey "Comparative Literature: Past and Future, American Colleges and Universities," *Studies in Language and Literature*, ed. G. R. Coffmann (Chapel Hill: University of North Carolina Press, 1945), pp. 62–73.

88. Babbitt's achievement was surveyed by Austin Warren in *YCGL*, 2 (1953), pp. 45–48.

89. A list of the twenty-four volumes which appeared through 1960 is found in *YCGL*, 9 (1960), p. 83f. Santayana as a comparatist is discussed by N. P. Stallknecht in *YCGL*, 15 (1966), pp. 5–18. The most recent volume (#32) is a collection of essays by Harry Levin, published under the title *Grounds for Comparison*.

90. An outline history of this department is given by Marjorie H. Nicholson in the *Comparative Literature Newsletter*, I/4 (March, 1943), p. 2f.

91. Woodberry's remarks were reprinted in *YCGL*, 11 (1962), pp. 5–7.

92. Ibid., p. 7.

93. *American Association of University Professors* (AAUP) *Bulletin*, 31 (1945), pp. 208–219. The passage cited is found on p. 208.

94. In 1922, H. M. Jones and R. Thomas wrote in the *Longhorn Magazine* on "The Comparative Study of Literature."

95. "The Comparative Study of Literature," *University* [of Cincinnati] *Studies*, 2nd Series, VI/4 (1910), pp. 3–26. The passage cited here is found on p. 7f. The speech, which was published in 1910 but not delivered until February 15, 1911, is reprinted in *YCGL*, 15 (1966), pp. 50–62.

96. "Littérature comparée et Littérature générale aux Etats-Unis," *Etudes Françaises* (Paris: Société d'Edition Les Belles Lettres), 6 (1925), pp. 43–60.

97. This is reported by Jones and Thomas in the *Longhorn Magazine* (see Note 92). I myself have been repeatedly addressed as Professor of Competitive [sic] Literature.

98. Guérard voiced his views on this subject in the introduction to his book *Preface to World Literature* (New York, 1940) and in the essay "Comparative Literature" in *YCGL*, 7 (1958), pp. 1–6.

99. *Essays in Memory of Barrett Wendell*, ed. W. R. Castle, Jr., and P. Kaufmann (Cambridge, Mass.: Harvard University Press, 1926), pp. 21–40.

100. *Books Abroad*, 10 (1936), pp. 132–141, 401–403. The articles are by S. Putnam ("Comparative Literature: Can It Come Alive?"), Chandler, Henry Smith ("Comparative Literature: Useful Tool in Skillful Hands"), and Harold S. Jantz, respectively.

101. A sketch of Christy's life is found in *YCGL*, 3 (1954), pp. 62–65. It somewhat resembles the story of Philo Buck, who grew up in India and headed the Comparative Literature Department at the University of Wisconsin from 1935 until his death. See Hazel Alberson's eulogy in *YCGL*, 5 (1956), pp. 35–38.

102. See "A Proposal for Organizing American Resources for the Study of Comparative Literature and Intellectual Relations," *Comparative Literature Newsletter*, vol. 3, pp. 43–47.

103. G. B. Parks, "Toward a Guide to World Literature," Ibid., vol. I, no. 3, p. 5.

104. Robert O'Neal, *Teachers' Guide to World Literature* (Champaign, Ill.; National Council of Teachers of English, 1966).

105. An overview of Friederich's career, penned by Oskar Seidlin, is found in *YCGL*, 9 (1960), pp. 77–79.

106. Pedagogical questions relating to Comparative Literature are touched upon in Phyllis Bartlett's essay "The Curriculum in Comparative Literature," *Comparative Literature Newsletter*, 4 (1946), pp. 49–55; in Henry H. H. Remak's contribution to a "Symposium on the Teaching of Comparative Literature" in *Proceedings II*, vol. I, pp. 222–229; and in the symposium "Graduate Study in Comparative Literature," *CLS*, Special Advance Issue, pp. 135–142.

107. In 1967, an eighth group ("Slavic-Western Literary Relations") was added. A ninth group ("Oriental-Western Literary Relations") rounds out the picture as it is presently constituted. Concerning the

prehistory of Comparative Literature within the MLA, see Friederich's article "The First Ten Years of Our Comparative Literature Section in the MLA," *YCGL*, 6 (1957), pp. 56–60.

108. From 1952 to 1960 (vols. 1–9), the yearbook was edited by Professor Friederich at the University of North Carolina. Since 1961, this responsibility has been borne by a group of comparatists at Indiana University. The present editors—as is evident from their comments in vol. 10, p. viii—no longer feel entirely bound by Friederich's program.

109. The proceedings of the first conference were published in the Special Advance Issue of *CLS*; those of the second conference partly in *ACLAN* (I/2 [1965], pp. 32–44) and partly in *CL* (17 [1965], pp. 325–345); and those of the third conference in *YCGL*, 17 (1968).

110. Carbondale: Southern Illinois University Press. Contains articles by H.H.H. Remak, E. D. Seeber, J. T. Shaw, H. Frenz ("The Art of Translation"), L. Edel ("Literature and Psychology"), N. P. Stallknecht ("Ideas and Literature"), M. Gaither ("Literature and the Arts"), S. Thompson, N. T. Pratt, Jr., A. Rey, and U. Weisstein. The second, revised edition of the book appeared in 1971. It lacks the essay by Agapito Rey, includes an article on "Literatures of Asia" by Arthur E. Kunst and substitutes Chapter Six of this book for the present author's survey of *Hamlet* criticism.

111. "Comparative Literature in the United Kingdom," *YCGL*, 3 (1954), pp. 1–12.

112. Hallam's study appeared in four volumes between 1837 and 1839. I quote from the two-volume fourth edition, published in 1880 (New York: A. C. Armstrong). In the "Preface to the First Edition," we read on p. vii: "France has, I believe, no work of any sort, even an indifferent one, on the universal history of her own literature; nor can we claim for ourselves a single attempt of the most superficial kind." The passage cited in the text is found on p. iii.

113. In the third volume of his *History of Criticism* (New York, 1904), George Saintsbury comments on this point (p. 294): "For Hallam was our first master in English of the true comparative-historical study of literature—the study without which . . . all criticism is now unsatisfactory and the special variety of criticism which has been cultivated for the last century most dangerously delusive."

114. "Stand und Aufgaben der vergleichenden Literaturgeschichte in England," *Forschungsberichte I*, p. 21.

115. *Works*, ed. G. W. E. Russell (London, 1904), vol. 13, p. 11.

116. New York. Like Max Koch in the following year, Posnett favored the creation of chairs of Comparative Literature (p. vii) and later believed that it was due to his efforts that this actually came to pass in France and the United States ("The Science of Comparative Literature," *The Contemporary Review*, 79 [1901], p. 856).

117. Posnett refers primarily to Maine's *Ancient Law* and to the

principle of a "progress of society from status to contract" (Ibid., p. 871), posited there.

118. Paris, 1894, p. 15.

119. The formulation comes from an essay by G. Rees in the *Modern Language Journal*, 37 (1953), p. 4.

120. See Saintsbury's *A History of Criticism* (New York, 1900–1904), vol. 3, p. 480. Dorothy Richardson wrote on "Saintsbury—Early Advocate of Comparative Literature" in the *Comparative Literature Newsletter*, 4 (1946), pp. 32–35.

121. *A History of Modern Criticism*, vol. 3, p. 462.

122. Saintsbury himself completed only the following three volumes of this series: *The Flourishing of Romance and the Rise of Allegory, The Earlier Renaissance,* and *The Later Nineteenth Century.* Brandes' *Hovedstromninger i det 19de aarhundredes litteratur* was published in six volumes in Copenhagen between 1872 and 1890. It was very soon translated into German, English, and partly into French.

123. In "The Science of Comparative Literature," p. 861, Posnett writes: "I cannot help regretting that up to the present time, no attempt has been made to produce an entire series of historical works treating all the great literatures of the world from the three standpoints of these leading principles."

124. Lee's book was published in 1910 by the Clarendon Press in Oxford, and the original version of Loliée's study by Delagrave in Paris (1903). M. D. Powers' translation appeared in 1906 under the title *A Short History of Comparative Literature* (London: Holder & Stoughton). The indigenous comparative tradition in English literary historiography stretches from C. H. Herford's *Studies in the Literary Relations of England and Germany in the Sixteenth Century* (1886), to F. W. Stokoe's *German Influence in the English Romantic Period 1788–1818* (1926), C. L. Waterhouse's *The Literary Relations of England and Germany in the Seventeenth Century* (1941) and Eudo C. Mason's *Deutsche und Englische Romantik* (Göttingen, 1959). Its focus is often placed on the study of Anglo-German relations.

125. "The Foible of Comparative Literature" appeared in the January, 1901, issue of *Blackwood's Edinburgh Magazine*, pp. 38–48. Eric Partridge identified the author in his previously mentioned essay in *A Critical Medley*.

126. "Some Notes on the Comparative Study of Literature" appeared in the *Modern Language Review*, 1 (1905), pp. 1–8. I mention H. V. Routh's essay "The Future of Comparative Literature" (Ibid., 7 [1913], pp. 1–14) only for the sake of completeness.

127. "Comparative Literature," *Times Educational Supplement,* March 26, 1965, as reprinted in *YCGL*, 15 (1966), pp. 63–65. A new development appears to be imminent, as witnessed by the lead article

"Not So Odious" in the *Times Literary Supplement* of March 12, 1964 (reprinted in *YCGL*, 14 [1965], pp. 72–73).

128. H. Gifford, "English in the University: The Use of Comparative Literature," *Essays in Criticism*, 12 (1962), pp. 67–74.

129. The study of Comparative Literature in Australia is reported on by W. P. Friederich in *RLC*, 30 (1956), pp. 237–239. Lately, comparative studies have been bolstered at the University of Tasmania through the initiative of Professor Hans Tisch, who is updating Van Tieghem's *Répertoire chronologique* in conjunction with the projected History of Literatures in the European languages. In the last five years, the Canadian Comparative Literature Association has become one of the most active branches of the ICLA. It publishes its own Newsletter and will shortly launch a magazine. The universities most active in comparative literature studies are the University of Alberta in Edmonton, the University of Toronto and Carleton University in Ottawa. Jointly with McGill University in Montreal, the latter institution has hosted the 1973 meeting of the ICLA.

130. Sayce (p. 63) defines "general literature" as "the study of literature without regard to linguistic frontiers" and "comparative literature" as "the study of national literatures in relation to each other."

131. *Il Ponte*, 2 (1946), pp. 120–134. The quote is taken from p. 127.

132. I might mention works like Arturo Graf's *L'Anglomania e l'influsso inglese in Italia nel secolo XVIII* (Turin, 1911) and Piero Rebora's *Civiltà italiana e civiltà inglese* (Florence, 1936).

133. Here I need to mention only Praz's study on European decadence (*La carne, la morte e il diavolo*), his *Ricerche anglo-italiane* (Rome, 1944), and his book *The Flaming Heart*. Praz' methodologically obsolete book *Mnemosyne*, which is concerned with the interrelation between literature and the visual arts, will be briefly discussed in Chapter Eight. Many of Praz's students (for example, his successor to the chair of English at Rome, Agostino d'Ambrosio) have turned their interests towards American studies.

134. Milan, 1948.

135. Milan, 1951. Recently a major step toward introducing Comparative Literature in the West German high school curriculum has been taken, through the initiative of Professor Hugo Dyserinck (Aachen), in the state of Rhineland-Westphalia.

136. "Benedetto Croce et la littérature comparée en Italie," *RLC*, 27 (1953), p. 3.

137. Graf's inaugural lecture was published in 1877 under the title "Storia letteraria e comparazione: Prolusione al corso di storia comparata delle letterature neolatine." Concerning Graf, see Arturo Farinelli's essay in his collection *Aufsätze, Reden und Charakteristiken zur Weltliteratur* (Bonn-Leipzig, 1925), pp. 293–321.

138. As Porta puts it on p. 35 of his book, "De Sanctis himself, although strongly aware of philosophical and methodological problems, did not concern himself with the theoretical formulation regarding the new form of literary criticism, perhaps because it was already implicit in his aesthetico-sociological system and was, therefore, considered as a natural development of the study of the work of art. And Graf was even less interested in the question, and with him the subsequent generation of comparatists—so much so, in fact, that this approach has always been vaguely understood in Italy . . . and considered as a spurious genre or identified with traditional literary criticism."

139. See Wellek's comment on p. 98 of his History of Modern Criticism, vol. 4 (New Haven: Yale University Press, 1966). Wellek devotes thirty pages to a discussion of De Sanctis' life and work.

140. Quoted by Simone, p. 6, notes 5 and 6. Concerning the term incomunicabile, cf. Höllerer's remarks in RLC, 27 (1953).

141. Croce on De Sanctis, as quoted by Porta, p. 44.

142. In vol. I, p. 134, of the Saggi critici, ed. Luigi Russo (Bari, 1952), De Sanctis writes: "I abhor criticism by parallels."

143. Quoted by Simone from Saggi critici, vol. I, pp. 83 and 262.

144. "Croce as a Comparatist," YCGL, 10 (1961), p. 63. Concerning the contradiction between theory and practice in Croce, see also Porta's comment to the effect that "Croce was too much a prisoner of his own system and that, since he could not reconcile the whole wealth of the real and ideal in his theory he overstepped the latter in his practice."

145. Quoted by Simone from La critica letteraria.

146. Ibid.

147. Briefwechsel Benedetto Croce-Karl Vossler (Frankfurt, 1955), p. 30.

148. La Critica, 1 (1903), pp. 77–80.

149. Ibid., p. 78.

150. Review of Charles Ricci's Sophonisbe dans la tragédie classique italienne et française (Turin, 1904), in La Critica, 2 (1904), pp. 483–486.

151. Quoted by Bernardo Gicovate, Conceptos fundamentales de literatura comparada (San Juan, Puerto Rico, 1962), p. 37.

152. "Croce . . . argued that it is only philosophy, and not poetry, that can operate as an influence from one culture to another. Poetry is essentially form, and form alone cannot influence culture. But the material of poetry, detached from its form, may operate as an influence; it is then no longer art but emotion or ideas." Gian N. Orsini in Benedetto Croce: Philosopher of Art and Literary Critic (Carbondale: University of Southern Illinois Press, 1961), p. 195.

153. Quoted by Orsini in YCGL, 10 (1961), p. 64; taken from Ariosto, Shakespeare e Corneille.

154. Quoted by Orsini (Benedetto Croce, p. 189) from the Nuovi saggi di estetica.

155. Quoted by Simone from *Petrarca, Manzoni, Leopardi* (Turin, 1925).

156. "Gli influssi letterari e l'insuperbire delle nazione," *Mélanges Baldensperger* (Paris, 1930), vol. I, p. 273.

157. A sketch of Orsini's career is offered by Haskell M. Block in *YCGL*, vol. 8 (1959), pp. 40–42, and Pellegrini's work is surveyed by Auda Prucher, ibid., vol. 7 (1958), pp. 40–41.

158. *Il Ponte*, 2 (1946), p. 131.

159. See, above all, the extensive quote from *Il Bocconiano* (April, 1950) on p. 84 of Porta's study, which is, however, factually unreliable and inadequate as a systematic study of the discipline.

160. "Quelques Remarques sur la littérature comparée," *Lettere Italiane*, 8 (1956), pp. 3–8.

161. From *La Critica*, 5 (1907), p. 466.

162. F. J. Billeskov Jansen wrote a brief obituary on Krüger in *YCGL*, 16 (1967), pp. 174–175, which was supplemented by a mimeographed statement penned by Henning Fanger and distributed to the members of the ICLA.

163. In this series, ten volumes have appeared so far, among them two studies each by Cornelis de Deugd, J. Kamerbeek, Jr. (*Tenants et Aboutissants de la Notion "Couleur Locale"* and *De poezie van J. C. Bloem in Europees perspectief*), and Mia I. Gerhardt.

164. Concerning the history and the present state of Comparative Literature in Holland, see the essays by A. M. M. D. van Eupen ("The Growth of Comparative Literature in the Netherlands," *YCGL*, 4 [1955], pp. 21–26) and A. van der Lee ("Zur Komparatistik im niederländischen Sprachraum," *Forschungsprobleme II*, pp. 173–177).

165. See Walter Thys' essay "A Glance at Comparative Literature in Belgium," *YCGL*, 9 (1960), pp. 31–43. F. de Backer's treatise "Littérature comparée: Questions de méthode," *Bulletin de l'Academie Royale de Belgique*, Literary Section, 5th Series, 45 (1959), p. 209f., is more theoretical.

166. I have used the second edition (Lisbon, 1914). The relevant chapter covers pp. 64–67. A sketch of Figueiredo's life is found in *YCGL*, 2 (1953), pp. 49–51.

167. The second chapter of the Lisbon (Edicão da Empressa Nacional de Publicade) edition is entitled "Da critica comparativa" (pp. 10–15). In 1967, the Brazilian scholar Massaud Moisés published a book entitled *A Criacão Literária: Introducão a Problemática da Literatura*.

168. Guillén wrote two important essays in Spanish on the theory of Comparative Literature. "Literatura como sistema," *Filologia Romanza*, 4 (1957), pp. 1–29; and "Perspectivas de la literatura comparata," *Boletín informativo del Seminario de Derecho Politico*, 8 (1962), pp. 57–70. The essay "Poetics as System" (*CL*, 22 [1970], pp. 193–222) harks back to "Literatura como sistema." It is included in the volume *Literature as*

System: Essays toward the Theory of Literary History (Princeton University Press, 1971). Gicovate's book, subtitled *Iniciacíon de la Poesia modernista*, has already been mentioned. Unfortunately, I was unable to locate an article by Eugenio d'Ors ("Las Sorpresas de la literatura comparata") which appeared in the Barcelona journal *La Vanguardia* on November 11, 1949.

169. *CLS*, 1 (1964), pp. 41–45. The author teaches at the University of San Marcos in Lima (Peru).

170. Čiževsky's *Outline of Comparative Slavic Literatures* (Boston: American Academy of Arts and Sciences) appeared in 1952. Roman Jakobson's "The Kernel of Comparative Slavic Literature" was published in the *Harvard Slavic Studies*, 1 (1953), pp. 1–72.

171. Gleb Struve's summary of the ideas of V. Kirpotkin are found in *YCGL*, 4 (1955), p. 7.

172. *La Littérature comparée en Europe Orientale* (Budapest, 1963). See especially the papers by J. Dolansky, T. Klaniczay, and B. Köpeczi on pp. 101–132 and the ensuing discussion (pp. 133–150). For a critical evaluation of the work accomplished at the Congress, see Ralph Matlaw's review ("Comparative Literature in Eastern Europe") in *YCGL*, 13 (1964), pp. 53–55, and that by David McCutchion ("Comparative Literature in Eastern Europe") in the *Jadavpur Journal of Comparative Literature*, no. 5 (1965), pp. 88–100.

173. Budapest, 1964.

174. The interest in Comparative Literature as a discipline, which several East European countries display, is demonstrated by the appearance of two methodological surveys, *Problémy literárnej komparatistiky* by Dionýz Durišin (Bratislava, 1967), and *Principii de literaturà comparata* by Alexandru Dima (Bucharest, 1969).

175. See the assessment of the Russian scholar's life and work by Victor Ehrlich in *YCGL*, 8 (1959), pp. 33–36. Veselovsky's inaugural lecture at St. Petersburg was published in an English translation by Harry Weber in *YCGL*, 16 (1967), pp. 33–43.

176. *Probleme der vergleichenden Literaturgeschichte*, p. 13.

177. "Comparative Literature in the Soviet Union, Today and Yesterday," *YCGL*, 4 (1955), pp. 1–20; "Comparative Literature in the Soviet Union: Two Postscripts," *YCGL*, 6 (1957), pp. 7–10; "More About Comparative Literature Studies in the Soviet Union," *YCGL*, 8 (1959), pp. 13–18.

178. The latest development is discussed by Robert Triomphe in "L'U.R.S.S. et la Littérature comparée," *RLC*, 34 (1960), pp. 304–310, and by Ralph Matlaw in *YCGL*, 13 (1964), pp. 49–53.

179. Regarding the situation in Yugoslavia, see especially Mirko Deanović's essay "La Littérature comparée et les pays slaves," *Proceedings II*, vol. I, pp. 70–79. See also the manuals by Hergešić (1932) and Ocvirk (1936) listed in the bibliography. Less informative are the pre-

sentations by Z. I. Zaleski ("La Littérature comparée en Pologne") and B. Munteano ("La Littérature comparée chez les Roumains") in *YCGL*, 2 (1953), pp. 14–19 and 19–27. Mieczislaw Brahmer discussed Comparative Literature in Poland in an essay published in the *Bulletin de l'Académie Polonaise* (Paris, 1953), which was unavailable.

180. G. M. Vajda outlines the history of Comparative Literature in Hungary in his "Essai d'une histoire de la littérature comparée en Hongrie," *Littérature hongroise, littérature européenne*, pp. 525–588.

181. An historical-critical study of Meltzl's work was presented by Vajda in *YCGL*, 14 (1965), pp. 37–45, and by C. Ijac in *RLC* 14 (1934), 733–745.

182. The Proceedings of this conference were published by the *Tamkang Review* (II/2 and III/1). "Comparative Literature East and West: An Appraisal of the Tamkang Conference" by A. O. Aldridge (*YCGL*, 21 [1972], pp. 65–70) is a firsthand report on that important meeting of minds and literatures.

183. "Comparative Literature in Japan," *Jadavpur Journal of Comparative Literature*, no. 3 (1963), pp. 37–45. For up-to-date information on Comparative Literature in Japan see the dialogue between A.O. Aldridge and Shunsuke Kamei in *Mosaic* 5 (1972), 149–163.

184. In this connection, I refer to an essay by Joseph K. Yamagiwa ("Comparative, General, and World Literature in Japan") in *YCGL*, 2 (1953), pp. 28–39. Regarding the statistical method, cf. Saburo Ota, "The Statistical Method of Investigation in Comparative Literature," *Proceedings II*, vol. II, pp. 88–97.

185. Ota in the *Jadavpur Journal* . . . , 3 (1963), p. 3.

186. Buddhadeva Bose, "Comparative Literature in India," *YCGL*, 8 (1959), pp. 1–10. The present chairman is Naresh Guha.

187. See especially Mohamed G. Hilal, "Les Etudes de littérature comparée dans la République Arabe Unie," *YCGL*, 8 (1959), pp. 10–13, and Gilbert Tutungi's review of Hilal's book length introduction to comparative literature, ibid., 13 (1964), pp. 64–67.

APPENDIX TWO

1. Chapel Hill: University of North Carolina Press, 1950.

2. 10 (1896), pp. 247–274, and 11 (1897), pp. 22–61, 81–108, 241–274.

3. Strasbourg, 1900.

4. 1 (1901), pp. 271–272, 381–384, 505–511; 2 (1902), pp. 121–128, 251–263, 387–392, 509–516.

5. Berlin, 1903.

6. Strasbourg, 1904.

7. *Comparative Literature*, 3 (1951), p. 90f.

8. Opinions on the work were voiced not only by Wellek but also by Basil Munteano in *RLC*, 26 (1952), pp. 273–286, and Sigmund Skard in

the *Journal of English and Germanic Philology*, 52 (1953), pp. 229–242.

9. Munteano, op. cit., p. 279.

10. "The current bibliography is restricted to items genuinely comparative in nature, pertaining to the field of imaginative literature (Belles Lettres), and published in 1960, although exceptions have been made for items dating from the preceding year. Since we wanted equal attention paid to emitters and receivers, it was decided to double or, as the case may be, triple list all relevant items," *YCGL*, 10 (1961), p. 99.

11. "Pour une Bibliographie internationale de Littérature comparée," *RLC*, 30 (1956), pp. 136–144. On p. 143, we read: "That means preparing two, three, or even four entries for the same article, such as the *Revue de Littérature comparée* has done, and as our colleagues in Utrecht have done even more systematically." On p. 142, Bataillon recommends a change of perspective: "If we wish to rejoin the living reality of literature, should we not substitute the point of view of the *receiving literature* for that of the great writer-emitter and exerciser of influence?"

12. "It will always be necessary to update, every five or ten years, a bibliographical handbook such as Louis Betz's *petit bagage*, which Baldensperger and Friederich wished to supplement for the scholars active in 1950." Marcel Bataillon in *RLC*, 30 (1956), p. 144.

13. Paris. Vol. I (incorporating the bibliographies for 1949 and 1950) appeared in 1957. To date, a total of five volumes have appeared (1949/50 to 1957/58).

14. "Of what use would be a bibliography that is not analytical? I would prefer it to be critical, but harbor no illusions in this regard," op. cit., p. 32. Bataillon (p. 139) had already called for international cooperation in the bibliographical field: "It is important that the whole world in which literary history is made should be covered by a network of organizations and institutions which would feel mutually responsible for exchanging information."

15. Meserole's contribution to the discussion of bibliographical questions appropriate to Comparative Literature at the Bloomington congress was published, together with the papers by D. W. Alden, Z. Folejewski, and P. M. Mitchell, in Volume Seventeen of *YCGL*.

Index

331